HUNGRY BENGAL

T0333341

JANAM MUKHERJEE

Hungry Bengal

War, Famine and the End of Empire

HURST & COMPANY, LONDON

First published in the United Kingdom in 2015 by
C. Hurst & Co. (Publishers) Ltd.,
41 Great Russell Street, London, WC1B 3PL
This paperback edition first published in 2023 by
C. Hurst & Co. (Publishers) Ltd.,
New Wing, Somerset House, Strand, London, WC2R 1LA
© Janam Mukherjee, 2023
All rights reserved.

Printed in the United Kingdom

The right of Janam Mukherjee to be identified as the author of this
publication is asserted by him in accordance with the Copyright, Designs and
Patents Act, 1988.

A Cataloguing-in-Publication data record for this book
is available from the British Library.

ISBN: 9781787389670

This book is printed using paper from registered sustainable
and managed sources.

www.hurstpublishers.com

"Unknown to me the wounds of the famine of 1943, the barbarities of war, the horror of the communal riots of 1946 were impinging on my style and engraving themselves on it, till there came a time when whatever I did, whether it was chiseling a piece of wood, or burning metal with acid to create a gaping hole, or cutting and tearing with no premeditated design, it would throw up innumerable wounds, bodying forth a single theme—the figures of the deprived, the destitute and the abandoned converging on us from all directions. The first chalk marks of famine that had passed from the fingers to engrave themselves on the heart persist indelibly."*

—Somnath Hore

* Sarkar, Nikhil. *A Matter of Conscience: Artists Bear Witness to the Great Bengal Famine of 1943*. (Calcutta: Punascha, 1998), pg. 32

CONTENTS

Contents

Contents

DEDICATION

I would like to thank first and foremost my late father, Dr Kalinath Mukherjee, without whom this work would not have been written. This project began, in fact, as a collaborative effort, which is how it also comes to conclusion. His always gentle, thoughtful and brilliant spirit has been guiding this work since his death in May 2002—and this is still *our* work. I would also like to especially thank his older brother, my *Jetha*, Narendra Krishna Mukherjee, who received me in Kolkata as a long lost and much beloved son. His love and respect for me changed my life and has kept me focused on this project throughout. In our many hundreds, if not thousands, of hours in sometimes heated and always lively discussion on that big bed in Hazra house, I learned an incalculable amount, not only about Kolkata, but just as importantly, I learned more about dignity, strength and perseverance from him than I have from any other individual I have met in my life. His colossal spirit has also been guiding me in this work since his death in October 2001. I also would like to give my very heartfelt and special thanks to his wife, my *Jethima*, Dolly Mukherjee, without whose astounding memory for detail and active engagement in my research, this work would also not have been possible. Her sweet and gentle spirit has been guiding me in her absence since November 2005. I would also like to thank the many men and women of this same generation, who lived through the unimaginable events that are the subject of this work, and who shared their memories and thoughts about these events with me, always graciously, conscientiously and with a sense of urgency and purpose that forms the core foundation of my own perspective towards the period under consideration. I was welcomed into each and every house of the many elderly people I interviewed with enough hospitality and warmth to last me a lifetime. It has been an inestimable privilege and honor. This book is for them.

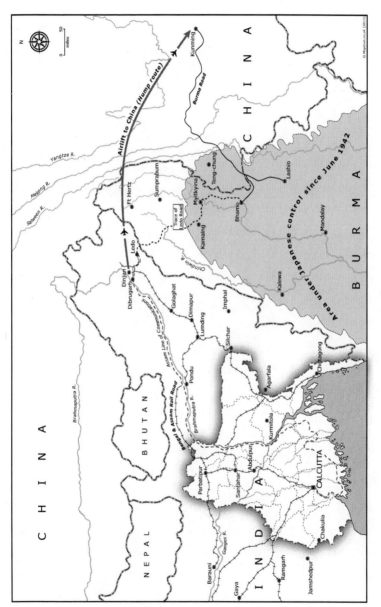

1. India-Burma Theater, 1942 (province of Bengal highlighted)

INTRODUCTION

IN SEARCH OF FAMINE

Framing Famine

There will be no pictures of emaciated mothers with child in this book on famine. I will not be looking to elicit pity, or to evoke a sense of charity. Even in the search for empathy, the existential bridges that would be necessary to cross are impossibly broad, and ultimately impassible. There are no such bridges. Famine preys on the poorest of the poor, the weakest of the weak, those whose very lives and life-stories are erased by marginality and neglect. Startling pictures and lurid descriptions of their suffering and/or demise, however moving, convey very little about the structures of inequality and injustice that define most famines. Famine, in the vast majority of cases, represents a complex form of human violence that merits much closer attention. It is not enough to gawk at the human wreckage that famine leaves in its wake. In all famines beasts of prey await the human carrion which is generated by brutal indifference, inequality and the Manichean mechanics of power. Instead we need to look intently into those mechanics, examining the structures and processes that bring about and perpetuate famine, rather than gaping at the work of hungry vultures in belated dread. To really know famine—and in this sense to imagine the possibility of its prevention—it is better to rigorously examine the intricate workings of mass starvation than to construct emotional requiems to the dead and dying. In this spirit it is my goal here to investigate the tightly wrought structures of influence

1

and indifference that gave birth to famine in mid-twentieth century Bengal; to unfold the dialectics of power and powerlessness—from the local to the global—that defined the trajectory of famine; and to trace the protracted and highly divisive consequences of a catastrophe that scarred the landscape of India for generations to come.

To date, historiography of India on the eve of independence has focused most often on the nationalist struggle, negotiations for a transfer of power, the maneuvering of the Indian National Congress and the Muslim League and/or the rise of communal rancor—all charted according to the irreducible teleology of eventual independence and the partition of the sub-continent into two distinct state entities, India and Pakistan. In short, the history of India in the 1940s has been trapped in the nationalist mode. The deleterious effects of world war have been relegated to footnotes or brief articles, and famine in Bengal has been removed from the course of events for occasional, if isolated, inspection. My objective here is to address this oversight and to demonstrate in clinical detail the deep and abiding impacts that both war and famine had on the course of events in India on the verge of independence. Famine in Bengal is not simply the story of a woeful human tragedy, it is just as importantly the story of how annihilating inequality and material deprivation both stem from and impact identifiable structures of power. The goal in this sense, is to return famine to the wider course of events and to illustrate that, far from being a side story for special study, the Bengal famine should be understood as central to the history of twentieth-century India and even global history. In this effort it might be possible to imagine that I am also attempting to restore the story of the most marginalized to the mainstream of history—even if in relief—as the story of the Bengal famine is in some definite sense their story.

Since the 1940s, scholarship on the Bengal famine has mostly focused on identifying the various "causes" of its occurrence. Famine is understood as a sort of historical aberration that needs to be explained. The complex political, economic, psychological and social forces that have been identified as causal in these several works, however, have never been narrated in full or analyzed in interrelated detail. Similarly, the effects that famine had on the politics and society of Bengal, and its deep entanglements in the broader history of India, have been largely ignored. On the other hand, in works dealing with modern Indian history writ large, the Bengal famine commonly receives a paragraph or two of mention. Because of its perceived nature as merely a humanitarian tragedy, perhaps, the extent to which famine impacted the wider historical context of pre-independence India has gone largely unexamined. Or maybe it is the very marginality of the victims of famine that make it a side story in histories that more commonly focus on the activities of great men. Whatever the exact reasons, until now, the complex political economy of famine in Bengal has received scant attention. But can it be that the mechanisms of power and exclusion that led to the annihilation of at least 3 million souls remain this marginal to the larger history of a nation in the making?

If not recognized as central to an understanding of mid-twentieth-century South Asian history as a whole, however, the Bengal famine has yet provided rich ground for important scholarly analysis. Most famously, in 1980, economist Amartya Sen published his seminal work *Poverty and Famines*, using the Bengal famine as a central example. Having grown up in Bengal during the 1940s himself, it is no wonder that famine has formed the cornerstone of his illustrious career. In *Poverty and Famines* Sen famously argued that, "Starvation is the characteristic of some people not *having* enough to eat. It is not the characteristic of there being not enough to eat. While the latter can be the cause of the former, it is but one of many possible causes."[1] That is; it is not enough to assume that famine indicates an actual shortage of food, all famine necessarily indicates is that certain sectors of a given population are—for one reason or another—forced to go without. In several respects the Bengal famine proved the perfect case study to substantiate this theory. Through a careful examination of the official record, Sen concluded that starvation, in this case, clearly resulted not from an overall deficit of food, but rather from sharp wartime inflation in India that left the poor of Bengal unable to *purchase* rice. This conclusion—that famine in Bengal resulted from a circumstance in which the poor starved because they had become acutely economically disadvantaged, not from a circumstance in which food was simply not available—might today seem somewhat intuitive, but at the time it was revolutionary enough to win him a Nobel Prize in economics.

Because his is an economic analysis meant to have certain modal implication as general theory, while Sen gives a cursory list of proximate causes for the wartime inflation that he identifies as famine's primary cause, little historical detail is included. In the present work, I examine in great depth (amongst other things) the several inflationary factors that Sen has also identified as primary. These included: the highly volatile mechanics of unregulated or poorly regulated wartime commodity markets; intense uncertainty (again related to war) which lead to panicked purchasing by government and industrial firms; related hoarding by corporate as well individual interests; a booming black-market that drove prices ever-higher; and a prevailing administrative chaos that fueled these and other forms of market withholdings, which led to deepening divergences, month by month, in the economic entitlements of different sectors of society. It is in examining these forces in action, I would argue, that the goriest details of famine might be found, as such an investigation lays bare the all-too-human face of annihilating structural violence. Branching out further from *Poverty and Famines*, I will also chart in detail the broader socio-political consequences of the structures of inequality that Sen expertly identifies as the root cause of famine.[2]

In a more recent work, journalist Madhusree Mukerjee has returned to famine in Bengal to examine the liabilities that might be assigned to the British empire, and Winston Churchill in particular. In her 2011 monograph, *Churchill's Secret War*, Mukerjee argues that this blame should be understood as considerable. Much of the work therefore is dedicated to tracing the policies hatched in the War Cabinet in London that denied imports to India and Bengal during the critical phase of famine. Mukerjee also charts something of the nationalist response, as well as the rebellions on the ground in the ever-restive district of Midnapore (southwest of Calcutta) and the subsequent ravages of famine there. In some sense, apart from the tragic scenes of famine-ridden Midnapore that she includes, hers is a macro-history of the Bengal famine. The actors that she identifies (and to whom she assigns corresponding blame) are mostly the "great men" of history such as Winston Churchill, his ever-present and nefarious advisor, Lord Cherwell, and the Secretary of State for India, Leopold Amery. The nationalist figures of India are drawn, in relief, as something like the good stewards of Indian popular interests and in this sense Mukerjee's account also falls into the nationalist mode of Indian historiography. It nevertheless provides moving insight into the colossal indifference, and at times sheer spite, that characterized London's attitude toward starving Bengal.

In my own investigations, I have been unimpressed with the response (and at times pointed lack of response) to the sufferings of the poor and starving of Bengal by the nationalist leadership.³ In fact, in as much as the nationalist leadership was deeply beholden to Indian industrial interests (reaping record profits in wartime Calcutta at the time), many of the policies and practices that precipitated famine in Bengal (particularly those that were related to keeping industrial Calcutta well-provisioned in the name of the war effort) met with little opposition from this same leadership. Furthermore, having been scarcely aware of (and almost entirely silent about) the dire material conditions that were prevailing in rural Bengal in the lead up to famine, it is, in fact, the expedient and at times nakedly self-serving uses of famine (once it had become a headline story) by political elites in India that interests me. That the present work and *Churchill's Secret War* diverge on these and other points does not need to be understood as a matter of discrepancy. An event as monumental as the Bengal famine deserves analysis from many different angles. In this light also, far from imagining the present work as definitive, it is my hope that it will generate further interest and scholarship on the Bengal famine. The period of famine in Bengal defines a fascinating and seemingly inexhaustibly fertile historical event, sown through and through with invaluable lessons about the nature of power and inequality.

While the macro-politics of famine in Bengal remain extremely important, the colonial aspect, and the guilt of empire at large, must ultimately be understood as only one particular aspect of the Bengal famine. Famine in Bengal, moreover, represents a much wider and more variegated story of power and disempowerment. Orders leading directly to famine came down from the War Cabinet in London, under pressure from Winston Churchill, it is true, and a healthy chunk of blame can be placed at the door of the Secretary of State for India, the viceroy in New Delhi and other high officials. But there were also a host of less exalted colonial officers throughout the province—both British and Indian— who enacted orders according to their own interests and capacities, contributing vastly to the economic chaos that precipitated famine. Their interactions with famine victims, moreover, in many cases proved to be riven with the same indifference and, indeed, contempt that Mukerjee identifies in Churchill's attitude. In addition, apart from being a cautionary tale of imperial impunity and colonial indifference, the story of the Bengal famine must be understood as the story of the enrichment of Indian industrialists, who themselves took avid part in repeated campaigns of rice appropriation that left the countryside to starve. In this sense, it was at least as much profit that motivated the rapacity that ravaged Bengal, as it was the colonial creed of racial and cultural superiority.

The fortunes that were made during World War II (and at the expense of famine), in fact, underpinned the influence that a handful of powerful capitalists exercised in the negotiations for independence. Moreover, viewed from a closer range, the Bengal famine was characterized by a shocking proliferation of local venalities: the hoarding of the middle classes; the cruel expedience of extortionary intermediaries; and the mute complicities of an increasingly callous society at large, increasingly inured to death, becoming increasingly more indifferent, month after month, and then year after year. It is also the story of a mushrooming and pervasive moral bankruptcy that stemmed from the burden of a thousand banal decisions made in the face of an increasing silence of despair. As such, famine in Bengal is a harrowing tale of the fracturing of an entire population along class lines (demarcated existentially), which could also be mapped rather easily along lines of caste, community and gender. It is this complex and dynamic story of famine in Bengal that I aim to reveal.

The analysis that I advance in the pages to follow then, is not so much simply about the causes of disaster, but just as importantly, is about how the disaster unfolded, what were its socio-economics, its political dynamics, how did these change over time, and in what ways did famine become entangled in the larger course of history in Bengal—and beyond? Above all what I aim to capture is the fact that throughout the period under study famine insinuated itself into every aspect of life, determining, more than any other single factor, the political, economic, psychological, and social landscape. For this reason what follows is a comprehensive history of the period, with famine (and, in as much as the two are intimately interrelated, war) as the primary hermeneutic. I should say that it is also my hope that my reading of famine in this context might influence parallel scholarship on poverty and inequality in other time periods and elsewhere. When I began this work, it surprised me that there was such a lack of critical work on the Bengal famine to be found. Lurking in this deficit, I detect a certain bias in historiography. How many books of history have been written on the political economy of the Great Depression in the United States, or on hyperinflation as a prelude to Nazism in interwar Germany? Why is it that economy is seen as so central to the socio-political dynamics of North America or Europe, whereas it is most often "culture" that is turned to in the analysis of non-western societies? What I hope to demonstrate here is that this is an oversight and the Bengal famine can and should be seen not merely as human tragedy, but just as importantly as a complex web of events deeply entangled in the history of South Asia. Its primary context, from a macro-historical perspective, was World War II.

Total War

Whatever were the concerns, contentions and calamities that confronted the Indian population during the period under study—from September 1939 until September 1946—the imperatives of the colonial state, throughout this same period, remained deeply enmeshed in a calculus of "total war." Defense, mobilization, security, and morale remained the primary mantras of authority, and the exigencies of war allowed an authoritarian resolve that served to accentuate and, in fact, accelerate the entrenched predatory dynamics of colonial rule—even as Empire itself was crumbling. Throughout the period it was also war—above all else—that determined the practices, priorities, and ideological orientation of the colonial state. From the commencement of hostilities in Europe in September 1939 onwards, the exigencies of Britain's war against the Axis powers remained central to how the colony would be governed—even as the specter of catastrophic famine loomed out of the martial landscape.

When war was declared against Germany on India's behalf in September 1939 this sharply exacerbated existing resentments of British rule in India. Shortly thereafter the Indian National Congress (INC), India's primary nationalist party, unwilling to concede war-time co-operation without representation, withdrew from governmental partici-pation and all political alignments in the country became increasingly entangled in the rhetoric of "defense." Opposition to Britain in the colony was now coded as opposition to the war effort, which, in turn, meant complicity with the "enemy." The colonial state, in this context, embraced the Muslim League, whom they understood to be more loyal to the British cause, as a counterweight to the "rebellious" Congress, which British authorities did their best to paint as a specifically Hindu organization. This dynamic conveniently reinforced the long-held colonial presumption of a subcontinent divided by culture, religion, and collective identification.

War also sharpened the tenor of colonial oppression, justifying the impunity with which the recalcitrant population could be dealt. The Defense of India (Criminal Law Act) of 1915, originally promulgated during World War I, was invoked throughout these years as well, giving colonial officials broad "emergency powers" in the name of defense. Provisions of the Act allowed for sharp authoritarian measure such as extra-judicial detention of opponents, the levy of "collective fines" against civilian populations, and the aggressive—and, where necessary, brutal—suppression of dissent. In Bengal these emergency powers were also used to mobilize hundreds of thousands of "loyalists" who would be deputized to do the bidding of the colonial state in the name of war-time "order." These same troops, however, were utilized most often, not to "defend" the population against enemy attack, but—throughout the period—to police society according to war-time colonial dictates.

The supposed exigencies of war were also used instrumentally to circumvent the nascent democratic process in India. The Government of India Act of 1935, which had established the principle of "Provincial Autonomy," allowed for the election of a Legislative Assembly in each province. At the head of the Legislative Assembly was to be a Chief Minister who was the principle elected Indian executive on the provincial level. As provinces had been—ostensibly—granted pervasive "autonomy," this democratically established executive was at the heart of the new system. In Bengal, however, war and famine were used repeatedly to side-step the principle of self-rule, and "provincial autonomy" proved contingent. Twice during the period the Ministry in Bengal was summarily dismissed and "Emergency Rule" (Section 93) declared. This allowed the province to be governed by executive fiat from the Government of India in New Delhi and, ultimately, His Majesty's Government in London. Throughout the period, moreover, the supposedly "essential" necessities of war were repeatedly cited as necessary grounds to enact drastic—and often disastrous—policies without any consultation with the elected provincial authority.

When Japan entered the war in late 1941, military rhetoric hardened. With Japan's quick succession of victories in Southeast Asia, Calcutta became increasingly central to the Allied war effort and the conceived "necessities of war" expanded exponentially. When Burma fell in early

1942, Bengal became the furthest easterly Allied front against the Japanese, and Calcutta became the industrial capital of Britain's failing war effort in Southeast Asia. Keeping the city's industries—textile, armament, transportation, steel and jute, in particular—running at full capacity became central to the prevailing rhetoric of "defense." The fact that enormous profits were being made in and around Calcutta at the same time, lent influence to arguments that the city needed to be maintained at any cost. The plan that the colonial administration devised to "defend" the city, however, had little to do with military re-enforcement. Instead the War Cabinet in London opted for a scorched earth campaign in Bengal—a scheme to "deny" Japan the resources that it might utilize to advance on Calcutta in the event of invasion. The "Denial Scheme," as it was called, is covered in extensive detail in chapter two of this work.

A primary aim of the policy was to confiscate all "surplus" stocks of rice in the vulnerable coastal districts of Bengal, so that an invading Japanese army could not feed its troops with locally confiscated stocks. Towards this end government agents went into the countryside and by force and coercion appropriated all the rice that they could lay hands on. This rice—ostensibly—would be used to feed Calcutta and keep the industrial labor force contented. Much of it, however, was merely removed from the open market and hoarded in corporate go-downs—even while starvation began to mount. Already by April 1942, the price of rice had risen dangerously and there was distress in both the city and the country-side. Denial upped the ante, putting further pressure on prices, disorganizing the traditional market system, and alerting an already uneasy population to the State's mounting anxiety. The second prong of "denial" dealt with river conveyance throughout the complex tidal delta of Bengal. The idea here was to "deny" potential Japanese landing forces the opportunity of seizing local transport to advance on Calcutta. In the period of a few short months more than 45,000 boats were sunk, destroyed, or otherwise removed from use, and the essential riverine transportation infrastructure of Bengal was entirely crippled.

Meanwhile, rice "denial" had failed to stem a seemingly insatiable governmental and commercial hunger for Bengal's rice. As will be charted in chapters three and four, repeated schemes of procurement—and ultimately confiscation—followed denial. In fact, throughout the entire period commercial agents, backed by governmental authority and martial force, never ceased scouring the countryside for rice under various rubrics of war-time authority. That Calcutta and its industrial workforce were deemed "essential" to the war effort justified all means. Any resistance to governmental schemes was understood as a threat to the war effort, and, as such, could be met with overwhelming force. Calcutta, in the process, was further centralized and the periphery further estranged. Meanwhile, the tenacity with which Government and industrial interests pursued rice in the Bengal countryside continued to destabilize prices, disrupt long-established trade relations, and fuel a thriving black market. As such, these campaigns for rice played a fundamental role in the manufacture of famine in Bengal. "Defense," in this sense, merely served as the ideological cover by means of which the poor of the province were disadvantaged to the point of mass starvation.

When the city was bombed by the Japanese in 1943, as I will detail in chapter five, the colonial State's rhetoric of "defense" was revealed to be extremely hollow. Calcutta was, in fact, almost entirely undefended, and Japan was able to mount a large-scale attack, in broad daylight, unopposed. Meanwhile industrial laborers of Calcutta, whose "priority" had been so central to the policies which had precipitated famine, were revealed to be of less than vital importance to either the industrial firms that relied on their labor, or the colonial administration, which had long cited the welfare of Calcutta's labor force as central to their war-time economic policies in Bengal. In the wake of the bombing, the bodies of dock workers were left unidentified and untended, and afforded little more concern than the hundreds of thousands who had died of hunger that same year. In this sense, the skepticism with which Britain's war effort was received by much of the population of India proved well-founded.

In short, the colonial state, at the tail end of its long tenure, used World War II instrumentally and at times extremely cynically to justify—and indeed amplify—the brutality and rapacity with which it clung to power in India. World War II, in this context, represented only a somewhat frenzied accentuation of the injustices that marked daily life under British rule since its inception. For the population of Bengal, moreover, it meant famine.

Introduction

"The Bengal Famine of 1943"

In order to establish the centrality of famine to the history of mid-twentieth-century South Asia, a primary aim of this work is to de-link famine in Bengal from the year 1943 and to demonstrate the extent to which hunger, scarcity, starvation and disease remained central to the torturous and volatile socio-political circumstances throughout this seven-year period. Though 1943 was the most graphic and extreme stage of famine in Bengal—particularly in the capital city of Calcutta—as Mike Davis has pointed out, famine is never a delimited spectacle or neatly contained "event," but rather "is part of a continuum with the silent violence of malnutrition that precedes and conditions it, and with the mortality shadow of debilitation and disease that follows."[4] Famine, in this sense, is inextricably woven into the fabric of famished populations, and as "part of a continuum" becomes deeply enmeshed in the political, social and economic structures of famine societies. The political economy of famine in Bengal is thus of central historical importance.

For the colonial administration, the effort to delimit famine to the year of 1943 was most pronounced. Denials, indifference, and administrative incompetence led to the highly consequential failure—by default or design—to recognize famine until as late as October 1943—once its eruption on the streets of Calcutta could no longer be ignored. In its *Report on Bengal*, the imperially sanctioned Famine Enquiry Commission found, a bit less conservatively, that the Bengal Famine had, in fact, begun "in the early months" of the same year.[5] Many years later, in 1982, historian Paul Greenough, in his work *Prosperity and Misery in Modern Bengal*, argued to expand this framework several more months, suggesting that the Bengal Famine could said to have begun in October 1942, in the wake of a devastating cyclone which decimated the district of Midnapore, south-west of Calcutta.[6] As early as 2 August 1942, however, the Chief Minister of Bengal, Fazlul Huq, was informing the colonial administration, that "at *the present moment* we are faced with a rice famine in Bengal."[7] Even this early recognition by the chief minister, however, should be understood as woefully late. Reports of famine from districts in Bengal had been wide-spread since at least two years earlier, and the abject impoverishment of the Bengal country-side and "the silent violence of malnutrition" that defines the long trajectory of famine, had been at least a decade in the making. As early as 1934, Bengali social scientist Satish Chandra Mitter had noted in his sadly ironically titled *Recovery Plan for Bengal* that the rural poor, even at that time, could not "but be hunger-stricken and starving."[8]

The "end" of famine in Bengal is a similarly slippery slope. With military aid to the famine-devastated province having begun in November 1943, by 18 December the Food Member of the Government of India could pronounce, "We are now faced with the problem of the future. The food crisis is probably over and I wish and pray that it may never occur again."[9] As I will show, however, starvation, and the myriad of diseases that prey on starving populations, remained a nagging reality well into 1946. In *Poverty and Famines*, Amartya Sen comes to a similar conclusion. Summing up his case study of famine mortality in mid-twentieth-century Bengal, he notes, "very substantially more than half the deaths attributable to the famine of 1943 took place *after* 1943."[10] In fact, though Sen's effort is essentially one of estimating the total fatalities of famine in Bengal in this piece, he writes, "What emerges most powerfully from our analysis is not so much the largeness of the size of total mortality, but its time pattern."[11] He continues, "if the turmoil of the partition of Bengal in 1947 and the displacement resulting from it make us reluctant to read the impact of famine in the excess mortality figures beyond 1946, we can be conservative and count the excess figures only during 1943–46."[12] That Sen punctuates his accounting of famine mortality with the Calcutta riots of 1946 is significant and relevant to the present work. Analysis of famine in Bengal under an expanded chronology is a necessary step towards detailing the extremely protracted entailments of famine on the socio-political landscape of Bengal.

Another prevailing trope that has had extensive currency since 1943 is the idea that victims of famine in Bengal, as in the words of eminent historian Sugata Bose, "died without a murmur,"[13] or as in the words of Paul Greenough, "accepted, virtually without protest, their victimization."[14] The notion that famine victims died passively, without resistance and without a fight, however, is a claim that cannot live up to historical scrutiny. In fact, I would argue, it is not possible for millions to die "without a murmur." Rather it is only a replication of the same forces that served to marginalize these same masses to the point of extermination that renders them "silent." In fact, and as I will demonstrate in all the chapters included in this work, famine was very much contested at every stage. Particularly when the chronology of famine is expanded, it can be seen that active resistance was widespread. From the earliest governmental and corporate schemes to denude the countryside of rice, the boats, lorries, and bullock carts employed in the effort were attacked and looted by outraged villagers who well understood the implications of these efforts. Paddy was also looted from small-scale capitalists who were hoarding stocks locally, even while poor villagers were beginning to die in large numbers. Government, fully cognizant of the threat that its policies posed to rural populations, could only move rice and paddy, much of the time, under armed military escort, which is a clear indication of the resistance it did face.

By the summer of 1942, members of the nationalist leadership, and Mohandas Gandhi in particular, were also openly contesting policies and practices that would lead to the further destitution of the Bengal countryside. Measures that directly led to famine—and were understood by Gandhi as promising the same—were, in fact, central to the stand-off between the Indian National Congress and the Government of India in 1942. Opposition to the "Denial Policy," in particular, was at the crux of tensions between Congress and the colonial state. These tensions eventually led to the arrest of the nationalist leadership in August and the widespread violence of the "Quit India" movement that ensued. In addition, as I will detail in chapter three, central to Gandhi's fast of early 1943 was concern for the "privations of the poor millions" in India— even if by this time that fact was ignored in most, if not all, elite circles. That these acts of protest failed to stem the progress of famine does not negate the fact that resistance was, in fact, prevalent.

Because the Bengal famine has all-too-often been delimited to the year 1943, on the other hand, the contention that victims of famine died without protest is mostly founded on the presumption that because victims at the height of famine, in the very last stages of bare life, riven by hunger and devitalized to the point of collapse, failed to attack rice shops in Calcutta, they did not "resist." The historiography of resistance, however, has undergone very productive development in the more recent past, particularly with methodologies pioneered by scholars such as Ranajit Guha and James Scott.[15] With a more subtle eye turned towards the agency of the most marginal citizens of Bengal, in chapter four I examine how famine victims resisted state authority, literally, until their last breath.

Once the international community had been alerted to the inconveniences of life in Bengal, the first priority of Government's "relief" mission in Calcutta was not to feed the starving, but to remove them from the streets of Britain's "second city," in order to wipe the story of their starvation from international headlines. Accordingly, the "sick destitutes" (as they were now officially called) were rounded up in military and police lorries, by main force where necessary, and removed to "repatriation camps" on the city's outskirts, where they were held, even, against their will. Many resisted these "relief efforts" to the best of their ability, escaping or evading capture and desperately clinging to the streets of Calcutta, rather than dying as detainees in god-forsaken government camps which supplied only starvation rations. Efforts to sanitize the city of starving villagers, in this sense, where thwarted by active resistance engendered by deep mistrust of governmental intentions. Famine in Bengal, after all, had not snuck up on anyone surreptitiously—nor did it "end" suddenly.

In the wake of 1943 famine became ever more deeply enmeshed in the structures and collective psyche of Bengal. The countryside lay in ruins, with the social fabric of rural society torn to shreds by disease, dislocation and death. Whole villages had been wiped out and hardship continued to take a devastating toll. With an "end" to famine declared in official circles, however, military relief efforts, begun late in 1943, were rolled back and imports to ward off further catastrophe were withheld from London. Provincial politics, meanwhile, became increasingly acrimonious, revolving around the highly charged issues of famine and the continuing hardships that residents of Bengal faced. With the Muslim League in control of the Ministry, moreover, the debate became increasingly more steeped in communal rancor. Accusations of bias in private relief, contentions about the communal make-up of rationing schemes, and dire predictions of a looming "second famine," became ever more dangerously entangled in opposing claims of "Hindu" versus "Muslim" interests. These communalized contentions reverberated in national politics, and lent a dark and elemental tone to negotiations in Delhi as well.

Also contributing to the entrenchment of communalist ideology during the period were the physical bodies of the dead. As the toll from famine mounted, so too did the corpses that government and society needed to process: materially, politically, and psychologically. The sheer enormity of the devastation wrought by famine had inured society to death, amounting to a collective "brutalization of consciousness"[16] that was deep and abiding. In the countryside, bodies lay were they had fallen, rotted in the sun, or were torn apart by wild animals. In Calcutta, which had its international image to maintain, however, corpses needed to be removed from public view, categorized and disposed of in orderly fashion. But because famine victims were the most marginal citizens of empire, the record kept of corpses collected by the authorities in Calcutta was extremely limited. In fact, the sole criteria used to classify the dead—as was also the case after the Japanese bombings—was religious affiliation. Ostensibly such distinctions were made in order to conform with religious practices concerning the disposal of the dead (Hindus cremate and Muslims bury), but given the total *lack* of concern or care that was afforded these bodies *before* death, such belated delicacy speaks of less culturally sensitive motivations as well. Even determining how authorities went about "identifying" the "religious affiliations" of these destroyed bodies is entirely unclear from the historic record. In this light, that the state was want to recognize these otherwise nameless and abandoned corpses as simply "Hindu" or "Muslim," must also be seen as an extension of the simplistic binary which they were want to categorize the population of India more generally. That even *corpses* were thus understood by the State, lent a certain biological "proof" to the long-advanced discursive argument that the Hindu/Muslim distinction, alone, was paramount in understanding the Indian population. Together with the cheapening of life that famine and war entailed, the contention that communal affiliation adhered to the very bodies of the citizens of Bengal represented a dark portent of the violence to come.

Among the population of Calcutta there was yet, however, a remarkable solidarity of purpose, which was expressed in large anti-colonial demonstrations that rocked the city in late 1945 and early 1946. The main political parties, Congress and the Muslim League, meanwhile, were busy jockeying for position in a future independent India, and so distanced themselves from the political will of the people, continuing to angle for a more narrowly "disciplined" constituency that would do their political bidding. The harvest of 1945, meanwhile, had been a bad one, and newspapers were again running headlines that millions were doomed to die of starvation in the coming year. A high-level Cabinet Mission had also been sent from London to negotiate a final settlement for a transfer of power, but had broken down around the intractable issue of Pakistan. In this context, with Bengal again careening into starvation by the summer of 1946, violence erupted in Calcutta on an unprecedented scale—and this time it was directed, not at the colonial state, but at fellow inhabitants of the city, Hindu and Muslim.

The Calcutta Riots

That the Calcutta riots of 1946 (often referred to as the "Great Calcutta Killings") were a catalyst and point of departure for the catastrophic violence that accompanied the partition of India, is a fact that is widely acknowledged by many historians, but about the Calcutta riots themselves very little has been written. Not a single full length monograph has been published, and minimal scholarship exists. Very little of anything that has been written on the topic, moreover, gives any plausible explanation of the extent and ferocity of the cataclysmic violence that devastated the city in August 1946. Participation was extremely widespread and defies the simple logic of political instigation, which is the most commonly attributed cause. The sheer scale of the violence committed is also not easily explained by political provocation. What were the larger socio-political factors at work? What was at stake for participants? What historical variables influenced the course of events? And why was the violence so pervasive? Towards an answer to these questions historian Ayesha Jalal notes that the Calcutta riots were "just one symptom of a more generalized and diverse unrest … (engendered by) the endemic rivalry of scarce resources."[17] The received wisdom on the riots, she contends, has proven insufficient: "everyone who describes these killings, runs for the shelter of communalism to explain the inexplicable, or more accurately the unacceptable, face of violence. But the killings still await their historian."[18]

The most commonly advanced theory to explain the Calcutta riots of 1946—which represented a scale of urban violence entirely unprecedented in India—is the acrimony between Congress and the Muslim League that followed in the wake of Britain's failed Cabinet Mission in the summer of 1946. According to this line of thought, the Muslim League's call for "Direct Action" after the collapse of negotiations is cited, de facto, as sufficient explanation for the violence that laid ruin to Calcutta.[19] The League's program of "Direct Action," however, was, in itself, merely an indefinite political posture taken by the central command of the All-India Muslim League. It included no explicit call for violence and was, moreover, intended as a mass movement against the British, at least as much as against Congress supporters, no less Hindus more generally. The Muslim League, above all else, wanted to prove that it, like Congress, could organize mass protest. In fact, Direct Action Day was observed peacefully all across India—while only in Calcutta was there mass violence. That Muslims—mostly poor and immigrant—comprised only 25 per cent of the population of Calcutta at the time, would also tend to make explanations of one-sided Muslim instigation implausible. It is, furthermore, generally accepted—though no reliable statistics were ever compiled—that more Muslims were killed in the violence than Hindus.[20]

In the most often cited, and most thorough work to date on the topic, Kolkata University historian Suranjan Das expands on the logic of political instigation. In his 1991 book, *Communal Riots in Bengal: 1905–1947*, Das engages in a meticulous and extremely well-researched survey of Hindu/Muslim conflict in Bengal during the twentieth-century, concluding with a chapter that is devoted primarily to the Great Calcutta Killings. Previous riots in Calcutta—most notably those in 1918 and 1926—Das contends, provided "a channel for an expression of the socio-economic grievances of the lower social order."[21] In these cases, Das argues, "the riotous crowd had their own perceptions [and] their participation in the violence was dictated as much by their own consciousness as by a response to mobilization attempts by communal leaders."[22] The 1946 riots, however, Das concludes, "were organized and overtly communal; religious and political, and not class or economic considerations, primarily determined the crowds' choice of targets."[23] The murderous mobs in 1946, he adds, "Hindu as well as Muslim—came to be motivated by a kind of *political* legitimization."[24] Das goes even further to suggest that in 1946 "the rioting crowd appears to have been broadly aware of the objective of the violence in which it was participating. It was inspired by the same sense of 'moral duty' as had motivated the French revolutionary crowd to perform tasks which the magistrates had shown themselves unwilling to do."[25]

But, in fact, the violence during the 1946 Calcutta riots was highly variegated and the list of motivations, objectives, grievances and expressions, is hardly exhausted by an examination of communally minded political instigation, and, most importantly, the socio-economic context in which the riots took place can not be so easily dismissed. This context, it should be understood, was defined above all else by famine. Das does mention the impact that famine had on the population of Bengal, noting:

> The 'man-made famine' of 1943 was [a] devastating experience for the Calcuttans, as thousands of hungry people from all parts of the province moved to Calcutta, begging even for gruel when they lost hope of being given rice. Great numbers starved to death on open streets, precipitating some of Calcutta's worst ever epidemics of cholera, malaria and smallpox… in popular perception these developments reduced the value of human lives. There was a brutalization of consciousness on a mass scale, as if the people were being prepared for the inhuman episode of August 1946.[26]

But Das's emphasis on the political aspects of the violence obscures the more pervasive structural relationship between famine and riots in Bengal. The Bengal Famine was not merely a psychological prelude to the riots, it was the primary feature of the socio-political landscape in which they took place.

By 1946 Bengal represented a society in which any idea of "moral duty" had been so attenuated by the ravages of famine and the uncertainties of war, that for many millions it can be said to have ceased to exist. Famine had not merely "brutalized the consciousness" of the population, it had distorted and deformed certain fundamental structures that define daily existence. Meanings of concepts like "health," "territory," "hunger," "home," "community," and "priority" (to cite just a few) had gone through many complicated and rapid layers of transformation in the tumult of war, starvation, and death. Famine and war had also transformed the geo-political importance of Calcutta. Millions had died—and continued to die—of deprivation and disease, so that Calcutta, the colonial war effort, and capital could thrive. With the countryside increasingly understood as merely a buffer zone to the city, both in terms of defense and supply, establishing a legitimate foothold in the city had increasingly meant the difference between life and death. "Belonging" to Calcutta meant "priority," which, in turn, meant survival. Meanwhile, bodies themselves became tokens of social value, with certain bodies—the bodies of the poor and disempowered—sacrificed for those deemed "essential." In this way, the bio-politics of famine also congealed identities, hardening distinctions in the furnace of necessity and survival, transforming, but at the same time cementing, affiliations of community, class, and caste. In chapter seven I trace these lineaments of war and famine in the context of the Calcutta riots.

Introduction

Perspective

I began my work on the history, culture and politics of mid-twentieth century Bengal in relation to stories told to me by my father, whose childhood in Calcutta was set against the chaotic backdrop of war, famine and communal violence. Having grown up in the United States myself and with little knowledge of Bengali culture or history, I traveled to Calcutta for the first time in 1999 to begin a long journey of investigation, analysis and inquiry that culminated in a PhD in Anthropology and History. Though my preliminary research as a doctoral student (begun in 2004) focused primarily on the Hindu/Muslim riots of 1946, at the frayed end of each and every lead that I followed, I was repeatedly confronted with famine. My search for an understanding of the Calcutta riots, then, was unavoidably and inevitably transformed into a comprehensive analysis of the Bengal famine and the extent to which starvation and its accompanying epidemics and dislocations impacted social structures, popular perceptions, political formations, and collective action in mid-twentieth century Bengal.

Because I came to this research from the perspective of personal experience, it has been, also, the personal experience of these times that has long been my primary interest. Along with the many relatives with whom I have spoken at length about this period, I have interviewed dozens of survivors from these times in Calcutta. When I began this journey, it was their stories that I had intended to tell. But for many reasons the effort to locate particular subject-positions within the complex nexus of destructive and violent forces that defined Bengal in the 1940s is difficult to do before the larger historical story is told. As such, the primary effort to reconstruct individual experience has devolved into the more academic exercise of detailing the anatomy of this historical period, mostly through access to archival materials. In this sense the secondary goal of trying to paint an adequate picture of the event—in which to later locate the individual—has here become primary. The compromised conclusion of such an endeavor is to elide the impact of structural violence on individual identity, while perhaps succeeding in theorizing something of its impact on collectivities. These were nearly impossible times to live through. To tell the story of any individual's passage before the historical story is told would be to set an inconceivably despairing voice afloat in the world without reference to the extraordinary circumstances that defined that passage. The historical account in the pages to follow represents the necessary pretext to understanding the individuals who, through their recollections, taught me the meaning of these events. Nevertheless, it is, above all else, the sense of injustice and disbelief that grounded their narratives that has informed this work. As such, this remains their story to me. Their individual stories, and the story of my family, as well as the story of my own journeys back and forth to Calcutta "in search of famine," are for another time. As a promise to return to their individual experiences, I include here just a very short and personal vignette, which briefly sets the stage for chapter one. Over the years that I have been doing this research and writing, I have always kept the child in this anecdote firmly in mind. The work is dedicated to him.

When Japan attacked the United States at Pearl Harbor, and Britain at Rangoon a few weeks later, my grandfather, Ramakrishna Mukherjee, made the decision, like so many others, to secure his family in the countryside at their village residence in order to shelter them from the dangers of war-time Calcutta. All but he and his oldest son made the difficult journey across several rivers and southeast into the Sundarbans to the village of Bahadupur in the district of Khulna. Ramakrishna had left the village in the second decade of the twentieth century and this was the first long-term return for any of his family. Kalinath, Ramakrishna's second son—and my father—was at this time eleven years old. He was a promising and intelligent boy. He was also engrossed in the world around him. In preparation for the trip to Bahadupur he manufactured a "radio" so that he might be able to follow the news from Calcutta in the village. From a magazine that he had come by, he painstakingly cut from cardboard the exact designs for all the components that were pictured in an illustration of a crystal radio. With equal precision, he hand-painted every component so that it looked identical to the illustration. The reproduction was so effective, in fact, that he was not the only one surprised when he turned the switch and no sound came. Nevertheless, he carried his radio to Bahadupur, crossing the wide river at Taki, and sailing by launch from Satkira through Budhhata and on down to the village from where his father had come. Life in the village was among the only fond memories that Kalinath would have of his war-torn childhood. The peace that he found there was transient, and the realities of his youth were far from idyllic. He returned to Calcutta some months later and lived through the worst of the war, famine and riots there.

Introduction

A passage from a popular children's magazine (that he very well may have read), published in the early forties, describes the circumstance that children of Bengal faced. The author, an "older sister," encourages her readers to keep faith in frightening times—as Bengal confronts war:

My Dear Little Brothers and Sisters!

A new month has come, and the old has gone.
In this way many more months will come and go.
And what do I have new to tell you?
The earth itself is being soaked in blood,
The sky has gone dark.
Bombs and gunpowder are piled in heaps.
All of India has been watching this war closely,
Knowing that we too are never far from peril.

Now the flames of war have come close to our land. The jaw of Calcutta is veiled in darkness. Bengal has been proclaimed what they call an 'essential area.' Civility and culture have been stricken to the root. And yet, I see, so many of you young boys and girls, remembering your faith, are speaking from your hearts, narrating dreams of happier days to come—even while the earth is stained with blood, even amidst the cries of distress and fear. You are like white lotus flowers, blooming in the sunshine, surrounded by the light of heaven, in harmonious strains—from the depths of this ignorance and darkness—singing of deliverance, praying for the gifts of logic and wisdom. I pray that your prayers will be answered...

Didi-bhai,
Magh 1348[27]

1

WAR

On 30 December 1940, in an industrial suburb of colonial Calcutta, a shabbily contrived Nazi aircraft circled low over a small formation of native huts erected in the shadows of the sprawling jute and cotton mills that line the banks of the river Hooghly. Across the river, in Calcutta proper, stood the grand, if now somewhat weatherworn, Victorian buildings that formerly housed the central administrative apparatus of the British Raj in India. As the plane came into view, according to the *Amrita Bazar Patrika*:

> Lighting restrictors who were tasking people of the peaceful hamlet over which the enemy aircraft was spotted flying met with opposition from a group of villagers who flashed their torch lights for locating their huts. Following this bombs were hurled by the bomber plane demolishing a number of huts and as a result, fire broke out in the locality. The entire personnel of the A.R.P. [Air Raid Precaution] organization handled the situation promptly, extinguished fires, demolished dangerous structures, rescued people from underneath debris, rendered first aid, and removed cases to Hospital in ambulance cars.[1]

A.R.P. trainees had performed admirably in this test of air-raid preparedness: "all the different parties, the messengers, the lighting restrictors, the reconnaissance party, the gas decontamination party, the fire extinguishing party and the first aid party all worked together in complete harmony as soon as the sirens were sounded on spotting the enemy aircraft."[2] If only the public could be educated to the necessities of maintaining order.

In subsequent press releases, and over the All-India Radio airwaves, strict regulations were iterated and reiterated to the public. On the sounding of the sirens—a series of five second blasts from street-side and factory "hooters":

1) Any person who has no duties and is within a building shall remain.
2) Any person who has no duties and is in the open shall take nearest cover.
3) All vehicular traffic shall pull to the left and stop.
4) All animals drawing vehicles shall be unyoked and tied to the nearest post.
5) Only police and Civic Guard vehicles, ambulances, fire engines and lorries, Rescue Party lorries, authorized Air Raid Precautionary staff vehicles, and defense service vehicles shall be permitted to proceed on roads.[3]

When the sirens sounded again on 30 January, however, again there was "opposition." In his notes on this second occasion, A.R.P. controller, N.V.H. Symons grumbled, "too much attention was paid to vehicular traffic and little or none to pedestrians. I found trams, buses, cars and lorries all well parked on the side of the road, but pedestrians were wandering all over the place under the very noses of the police."[4] To add insult to injury;

draft animals were not unyoked…large numbers of the public stayed under verandas and in doorways instead of going into houses [and] too many people, amongst whom women were noticeable, were gazing out of windows…on the whole [police] constables were very lazy…they frequently were found standing about doing nothing…they need more instruction as to the reasons for all these orders and as to how to enforce [them] by reasoning with the public and polite requests rather than shouted commands.[5]

Laborers were found to be less lethargic, if just as lacking in discipline: "in Strand Road, North, coolies were still loading jute onto carts at 3:50 P.M…and near the Talla Bridge a gang of men were found pumping water."[6]

This exercise, a second test of war-readiness in Calcutta, had been a failure. Great Britain was at war—and with it India—and yet, in Calcutta, the putative "second city" of empire, the general public remained apathetic. Urgent work was needed to "train the general public in their duties."[7] Even the sirens were deficient, Symons noted, they were "very faint, and might easily go unnoticed in a rain storm…there is nothing about them to startle anybody into a realization that danger is imminent."[8] A.D. Gordon, Inspector General of the Bengal police, concurred that the idea that danger was imminent needed to be "dinned into their minds by constant propaganda."[9]

The fact that Nazi Germany was, in fact, an extremely remote "enemy," however, made the war a difficult sell. Resources meanwhile limited imagination and measures taken to discipline the recalcitrant public remained fanciful. The majority of the population of Bengal was beyond the state's rhetorical reach—and would remain that way throughout the period. In London, on the other hand, farsighted and well-resourced preparations for war had been underway for quite some time.

Food Security

Winston Churchill, for one, had long experience with the role that a nation's food supply could play in war. As England's First Lord of the Admiralty during the First World War, he had overseen the British naval blockade of Germany. This "maneuver"—as he later wrote—had "treated the whole of Germany as if it were a beleaguered fortress, and avowedly sought to starve the whole population—men, women, and children, old and young, wounded and sound—into submission."[10] For his role as the architect of such blockades he had earned the nickname "the famisher" in France.[11] He and other British war-planners knew well that hunger was a working weapon in the arsenal of modern warfare, and that a combatant nation's food security was a top priority in preparation for war.

With tensions in Europe bristling, early in the summer of 1936 a subcommittee on rationing was formed, with Sir William Beveridge, Permanent Secretary to the First Ministry of Food (during WWI), as Chair. Beveridge argued that the need to "think out in advance, *and as a whole*, the civilian side of the next war is as important as to design measures of military attack and defense."[12] A Food (Defense Plans) Department of His Majesty's Government (HMG) was established in December of the same year. The objective was to ensure that "every member of the public would be able to obtain a fair share of the national food supply at a reasonable price."[13] Nineteen regional administrative divisions were demarcated and 1,400 local food committees organized to meet the department's "fair share" goal.[14] Detailed schemes for the flat-rate rationing of sugar, butter, bacon, ham and other meat were drawn up, and arrangements were also made to provide a heavily subsidized "buffer" of bread and potatoes.[15]

As importantly, the plan included strict measures to control bulk purchasing. Bulk purchasing by vested interests and commodity speculators, it was well understood, could radically destabilize markets during wartime, leading to uncontrolled inflation and ultimately shortages. As such, detailed plans were drawn up for governmental appropriation and storage of large quantities of food grains in order to control markets. The pace of preparations was accelerated after the Munich Crisis in September 1938, at which time more food was stockpiled and arrangements for the transport of large shipments of grains were elaborated.[16] As further guarantee the Food Department's plans would meet with smooth transition, it was agreed that a Second Food Ministry (second to the First in WWI) would be established "within hours of the outbreak of hostilities."[17]

Accordingly, Britain's Second Ministry of Food was established almost immediately on the declaration of war against Germany. Ration books, which had been printed in advance, were distributed and the rationing of sugar, butter, ham, and bacon began in January of 1940. Meat was included in March and tea, margarine, and cooking fats in July. Early in 1941 preserves and cheese were rolled in, and the rationing of cloth began. Differential access to non-rationed foods created some discontent, and so a "points-rationing" system was also introduced in December for the purchase of items like canned fish, dried fruits, rice, and biscuits. A scheme for rationing chocolate and confectionaries was launched a short time later.[18] In the industrial sector, heavily subsidized canteens were set up and agricultural laborers were given a supplementary ration of cheese.[19] Children under five were guaranteed free fruit juices and cod-liver oil, and daily meals served to schoolchildren increased from approximately 160,000 before the war to 1.6 million in 1945.

The results of such foresight and initiative were remarkable. Despite routine bombings and thinly stretched resources, by the end of the war an overall improvement in public health in Britain was evident.[20] The Ministry of Food, in retrospect, noted, "general health was good throughout the period of war [and the] fitness of babies and school children was particularly striking."[21] Moreover, despite the fact that food imports had fully halved during wartime,[22] average per capita spending on foodstuffs, due to the success of the rationing system, had declined.[23]

With the lack of any similar initiatives in India, the only real guidelines for managing the food supply in Bengal during World War II was the Bengal Famine Code: first published in 1897, updated once in 1905, and then lastly in 1913. The Code was the product of Britain's long experience with starvation in India.

The first and most spectacular mass starvation in British India followed close on the heels of the East India Company's victory at the Battle of Plassey. Between the years of 1769 and 1771 as much as one third of the population of Bengal—then estimated to be about 30 million—was wiped out by famine.[24] Only seven years earlier the Company had gained *diwani* rights over Bengal and Bihar from the Mughal Emperor, which gave them exclusive revenue collecting authority in the new colony. William Wilson Hunter, British civil servant and compiler of *The Imperial Gazetteer of India*, was author of one of the few colonial descriptions of the "1770 Bengal Famine" in his *Annals of Rural Bengal*, written in 1868. The enormity of the death from starvation and disease of 10 million or more of the Company's newly acquired subjects, placed in new light, Hunter explained,

> those broad tracks of desolation which the British conquerors found everywhere throughout the Lower Valley; it enfolds the sufferings entailed on an ancient rural society by being suddenly placed in a position which its immemorial forms and usages could no longer apply; and then it explains how, out of disorganized and fragmentary elements, a new order of things was evolved.[25]

But the fact that depopulation through starvation had made Bengal something of a "clean slate" for the colonial enterprise was not entirely a surprise. The Famine Commission of 1878, investigating events leading up to the 1770 famine reported:

> In October 1769, very gloomy reports were received from Behar and North Bengal. In November the Collector-General "saw an alarming prospect of the province becoming desolate" and the Government wrote home to the Court of Directors in the most alarming terms. They resolved to lay up six months' store of grain for their troops and sent in December to Dacca and Backergunj to buy rice.[26]

These efforts at martial appropriation were not entirely effective, however, and the "laying up" of grain continued. Even as "day and night a torrent of famished and disease-stricken wretches poured into the great cities:"[27]

The troops were marched from one famine-stricken part to another, the movement being represented to the king as made for his benefit; and so far from the English administration having laid in a sufficient stock of grain for the army at the commencement of the famine, the peasantry complained that the military wrung from them their last chance of subsistence.[28]

"In 1770," Hunter notes, "the English Government knew very little about the country, and did still less for its inhabitants."[29] He goes on to explain eighteenth-century British priorities succinctly:

Until 1772 Bengal was regarded by the British public in the light of a vast warehouse, in which a number of adventurous Englishmen carried on business with great profit and on an enormous scale. That a numerous native population existed, they were aware; but this they considered an accidental circumstance.[30]

The accident of the population's starvation, then, demanded little reflection. "The utmost that could be expected from Government," wrote the Company's Council from Calcutta, "would be a lenient policy towards the husbandmen whom a bad harvest had disabled from paying the usual land-tax."[31] This "relief," as might be expected, proved grossly inadequate, and in subsequent years the Company found that "the remnant of the population would not [even] suffice to till the land."[32] In 1771 the President of the Council in Calcutta mourned to the Court of Directors in London that there had been "such a mortality and desertion among the ryots [peasant cultivators] as to deprive the [revenue] farmers of the possibility of receiving rents in arrear."[33] Ten million were dead and revenues remained moribund. It was only toward this latter casualty of famine that the Council directed its imagination and began hammering out a "permanent settlement" of Bengal's land tenure in order to guarantee the Company's revenue.[34]

In the next 127 years there were no fewer than twenty-five officially recorded famines in colonial India, with those of 1783, 1873–4, 1866, and 1896–97 (the largest since 1770), all affecting Bengal to varying degrees.[35] In 1880 a Famine Commission was established in Bengal to outline measures of redress. According to the commission's findings the *Bengal Famine Code* was published some sixteen years later—in the midst of the most devastating famine since 1770. Meanwhile, from the year before the Famine Code's first publication in 1896 until its revision and republication in 1903, it is estimated that up to 19 million people died of starvation and disease in India.[36]

Of primary importance in the *Bengal Famine Code* was to train administrative personnel how to identify famine in the offing. In this regard, protocols were established for bi-weekly reporting on crop conditions, rainfall, "the health of the people" and the "existence of any scarcity or distress." Particular instructions were given to promptly report any "rise in prices above 20 percent over normal rates." Statistical compilations of records that should be used to determine "normal rates" were sketched in detail, and if these statistically established normal rates failed to apply, a detailed report was to be made and sent to the Government of India. In the event that prices continue to remain abnormal, prompt reporting of early signs of imminent famine was required. These signs included:

1) The contraction of private charity indicated by the wandering of paupers.
2) Contraction of credit.
3) Feverish activity in the grain trade.
4) Restlessness shown in an increase of crime.
5) Unusual movements of flocks and herds in search of pasturage.
6) Unusual wandering of people.[37]

When any combination of these occurrences was observed, according to the Code, a Famine Commissioner was to be immediately appointed and District Officers were required to open "Test Works" to determine the extent of need. The nature of the "Test Works" (essentially labor-camps for the hungry) is also outlined in detail. The test works were of ultimate importance, because if such test works attracted applicants in large numbers, famine was to be officially declared and various schemes of famine relief were to commence at once—the "test" had proved positive.

Importantly, although according to the Famine Code relief was to be run through local channels, it was duly recognized that famine entailed distinct extra-local, as well as extra-provincial, and ultimately imperial responsibilities. In this regard local officials were directed to notify their superiors, and their superiors to notify the Government of India promptly of:

1) The extent to which Imperial aid is likely to be required…if there is any reason to believe that the Provincial funds will prove insufficient to meet the exigencies of famine.
2) The extent to which suspension or remission of land revenue may be considered necessary. [And,]

3) The extent to which the Provincial staff requires to be increased by drafts from Imperial departments or otherwise.[38]

In all the *Bengal Famine Code* was a fairly comprehensive and pragmatic document. I include mention of it here because it was—ostensibly—the only guideline for food security available in Bengal during the war-period. Discussion of the Code here is a somewhat moot point however. Famine was never declared in the 1940s in Bengal and the Code failed to apply. As will be seen, a few "Test Works" were opened on an ad hoc basis along the way, but the Famine Code was never enacted, and there was almost no discussion of its implementation by colonial or provincial authorities. In fact, as K.C. Neogy, Bengal MLA[39] testified to the Famine Enquiry Commission in 1944, the last official revision of the Bengal Famine Code (1905)—at the time of this particular mass starvation in India—was found to be out of print.[40] A somewhat mysterious, and provisional "Famine Manual" stamped "for official use only" had been drafted in 1941, but was not readily available for consideration in 1943. Neogy himself could only get a hold of it "surreptitiously."[41] In any case, he testified, the elusive Famine Manual began: "This Manual is not intended to displace the Bengal Famine Code but to indicate how its leading principles ought to be applied." This despite the fact that Neogy, when he inquired about consulting the Bengal Famine Code during the height of famine in 1943, had been told by the Revenue Minister of Bengal that it had been superseded since the advent of "Provincial Autonomy."[42] Such confusion and obfuscation clearly illustrates the real lack of effective will or policy to deal with famine in colonial India at the time.

Enforcing Morale

Short of a comprehensive plan to secure the public welfare in terms of the food supply, war planning in Bengal consisted primarily of the establishment of "Civil Defense" forces; organizations of locally recruited young men who would constitute a somewhat ad-hoc, loyalist, native police force, which over the years would serve the aims of empire in diverse and creative ways—few with any direct relation to the "war effort." The structure, authority, and partiality of these organizations would also sow seeds of conflict in society at large, exasperating increasingly deep divisions among the population which would periodically erupt into violence—class, communal, or otherwise—which these same services would then be called on to police.

The A.R.P.

The first of these forces to be established was the Air Raid Precaution services, or A.R.P. In July 1938, even before war had broken out, a committee was appointed to sketch out a plan for the A.R.P. in Calcutta and its surrounding suburbs, most importantly the docks at Kidderpore and the industrial belt spanning both sides of the River Hooghly. The Commissioner of the Presidency Division[43] was appointed Chair of the coordinating committee, and District Magistrates of Howrah, Hooghly and the 24 Parganas were responsible for development in their respective jurisdictions. The municipality of Calcutta was to be managed by the Commissioner of Police—a delegation of authority that created an outcry. Members of the Calcutta Corporation[44]—always a hotbed of political contention—argued that the Mayor of Calcutta, appointed by the democratically elected Corporation, should be in charge of the Calcutta A.R.P., rather than the Chief of Police, a colonially appointed official. Concessions were made, but at length the Corporation condemned the scheme as "unscientific and puerile,"[45] and refused to take part, discounting, in any case, the likelihood of an "enemy" attack on Calcutta or its suburbs.[46]

Nevertheless, "the whole of 1940 and 1941 saw the expansion and development of the Air Raid Precautionary measures [and] during this period an intensive propaganda campaign for recruitment of volunteers was undertaken."[47] Recruitment in Howrah and the suburbs went well, but in Calcutta it did not.[48] The rift with the Corporation had damaged the A.R.P.'s reputation, and the Corporation's affiliation with the Indian National Congress and its program of "non-cooperation" entrenched the situation further. Furthermore, as one organizing member noted, "it was no easy task educating the public. There was a common belief that once recruited in the A.R.P. they would be sent abroad as fighting forces."[49] On 10 December 1941 a system of pay was introduced and later allowances for subsidized food grains were added. Recruitment picked up. In the coming years, with rapid inflation taking hold and increasing scarcity beginning to bite, a remunerative position of local authority, sanctioned by imperial authority, in and around Calcutta became increasingly more attractive. By the time of its demobilization at the end of 1945, in addition to at least 66,000 volunteers,[50] the paid A.R.P. ranks numbered over 26,000, the majority of whom were engaged in "administrative" work.[51]

In the early days of war, given that the Indian Army itself was at the time "starved of money and poorly equipped,"[52] the A.R.P. had its work cut out for it. Along all the main thoroughfares of Calcutta and the industrial districts, "slit trenches" were dug to serve as shelters in case of bombing.[53] The slit trenches were no more than six foot deep gulleys, without overhead protection or drainage. They were protected on the sides by "baffle walls" made of local brick, and reinforced with sand bags. Baffle walls were also constructed at the entrances to governmental and residential buildings in the downtown area. As a back-up to the Corporation's water treatment facility, arrangements were also made to sink 2,000 deep tube wells (at an average depth of 250 feet) and 500 shallow tube wells (averaging 70 feet in depth): a mammoth task. In Calcutta, 20 hospitals were selected and asked to reserve 100 beds on their premises strictly for A.R.P. purposes. Officers were appointed to serve as local Wardens, and managers were assigned to various work crews to oversee and execute lighting restrictions, fire fighting, rescue and demolition, medical treatment, gas decontamination, and corpse disposal. Mass burial pits were dug at Gobra on the northern outskirts of the city to accommodate many thousands of corpses,[54] and vague plans were outlined for the maintenance of essential services such as sewage, gas, electric, and food supply.[55]

Officers' uniforms consisted of khaki drill tunics fastened with four silver A.R.P. buttons, khaki slacks, shirts, socks and neckties, brown shoes, and a steel helmet bearing the A.R.P. insignia. Officers and all other members of the forces were to wear a "navy blue brassard on which the prescribed Air Raid Precautions Service Badge shall remain imposed," this would "remain the property of the crown."[56] Such measures ensured that the A.R.P. attained an aspect of pseudo-military authority, becoming a kind of civilian militia operating under Crown auspices. In addition the Viceroy of India, Victor Hope, Second Marquess of Linlithgow, signed an ordinance in 1941 granting members of the A.R.P. pervasive immunity in relation to their nebulously defined civil authority. The ordinance read: "no suit, prosecution or other legal proceeding shall lie against the Controller or any member of an Air Raid Precautions service for anything which is in good faith done or intended to be done in pursuance of this Ordinance or any rules made there under."[57] Over the next several years, as the "emergency" of war became ever-more pressing, the A.R.P. would be used in diverse ways to patrol, police and propagandize the cities and larger towns of Bengal—often in relation to "disorders" having little to with their initial mission of "defense."

The Civic Guards

Shortly thereafter the colonial government also began organizing a second mechanism to maintain order amongst urban populations in the province; the Civic Guard. On November 1st, 1941, it was announced in a government press release that the Governor, Sir John Herbert, "had made certain rules for the Civic Guard organization in Bengal."[58] This executive decision (announced in the past tense) had been possible in relation to the exercise of powers conferred to him in the Civic Guard Ordinance of 1940, which until that time had not been utilised. According to Herbert's scheme, the Commissioner of Police would be responsible for units in Calcutta, with local Superintendents, under the direction of District Magistrates, organizing in smaller cities. Recruits, it was also announced, would "be formally enrolled with due ceremony on parade and during this ceremony each recruit shall take the oath of allegiance to His Majesty the King Emperor."[59]

At the time of this announcement the duties of the Civic Guard were few, but broad in scope. They were:

1) to assist the regular police force in the protection of the civil population against the forces of crime and disorder
2) to work in close touch with air raid precautions and to maintain and enforce order during black-outs and air raid alarms, [and]
3) to perform such duties in connection with the protection of persons and property, or the public safety, as the Provincial Government may from time to time assign to them.[60]

A few weeks later, "the promotion of communal harmony," the prevention of "the spread of false rumors," and the circulation of "accurate war news" were all added to their duties. Additionally, it was expected "that every member of the Civic Guard [would] consider himself a servant of the public at all times, and be ready to help, without hope of reward, anybody who is to be found in distress or difficulty."[61]

The lack of reward, however—and again—did seem to hamper recruitment. In the government's quarterly "War Diary" the Inspector-General of the Bengal Police explained:

> In most districts the Civic Guards have been inactive; little progress has been made with training in drill and law, while physical training has been neglected…it is hoped that with the posting of Adjutants and Quarter-Masters, the issue of new uniforms, *and a scheme of allowances*…the waning enthusiasm will be revived.[62]

Taking into consideration the additional privileges that can be assumed to have accrued to positions of imperially recognized authority during a period of acute scarcity and administrative chaos, it can be ventured that the non-monetary benefits of membership in the Civic Guard were also increasingly significant. By the next year the ranks of the Civic Guard in Calcutta alone numbered close to 5,000, and they were reported to be acting as an effective "special police" throughout Bengal.[63]

The Home Guards

Control in the countryside was a more complex question. With its more than 90,000 villages and 20,000 miles of water communications winding through thick jungle, and its human geography an "infinite variety of local agrarian structures,"[64] much of the province had proven a governmental conundrum from the earliest days of European penetration. From the earliest times of the East India Company adventures in India until the advent of WWII, colonial forays into the Bengal countryside had remained "a journey into the unknown in more than one sense."[65] Moreover, with the "Permanent Settlement" of land tenures in 1793, revenue collecting responsibilities had been conferred on local landlords and Government was able to maintain a light administrative footprint, intervening directly only as necessary—most often to enforce "order."

Order in rural Bengal, however, seemed chronically beyond colonial reach. "Special Officer" L.G. Pinnell—who would play a fateful role in the lives of many millions of Bengalis—narrated his equivocal record of administration in the Bengal countryside during the war and famine tellingly:

> I do hope that some of the members of the Commission will go on tour by the watercourses along the coastal routes of Bengal; if they do so they will

appreciate how impossible it is to administer that area in detail with the staff that exists...the whole area is a network of tidal *khal* [inlets, canals and bayous] running between very big and dangerous rivers and your staff consists of the sub-divisional officer, perhaps a couple of circle officers for an area of 600 square miles, and a *thana* [police precinct] staff of a sub-inspector with perhaps one assistant for an area of—I would not like to exactly say....

However, as the rural population comprised at least 90 per cent of Bengal's population at the time, Government could not content itself with civil defense measures that focused on cities alone. In this context, the Governor of Bengal, acting under Government of India authority, and ultimately the War Office in London, introduced, in addition to the A.R.P. and the Civic Guards, the Bengal Home Guard, or *Bangya Griharaksha Dal*. The duties of the Home Guard were officially outlined as:

1) the preservation of peace and order
2) aiding and assisting evacuees or refugees who may pass through the area
3) raising and stiffening the morale of the people, discounting and denying false rumor and rumor-mongering generally, and;
4) in the areas near the coast and eastern frontiers, watching for and reporting anything of a suspicious nature.

Additionally, "if necessary," it was later added, "in times of emergency, they would also be available for maintaining the food supply and similar activities."[66] No specific plans for this last function were outlined.

The Home Guard would be organized under police supervision and would operate in rural areas only. Local officials, under the direction of District Magistrates were responsible to enlist ranks in the following, highly divisive, manner:

> within the area of a police station they will co-opt two influential non-officials, of whom one will be Hindu and one Muslim...in consultation with these co-opted members Circle Officer and Circle Inspector of Police will select a suitable local man to be the Captain...the Captain will be entrusted with enrolling a group of at least 25 effectives.[67]

In this way Government would be able to extend its authority, if not its own human resources, into the far reaches of the countryside. Home Guard members would be required to wear an identifying badge "indicating in Bengali letters the title of the organization," and would be armed with *lathis* [canes], but—initially—were to receive no pay. Based on previous experience with recruitment in such volunteer organiza-tions, however, it was added that, "if the Home Guards prove a success and establish themselves in the esteem and affection of the persons [in] whose services they are enrolled, there is no need to anticipate insur-mountable difficulties in the way of providing them with uniforms and possibly other amenities...."[68] By the end of the war the Home Guards in Bengal numbered close to 200,000.

Hearts and Minds

For a significant portion of the population, however, cooperation with the war effort amounted to colonial collaboration and, as such, national betrayal. Increasingly confrontational anti-colonial movements had been gaining steam for decades, and when in 1939 the viceroy declared war on India's behalf without any consultation, long-standing resentments of colonial rule only sharpened. Radical Bengali nationalist, Subhas Chandra Bose, resigned from the All-India Congress leadership when Gandhi refused to launch a mass movement to denounce the war, and in Bengal founded the breakaway Forward Block.[69] Opposition to the war was widespread and resistance and rebellion increasingly entrenched. Understanding the risks to an empire at war of a restive population, in June 1940 the War Cabinet in London approved the viceroy's scheme for a Revolutionary Movements Ordinance, "conferring extraordinary powers [on the Government of India] in the event of civil disobedi-ence."[70] About this, maverick British journalist Arthur Moore wrote to the incoming Secretary of State for India Leo Amery ominously:

> the idea that, with their base in England largely out of the reckoning, the handful of British here can, by invoking a Defense of the Realm Act, keep army and police control and hold the country down, is dangerous madness.[71]

In October 1940, riding the wave of discontent, the Indian Congress High Command announced the resignation of all its elected representa-tives in protest against unrepresentative cooption into Britain's war against Germany. Seven provinces had elected Chief Ministers who were members of Congress, and as such these ministries were effectively dis-solved by the resignations. Consequently, Section 93 of the Defense of India Rules was invoked, giving the imperially appointed Governors of these seven provinces emergency rule. Provincial Autonomy, established in 1935, was turning out to be something less in practice than what it had been imagined in theory. Linlithgow himself, panicked by the breakdown in governmental order, "was getting very desperate, felt he could do nothing and wanted to resign and come home."[72] Perhaps his high sense of dignity could not accommodate the nitty-gritty of holding empire together in times of war and rebellion. As Reforms Commissioner, Henry Hodson describes him, the viceroy "was a formidable-looking man. Very tall, ungainly in motion, with a long solemn face like a sad clown that belied his rich humor, he displayed the deterrent reserve of a naturally shy man. As if this were not enough to awe an official caller at Viceroy's House, he always sat on a big throne-like chair raised several inches on a dais behind a massive desk."[73]

Material concerns, meanwhile, motivated the majority of the population of Bengal and a deep apathy towards the war prevailed. During an A.R.P. exercise in Sovabazar, not only were "numbers of *bhadralok*[74] walking about on their business and ignoring the exercise," but even more alarmingly, "two *chokras*[75] aged 13 or 14 were seen wearing A.R.P. armlets."[76] An investigation was launched and it was found that at least seventeen firms in Calcutta were selling unauthorized A.R.P. brassards and badges to civilians. An order under the Defense of India Rules was issued prohibiting the manufacture or sale of unauthorized badges, and a directive was circulated stating that "it should be made clear that anyone found in unauthorized possession of such articles shall be severely dealt with."[77] Several orders followed, detailing the exact procedure of authorization and distribution of badges and other identifying paraphernalia related to A.R.P. and Civic Guard membership—to what effect it is difficult to discover.

In rural Bengal, where anti-British sentiment had long been sharp, there were also more alarming signs of disorder. Posters were hung in 1940 warning:

> The British Empire Is On The Verge Of Annihilation: Don't Be A Recruited Soldier!"[78]

Leaflets, entitled "Civic Guard or a Treacherous Force?" were circulated, and strident anti-war appeals were openly publicized:

> If the British Agents Would Approach You for War Contributions
> Turn them Out!

> Do Not Betray Your Country by Enrolling Yourself in the Civic Guard!

Killed by Hitler on the other side of the ocean,
the British Raj has greatly increased repression on us.
Let us get ready to retaliate![79]

Significant contributions to the war fund failed to materialize, and withdrawals from post office banks further undermined the finances of war.[80] Measures to improve "morale" continued to meet with failure, and repeated calls to "stand to" were met with the contrary inclination to flee. Even after Japan's entry into the war, while there was considerable anxiety and uncertainty in the province, the alarm with which the British looked east from Calcutta was not shared by many among the Indian population. In fact, the vulnerability of the British Empire was greeted with a measure of glee as well as cynicism. Even as the A.R.P. and Civic Guard paraded in the streets, behind closed doors, in schoolrooms, playgrounds, and in Bengali kitchens, a humorous ditty—that few would forget[81]—made the rounds:

Sa-re-ga-ma-pa-dha-ni
Bom phelechhe Japani,
Bomar maidhe keute sap
British bole bapre-bap!

Do-re-mi-fa-so-la-ti
A bomb was dropped by the Japanese
In the bomb is a cobra snake
The British shout "For Heaven's Sake!"

The Countryside

Particularly in the countryside, concern for the war was attenuated by the more pressing struggle for basic survival. In 1934, Satish Chandra Mitter published a book with the retrospectively ironic title *A Recovery Plan for Bengal*. In his appended, hand typed appreciation of the work, Rabindranath Tagore called *Recovery Plan* "the best possible book one can wish for," at a time when "our villages are driven to desolation [and their inhabitants] are grown inconspicuous by the deadly pallor of their anemic existence."[82] Mitter himself paints a grim picture of rural Bengal circa 1934. "It is evident to anyone familiar with agricultural conditions…and with the lives of the cultivators," he writes, "that they exist rather than live, and that the margin between starvation and existence is an extremely small one."[83] The index of jute prices, set at 100 in 1914, had plummeted to 40 by 1934,[84] and jute producers were pushed to the brink. Rice prices, similarly, were perilously deflated, with the value to the cultivator in 1934 half that which it had been five years earlier.[85] Malaria had depopulated important sectors of the economy, and the fishing industry was a shambles.[86] Milk cows were being slaughtered out of economic necessity, and, with the cost of living at 150 per cent of pre-WWI levels, inhabitants of Bengal's countryside, Mitter cautioned, "[could not] but be hunger-stricken and starving, and eventually insolvent."[87]

In the first two decades of the twentieth century, due to increasing commercialization in grain markets and slumping jute prices, "many peasants fell into debt and could only carry on by borrowing seed and grain from year to year; and in course of time, were reduced to a position close to that of landless laborers."[88] Cultivators were trapped in a cycle of debt and repayment that left them on the verge of starvation between crops; forced to sell their products at deflated prices during the post-harvest glut, in order to pay loans taken during the pre-harvest "starvation" season. Meanwhile, restrictions on rent increases mandated by the Bengal Tenancy Act of 1885, compounded by the increasing pressures of population growth and the diminishing size of land holdings, had made it increasingly difficult for landlords to profit from rent extraction. The rural gentry had thus increasingly turned to usurious relationships with their tenants to stay afloat,[89] further straitening the already impoverished peasantry, and further entrenching class—and communal[90]—resentments.

Subsequently, by the late 1930s the rural credit market had all but totally collapsed.[91] Deflation of prices in rice and jute markets, throughout the decade, meant unpaid credit balances. While "recovery" from the Great Depression had been achieved in the U.S. and Europe, credit relations in Bengal failed to rebound and poverty deepened.[92] By the turn of the decade moneylenders "had shut their money-chests…[and] the supply of grain had largely been taken out of the orbit of credit and subjected to the convulsions of a wartime product market."[93] In the meantime, the cycle of subsistence and starvation remained, with many millions of cultivators now falling into abject destitution. To make ends meet in the absence of credit, cultivators entered into cynically usufructary mortgages and lost their lands, or managed to hang on by selling off family ornaments, brass-wear and other moveable possessions. The poor of Bengal had been through a devastating decade, and even in the late 30s many were already starving.

With the declaration of war in 1939 and dislocations in commodity markets related to the same, the price of rice rose 33 per cent in a single year[94]—a shock that the rural population could ill afford. In October 1940, Mihirlal Chatterjee, member of the All India Village Association issued an appeal to the provincial government in the *Amrita Bazar Patrika*, warning that "the gloom of a frightful famine [had] cast its shadow all over Birbhum. He went on:

> it is high time that the authorities at the head of the Provincial Government should gather first hand knowledge of the exact situation and do everything in their power to combat the famine. Let it never be said to the eternal disgrace of the responsible ministers at the head of a provincial autonomous Government that, like the bureaucratic administration of the past, they have also studiously refrained from declaring famine when actually that condition prevailed.[95]

Dr Profulla Chandra Ghosh, ardent Gandhian and future chief minister of independent West Bengal, set up the West Bengal Famine Relief Committee to raise relief funds for the "famine-stricken people of Midnapur, Birbhum, Bankura and Murshidabad."[96] Floods during the monsoon season had compounded the difficulties of inflation, and scarcity was taking a toll.

A year later, in September of 1941, the price of rice had risen another 36 per cent, and distress deepened in rural Bengal.[97] In its quarterly diary of war activities, the Government of Bengal reported:

> In the districts the abnormal rise in prices of paddy, rice and piece goods has hit the poorer section of the people very hard. Though the general rise in prices is taken to be an outcome of the war, the failure to exercise any effective control over the price...has been a great disappointment to many.[98]

In Noakhali and Tippera (in eastern Bengal) with jute prices failing to follow the inflationary curve, the rice-purchasing power of cultivators plummeted dangerously. The Commissioner worried that "economic distress and the high price of rice may lead to organized goondaism."[99] "Test Works"—the primary indicator of famine laid out in the Bengal Famine Code—were opened in both Tippera and Noakhali. Rates of recompense were negligible, but the works drew "considerable numbers."[100] The "test" had proven positive, but no further resources were expended and famine was not declared. Hunger marches were organized to demand relief,[101] and in north Bengal sharecroppers and landless laborers looted rice paddy from the storehouses of rich landholders (*jot-*

edars).[102] Prices of sugar, cooking oil, kerosene and pulses of all varieties had also risen steeply,[103] and "the price of yarn hit the hand-loom weavers in the province so hard that they had to suspend business."[104]

In the same quarter, the War Diary reports, "25 important articles on A.R.P., war, war funds, etc. were published, 38 press notes were issued and 22 leaflets, pamphlets, etc. were distributed, and movie-tone war news reels and war films, prepared, purchased, or hired, continue to be displayed by the National Welfare Units."[105] For this last purpose Government had at its disposal not only six publicity vans, but also eight bullock carts, and four river boats, commissioned to spread the word of imminent danger down into the countryside.[106] One can only imagine how such efforts might have been received. According to the Director of Public Instruction, literacy rates in Bengal were not more than 15 per cent, and life expectancy no more than 27 years.[107] In this context, there is little doubt that distinct knowledge of, not to mention support for, the British war effort was extremely limited.

When Japan entered the war, things disintegrated further. "The slogan 'resist Japan'," as Sunil Sen has suggested, "[could have] hardly made any sense to the [impoverished, illiterate and disenfranchised] peasant."[108] Such a disconnect is suggested in a poignant scene in Satyajit Ray's 1973 movie *Asani Sanket*,[109] wherein, in a typical village of central Bengal, circa 1942, the population is struggling to survive. Prices have risen prohibitively and the poorest have already begun to starve. An educated member of the village reads a newspaper to a gathered crowed. "The British have been defeated! Singapore has fallen to the Japanese!" The news is accompanied by much excitement. One naive member of the audience enquires hesitantly, however, "…but where is Singapore?" The newsreader pauses to consider, then responds confidently, "not far from Midnapore…."[110] Apparently the bullock vans had not made their way yet to this particular village.

Establishing Priorities

In the factories surrounding Calcutta there were also acute economic anxieties. From the earliest days of the war, strikes for wage increases, "dearness allowances," war bonuses, and the opening of "controlled shops"[111] were common. The dominant industry in Bengal was jute manufacturing, employing more than 285,000 workers, the majority of whom were migrant laborers from Bihar, the United Provinces and

Orissa.[112] As in the jute mills, in the all-important cotton mills,[113] workers were primarily migrant, unskilled, and easily replaceable. But war meant profit, and maximization of profit demanded maintaining a stable labor force, which was not always easy to achieve.

In November 1939 a strike involving more than 11,000 workers at the Hukumchand Jute Mill in the northern suburbs of Calcutta drew a quick response from the Indian Jute Mills Association (IJMA). Bengal's jute production at the time accounted for more than half the supply of jute world-wide,[114] and as such production in Calcutta was considered essential to the war effort. The IJMA quickly settled the strike and instituted a flat-rate wage increase of 10 per cent throughout the industry, which, however, did not succeed in dampening widespread labor actions. In May 1941, 9,000 workers at Baranagar jute mills went on strike and in July 12,000 workers at the Anglo Indian Jute Mills followed suit.[115] Earlier, in March of 1940, 20,000 workers of the Calcutta Corporation—street cleaners, sewage workers, and other menial laborers—had also gone on strike, and in September workers of the Calcutta Tramways and Calcutta Port Trust began petitioning for war-bonuses as well. The President of the Bengal Labor Association had moved a resolution in the legislature asking for the grant of a 25 per cent war-bonus to *all* factory and mill labor,[116] but the resolution was defeated and discontent simmered.

The appeal of remaining in oppressive mills and factories, and running the additional hazard of being targeted by "enemy" aircraft, began to pale just as labor requirements were increasing. Consequently, in February 1941 the "Essential Services Maintenance Ordinance" was promulgated by the Government of India. The Ordinance defined as essential "war industries" including: cotton and jute mills, armament factories, engineering firms, paper mills, printing facilities, and even tobacco factories, gin presses, food service workers, and stone masons, as well as employees of municipal, provincial or central governments.[117] All of these workers, because deemed "essential" to the war effort, were put under extraordinary restrictions:

> The ordinance makes it an offence punishable with imprisonment for a term which may extend to one year and with fine, for any person [covered under the ordinance] to abandon such employment or absent himself without reasonable excuse. The fact that a person apprehends that by continuing in his employment he will be exposed to increased physical danger does not constitute a reasonable excuse.[118]

In declaring the workers essential, the government was also signifying them as "priority" citizens.[119] Such a designation would have an increasingly important significance in the coming years, as the differential "priority" of citizens of Calcutta became almost the sole measure of life and death.

But, to date, very little had actually been done regarding the actual defense of Calcutta—the idea of which played such a central rhetorical role in colonial governance at the time. The British themselves, though they had mobilized a native police force of close to 300,000 in Bengal, were less than well-organized on the military front. In his *Official History of the Indian Armed Forces in the Second World War*, Bisheswar Prasad admits, "till the end of 1941 no effective measures for the defense of Burma or India on the eastern side had been adopted."[120] For all the fanfare, the Empire's Second City remained largely unprotected. "There were virtually no anti-aircraft guns, air-raid flood lights, or radar sets, and the Royal Indian Air Force could only deploy 8 'serviceable Mohawks' to defend Calcutta."[121] Historian Eric Stokes, who himself served in the British armed forces in India during the war, places further doubt on the urgency of British preparedness. Bayly and Harper note:

> Throughout the war India Command's fortnightly situation appreciations conventionally began with an account of operations on the North West Frontier in which British officers pursued shadowy Mullahs over the hills and frustrated the plots of obscure tribal insurgents. Stokes felt that the Faqir of Ipi, a Muslim rebel [in Waziristan] and long time thorn in the imperial flesh, seemed to loom as large in their minds as Tojo and Hitler even when the Japanese stood at the gates of India.[122]

[Some things don't seem to change.]

The Fortress Falls

Above all, Britain's strategy for the defense of its colonial possessions in South and Southeast Asia hinged on the presumed invulnerability of 'Fortress Singapore.' Originally under the administrative ambit of the Bengal Presidency, Singapore became a crown colony in 1867, and by 1930, 23 per cent of all British trade passed through this single port.[123] The naval base built at Sembawang (on the northern coast of the island) boasted the largest dry dock in the world, and the southern coast was fortified with a battery of huge artillery guns poised to repel naval attack at long range—but, importantly, only if that attack came from the south.

In 1940 Japanese officers on a reconnaissance mission to the area informed their commanding Colonel, Masanobu Tsuji, that Singapore was indeed vulnerable to attack—from the Johore Strait to the north.[124] Later the same year, when the British commander of Malaya, Lieutenant-General Lionel Bond, surveyed the situation he similarly concluded that Singapore remained perilously vulnerable to invasion from the north, and advised swift preparations to defend against this line of attack. But only symbolic measures of defense were taken. Bond had suggested that a minimum of 336 first-line aircraft were needed to secure the peninsula, but in January 1942, Malaya was defended by only ninety antiquated "Brewster Buffalo" aircraft, which had been rejected for service in Europe. The seas were patrolled by the ad hoc 'Force Z,' consisting only of two battleships, the HMS *Prince of Wales* and HMS *Repulse*, backed by four destroyers. There were no aircraft carriers within range, and not a single tank on the ground. In November 1941, when approached by "frantic" Australian generals about the situation in Singapore, Churchill pointedly declined to reinforce the Southeast Asia defenses, citing the urgency of war in the Middle East.[125]

Several hours before the attack on Pearl Harbor, Japan launched an ambitious assault on the northern coast of Malaya at Kota Bahru, raining bombs down on unprepared British aerodromes and landing infantry battalions on unguarded beaches: marshaling 125,000 men, 534 aircraft and 79 tanks.[126] The British were caught completely unawares. Sixty of ninety Allied aircraft were destroyed in their hangers. The Indian troops of the 1st Hyderabads fought to defend the railhead, then in disorganized retreat shot and killed their British commander.[127] Force Z steamed from Singapore on the afternoon of 8 December and, without air support, engaged the Japanese naval force off the northern coast of Malaya. The *Prince of Wales* and *Repulse* were quickly sunk, and Admiral Phillips and 840 of his men were killed. Word of this startling defeat shook the Empire. The following day in the House of Commons, Winston Churchill mourned, "in my whole experience I do not remember any naval blow so heavy or so painful as the sinking of the *Prince of Wales* and the *Repulse* on Monday last. These two vast, powerful ships constituted an essential feature in our plans for meeting the new Japanese danger as it loomed against us in the last few months."[128] In the subsequent days, Kota Bahru was abandoned and Japanese forces landing in Thailand pushed south to reinforce the invading army.

Japanese divisions, each equipped with 6,000 bicycles and light tanks, advanced down the Malaya peninsula rapidly. Several lines of defense were hastily erected, but fell quickly to the swift advance of Japanese troops. At Jitra British/Indian defenses were consolidated, but collapsed in fifteen short hours. Retreating soldiers left behind vast stores of tinned food, petrol and other military supplies that Japan swept up as they moved south. The Japanese air-force, meanwhile, pummeled British staging grounds at Penang and Singapore. The colonial administration, in a state of panic, hastened to evacuate Europeans from the line of fire, leaving Malayans and Indians to their own devices.[129] On 27 January, 1942 Malaya was surrendered, and Allied forces, demolishing the bridge behind them, retreated to 'Fortress Singapore.'

Singapore itself had been under air-attack since 8 December, and many of its European residents had already been evacuated. The big guns on the southern coast remained silent, and the Japanese air-force redoubled its assault, blanketing the island from high altitudes. Communication lines were knocked out and hospitals overflowed with wounded soldiers and civilians alike. Rumors of gas attacks circulated and, as menial labors began to flee in mass, civic services collapsed. The remaining Europeans gathered in luxury hotels and country clubs, guzzling whiskey from basement casks and cursing their commanders.[130] In the Asian quarters, corpses rotted on street corners and families hunkered in hand-dug earthen pits. The fall of Singapore, however, could not be countenanced. On 10 February, Churchill telegraphed his regional Commander in Chief, Archibald Wavell:

> There must be at this stage no thought of saving the troops or sparing the population. The battle must be fought to the bitter end and at all costs... Commanders and senior officers should die with their troops. The honor of the British Empire and the British Army is at stake.[131]

Churchill's orders, however, were met with skepticism. The Governor himself argued for capitulation. Allied troops, demoralized by defeat, looted city shops and threatened their own officers with revolvers.[132] Surrender came on the afternoon of 15 February 1942. In all, the British Army had lost as many as 130,000 troops to death or capture, many of them Indian forces, and also the Crown possessions of Malaya and Singapore. Churchill called the defeat "the worst disaster and the largest capitulation in British history."

Burmese Days

Reginald Dorman-Smith had been appointed Governor of Burma in May 1941. Before his inauguration he frankly admitted his pervasive ignorance of the country: "my knowledge of Burma was precisely nil…I knew approximately where it was on the map, that its capital was Rangoon, and that the Irrawaddy flowed through it, but my knowledge did not extend beyond this."[133] Unsurprisingly, when Japan began bombing Rangoon in the last week of December, chaos broke out immediately. The Burmese population fled the city in droves, retreating to monasteries and homes in the countryside, and the majority Indian population of the city "simply scattered in terror."[134] Rumors of violence against Indians by Burmese nationals circulated widely, and the British began evacuating all their own "non-essential" personnel in preparation for a long siege.

With success in Malaya well in hand, Japan turned more of its military might in the direction of Burma and the fissures in the British system opened further. Inexperienced and disaffected British troops put up only sporadic and uninspired resistance, and Indian troops, paired with Burmese recruits, were hampered by language difficulties that plagued their bi-national battalions. American volunteer forces, in Burma to secure the Burma Road, were openly critical of British military prowess, going so far as to burn "lend-lease" vehicles rather than allow their use by British forces.[135] Furthermore, British heavy artillery, though impressive in theory, was unsuitable for the conditions. Dorman-Smith reported with dismay that Japanese troops were able to simply "walk around" British defensive positions—their tanks and heavy guns sunk deep in mud—as they made their way towards Rangoon.[136]

As Japanese forces approached the city, life in the capital deteriorated precipitously. Disease spread as sweepers fled in terror, compelling Dorman-Smith to conclude that life in a colonial metropolis "begins with the sweeper. That lowest of all human beings who holds in his hands the difference between health and disease, cleanliness and filth."[137] Calcutta would learn the same lesson in the months to come. The British army withdrew large contingents of troops to the north in order to regroup, while the US consul departed for Chunking. The bombings continued. Telecommunications broke down and chaos reigned. The official report of 21 February explained: "the docks during the night were in a state which it is hardly believable could have existed in any

British possession…I do not think there was a single sober man anywhere. The crews of the boats alongside and the troops had looted liquor and were rolling about the place in the last stages of drunkenness."[138] The city was surrendered on 7 March.

It is estimated that at least 600,000 Indian refugees fled Burma after the British defeat, with at least 400,000 forced to travel the 600 miles of perilous mule tracks and cart-roads, across the high mountain passes and thick jungle of eastern India on foot, eventually filtering into the villages and by-lanes of rural Bengal.[139] Along the way there was no shelter, no medical aid, and little or no food. People traveled with whatever possessions they could carry and left their dead on the side of the road. British caravans, complete with local porters and pack animals, edged starving families to the side of the road as they hurried past to safety.[140] At improvised refugee encampments, dysentery, small pox and malaria flourished.[141] When the rains came, the road was washed away in places and some had to make their way on their knees through mud and along perilous precipices. The Government of India sent no help. They had now conceded Burma, and the fate of the British Indian citizens stranded in that country was not a priority. At least 80,000 died in transit.

Those who survived the journey to India, according to a British Army Brigadier who witnessed their arrival in Bengal, were in a sate of "complete exhaustion, physical and mental, with disease superimposed…all social sense lost…they suffer from bad nightmares and their delirium is a babble of rivers and crossings, of mud and corpses…emaciation and loss of weight are universal."[142] In this state they entered into the villages of Bengal, begging at the bazaars, and telling stories of Japanese atrocities—and British capitulation.

Nobody's Home

As Japan breezed through British defenses in Asia, attitudes—both administrative and popular—underwent a rapid change, and the strategic importance of Calcutta to the war effort expanded exponentially day by day. With the loss of Burma, the city was now the last eastern industrial frontier of the British Empire, and, as such, vital to the fight (back) against Japan. Of utmost importance was to keep the factories, writing desks, and ports of Calcutta operating at emergency pace, and the handful of British who "held it down" were unequal to the task. "Native" allegiance to the city of Calcutta, however, proved a slippery problem. The British, much to their chagrin, quickly found that, though they had built it, and the people had come, Calcutta was not yet "home" to the the complex array of migrants who had made their way to the city for many decades past in search of economic survival, and the personnel that they required to run their factories and offices in and around Calcutta proved less than "patriotic."

Between the mid-nineteenth century and the mid-twentieth, the population of Calcutta had grown from approximately 400,000 to over 2,000,000. Economic pressure and lack of opportunity in the vast hinterland had driven waves of immigrants into the city in search of the means of survival. Laborers from Bengal itself provided the bulk of the industrial workforce early in the nineteenth century, but by late-century cheaper, semi-transient laborers from Bihar, Orissa, and the United Provinces began to outnumber Bengalis. In the jute mills, by 1941, Bengalis comprised less than 25 per cent of the labor force, and in textile mills and other factories the demographics were similar.[143] By the 1940s the Bengali population of Calcutta consisted primarily of Bengali *bhadralok* (the "middle-class") who had left the countryside in search of education and white collar employment. They too, as such, were semi-transient, migrant workers themselves. As the saying went, Calcutta was their *basa* ("nest"—temporary dwelling) but in their districts of origin were their *barhi* (homes). Marwari traders, with roots in Rajasthan, had also come to the city in increasing numbers late in the nineteenth century, and by the mid-twentieth were the primary Indian capitalist class in Calcutta. By the outbreak of war they dominated the jute and textile industries,[144] and were deeply entrenched in the grain trade as well. Their speculations in commodity markets—known as *fatka*—were legendary and could influence prices sharply.[145]

When Japan attacked Pearl Harbor, and a few weeks later Rangoon, a crisis of confidence ensued and the immigrant-dependent mosaic of labor, industry and administration began to unravel. On 18 December 1941 Calcutta and its suburbs were declared a "dangerous area," and despite all calls to stand-to, residents of Calcutta began to flee the colonial city in large numbers. The war had at last entered into popular consciousness, and clinging to Calcutta had risks outweighing the penalties established by the Essential Services Maintenance Ordinance. Non-Bengali laborers boarded trains and congested roads and headed for their native provinces.[146] Defections from the Ishapore Rifle Factory and the Cossipore Gun and Shell Factory were cause for alarm.[147] On 1 January 1942 the Mayor of Calcutta issued an appeal, calling on laborers to remain at their posts, but the exodus continued.[148] "Marwari businessmen in Calcutta were selling their stocks at reduced prices, closing down their businesses and moving in large numbers to central and north India."[149] This meant the immobilization of a significant sector of Calcutta trade, including in rice. The air was rife with rumors of Britain's imminent defeat, "black-outs" were observed every night, and the Bengali middle-class too fled to the countryside in numbers, leaving only earning members, as necessary, behind.

Meanwhile, the British themselves were making plans for hasty retreat. I.C.S. Special Officer, L.G. Pinnell, whose assorted appointments by the Government of India would have deep implications for Bengal, hustled off to Darjeeling with his family—even as he wondered at the Indian exodus. "Before Burma had actually fallen," he testified later, "the trains leaving Calcutta were crowded beyond capacity with people trying to get away…and to get their valuables away. Large numbers of merchants and traders left and I was told that ordinary shop commodities in Calcutta could be bought for nothing."[150]

A scene in Bimal Kar's novel, *Dewal*, depicts the chaos of exodus more intimately:

> Burdened down with any belongings they can carry, people are boarding taxis, and lorries, horse-drawn buggies and ox-carts and *moving on*. Their faces are dark and lined with worry. Small children stare dully and cry. Girls, abandoning their accustomed modesty, push desperately onto fly-swarmed railway cars, tearing their saris or falling into strangers' laps. Feverish babies cry and vomit. Old folks gasp for breath, more dead than alive. Men are running in every direction, withdrawing money from banks, handing out bribes for favors, and falling at the feet of taxi drivers to beg them for consideration. Yesterday's fare of five rupees has become twenty-five today.[151]

Those left behind, mostly those without the means to flee, dwelt in a city depopulated, houses were boarded up and dark, the streets desolate, and the mood apprehensive.

Provincial Politics and War

The elected Chief Minister of Bengal, Fazlul Huq, was a well-seasoned politician with a wide base of rural support. He had been a founding member of the Muslim League in 1906 and had served as its president from 1916 to 1921. He had also served as joint secretary of the Indian National Congress. Throughout his career he was decidedly anti-communal, and the League's increasingly divisive communal idiom did not sit well with him. Prior to the 1937 elections Huq canvassed and consolidated the *Praja Samitis* ("peasant organizations") of eastern Bengal and established himself as the leader of the newly formed Krishak Praja Party (KPP), which opposed League candidates directly.[152] The KPP campaigned on a platform of tenants' rights, the abolishment of land settlement, fixation of rents, and other populist issues.

The existing *praja samitis* provided a ready network for canvassing rural support, and the KPP gained fast traction throughout the countryside. In response to the League's call for "Muslim Unity," Huq and the KPP raised the slogan of "*dal bhat*" ("pulses and rice"), promising food security and economic justice.[153] Such a message had broad appeal among the impoverished masses of Bengal—Muslim and Hindu alike. Scheduled caste tillers joined fellow Muslim peasants in support of the KPP as the election approached. The Muslim League, with its urban, elite base, struggled to counter, accusing Huq—in rejecting the League's political agendas—of currying Hindu favor. Huq stuck to his message: "It is not all a civil war in the Muslim community but it is a fight in which the people of Bengal are divided on a purely economic issue…the problem of 'dal and bhat' and some kind of coarse cloth to cover our nudity is the problem of problems which stares us in the face and which must be solved immediately."[154] Huq also argued that considering that 90 per cent of Muslims in Bengal were peasants, the causes that the Krishak Praja Party were advancing *were*, indeed, Muslim causes, as such.[155]

The results of the 1937 election, the last until 1946, proved a disappointment for the Muslim League. The Muslims of Bengal had failed to "unify" as a political unit. Huq's party won 31.5 per cent of the popular Muslim vote to the League's 27 per cent.[156] Congress took the most seats, but entangled as they were with landed interests in the province, could not come to terms with the KPP. The war had also divided their base between the Forward Block and the Bengal Congress Party, which caused deep divisions in their own ranks. In the end, a rather awkward alliance was struck between the Muslim League and the Krishak Praja Party, and Fazlul Huq became the first Chief Minister of Bengal under Provincial Autonomy. Given the bitterness of the election, and the qualms that All-India Muslim League President Muhammad Ali Jinnah, in particular, had about Huq, it was an unlikely alliance, and one that war would severely test.

In 1939 when Congress withdrew its ministries in protest of the war, Jinnah was jubilant, announcing a "Day of Deliverance" to celebrate relief from "Congress oppression."[157] Members of the Bengal Provincial Muslim League, however, were less sanguine. Abdur Rahman Siddique, one of only three Bengalis on the Working Committee of the All-India League, resigned in protest at Jinnah's announcement, calling it "an insult to national prestige" and a "flattery of British Imperialism."[158] Anti-colonial sentiment ran deep in Bengal and such open contempt for principled opposition to British rule could not be countenanced along lines of communal association. Furthermore the All-India Muslim League's position on war support was itself equivocal.

Fazlul Huq, though he had fought bitter political battles with League candidates in 1937, became a member of the All-India League's Working committee following the formation of the KPP/Muslim League joint Ministry. As as chief minister of a still divided house, he struggled to balance his populist KPP election pledges with the more narrowly communal considerations of the Muslim League. The war situation strained his efforts to the breaking point. The League, while publicly supporting the war, had deep disagreements with Linlithgow's government. Jinnah felt cheated that the viceroy had established emergency rule in the formerly Congress provinces rather than inviting the League to form new ministries. In addition, Britain's issuance of the 1939 White Paper in Palestine had angered many Muslims in Bengal.[159] To register these various grievances, in June of 1940, the All-India Muslim League Working Committee passed a resolution barring Muslims from participating in war committees.[160]

At the viceroy's invitation, however, Fazlul Huq agreed to serve on the newly formed National Defense Council with other chief ministers, and traveled to Delhi in August of 1941 to represent Bengal's interests in warplanning. Jinnah was enraged by Huq's indiscipline and the Working Committee convened to demand Huq's immediate resignation.

Huq resigned from both the All-India Muslim League Working Committee and the National Defense Council, and penned an acerbic letter to the League's Secretary, Liaquat Ali Khan, defending his decision to represent *Bengal* in Delhi. Huq argued against Jinnah's accusation that he had contravened the Working Committee's prohibition against "Muslims" serving on war committees. Defending himself and the Chief Ministers of Assam and Punjab, who were also Muslim, Huq noted that "despite [Jinnah's] declaration that we were selected as Muslim representatives, I maintain that we were selected as Premiers. From this point of view membership in the Defense Council does not involve violation of League principles and policy."[161] In more direct language Huq squarely condemned the "unfair and unconstitutional" policies of "political dictators" who sought to gain "omnipotent authority" over Muslims in India.[162] Huq further denounced as "baseless" Jinnah's suggestion that in accepting a representative post outside of the League's political jurisdiction, he was creating a "split in ranks of Muslim India." Rather, Huq went on to suggest, Jinnah and other League leaders coming from Muslim minority provinces, were subverting democratic representation in their efforts to control the political expressions of leaders in Muslim majority provinces.

Such attacks were not well received by Jinnah. The All-India League leadership threw their weight behind more faithful Bengal members, two influential Ministers in Huq's cabinet: Home Minister, Khwaja Nazimuddin, and Minister of Commerce and Labor, Huseyn Shaheed Suhrawardy. On 11 September 1941, Suhrawardy held a meeting on the Maidan condemning Huq's letter, and on 29 November Huq's followers retaliated in the legislature, joining with Hindu members to table a resolution of no-confidence against both Suhrawardy and Nazimuddin. A few days later the Muslim League members of Huq's cabinet resigned and the ministry was dissolved—on the eve of the Japanese bombing of Pearl Harbor and invasion of Malaya. Huq, the consummate politician, struck a hasty deal with Congress leader Sarat Chandra Bose and Hindu Mahasabha Member, Shyama Prasad Mookerjee to form a new Ministry. Bengal Governor, John Herbert, delayed just long enough for Sarat Bose to be arrested and on the same day sanctioned the second Huq Ministry, which consisted now of the highly unlikely partnership between stalwart Muslim populist, Fazlul Huq, and polarizing, Hindu nationalist, Shyama Prasad Mookerjee.

Meanwhile, while Calcutta emptied out and refugees poured into Bengal, plans beyond consultation with elected government were being made to take the war and its priorities deep into the countryside—and things began to unravel at an alarming pace.

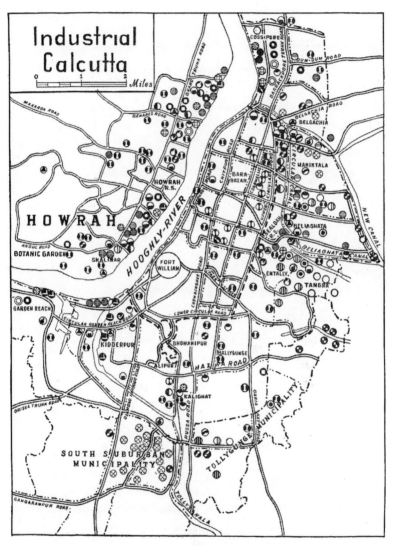

2. Industries in the Calcutta/Howrah area during the war

THE CALCUTTA INDUSTRIAL REGION

Rice Mills
Jute Mills
Jute Press
Cotton
   " Ginning & Baling

Flour Mills
Tobacco
Soap
Paint
Pottery & Cement
Brick-fields
Printing
Docks
Shell Factory

Railway Workshop
Chemicals
Iron & Steel rolling
Paper Mills
Glass
Rubber
Matches
Oil Mills
Hosiery
Silk
Saw Mills
Leather & Shoe
Tanneries
General Engineering
Power Generating

Key to Map 2

2

DENIAL

By December 1941, the price of rice had risen by nearly 75 per cent since the declaration of war.[1] Rice was in high demand as part of the war effort, particularly to feed industrial labor. Wheat prices had risen still more sharply, and so rice was also in high demand in western India and the Middle East as a hedge on wheat. This precipitated a drain of rice from eastern India, exasperating other difficulties in the food supply that war entailed. Coinciding with the onset of war against Japan, the export from Bengal of a record 45,000 tons of rice in January 1942 represented a quadrupling of exports for the same month in the previous year. In February exports increased again to 60,000 tons, in March to 61,000 tons, and in April to more than 66,000 tons.[2] Meanwhile, the influx of Calcuttans, with their relatively substantial economic resources, into rural districts was stressing local commodity markets further, as poor villagers were now forced to compete with rich city folk for increasingly dear provisions. Refugees from Burma also continued to pour in, and local shortages of sugar, coal, matches, raw cotton, cotton yarn, piece goods, paper, and cooking fuel, were making life increasingly difficult for many millions.

With war fueling inflation and threatening the economic stability of India as a whole, the viceroy convened a "Price Control Conference" in New Delhi on 6 February. It was, in fact, the Fourth Price Control Conference, the preceding three having accomplished little to stem rising prices. At this time the Government of India had no Food Department, and so the question of civilian food supply fell under the auspices of the Commerce Department—which created something of a tautological outcome to the Conference.

No price control was adopted. Instead it was concluded that a broad facilitation of "free trade" would solve the problem. A pervasive decentralization of authority over the purchase and movement of foodstuffs was recommended and provinces were encouraged to lift bans on exports and allow foodstuffs to move freely about the sub-continent. The difficulty of transportation during wartime was also addressed. A Central Transport Authority was established and protocols for the priority movement of food grains were established. The idea was that these measures, alone, would cause prices in deficit provinces to stabilize. As for the more immediate "scramble for supplies, rising prices, competitive buying, reluctance to sell, and speculation,"[3] that were all making the lives of the poor increasingly difficult, the President of the Conference advocated a "process of tightening up the belt."[4]

In the coming months food did, in fact, begin to move—and the belt did tighten. Major General Wood, in charge of military transport, testified before the Famine Enquiry Commission that he "was procuring and moving a considerable amount of food all the time, and in 1941–42 commenced to wonder why."[5] That the Major-General himself was uncertain why such quantities were being shifted—and to whom—is telling. What was manifest was that food grains were, in fact, moving out of the hands of those who needed them most—the rural poor—and into the warehouses of large capitalists, the military, government, and also unspecified points outside Bengal. In this regard, Major-General Wood later argued before the Famine Enquiry Commission that the deregulation of the movement of food grains established at the Fourth Price Control Conference was "the most significant single factor that led to the food crisis."[6]

In Calcutta it was now clear that rice had become a central strategic necessity in the increasingly complicated chessboard of war in Asia. War-related labor actions were nothing new, but now that war production was in full gear, government and industrial employers were quicker to grant demands for wartime concessions. In February 1942 Calcutta Corporation workers, whose strike in March of 1940 for wartime "dearness allowances" had ended in police shootings, again threatened a strike for access to subsidized foodstuffs. In response this time, the Corpora-tion quickly opened food stores to sell rice and other staples to its employees at concession rates.[7] This kept sweepers, waste workers, and other essential city services working, which was now well known to be necessary to the prosecution of war. But labor actions continued to be widespread—particularly in relation to "dearness allowances" and sub-sidized food stores.[8]

On 3 March 1942, the Government of India, fully cognizant of mounting difficulties, advised the Bengal Chamber of Commerce that "industrial concerns should adopt the practice of making themselves responsible for feeding their employees."[9] Toward this end it was sug-gested that industrial firms should keep three months of food grains, sufficient for all its employees, in stock. This injunction, according to the Bengal Chamber of Commerce, was not a warning based on a short-age of supplies, but rather was a precautionary measure related to A.R.P. planning. Beginning in March the appeal was broadened to include the general public, and uncertainty proliferated.[10] This warning, according to the Calcutta Municipal Corporation, had "extremely adverse" effects on the food supply, and widespread hoarding soon began by industrial interests and private citizens alike.[11] Azizul Haque, former speaker of the Legislative Assembly in Bengal and at that point High Commissioner for India in London, pointed to the deleterious effects on the food supply that the injunction to stockpile had entailed: "if a Government asks its people publicly to hoard stocks for three months," he testified, "the tendency [will] be for everybody to store up stocks for six months or more, and to that extent the stocks are immobilized."[12] By June the price of rice had risen an additional 30 per cent.[13]

Concurrent with the A.R.P.'s call for stockpiling food were intensive negotiations at the national level. Sir Stafford Cripps, sanctioned by the House of Commons in London, arrived in Delhi in March to attempt to broker a political solution to the impasse between India and Britain. At length, negotiations with the Indian National Congress broke down around the all-important question of war support.[14] Government of India Reforms Commissioner, Henry Hodson, discussing the failure to reach agreement noted that "Linlithgow's opinion of Indian character and political sense was," in any case, "not high."[15] Nor did his office seem to have any understanding of the difficulties that the Indian popu-lation was facing. On the ground in India, food security was increasingly the over-determining problem of the day. A telling anecdote by Hodson illustrates the disconnect and is worth quoting at length:

> A grand charity ball was announced to take place at Viceroy's House in New Delhi during the visit of Sir Stafford Cripps in March 1942. When it was cancelled I assumed that Cripps himself had protested, but the *Times* resident correspondent told me that he had been responsible. He had warned the Viceroy's private secretary that demonstrations against the ball were planned, denouncing the scarcity and high price of food and mocking the lavish supper menu that had been published in the press; his advice that this would do great harm to the image of British rule at a critical time had been reluctantly accepted.[16]

The ultimate failure of the Cripps Mission was disappointing, but Linlithgow was pragmatic; "We can carry on easily enough," he told Hodson, "so long as the war lasts and people are afraid of stirring up too much trouble."[17]

"Denial"

Under the mandates of the Government of India Act of 1935, Ministers of provincial Legislative Assemblies had been given a wide range of administrative responsibilities that comprehensively limited the central government's accountability in regards to regional affairs. The real limits of the power allocated to elected officials by the Act, however, proved to be surprisingly contingent. The Governor—appointed by His Majesty's Government (HMG) in London—retained certain broad "discretionary powers," including the authority to suspend ministerial authority altogether and enforce emergency rule in accordance with Section 93 of the Act, as had been done in the seven former Congress provinces. Furthermore, in the "special circumstances" related to the prosecution of war, the breadth of emergency powers available to the Governor—even without Section 93—proved expansive.

Sometime toward the end of March 1942 Governor Herbert was instructed through central government channels to begin a scorched earth campaign in coastal Bengal. The vast deltaic coastline of Bengal, until this time, had been left almost entirely undefended by the British military.[18] The recommendation was, however, not for a concerted effort at organizing military defense, but rather for an ad hoc campaign of "denial." In their landings in Malaya and Burma, Japanese forces had made expedient use of existing resources on the ground to facilitate their advance. In Bengal, no doubt, they would do the same. If—the rhetoric went—the colonial government itself could make a preemptive strike and denude the coastal region of the resources that might enable invasion, they would be able to discourage attack without unnecessary expenditures on military defense. "Denial" was the term used for the various measures undertaken by the Government of India ostensibly to deprive invading Japanese forces the means of sustaining an advance on Calcutta in an over-land attack.

Rice

In March 1942 Governor Herbert—without any consultation with elected officials—appointed British civil servant, and former Personal Secretary to the Viceroy, L.G. Pinnell, "Special Officer" in general charge of "denial" operations in Bengal. Shortly thereafter, Herbert summoned the Joint Secretary of the Commerce and Labor Department, M. K. Kirpalani—also appointed by the Governor himself—and assigned him the more specific task of implementing the first prong of "denial," the appropriation of all "surplus" rice throughout coastal Bengal. Kirpalani later testified that he "was asked to get this done almost immediately by the Governor."[19] The members of the Bengal Ministry, meanwhile, were out of session for the Easter recess, and by the time they had returned "denial" operations were already underway.

Kirpalani estimated that in the three districts involved—Midnapore, Khulna and Barisal—there would be a surplus of at least 123,000 tons of rice, the "denial" of which posed an estimable challenge.[20] Kirpalani approached M. A. Ispahani, whose firm had considerable experience in the rice markets of Bengal, though limited experience procuring in any of these three districts. More worrisome was that Ispahani was a staunch supporter of the Muslim League with intimate ties to Muhammad Ali Jinnah.[21] His appointment was sure to draw fire from Huq, Mookerjee, and Congress supporters. Ispahani himself recognized the potential for contention, and so suggested that the commission be given, in name, to an agent of his, Mirza Ali Akhbar, while Ispahani Ltd. would guarantee the standing accounts.[22] Because the Governor was anxious to get the work underway at once, the Joint Secretary quickly agreed and advanced 2 million rupees to Ispahani's man to expedite the process.[23]

When Ministers got word of the plan already underway, there was a great "hue and cry" in the Assembly. Fazlul Huq accused Herbert of having acted "as if the Government of India Act in Bengal had been suspended, and he was at the head of an administration under Section 93 of the Act."[24] Members of the opposition, particularly Hindus, decried the Governor's appointment of "political opponents" who, they said, would use the platform of "denial" to penetrate the countryside in order "to make political propaganda there."[25] The protests were loud enough to force the Governor's hand. Four other agents were quickly appointed; one, H. Dutta, was a Hindu Mahasabhite put forward by S. P. Mookerjee, another, B. K. Poddar, was advanced by the Scheduled Caste Ministers, a third, Ahmed Khan, was a (Muslim) Congress man, and lastly, Ashutosh Bhattacharjee made the list by dint of his commercial connections.[26] The contentious political nature of these appointments, together with the inexperience of several,[27] contributed greatly to the pervasive chaos and corruption that characterized the whole "denial" scheme.

In Bengal there are three seasons of paddy production: the *boro* crop planted in the winter and harvested in spring, the *aus* crop, planted in early spring and harvested in late summer, and the *aman* crop, planted in late spring and harvested in winter. Because the *aman* crop is planted just prior to the monsoon season and receives rain-fed irrigation, it was the most consistent and abundant of the three crops, accounting for at least 75 per cent of the total rice production in Bengal.[28] For cultivators, once the *aman* crop had been marketed, or consumed, a long season of hardship often followed. The *aman* crop, harvested between the end of November and the beginning of February, for this reason, was desperately anticipated in the "starvation" months, when most cultivators also had to take loans in order to survive. According to Ispahani, "the Bengal cultivator, [even] before the war, had three months of feasting, five months of subsistence diet and four months of starvation."[29] The merchants (*paikars, beparis,* or *farias*) who bought the cultivators' paddy were also money and rice lenders, which made trade relationships that much more intricate. The difficulty was compounded in that, during the lean months the price of rice and paddy would inevitably increase, so that a loan taken at this time was a disproportionate burden to pay off. Then with the *aman* harvest in, an abundance of paddy would make its way to markets and prices would again sink, and the individual indebted cultivator was forced to sell at deflated prices to pay off debts—starting the cycle of feast and famine yet again. The relationships that cultivators were able to forge with merchants and creditors were critical to their very survival. Furthermore, in Bengal there were tens of thousands of petty traders who bought from cultivators,[30] and relationships were highly personalized. A memorandum drafted by the Bengal Rice Mills Association describing these relationships—before "denial"—is worth quoting at length:

> In Bengal, as probably in many parts of the world, the trade is not carried out as a single unconnected transaction. Most of the *beparis, paikars*, merchants, etc. have got an undefined but fairly rigid area of operation, for each and every person in the trade has got his own sellers, *beparis, paikars* and mills which he has been in trade association with for many years. Frequently this association has not merely meant the sale and purchase of the goods year after year for many years...such transactions have frequently been carried out as partly cash and partly credit transactions on the basis of a running account. The association has been in many cases one of several generations. Mutual influence and obligations between the parties in such cases...has therefore been enormous.[31]

In 1942, agents and sub-agents for denial operations were enlisted indiscriminately and according to political manipulations, and these existing market systems were completely ignored. Credit relations, patronage, commercial familiarity, and existing patterns of trade all collapsed, leading to a dangerous breakdown in the operations of the rice trade in Bengal, almost overnight. Resistance to governmental schemes was met with force, and without the necessary expertise or knowledge of existing agrarian relations, extraordinary means were often resorted to:

> Persons acting on behalf of Government [did] not always act either tactfully or fairly and the [Bengal Rice Mills Association] got the information that in many cases undue pressure was used on the growers and sellers to compel them to sell to people entirely unknown to them...this further stiffened the resolve of the growers. A few of the agents of Government...did not know the real and actual sources whence substantial stocks could be collected and were further handicapped by the attitude of the sellers...this exasperated them and also enraged them especially, because...Government was putting pressure on them for showing better purchases. At this stage it was reported that considerable pressure amounting in some cases to oppression was used on many people for obtaining stocks and it was not un-often said that such action was not merely countenanced and tolerated, but backed by local officers of Government who had been instructed to help the agents.[32]

Not only were growers reluctant to part with their product, but the pre-existing petty merchants approached by denial agents where likewise harassed to sell under Government conditions. Their stocks were reported to have been summarily seized for non-compliance.[33]

Special Officer L. G. Pinnell, for his part, rued that "for anyone who knows the Bengal cultivator it was a completely heart-breaking job."[34] But a job is a job, and as such he also, "had no objection to 'taking the gloves off.'"[35] For the most part, however, Pinnell was careful to gauge the threat of resistance and adjust to the opposition. "If we had moved along certain routes," he noted, "the transport would have been obstructed or looted by the people."[36] In many areas, however, despite the threat—and at times reality—of looting,[37] Government was able to exercise their scheme without direct violence. In this regard Pinnell testified: "We got away with it by luck and money."[38] At the beginning of the denial scheme the maximum price to be paid by denial agents was fixed at the current market price, plus 10 per cent. But with the contagion of agents combing the countryside looking to snap up all "surplus" rice, this ceiling soon became market price, and prices kept rising.[39] As the Bengal National Chamber of Commerce noted: "the fact that it was the Government who were buying in the market… was sufficient to induce both a rise in prices and a feeling of panic among the general public."[40]

Charges of corruption were also rampant, and not easy to dismiss.[41] Nawab Habibullah Bahadur of Dacca, Government of Bengal Minister of Agriculture, testified before the Famine Enquiry Commission that denial agents had been operating well outside the stipulated "denial" zone, "pretending in other areas that they were buying on behalf of Government."[42] In addition, "owing to the practical monopoly of Government agents in [denial] districts, others flocked to non-denial areas and affected markets, established organization and connections."[43] In short, though the objectives of "denial" were ostensibly limited to certain coastal districts, denial created sharp dislocations in the trade that threw Bengal rice markets, as a whole, into a state of complete disarray. Despite protests from many quarters, including the Bengal Chamber of Commerce, "denial" continued unabated for many moths to come.[44]

The question of the real impact on actual stocks of paddy and rice that denial represented is impossible to determine. By official account the total of purchases transferred to Government warehouses, was rather small—40,000 tons.[45] This number, however, does not represent the actual extent of purchases made. Much of the *paddy* that Government purchased remained where it was in the countryside due to a weak mill capacity and difficulties with transportation during the war, effectively frozen from the market, but unrecorded. No records exist either to determine what percentage of the record exports leaving Bengal at the time were related to purchases made—officially or unofficially—under the nebulous umbrella of "denial." Pinnell himself testified that exports were taking place without Government authorization and that back-room deals were being struck between large-scale dealers and transportation officials.[46] In the 24 Parganas district south of Calcutta, by 1 May, at least one hundred boat-loads of rice per month were "getting away." The District Magistrate, in a secret memo to the Joint Secretary, estimated that if this pace could be maintained through August all "surplus" rice would be cleared by the end of the summer.[47] But though this massive effort was being undertaken under Government authority, and in relation to "denial," none of the rice or paddy involved appears to have been destined for government warehouses. Instead, special permits for boat transport were being granted to rice mill owners and large stockists so that they could "buy up and remove most of the surplus stock."[48]

Boats

The special permits mentioned above were necessary in relation to the second main prong of the Government of India's scheme: "boat denial." The coastal region of Bengal lies in the vast and volatile Ganges river delta. The silt of the Ganges and its tributaries has fertilized the delta for millennia, and as such it is one of the most productive agricultural regions in India. The Padma, Jamuna and Meghna rivers, with rich cultural as well as economic significance, converge in a seemingly infinite and shifting series of tidal estuaries, bayous and backwaters that constitute the coastal belt of Bengal. The people of this region are deeply connected not only to the land that sustains them, but just as importantly to the waters that move them, that bathe them, that feed them, and that connect them at all to the world beyond. The "country boats" of Bengal, in this context, were as much an inextricable part of the landscape as the waterways themselves.

Potters in Chittagong depended on country boats to move the earth that was necessary for their livelihood. The *khalasis* of Noakhali, expert at navigating the shifting deltaic tides from Midnapore to Burma, also depended on country boats to survive. The *char* cultivators of Khulna and Bakargunj transplanted their paddy and harvested their crops from extremely fertile islands off the coast by means of country boats, and even the *babus* of Calcutta moved to and from their native villages onboard these same river-craft. Jute also moved to and from markets on country boats, as did paddy and rice. The fishermen of Bengal, the largest producers of foodstuffs other than rice, also depended on these boats, both for netting in the rivers and bayous, as well as for voyaging out to sea. In short, country boats were an unequivocally essential component of the economy of Bengal.

On 2 April, after plans for "rice denial" had been leaked in the press, Governor Herbert stood before the Bengal Legislative Assembly and announced: "The other form of denial to the enemy that is intended is to prevent any means of transport from falling into his hands."[49] A Press Note was released the following day informing district officials that all country boats capable of carrying ten or more persons should be registered in the coastal districts of Midnapore, Hooghly, Howrah, 24 Parganas, Jessore, Khulna, Bakargunj, Faridpur, Tippera, Dacca, Noakhali, and Chittagong—all districts where water-conveyance constituted, by far, the most important means of travel and trade. In the subsequent weeks 66,563 watercraft were registered. The active implementation of "boat denial" was announced on 1 May, and though the plan was to be executed only in the event that "the invasion of any district in Bengal [was] imminent,"[50] the confiscation and/or destruction of thousands of country boats began in Bengal almost immediately.

The "denial" of country boats was the specific job of Special Officer, L. G. Pinnell. His license of autocracy again drew quick protest. In a letter to Herbert, Fazlul Huq complained that in relation to "boat denial," the Governor "seem[ed] to have been consulting with Military authorities in secret and discussing plans with permanent officials... without taking Ministers into confidence."[51] Military authorities, meanwhile, had expressed it necessary to "reduce the boats to the absolute minimum required for the subsistence of the people."[52] By what matrix military authorities were able to gauge the subsistence requirements of an already impoverished Bengali population is impossible to guess, but "what was definitely and openly allowed [was] about 6,800 boats."[53] In the coming weeks 46,146 country boats were confiscated; some were sunk, others burnt, and still others warehoused in military compounds were they rotted in the open air.[54] Some 20,000 boats, Pinnell admitted "were hidden and could not be traced."[55] Had this not been the case, things may have been even worse for Bengal.

However, if the initial objective of denial in the months, and years, to come—as was officially stated—was the "complete destruction of internal economy, trade and administration,"[56] nothing could have furthered that goal more effectively than the removal and destruction of Bengal's country boats. From the beginning, the Famine Enquiry Commission reported, "it was recognized that the removal of a large number of boats from the delta, in which communications [means of transport] are almost entirely by river and not by rail or road, would cause considerable hardship and difficulties."[57] And that it did. "In the districts of Khulna, 24 Parganas, Bakargunj and Tippera, it completely broke the economy of the fishing class."[58] In districts where people were involved in pottery making, an important and substantial industry that required large inland shipments of clay, many people "were put out of trade and…their families became destitute."[59] The productive and important paddy fields at the mouth of the delta in several districts could not be cultivated, and the primary means of transportation of people, as well as goods and services, was almost entirely crippled.

Compensation was initially only given to the owners of boats, which meant little to those who made a living from these same boats. Owners were often from the wealthier strata of society and boats were leased to those whose livelihoods depended on them (fishermen, *khalasis*, potters, cultivators, *paikars*, etc.). These workers at first received nothing. After protests from several quarters, however, it was decided to give them three months' compensation. For this segment of the population, already living on the margins of bare subsistence, three months' compensation meant little. The livelihood of generations was lost in a matter of weeks, and for that loss, three months of wages were received—wages that even before they were dispersed had lost considerable value against a continuingly increasing cost of living—and many began to starve. Apart from the catastrophic consequences of such a policy on the existing economic and social structures of Bengal, the enormity of the undertaking also brought home to residents of the countryside the extent of British fears—as well as their ruthlessness. For now, it looked to many, as if it were the British—not the Japanese—who were launching an attack on the Bengal countryside.

Territory

At the same time, the military was entrenching itself in and around the commercial and strategic centers of the province, while administrative workers were removing their own kin from "non-family areas," and non-essential government employees were receiving "exodus allowances" to relocate.[60] Meanwhile, aerodromes, army encampments and supply dumps were carved out of the heavily populated countryside south of Calcutta—the same area from which rice had been "getting away" by the boat-load. The Minister of Commerce received directions from the Governor that a total of forty-seven areas had to be cleared in as little as twenty-four hours.[61] In Chittagong District a sub-divisional officer received a similar order: he was to evacuate twenty villages within forty-eight hours. In Diamond Harbor an order for military appropriation of land resulted in the summary eviction of at least 36,000 people. In Noakhali another 70,000 were dislocated.[62] The total number of mostly poor tenants evicted from their lands in relation to such measures, however, is not possible to determine.[63] The impact on those dislocated, according to the Famine Commission, was more easily assessed: "compensation was of course paid, but there is little doubt that the members of many of these families became famine victims in 1943."[64]

Uneasy about the military's image in the countryside, Government issued an order in May to appoint police guides and interpreters "to facilitate the work of troops and at the same time to reassure villagers against any apprehension or panic."[65] In addition, Herbert sent out a memorandum to all District Magistrates reminding them that "everything possible should be done by propaganda…to instill into the general public the lesson that troops are their friends and that they have nothing to fear from them."[66] However, the circular went on, the public should also be warned that troops would not be confined to "evacuated" areas, and in this regard, when and where military exercises were underway, "it would be far more satisfactory for [the public] and everyone else concerned if they remain in their houses, as otherwise they might only get in the way and suffer unnecessary inconvenience."[67] The Bengal Home Guard was also being organized just at this time, and arrangements for the guards were creating tension between the representatives of the provincial government and the King's representative, John Herbert. Fazlul Huq complained of "the mischief of officialisation of Home Guards" as yet another example of the Imperial Government making a "mockery of Provincial Autonomy."[68]

Meanwhile, national politics were also becoming ever more embroiled in controversies emerging from "denial." Resentment simmered in the wake of the failed Cripps Mission and relations between the Indian National Congress and the colonial government were strained to the breaking point. Even before the official announcement of denial policies, Gandhi was warning against the intended measures in his weekly *Harijan*. In the 22 March edition, sub-titled "Scorched Earth," he reminded his readers, "India is not fighting. Her conquerors are."[69] He continued crossly, "are we to contemplate with equanimity, or feel the glow of bravery and sacrifice in destroying life or property at the prospect of India's earth being scorched and everything destroyed in order that the enemy's march be hampered?"[70] Three weeks later, again in *Harijan*, Gandhi warned that the people of Bengal were already "suffering from famine," and explained that military evacuations taking place in eastern Bengal were being "left in the hands of many and petty officials," creating local acrimony and severe hardship.[71] By 3 May the consequences and scope of "denial" were becoming ever clearer, and Gandhi wrote with increasing alarm: "No promise of compensation can be any comfort for the dispossession of...tenements. To the poor people it is like taking away their bodies. The dispossession of the country boats is almost like that of tenements. To deprive the people of East Bengal of their boats is like cutting off a vital limb."[72] Similarly, the "denial" of rice, Gandhi wrote, could not be countenanced: "people cannot be asked or advised to starve or die of thirst for fear of the Japanese helping themselves to the people's provisions or water."[73]

"Denial," however, continued unabated. Instructions were given in May for the confiscation, destruction, or removal of all mechanical transport—private cars, bicycles, carriages and bullock carts "not required for Military or Civil Defense purposes,"[74]—the Victoria Memorial was "camouflaged" in cow dung, and plans were hatched to blow up as many as seventeen bridges in and around Calcutta.[75]

The Denial Resolution

It is a point that has received scant historical notice, but the colonial government's "denial" policy played a very central role in the dynamics of the fiercest conflict between the Indian population and their colonial rulers since the rebellion of 1857. Following Gandhi's cue, the leadership of the Indian National Congress took direct aim at the scorched earth campaign in Bengal, and these protests had a profound impact on the way that the "Quit India" movement played out. Though the All-India Congress Working Committee's resolutions of 14 July and 8 August 1942 are most often cited as the signal events that led to the "Open Rebellion," the repressive and absolutist strategies of the colonial state, were forged in reference to an earlier resolution—that of 10 July—known in official circles as the "denial resolution."[76]

After the failure of the Cripps Mission in April, the Secretary of State for India, Leo Amery and Viceroy Linlithgow, waited apprehensively for Congress's next move. On 10 July the Working Committee met at Wardha, and on the same day passed a resolution that was subsequently published in the nationalist media. The resolution, echoing Gandhi's earlier publications in *Harijan*, began with "denial:"

> Whereas various complaints have been received regarding Governments orders for evacuation of villages, lands and buildings without due notice and proper compensation, seizure and destruction of country-boats, even where life is impossible without them, requisition of vehicles without proper compensation and regard for needs of civil population, Working Committee issue following instructions for guidance of the people concerned…with regard to evacuation and other orders involving temporary or permanent loss of landed property full compensation should be demanded…there should be no interference with use or disposal of private property except with consent of owner or on adequate payment of compensation. In case of requisition of boats full compensation should be demanded and no boats should be surrendered until question of compensation is settled. In areas surrounded by water where boats are indispensable for normal everyday life they should not be surrendered at all.[77]

When Amery received the draft of this resolution in London, he wrote to Linlithgow in alarm. Such a resolution by Congress, he warned the viceroy, amounted to the declaration of a "parallel authority acting in defiance of established Government in respect of measures necessary for the prosecution of war."[78] Amery, while anticipating a "more general" resolution from Wardha, urged Linlithgow to take "drastic action with Gandhi and the Working Committee—such as immediate arrest pending prosecution—and with Press—in any case it would seem necessary to impound so far as possible all copies of papers carrying the Resolution."[79]

On the same day, he quickly penned a minute to Winston Churchill warning the prime minister, "we are dealing with men who are now definitely our enemies…to appease them or delay in striking at them can only discourage the army and all other loyal elements."[80] The secretary of state also personally authorized extending the viceroy de facto emergency powers to deal with the situation immediately and forcefully. In the meantime, he brought the question of such authority before the War Cabinet in London for advice. The War Cabinet convened on 13 July and supported Amery's authorization of Linlithgow's emergency powers, agreeing that the "denial resolution" amounted to treason.[81]

Fearing that the immediate arrest of Congress leadership would precipitate (perhaps violent) mass movements, the viceroy argued for restraint, while promising prompt action in the event that directions to resist denial given in the resolution were actually executed.[82] Amery reminded the viceroy that "feeling may inevitably run high among ignorant villagers and people on whom hardship will *necessarily* be inflicted,"[83] and he urged Linlithgow to adopt harsher measures with Gandhi and the Working Committee rather than "merely punish[ing] the wretched villager who refuses to hand over his boat or his bullock cart."[84] Linlithgow, in response, noted the "regrettable spirit of defeatism" that had gripped the country, and again argued that a militant response to the 10 July resolution would only inflame anti-colonial sentiment further. The policy should be to wait and see. Amery deferred to Linlithgow for the time being, but the 10 July resolution would remain central to the colonial response to Congress initiatives.

On 14 July the "general resolution" came out.[85] This main resolution did not deal directly with "denial," but was, instead, a plea for Indian independence, deeply couched in the prevailing rhetoric of "defense." In the wake of the Cripps Mission, the Working Committee warned, "a growing satisfaction at the success of Japanese arms" was sweeping the nation. In this context, the resolution continued, "Congress is anxious to avoid the experience of Malaya, Singapore and Burma." The only means of defending India, Congress concluded, was for Britain to agree to grant the nation complete independence, at which time a treaty could be struck with the Allies for the continuance of war against Japan. Without such an agreement there could be no partnership, the defense of India would remain an impossibility, and India would fall to the Axis powers. Finally, Congress warned rather vaguely of a "widespread struggle…under the leadership of Mahatma Gandhi" if Britain refused to come to terms. An additional meeting was scheduled for 7 August.

In a telegram to Linlithgow on 16 July, Amery adopted a dismissive attitude toward this "main resolution." It might be the case, he wrote, that the main resolution would necessitate no immediate action, but that of 10 July, he again insisted, could easily be understood to be in direct breach of Defense of India Rules 38 (1) (a), dealing with acts "prejudicial" to the authority of His Majesty's Government. Amery again advised Linlithgow that he "already [had] ground for action if and when expedient."[86] Linlithgow continued to argue for restraint, finding some encouragement in the "conciliatory" tone of the 14 July resolution.[87] He also saw a possibility that the 14 July resolution could be used to drive a wedge between religious communities. He assured Amery that he was doing everything possible to "energize propaganda" against Congress in the hopes of "stimulating" open denunciations of the main resolution amongst "Muslims, Depressed Classes & co.," who were assumed to be more loyal to the war effort.[88] The viceroy sent a special telegram to Bengal Governor, John Herbert, enlisting him to encourage Fazlul Huq to issue a public condemnation of the Congress resolution.[89] Huq declined, preferring to maintain his pluralist position in Bengal, and resisting government bait to publicly cross Congress.[90]

With his propaganda campaign showing mixed results, Linlithgow was, meanwhile, making less rhetorical preparations against Congress. Consulting with his own legal council, the viceroy confirmed Amery's opinion that the Defense of India Rules could be invoked against Gandhi and the Working Committee in response to both resolutions. The "denial resolution," however, represented a more clearly actionable offence in that it contained "direct and authoritative instruction to the people to interfere with the administration of law."[91] As such, the resolution of 10 July fell foul not only of the Defense of India Rules, but also of the Criminal Law Amendment Act, which gave the colonial government grounds to declare the Congress as a whole, not merely the Working Committee, an unlawful association, greatly expanding the emergency powers with which to suppress any eventual popular movement.

The resolution of 10 July was thus central to the three-stage plan that Linlithgow developed to deal with the "open rebellion," and the proposed resistance to "denial" was central to the brutality with which the "Quit India" movement would be dealt. The first stage, a propaganda campaign against Congress, was gaining little traction. The second stage would involve not only the arrest of Gandhi and the Working Committee, but also the arrest of the leaders of Provincial Congress Committees under the Criminal Law Amendment Act. The third stage would be to promulgate the Emergency Powers Ordinance, which would allow broad impunity to suppress any movement that followed the second stage.[92] Secretary of State Amery brought Linlithgow's plan of action before the War Cabinet in London on 5 August and won approval the next day. The course of action that government would take against Congress and anti-colonial protest was thus established even before the Working Committee had convened to issue their much more famous 8 August declaration.

Quit India

Winston Churchill needed little convincing that the hard line proposed by the Government of India was warranted. The prime minister had been a long-time and particularly staunch advocate of Empire. "India," he had said some years earlier, "is a geographical term. It is no more a united nation than the equator."[93] The Cripps Mission had been salt in Churchill's wounds after losing Singapore. Cripps, a political opponent of Churchill's, had become Speaker of the House of Commons and a member of the War Cabinet only after the defeats in Southeast Asia. His appointment as emissary to negotiate a political settlement in India in March of 1942 was further evidence of a lack of parliamentary confidence in Churchill's own imperial acumen. During the mission, Churchill worked behind the scenes directly with Linlithgow to undermine Cripps' positions.[94]

The "denial resolution" had prompted the Secretary of State to warn the prime minister that the leaders of Congress were dangerous, but it is likely that Churchill understood freedom fighters in India as "enemies" even without further advice. Already entrenched in pitched battles on three continents, the unrest in India struck Churchill as yet another front in a "total war" that Britain had yet to master. On 11 August he chastised Amery for using the word "independence" in a broadcast from London, and on 2 September, while preparing a statement for the House of Commons on the worsening situation in Quit India, he exploded to his Secretary of State, "I hate Indians. They are beastly people with a beastly religion."[95]

What became known as the "Quit India" resolution was passed in Bombay by the All-India Congress Working Committee on the night of 8 August 1942. The terms of the resolution were very similar to those put forward in the 14 July resolution and the nature of the movement that would follow if Congress demands were not met remained vague.[96] Early the next morning, the leadership of Congress was rounded up and summarily jailed and the Congress organization, as a whole, was declared illegal. Maulana Azad, President of the Working Committee, admitted that this swift move by the British had caught the leadership on the back foot. "If the Government," he wrote, "had at least shown a conciliatory attitude there would have been scope for further discussions."[97] The sudden over-determining response by the colonial state came as a surprise. Of the 8 August resolution historian Sumit Sarkar too has argued, "far from ruling out further negotiations, the whole thing may conceivably have been an exercise in brinkmanship and a bargaining counter which was followed by an explosion only because the British had decided on a policy of wholesale repression."[98] The fact of the matter is that even before the August resolution had been issued, in response to the "denial resolution," the die had already been cast.

Without leadership, nationalist and anti-colonial elements across the country were left to their own devices and interpretations. Gandhi's appeals to non-violence had been recently attenuated by his increasingly and uncharacteristically extreme rhetoric throughout 1942. Ever since the spring Gandhi had been urging Britain to "leave India to God or anarchy," expressing a final willingness to risk "complete lawlessness" if such would be the price of freedom.[99] On 8 August he gave his now famous "Do or Die" speech, which, while still advocating non-violence, expressed a tone of finality that would increase the intensity of the movement.[100] With the arrest of Gandhi and both national and provincial Congress leadership, the masses of India proceeded with their own interpretation of "Do or Die." Disruptions of transport, communication lines, factory operations, and open challenges to police and governmental authority began in most urban centers immediately. Violence moved into the countryside subsequently, with peasants participating in open rebellion in large numbers. In rural districts of Bihar and the United Provinces railway tracks were cut, telegraph poles were downed, goodssheds were looted and police stations ransacked. By 15 August things had spiraled out of control to the extent that Linlithgow had authorized the military, in aid of civil power, to begin machine-gunning saboteurs from the air.[101] But the movement only continued to gain strength. On 31 August Linlithgow telegraphed Winston Churchill and confided, "I am engaged here in meeting by far the most serious rebellion since that of 1857, the gravity and extent of which we have so far concealed from the world for reasons of military security."[102]

In Bengal, the pattern of disturbances followed the all-India model, with disturbances breaking out in Calcutta and Dacca shortly after the arrest of Congress leaders, and violence spreading to the countryside subsequently. Student demonstrations began on 10 August in both cities, and picked up momentum in the following days. The police and the Civic Guards were mobilized to deal with widespread transportation disruptions and vocal demonstrations. Military reinforcements were requested as the violence escalated. Scuffles broke out between the public and the police, and on 14 August police firings killed two in Calcutta.[103] Marwari industrialists, led by Gandhi's staunch ally in Calcutta, G.D. Birla, organized strikes at jute mills and steel works in and around the city. At the Kesoram Cotton Mills, Birla's own textile mill in Metiabruz, striking workers clashed with police on the 24 August, and other serious incidents were reported from the jute mills at Cossipore and Chitpur. The Imperial Tobacco Company was also attacked by a mob of at least 1,000, and five were killed in police firings. In Calcutta alone, by the beginning of September, twenty protesters had been killed by the police, and 229 injured, including seventy-four policemen.[104]

By the end of the month, demonstrations had petered out in urban areas but were gaining strength in the countryside. In Midnapore, a district just south-west of Calcutta, the "open rebellion" took firm root. Local activists organized attacks on police stations, post offices, transportation facilities, and other symbols of imperial rule, and under the remnants of Congress leadership, an alternative "national government" (the Tamluk Jatiya Sarkar) was founded. A weekly journal, *Biplabi*, was also established to report on socio-political events in the district. With fifty-seven army battalions mobilized across India, the "Quit India" movement was suppressed in many rural areas of the country by main force, but due to organizational sophistication in Midnapore, the movement held together and proved an enduring problem for colonial authorities for years to come. Rebellion had a strong foothold in

Midnapore, and denial policies, increasing scarcity of essential commodities, and outrage at military heavy-handedness, created conditions for a sustained movement under dedicated leadership.[105] In other parts of the province many of these same factors blunted overt political expressions among the peasantry, as the hardships of material scarcity began to unravel social networks and undermine political solidarity.

Economic Warfare

In the districts rice and paddy prices continued to rise precipitously as the lean season fast approached. A statutory ceiling on rice and paddy prices was established on 1 July and exports from the province banned later in the month. But prices were moving too fast for government to keep up. The controlled price announced on 1 July was already below prevailing market rates, which drew protests from stockists who would be operating at a loss for recent purchases if they sold their grains. The price was adjusted accordingly, but black markets had already begun functioning on a large scale.[106] By August official stocks of rice in Calcutta were exceedingly low, and Government began worrying in earnest about feeding labor in war-production factories.[107] About 100 privately owned, government sanctioned and supplied "control shops" were established in the city to feed a large number of industrial employees, and a Directorate of Civil Supplies was haphazardly set up. "Denial" mastermind, L. G. Pinnell, was appointed Director of Civil Supplies and large purchases were made on government account from Birbhum district, north of Calcutta, at prices well above the price ceiling fixed by Government in July.[108] Rumors spread. The fact that the government itself was buying at highly inflated prices led to increased panic in rice markets across the province and furthered the proliferation of black markets, which again fueled inflation.

At this time the Directorate of Civil Supplies had little real organizational capability to manage even its own affairs. Established under the authority of the Department of Commerce and Labor, it had no minister of its own; only Pinnell as Director, D. L. Mazumdar as Deputy Director, one Assistant Director, and two trained clerks. "Briefly speaking," Pinnell admitted, "the department never even had 'the staff to ask for the staff' for months."[109] Recruitment was further handicapped by Pinnell's reluctance to comply with communal ratios, which would have necessitated hiring an equal proportion of Muslims to staff the director-ate.[110] Pinnell's attitude drew ire from the Muslim League, which further complicated administrative execution. Moreover, the very establishment of the Directorate spurred alarm. "Civil Supplies," it was well under-stood by now, meant only supply to "essential" industrial labor in and around Calcutta. The rest would be left to fate. Government alarm was read as inside information—if the government can't even feed Calcutta, what of the remaining 56 million in the province? Many of the big industrial firms had been granting "dearness allowances" and opening control shops since the beginning of 1942. Now, with prices failing to stabilize—and Japan within striking distance—anxieties proliferated.

The Bengal National Chamber of Commerce, representing all the major jute mills, the Paper Makers Association, the Engineering Association, the Tramways, and other industries, initiated its "Chambers Foodstuff Scheme" in late August 1942. According to this scheme, the Chamber itself began making large purchases of rice and paddy from districts and supplying it to its members directly. Constituent firms, meanwhile, continued bulk purchases on their own accounts, doubling down on the most essential commodity in the province. Some months earlier the Central Government had imposed an Excess Profit Tax (E.P.T.) to raise revenue from industrial firms recording record profits in war industries. Now, with developing difficulties in the food supply, the Labor Department notified employers in August that expenditures on foodstuffs for "essential" employees could be written off against the E.P.T. And so, with the provincial government showing an "extremely panicky mentality themselves,"[111] high prices were freely paid on bulk purchases by industrial interests with priority access to transportation facilities, and the expenditures were subsidized in the form of tax credits. Speculation in increasingly volatile commodity markets fueled the fire still further.

Between 7 July and 21 August alone, the price of rice rose 65 per cent[112]—and the "starvation season" in Bengal was about to begin.

In its first issue of *Biplabi* the Tamluk Congress Committee reported the attack and attempted sinking of a boat trying to carry rice away from the Danipur rice mill by a group of villagers on 9 September. Police, backed by armed soldiers, had been making arrests in the sub-division for a week past. The villagers were fired on by troops and three were killed.[113] On 14 September, in Dinajpur, north Bengal, a crowd of as many as 10,000 villagers armed with lathis and other weapons attacked government buildings and looted hoards of rice and paddy from stockists in the countryside.[114] Two weeks later a similar crowd gathered in Jalpaiguri, the chief grievance being a scarcity of paddy in the locality.[115] Local officials requisitioned paddy from large stockists and released it on local markets, pacifying the restive mob. In a weekly report during the same quarter the provincial Deputy Inspector General of Police noted a sharp rise in "dacoity cases." "It is a very significant sign of the times," he wrote, "that in not less than 33 cases utensils and/or cloth are specifically mentioned amongst the stolen property and in seven cases foodstuffs were either the sole objective or were taken along with other things. It is many years since dacoits bothered themselves with such items."[116]

Faced with increasing disorder in Bengal, the Government of India adopted novel measures in accordance with the Defence of India Rules, and on 8 September 1942 the Collective Fines Ordinance was executed for the first time in India. A fine of 10,000 rupees was imposed on the inhabitants of Bolpur in Bengal for unspecified "Congress-inspired disturbances."[117] A similar fine was imposed on the inhabitants of Birbhum district a week later, and collective fines were subsequently levied in Malda, Burdwan, Midnapore, Tippera, Dinajpur, Faridpur, Murshidabad, Hooghly, and Dacca. The concept of the collective fine was to create a backlash against political agitators, who were known to be in a minority in most districts, at the (literal) expense of the already impoverished masses.[118] In this way a wedge could be driven between the poor and the "political."

Other measures were adopted for those with better resources. In September a secret memorandum was sent out by the central government to all provincial governors outlining general guidelines for "economic warfare" against all corporate entities with anti-colonial leanings.[119] Provincial governments were requested to black-list companies associated with the nationalist movement, confiscate the funds of "unlawful associations," prosecute all contributors to the same, withhold advertisements from newspapers printing "anti-government reports," and otherwise seek to economically disadvantage sectors of the population in non-compliance with wartime authority. It was noted, furthermore, that "no public notice or warning of the action [to be taken] should be given in advance…and economic sanction [should] be enacted without publication of intent to do economic damage."[120] This makes it difficult to determine, in retrospect, to what extent such orders were executed—certainly the landscape of Bengal began to look more and more like a battlefield of "economic warfare" in the months and years to come.

At the same time, the more overt economics of warfare were undermining the financial system of India still further. Since the beginning of the war, India had been providing Britain with a large number of troops and supplies for its campaigns in the Middle East, North Africa and Southeast Asia. Because India was recognized as a sovereign state, Britain was under obligation to pay for the Indian resources (both human and material) that it was utilizing across the globe. The Exchequer in London, however, was reluctant to part with the money that such exports from India entailed, knowing that the outlay of so much cash to India could spur inflation back home. Britain opted, instead, to float a massive I.O.U. to India in the form of "sterling balances" held on account by the Exchequer in London. In the meantime the Indian Government paid out large sums in relation to the war on Britain's (frozen) account. In order to cover these expenses, the Reserve Bank of India printed money at an accelerating pace and by the end of the war the currency in circulation in India had increased six-fold.[121]

With inflation whittling away at the security of the sub-continent, Amery pressed the issue of sterling balances owed to India in the War Cabinet. Churchill, however, could not be convinced that anything at all was owed to India, but rather "burbled away endlessly" that Britain was India's protector not its debtor![122] India should simply be grateful that Britain was there to defend her. "It is an awful thing," wrote Churchill's Secretary of State for India,

> dealing with a man like Winston who is at the same moment dictatorial, eloquent and muddleheaded. I am not sure that I ever got into his mind that India pays for the whole of her defense including British forces in India, or that there is no other possible way of reducing these accumulating balances except by stopping to buy Indian goods or employing Indian soldiers outside India.[123]

As for the rest of the Cabinet, Amery noted, "none of them ever really have the courage to stand up to Winston and tell him when he is making a fool of himself."[124] Needless to say, sterling balances on India's account continued accumulating in London, while rupee notes continued flying off the presses in India.

In the last week of September large demonstrations against colonial rule rocked Midnapore. Thousands of villagers marched on police stations and government offices in Tamluk, Nandigram, and Contai subdivisions. Troops stationed in the area responded with overwhelming force, killing at least forty-four in Tamluk alone including Matangini Hazra, a 73 year old woman who would become an icon of the anti-British movement.[125] Villagers fought running battles with police and soldiers, blocking roads, burning down police *thanas*, and raising nationalist flags over government offices. The violence spread and was also directed against big landholders. The rent-collecting offices of the *zamindar* of Mahisadal were gutted, and the granary looted. Rice and paddy were distributed amongst the crowd and the grain bin was burnt to the ground.[126] *Chowkidars'* tax record offices and Debt Conciliation Boards were attacked, documents destroyed, and uniforms of local police agents were burnt in effigy in many places across the district.[127] Indiscriminate police firings were widely reported and evidence of military atrocities multiplied. In the pages of *Biplabi* there were stories of rape, looting, arson and cold-blooded murder perpetrated by military troops. The situation was spiraling out of control.

Storm

On 16 October a strong wind was blowing and unseasonal rains were falling in Calcutta. On the same day, Midnapore went silent. Not a word of news about prevailing conditions there reached Calcutta for the next several weeks. Even the chief editor of Calcutta's premier newspaper, *The Statesman*, heard neither fact nor rumor about what was happening in the rebellious region.[128]

It was some weeks later revealed that on 16 October a massive cyclone and accompanying tidal wave had swept through the district of Midnapore, destroying paddy, houses, cattle, and communications.[129] The Bengal Government later estimated the death toll to be 14,443, but accurate information was difficult to gather. Corpses lay scattered over several thousand square miles of devastated land, 7,400 villages were partly or wholly destroyed, and standing flood waters remained for weeks in at least 1,600 villages. Cholera, dysentery and other waterborne diseases flourished. 527,000 houses and 1,900 schools were lost, over 1,000 square miles of the most fertile paddy land in the province was entirely destroyed, and the standing crop over an additional 3,000 square miles was damaged.[130] Amongst the worst hit sub-divisions were Tamluk and Contai, the same areas were revolutionary activities had been most violent: 786 villages in the two sub-divisions had disappeared without a trace.[131] In all as many as 2.5 million people were killed, displaced, or otherwise dispossessed by the cyclone.

When the devastation was finally announced, the Secretary of the Revenue Department, B. R. Sen, was put in charge of relief operations. The most pressing issue of concern was getting food into the cyclone-struck area. Sen approached the newly inaugurated Directorate of Civil Supplies for help, but was told that "since the Department of Civil Supplies found it impossible to cope with the demands made on them by different authorities, I should myself go into the market and buy what I could."[132] The idea of simply "going to the market" in relation to a catastrophe of that magnitude was a patent absurdity, and many began to starve. In his *Prosperity and Misery in Modern Bengal,* one of the few full length scholarly works on the Bengal famine, Paul Greenough argues that the cyclone that struck Midnapore might be understood as the "first stage" of the famine. The question of the beginning and end of famine in Bengal, however, is an extremely complex one, and one that defies the fixing of any particular event as a sign post.

On 28 October, even before the Midnapore cyclone had been reported, the American Economic Warfare Board sent a communiqué to the Indian Government expressing deep concern about the "critical" food situation in India. The Government of India, however, and despite acute British concern about American perceptions, remained entrenched in denial. At the Sixth Price Control Conference, it was admitted that Central Government needed to concern itself with the civilian food supply, and a "Basic Plan" was outlined for government control of inter-provincial trade. But no real measure towards feeding an increasingly hungry population were enacted. "Such food shortages as occur," the External Affairs Department responded to the American Economic Warfare Board, "are local and mainly experienced by relatively small *urban* populations."[133]

Three days later, however, and a full three years after the war had begun, the viceroy approved the establishment of a separate Government of India, Department of Food. No independent Food Member was, as of yet, installed; instead, the Food Department portfolio was assigned to the Commerce Member of the Government of India, Nalini Sarkar. Sarkar, earlier in life, had been President of the Bengal National Chamber of Commerce as well as Commissioner of the Calcutta Port. The War Transport Member of the Government of India, Sir Edward Benthall, was, similarly, a Calcutta-based industrialist, whose firm Bird & Co. on the Hooghly River was a major player in war production. As such, the Government of India did appear to be staffed with crucial personnel who had both the resources and incentive to keep the industrial population of Calcutta fed at all cost. The question of the Bengal countryside was another matter.

Reports of death from starvation, quite outside the cyclone-decimated area, were being reported from several districts.[134] In fact, every indicator outlined in the Bengal Famine Code had already been met by October 1942. The impact of disaster, war, and want had dislocated several hundreds of thousands who wandered the rural districts looking for shelter, work, food, and safety. Credit in rural districts had contracted to the extent that the poor were selling off their household possessions in large numbers. Speculation, black-marketing, and a general atmosphere of uncertainty and fear had rendered rice markets increasingly volatile. There had been a high spike in crime, including the theft of foodstuffs. Looting of food stores and transportation facilities had been reported widely across several districts, and "test works," the final measure of prevailing distress, had been opened in several places as early as 1941 and had drawn large numbers, indicating, according to the Bengal Famine Code, that famine should have officially been declared and appropriate steps taken to alleviate its predations.

On 3 December 1942, the viceroy cabled the secretary of state to relay a "serious deterioration in the food situation in India."[135] Amongst the causes of the "acute difficulty" Linlithgow listed prominently "the tendency on the part of small subsistence farmers to keep back more of his grain than usual for his own consumption, a course rendered possible by enhanced prices realized by such part of his produce he sells."[136] "The food situation is so acute," he went on, "that immediate substantial assistance is essential if war work in India is not to be seriously disorganized and law and order gravely menaced."[137] This pairing of the "food situation" with both "law and order" and the prosecution of war, became the only working "famine code" in India during this time. According to this code, the threat to war industries and internal security that scarcity might entail were extremely serious matters that demanded imperial attention and immediate action. In contrast, as long as war work was progressing smoothly, and threats to law and order remained in-check, the country could push on with the status quo, even if that meant abject destitution and eventually starvation.

On 12 December "an acute scarcity of rice" was reported in Burdwan, just north of the city.[138] On 15 December, at a meeting of the Calcutta Corporation a recommendation for rationing the city was tabled.[139] On 16 December, the Bengal Government admitted to "large scale un-coordinated buying all over the province," as well as "widespread speculative buying in both Calcutta and the rice-growing districts."[140] On 18 December the Employers' Federation of India met in Calcutta and recommended that employers adopt a policy of paying dearness allowances in kind rather than cash, as access to food was becoming highly contingent.[141] "Akin to the problem of foodstuffs," it was noted, "and second only to it in urgency, was that of cloth, the prices of which had risen to an abnormal extent."[142] A "cloth famine" had begun.[143] On the 19 December a joint meeting of all Chambers of Commerce operating in Bengal was convened. "Grave alarm" was expressed at the "unprecedented and unnatural" rise in the price of foodstuffs.[144] A few days earlier, the British Indian Association had sent an urgent memorandum to the Government of India in Delhi warning of a "grave situation that threatens the Province of Bengal in the matter of steep rise in price of rice and apprehended famine conditions."[145] The following day the viceroy left for Calcutta.

Christmas in Calcutta

"When Lord Linlithgow traveled from Delhi in the cold weather as he always did to Calcutta around Christmas," wrote his Reforms Commissioner, Harry Hodson:

> he used the famous white train, preceded for security's sake by another locomotive and guarded by armed policemen stationed at short intervals along the route. The vice-regal establishment occupying the train on these journeys was reputed to number 500. When you consider that His Excellency's entourage included official staff from private secretary to typists and cipher clerks, the Viceroy's Bodyguard of cavalry with all their appurtenances, chaprassis, syces and servants domestic and personal, together with servants of the ser-

vants in the caste-bound Indian tradition, five hundred begins to seem too few…in 1941–42 the Viceroy was still a great potentate, successor to the Mogul throne, surrounded by a court whom his unfortunate hosts had to entertain, as aforetime grandees in England were obliged to lodge the train of a medieval or Tudor monarch.[146]

In December 1942, Linlithgow found Calcutta "in very good trim… the streets" he wrote to secretary of state Amery, "were full of British soldiers and airmen, there was any quantity of military transport, jeeps & c. about; and in the center of Calcutta one of the principal avenues has been made into a runway."[147] The city was well prepared for war, the viceroy thought. However, Linlithgow noted in the same correspondence, he continued to be "greatly exercised about the food position… we are terribly hampered by the absence of personnel with expert experience in this line… I hope very much that you may be able to borrow me a man from the Ministry of Food [in London]."[148] No man was sent.

The admirable preparedness of Calcutta was severely tested the very day after the viceroy left the city. On 20 December air raid sirens began to sound throughout the city and industrial areas, but residents of the city had become inured to false alarms, and largely went about their business unperturbed.[149] An hour later, however, the air filled with the rumble of Japanese fighter planes and bombs fell in several parts of the city and the industrial suburbs. An hour later the "all-clear" signal sounded. News about damage from the raids was censored from Delhi, with official reports denying any significant destruction or dislocation.[150] After the first air raid it was reported only that "the number of casualties was very small."[151] Night time air-raids followed on 21, 23, 24, and 28 December. The third air raid, on Christmas Eve, was the heaviest, coming in two waves of attack, with "sticks" of heavy explosive bombs falling "slap across the middle of the city."[152]

"Fear of the unknown seized the industrial labor in and around Calcutta, the members of essential services including A.R.P. organizations, the members of public utilities services like Tramways Corporation, and even the constabulary and warders in Jails."[153] An exodus from the city was again underway with people packing their belongings and setting out on foot, traveling trunk roads out of the city with whatever belongings they could carry perched on their heads. By 23 December "every imaginable vehicle seemed to be in use."[154] The Bengal Chamber of Commerce called the exodus "immense," estimating that between six and seven hundred thousand people left the Calcutta area.[155] Sir Edward Benthall, War Transport Member of the Viceroy's Executive Council, had given a figure of 300,000 fleeing by rail.[156] With the exodus of "sweepers" as well, the depopulated city had been left to "crows, kites and pi-dogs squabbling over the debris amidst much smell."[157]

Linlithgow, however, congratulated the citizens of Calcutta for their fortitude: "Well done Calcutta!"[158] On 23 December a press release was issued from Delhi commending the fact that there had been "no evacuation" from the city.[159] Ian Stephens, editor of *The Statesman*, took Government denials to task over the next several days. "We do not know what the term 'evacuation' officially means," an editorial of the next day read, "but large numbers of people could be seen leaving the city."[160] On 27 December a second editorial was published, roundly condemning Government's air-raid publicity. After the heavy raids of 24 December, no information about damage had been released for a full twelve hours and the announcement that eventually came was "of the most meager sort."[161] Photographic evidence was censored and claims about the lack of exodus from Calcutta continued to be circulated. "When authority fails to put forth reliable information promptly or in adequate amount about outstanding local happenings," *Statesman* reporters argued, "it is inevitable that rumors should gain currency…the population would have been less suddenly depleted had rumor been less."[162]

Lurking behind governmental denials were simmering anxieties that were about to explode. Though, by all contemporary accounts, material damage from this first series of Japanese bombings was "slight," the ramifications of Japanese attacks on Calcutta in December 1942 were extremely profound. In some sense, it could be argued, these air-raids were among the most devastating of World War II, and can be implicated in the death of as many as 3 million residents of Bengal.

3

PRIORITIES

The fourth bombing of Calcutta, on 24 December 1942, was the heaviest in Japan's first round of raids, and in its wake panic ensued. The city had gradually been repopulated after the mass exodus in February, after the fall of Singapore and the Burma, but now, again, Calcutta began to empty out. Laborers again boarded trains and ferries, or set out on foot to escape the danger of proximity to Allied efforts, and sweepers, menial laborers, and domestic employees also deserted in large numbers. With the exit this time of Marwari commodity merchants, in particular—who shuttered their establishments behind them—the increasingly crucial circulation of goods and services in the city was crippled. Calcutta was now the central collection point of personnel and resources for Allied military mobilization against Japan. Hundreds of thousands of British, American, African, Middle-Eastern and Indian troops passed through the city on their way to and from the front. The port at Kidderpore was operating at full capacity and the city served as the gateway to vital coal and iron ore fields to the west, which fed industrial production essential to the war effort. Its factories were running at full tilt and huge profits were being made. Meanwhile, stocks of rice were already running low, and the question of feeding industrial Calcutta had been weighing ever-heavier on government officials for some time. The food supply in India as a whole was in shambles, imports were heavily curtailed, and now—with bombs falling on Calcutta and large stockists locking their doors and fleeing Bengal— Director of Civil Supplies, L.G. Pinnell, rolled the dice.

On 27 December an order was issued giving agents of the Directorate authority to break the locks on shuttered shops and storage sheds in and around Calcutta.[1] Specifically, any and all warehouses or shops dealing in rice, wheat, *atta*, flour, *dal*, mustard oil, salt, coke or matches that had failed to open for business within twenty-four hours of the "all clear" signal would be subject to forcible entry and confiscation of goods. Rice mills were also subject to government seizure in the event of closure. The A.R.P. and Calcutta Police would assist the Directorate, and the Directorate of Civil Supplies would have the authority to dispose of the seized commodities "in such a manner as they consider expedient."[2] A second order restricted the bulk sale or movement of any food grains by owners or persons in charge of storage facilities except under written permission of the Director of Civil Supplies. In order to monitor inventories, all imports into Calcutta and Howrah were also restricted, prohibiting delivery of any rice arriving by rail or steamer to any consignee, except under the authority of the Directorate. These orders essentially amounted to a state of martial law in the commodities markets of Calcutta and Howrah. In the days that followed a full two thirds of "visible" (non-black market) stocks of rice in and around Calcutta were seized by the Directorate of Civil Supplies.[3]

Little if any warning had been given and the scheme was enacted with such speed and impunity that affected parties had little opportunity to protest. The seizure of grain from rice mills around Calcutta was especially pernicious:

> Instead of sending for the mill owners and seeking their co-operation to maintain supplies in the city, Government sent around a large number of police staff who descended on the mills without notice and sealed godowns of a large number of mill owners. The action destroyed all faith the mills still had in Government's good dealings. The usual channels through which the mills supplied the Calcutta market immediately dried up.[4]

A letter of protest from the Rice Mills Association followed stating that "the sudden seizure of rice by Government and payment of an arbitrary rate to stockists and mill-owners in Calcutta...created panic in the minds of all owners of paddy and rice and [other] legitimate trade interests."[5] In its 1945 *Report on Bengal*, the Bengal Famine Enquiry Commission concurred: "On the 27th of December, the Government of Bengal, in order to maintain the distributions of supplies in Calcutta, were reluctantly compelled to requisition stocks from wholesale dealers and *from that moment* the ordinary trade machinery could not be relied upon to feed Calcutta. The crisis had begun."[6]

The manner and extent of requisitioning in Calcutta had deeply alienated "legitimate trade interests." All the stocks that had been seized had been identified in relation to applications duly filled out under the Foodgrains Control Order (these were what Pinnell called "visible" stocks). Consequently, the already thriving black-market—which had been untouched by requisitioning—began to expand rapidly as the potential liability of playing by government rules was laid bare. "Visible" stocks in the city began to decline as traders, mill-owners and large stockists became increasingly mistrustful of government interference. In turn, government estimates of the rice position in Calcutta became increasingly speculative and unreliable—further fueling governmental, as well as public, anxiety. The need to balance escalating uncertainties with large stocks of rice-in-hand increased again, and again more rice went "underground." Seeking to break this cycle—at least in Calcutta—Government again turned to the countryside.

Rajshahi, a productive agricultural district in the Dinajpur division north of Calcutta, was cordoned off just a few days after Calcutta had been bombed and soon thereafter agents of the Civil Supply Directorate entered to buy up large quantities of rice and paddy for Calcutta. Competition was excluded by a permit system, and government agents were backed by the threat of requisitioning if their restricted price structure was contested.[7] The region, while normally a surplus district, had in the past provided little rice to Calcutta.[8] That Government was now making large purchases there for Calcutta, alone, was cause for alarm. When word got out that they were resorting to strong-arm tactics, anxieties mounted. Rumors spread that Government was buying to supply massive military requirements elsewhere, or that the British were planning to withdraw from Bengal altogether, and were taking all the rice that they could lay their hands on with them.[9] Such "extraordinary measures" created tremendous hardship and also sharpened public distrust of colonial officials as tensions continued to mount.

The "Steel Frame"

The losses in Singapore, Malaya, and Burma had deeply shaken the confidence of members of the Indian Civil Service, or I.C.S.; an elite network of colonial officials (Governors, District Magistrates, "Special Officers," etc.) who comprised what was known as the "steel frame" of colonial rule in British India.[10] Since at least WWI, however, the I.C.S. had been a fairly moribund and anemic corps.[11] Officers of the I.C.S. rotated through positions and postings that were dependent on social networks at least as much as on administrative competence, leading to persistent maladministration and pervasive discontent. Particularly in the vast province of Bengal, the I.C.S. was undermanned, poorly equipped, and, increasingly, ill at ease. Local populations were disaffected, starving and rebellious. The war was going badly, and on their shoulders rested the prestige of colonial rule in South Asia. Colonial officers in Singapore and Burma were understood to have been apathetic, ill-prepared and ultimately timorous in the face of Japanese threat. Their chaotic and desperate evacuations had been sordid and humiliating. Many had made their way to Calcutta, sometimes in a desperate condition, with hair-raising stories to tell. With morale among colonial officials in Bengal already at a low point, this influx of disillusioned comrades from further east only served to compound the enervation of war, rebellion, and administrative impasse. Would they be next to be driven from their posts and suffer the humiliation of enemy defeat in a foreign land? Whatever the outcome, as long as the industrial production in Calcutta could be maintained, they knew, the war could be won. The "defense" of Calcutta, they also knew, was as much about rice as it was about anti-aircraft guns.

Early in January 1943 a Food Grains Purchasing Officer with far-ranging authority was appointed by Governor Herbert in order to scale up procurement for Calcutta. A scheme was outlined for bulk purchasing in the countryside. The new appointee, A.A. McInnes, I.C.S., would work under L.G. Pinnell (also I.C.S.) in the Directorate of Civil Supplies. McInnes had been in service in India for twenty-four years. He had no experience in food grains purchasing, but he did have great confidence in his understanding of things Bengali. Something of a lay anthropologist, McInnes boasted that he had always "made a special hobby of spending weekends and holidays living among the villagers and studying life from their point of view."[12] Along the way he had learned some Bengali and imagined that his linguistic achievements would stand him in good stead. Rice procurement was tough business, however, and villagers remained unimpressed by his assurances in broken Bengali. As he later relayed, "they thought that more and more of their supplies [were] going to be in danger, and they had no confidence in us."[13] Pinnell, having ample experience during "denial," was less of a romantic. He had no illusions about the difficulties that he and McInnes were likely to face in the countryside and was happy to be able to "pitch into the villagers…in their own language which," he admitted, "I find I can speak with force if not with grammar."[14]

Before the rural procurement scheme could get underway there were again disagreements between Government and the Bengal Ministry about agency appointments.[15] Again Pinnell wanted to enlist Ispahani's firm as a primary agent, and again this caused a backlash from the Huq Ministry and Hindu parties. At length, seeking to ameliorate tensions, Pinnell opted for a "Dutch Auction" to select agents. Seven of the agents involved, who were thought to have the highest turn-over in the province, were given exclusive contracts to purchase on Government's behalf. Each was assigned a particular area of operation and charged with buying up as much rice as possible in that zone. To minimalize competition, "free run" was given to agents in their respective zones and "considerable restriction on other people" was enforced.[16] In addition, embargoes were placed around purchasing areas, and even in areas not covered by the scheme, embargoes were levied in order to prevent speculative purchasing by non-government agents there.[17] In "denial" areas special passes were given so that agents could bring boats into coastal areas to remove even more rice and paddy. A ceiling price was fixed and purchases and sales above that amount were outlawed with threat of arrest and confiscation.

Subsequently, in late January 1943, less than one year after "denial," and with the essential *aman* crop again making its way to markets, agents employed by the government, protected by executive orders, and backed by police and ultimately military authority, again began to fan out across the province in order to buy up—or seize by force if need be—the "surplus" rice of Bengal. A special deal had been struck between the Bengal Chamber of Commerce and the Bengal Government for the Chamber to cease purchases during the drive, but no deal was struck with their constituent members who continued bulk purchasing in the countryside on their own accounts.[18] Jute and cotton mills, paper factories, the Calcutta Port Trust, the big railways, the military and even the Revenue Department of the Government of Bengal itself, continued heavy purchasing, with industrial firms writing off the expenditure against the Excess Profit Tax.[19] The drain of the countryside that had begun with "denial" continued.

Durbhikkho

With rumors about governmental intentions swirling, the frenetic purchasing of agents, sub-agents and district officials, was received with alarm. It was well understood that Government was in a state of panic and would use any means at its disposal to acquire rice and paddy from the countryside—even while conditions in the districts continued to deteriorate. The Rajshahi scheme had ended, but in Chittagong the Collector had begun "requisitioning hard" from cultivators. "This caused strong local resentment—people on their knees weeping or cursing before the District Magistrate."[20] A shortage of kerosene across the province was becoming acute and made the cooking and consumption of rice that much more difficult. Sugar, lentils, coal, and matches were also growing increasingly scarce. In Rangpur District it was reported that desperate farmers had eaten up their seed stocks and had nothing to sow for the summer season,[21] and in parts of Rajshahi, famine conditions were being reported, with as many as 50 per cent of households in some areas without any rice stores left at all.[22]

Even in Calcutta queues had begun to increase and supplies were being shifted without explanation. At certain shops, government lorries, aided by police officers, removed wheat to unspecified locations, leaving nothing at all behind for local residents.[23] With provisions for "essential" laborers at large industrial firms enjoying rhetorical precedence, sweepers, servants, contract laborers, and other menial workers employed in private residences *and* factories were left to fend for themselves. They had little security, either in terms of food or even shelter. The hardships of white-collar workers, on the other hand, did receive certain attention. Newly minted Member of the Food Department, Nalini Sarkar, visited Calcutta in early January to inaugurate a canteen system for the "middle-class" public, who, he said without a hint of irony, had "been so badly hit by food shortages, high prices, disruption of the family, and, lastly, the exodus of servants."[24] Meanwhile, even as Sarkar was inaugurating his middle-class canteens, J.C. Roy, president of The Refuge, an organization feeding homeless people in Calcutta, applied to the Directorate of Civil Supplies to obtain a permit to purchase food grains at subsidized prices and the permit was refused without comment.[25]

By January 1943, Calcutta was filling up with "beggars." A string of letters written to *The Statesman* complained that these "gentlemen of leisure" were increasing, spreading filth throughout the city, squatting in air raid shelters and pestering hard-working citizens with their plaintive grumblings.[26] The newspaper reported that while urban poverty was an "old evil" in Calcutta, the numbers of desperate immigrants had sharply increased in recent months. A Press Note on the topic was released by the Government of Bengal explaining that Government had every good intention to round up the "beggars," but were faced with certain administrative obstacles. Suggestions that they should be "kept under restraint" in relief centers built for air-raid refugees were impractical.[27] Air raid shelters had been built for evacuees "on the move" and did not have the sanitation or logistical facilities to house Calcutta's mounting indigent population. Furthermore, the shelters were rudimentary and would have to be fortified with compound walls, as, it was noted, "beggars will not remain voluntarily in detention."[28] The prospect of building new detention facilities for the poor was fraught with difficulties. Bricks were in short supply and the location of camps was tricky. In the meantime Government could only reassure the more fortunate public, that "it [was] fully conscious of [the] urgency and [was] constantly considering possible ways and means for the earlier collection and detention of at least those beggars who are suffering from dangerous or infectious diseases."[29]

Another editorial in *The Statesman* read, "there seem more beggars than ever in the city's streets and dirtier than ever; many are more importunate in plying their calling. A census to find from whence they come would be interesting, but unprofitable."[30] The question of profit aside, it would not have been difficult to determine where they were coming from: they were coming from the cyclone ravaged towns of Midnapore to the west, the militarily evacuated regions of Diamond Harbor to the south, and the impoverished districts of Rangpur and Rajshahi to the north. Across the province as a whole, in fact, the price of rice had risen far beyond the reach of many millions, and as the government strained ever-more fitfully to bring that rice into Calcutta, there followed an ever-growing stream of starving people from every corner of the province. But in the city too there was brutal hardship, and compassion had become extremely strained.

The most common Bengali word for scarcity, often translated as "famine" is *durbhikkho*; a word that might be more literally translated as "scarcity of alms." In a province historically ravaged by hunger, the poorest members of society had long depended on the charity of the wealthy to survive hard times. When times were especially hard, however, they found no help, and starved in large numbers. Now with the dislocations of war, governmental and capital predations were taking a brutal toll. Compassion had dried up, Calcutta was filling up with "beggars," and their plaintive moans were increasingly going unheard: *durbhikkho* was well underway.

Imports

The Government of India in Delhi had few illusions. Linlithgow, in his official capacity as head of the (only days old) Food Department, wrote to the Secretary of State in London on 9 December 1942 informing him that the food situation in India as a whole had "deteriorated seriously," and was causing "acute anxiety."[31] He asked for the immediate import of 600,000 tons of wheat. For "psychological effect," he suggested, the request should be made without specific reference to military or civilian allocation. The Food Department, the viceroy assured London, "will see that military needs are given preference."[32] Using the peculiar "famine code" that prevailed he noted, "the food situation is so acute that immediate substantial assistance is essential if war work in India is not to be seriously disorganized and law and order gravely menaced."[33] Amery replied that imports would, unfortunately, be impossible, given the "cost to the main war effort" that they would entail. The Government of India was on its own, he continued, and "should therefore lose no time in setting on foot measures which, *though drastic*, will serve to place maximum food supplies at disposal of Government."[34]

Linlithgow sent several more telegrams, pleading the case. If nothing was done, he warned, there could even be the possibility of "shortage being felt by the armed forces."[35] Amery remained skeptical, wondering whether or not the statistics that Linlithgow was using were of any merit: "Judging by the use which the Congress people have made of the Midnapore disaster," he replied, "they are no doubt capable of doing their utmost to aggravate the food situation by encouraging hoarding on the one hand and, on the other, [by] denouncing the Government for deliberately starving the people."[36] Linlithgow persisted, enlisting the influence of the Commander-in-Chief for South and Southeast Asia,

Field Marshall Archibald Wavell, who agreed that the situation was grave. Military rations, Wavell informed the War Cabinet, were already being cut for both men and draught animals.[37]

On 8 January 1943, Amery sent a memorandum to the Minister of War Transport in London, Lord Leathers, outlining Linlithgow's entreaty. "It is the urban population," Amery wrote,

> who are the first to experience any shortage, and since it is the urban popula-
> tion on whose labour the Indian munitions and supply industries depend,
> any marginal shortage of food tends to reduce the output of those industries.
> Such a shortage may have the effect of driving labour from factory centres
> back to the country where they may be lost to industry and constitute a
> threat to law and order with the possibility of food riots.[38]

This, then, was Government's "famine code" encapsulated.

A meeting of the War Cabinet was held and at length it was agreed that in lieu of the 600,000 tons of grains requested by the viceroy, a maximum of 130,000 tons might be made available by the end of April.[39] In return for these minimal promises, the War Cabinet pressed for Indian assistance on Ceylon. Ceylon was also a critical strategic base against Japan and there too rice was in short supply. The 130,000 tons of grains promised was specifically for wheat to supply western India. Rice from Bengal would be the trade-off. The viceroy approached Fazlul Huq with the Ceylon problem: "Mindful of our difficulties about food I told him that he simply *must* produce some more rice out of Bengal for Ceylon, even if Bengal itself went short! He was by no means unsympathetic," Linlithgow wrote hopefully, "and it is possible that I may in the result screw a little out of them."[40]

Having failed to gain any traction on the over-all "food situation," the viceroy wrote to all provincial governors to advise them on how to proceed. "The Central Government," he warned, "regard the position more seriously than might be supposed from their communications to the general public."[41] Wheat imports were promised but would necessarily be far less than adequate. "As for the problem of rice," he added, "no help can be expected from outside the country and we are forced back on our own resources."[42] It would be imperative for provincial governments to use all means necessary to get control of as much food as possible. Rather than working with elected officials, however, the viceroy advised governors that "for the fullest measure of success" they should rely on the I.C.S. for the execution of procurement.

With this, Linlithgow contented himself with the "food position" for the time being. Other vastly more spectacular events were on the immediate horizon, and it was to them that all administrative eyes now turned.

Starving Indians

Even before Gandhi was arrested on the 9th of August, 1942, plans for what course of action to take if he chose to hunger-strike were being urgently discussed in New Delhi and London. The viceroy, fearing mass unrest if Gandhi were to die of hunger in custody, conveyed to London his intention to follow the officially codified "cat and mouse" procedure: releasing Gandhi if his health declined enough that he was in danger of dying on Government hands, then re-arresting him if he survived.[43] The War Cabinet rebutted Linlithgow, staunchly advocating allowing Gandhi to fast to death in detention, if it came to that. The political implications of his death in custody could be blunted, the War Cabinet argued, if Gandhi could be deported upon arrest and detained in Yemen or Sudan—where news of his demise could be carefully censored.[44] The War Cabinet also expressed its jurisdictional primacy, noting that the treatment of State Prisoner Gandhi "was a matter in which His Majesty's Government must be responsible for the decision taken."[45]

The first inklings that Gandhi would venture to starve himself while in custody came in an uncharacteristically angry letter to the viceroy on New Year's Eve of 1942. In this letter Gandhi focused on the 9 August arrest of Congress leaders. The arrests, Gandhi argued, were unjust unless and until some objective proof could be given that the leadership of Congress had directed any violence at all, which, he said, they had not. Instead, he blamed Government's authoritarian stance for the violence that was sweeping the country, and added that a fast would be his "last resort" to redress governmental injustice. The viceroy replied tersely to Gandhi, accusing him of merely trying to evade responsibility, and suggesting that he should, at once, denounce the popular movement that *his* actions had instigated. Gandhi again replied that Government heavy-handedness, not Congress instigation, had precipitated the uprising, and added that as a "helpless witness to what is going on in the country, *including the privations of the poor millions owing to the universal scarcity stalking the land*,"[46] he was morally compelled to fast.

The last word on how to deal with the eventuality of a fast by Gandhi had been given by the War Cabinet months earlier: he should be allowed to die in custody. Governor of Bombay, Sir Richard Lumley, under whose jurisdiction the immediate matter of dealing with the intricacies of Gandhi's detention fell, however, now argued frankly against the decision, warning that in Bombay, if not across India as a whole, Gandhi's death under arrest would be sure to create considerable unrest. He also warned New Delhi that the Surgeon-General of Bombay had alerted him to the fact that at his age, and given his high blood pressure, Gandhi would be unlikely to last more than three or four days.[47] Gandhi would almost certainly die during this fast, and mass movements would follow. Linlithgow seconded Lumley's apprehensions, and submitted a memorandum to the War Cabinet in London, urging reconsideration of the case given sentiments on the ground in India and the likelihood of an impending fast.[48]

Amery knew that the case for release would be a hard sell, particularly with Winston Churchill at the helm. Churchill, it was well understood, was deeply opposed to Indian independence, and had a particularly arch opinion of Mohandas Gandhi. When Gandhi had met with a previous viceroy to negotiate a detente between nationalist forces and the colonial government, Churchill had been aghast: "it is alarming," he commented, "and also nauseating to see Mr. Gandhi, a seditious Middle Temple lawyer, now posing as a fakir of a type well known in the East, striding half naked up the steps of the Viceregal palace, while he is still organizing and conducting a defiant campaign of civil disobedience, to parley on equal terms with the representative of the King-Emperor."[49] Amery's memorandum, moreover, was considered by the War Cabinet on a day that seems to have found Churchill in a markedly acrimonious mood—particularly on the topic of Empire.

The War Cabinet began discussions with a proposed joint declaration on general colonial policy. Amery, himself a conservative with close ties to the prime minister, was dismayed to find Churchill "at his worst as a Chairman" that day. He had "not really read the Declaration itself," but, in any case, "started off with a terrific tirade against apologizing for the Empire, appeasing the Americans, etc."[50] Amery tried to keep the meeting on track, but confessed:

> when he is really stupid like that and simply cannot see obvious points, I find myself getting very impatient...At one moment he got onto a long discourse on Imperial Preference and Ottawa and could not see that this was not raised one way or other by the declaration. In the end after an hour and a half or

more of time wasted it was decided that a revised draft with one or two further amendments should again be submitted. We then got on to Gandhi.[51]

Unsurprisingly, the War Cabinet stuck to its guns and found that
Gandhi should remain in detention, until death if need be. At a subsequent meeting they urged the viceroy to reply to Gandhi in the strictest
terms. If he would admit Congress's blame for the violence that was
wracking India, and personally disavow the same, negotiations would be
possible for release.[52] (Coincidentally, at the same meeting the "Food
Situation" in India was discussed "for another ten minutes or so."[53]
Despite dire warnings by the Secretary of State, the War Cabinet decided
that new imports that Linlithgow had requested would be impossible).[54]

Gandhi responded to the viceroy's letter promptly, roundly rejecting its
premises.[55] Again he blamed Government's excessively belligerent posture
of the previous August for the nature of the violence. The inclination to
fast, he assured the viceroy, was not simply the result of the injustices
being done to him but was also the result of his frustration at being incar-
cerated when "universal scarcity [was] stalking the land."[56] Linlithgow sent
back a blunt response, urging Gandhi to "face the facts" and accept
responsibility for the "sad campaign of violence and crime."[57] He did not
mention the "food situation" nor, for that matter, Gandhi's threat of a fast.
Later in the day, however, he grumbled to his secretary of state that
Gandhi seemed to be hell bent on a hunger-strike, even "in connection
with the food situation if he is deprived of an excuse for fasting on political grounds."[58] The secretary of state was sympathetic, agreeing that the
Mahatma did look to be intending a fast only "in order to focus the
limelight on himself again."[59] That Gandhi would be actually concerned
with the deprivation of millions of Indians was somehow inadmissible.

The violence in India, Gandhi rejoined, stemmed from the "leonine
violence" of the government's summary arrests and subsequent brutal
repression of the population. Such authoritarian measures had "goaded
the people to the point of madness."[60] The madness of the people, he
argued further—and again—had been significantly compounded by
hunger. The scarcity stalking the land was violence in its own right. The
injustice of hunger, Gandhi insisted furthermore, "might have been
largely mitigated, if not altogether prevented, had there been a *bona fide*
national government responsible to a popularly elected assembly."[61] The
fast would begin on 9 February. If he survived, it would end twenty-one
days later, on the 2nd of March.

Linlithgow hastened to finalize Government's plan. That Gandhi was insisting on making "publicity use of the food situation," was deplorable, but "however flimsy the justification," the Government of India needed to proceed with great caution to avoid popular unrest.[62] Linlithgow informed Amery that for his part he had "never wavered that Gandhi, if he desired to do so, should be allowed, on his own responsibility, to starve to death,"[63] but he noted that there were intricate strategic considerations that could not be ignored. Lumley had written another series of telegrams arguing that Indian opinion would be perilously inflamed if Gandhi were to starve to death in prison, and Lumley's estimations carried weight. Furthermore, Gandhi's death in detention was an eventuality that the political left in Britain would make hay out of and Washington revile. What was required was for the Government of India to present a united front. Towards this end the viceroy felt it necessary to invoke the opinions of his Provincial Governors, and most importantly, the compliance of his Executive Council.

The Viceroy's Executive Council, established by the Indian Councils Act of 1861, was an advisory body of appointed Members, vetted by the Crown, who were assigned governmental "portfolios" deemed essential to the various tasks of central colonial administration. At its inception the Executive Council consisted of six British members whose duty was to advise the viceroy on colonial governance according to their respective "portfolios." In the first half of the twentieth century, "Indianization" of the Council had become a bargaining chip in the struggle for independence, and gradually Indians had been incorporated into the Council, presumably to groom them for eventual self-rule. In 1941 Linlithgow advanced the most comprehensive expansion of the Council, adding four additional portfolios: Supply, Civil Defence, Information and Broadcasting, and Indians Overseas. All the new positions were to be filled by Indians, shifting the overall composition of the Viceroy's Executive Council from five Europeans and three Indians, to four Europeans and eight Indians. The Executive Council, at this time, however, remained a loyalist body with little public accountability. The ramifications of a fast by Gandhi, and the disruptions that any mass movement on his behalf might have, in fact, represented a particularly pressing dilemma for the Council, many of whom had vested political and economic interests in maintaining a "peaceful" status quo, particularly in industrial Bengal.[64]

At short length it was unanimously decided that the Government of India could not be burdened with the responsibility of Gandhi's health in the event of a fast: "if he decides to do so," they concluded, "he must do so at his own risk, and under his own arrangements." The decision was for release in order to dampen the potential for widespread unrest.[65] In a brief nod to Gandhi's own inclusion of the "food situation," the Council noted that the violence that Gandhi had instigated had itself "aggravated the difficulties of the food situation."[66] The viceroy sent their considerations along to London.

When Winston Churchill got wind of the Council's decision he was apoplectic.[67] At a special meeting of the War Cabinet he argued angrily for an immediate contravention to "force the Viceroy to override his Council."[68] He ordered Amery to draft a telegram to Linlithgow at once. Amery went off and composed what he deemed "a telegram of the most dictatorial kind," and returned to Churchill to argue his case further before transmitting. Solidarity with the Executive Council, he argued, was an essential tactic in dealing with the Gandhi affair. If a hard line were to be dictated from London, it could lead to resignations in the Executive Council which would destabilize the entire concept of the "Indianization" of rule. Churchill was unimpressed and accused Amery of weak-kneed appeasement, "as for the Council," he barked, "what did it matter if a few blackamoors resigned!"[69] Linlithgow was ordered to "suspend action on [his proposal] until further notice," and Amery's "dictatorial telegram" contravening the authority of the viceroy and Governor General of India was duly posted.[70]

While this drama is an instructive example of the colonial chain of authority, its practical import was mooted. Linlithgow had broken from the War Cabinet in London and had already communicated an offer of release to Gandhi, but Gandhi had refused, preferring to undertake his fast in detention rather than playing cat and mouse. The viceroy convened his Executive Council in the middle of the night and they voted, by majority, that since Gandhi had refused Government's offer once, he should now be held in detention for the duration of the fast, even if he died in custody.[71] Amery breathed a sigh of relief at not having to override the Government of India from London and lay bare the realities of colonial rule in India.[72]

Hunger Artist

After the flurry of activity leading up to the fast, Gandhi's hunger-strike began on 10 February with little fanfare. Lumley telegrammed the pre-arranged code word ("repudiation") to convey that Gandhi had begun, and thereafter Government shifted into a tense and ironic mode. Amery, in his diary of the day, jotted a single line: "The fast seems to have begun in a most amiable mood on the part of Gandhi and all concerned."[73] Linlithgow wrote a "Private and Personal" telegram to Churchill, apologizing for his "flank march," and also for his Executive Council, which, he reminded Churchill, was the true source of the prime minister's disquiet.[74] "They are not precisely the troops I would choose for a close encounter," he admitted, "but I think we shall manage well enough. May you never have to handle a Cabinet of NO-men. Love and good hunting. [signed] Hopie."[75]

Much to the viceroy's relief, the Indian general public remained calm as well. Reports from previously volatile provinces, including the United Provinces, Bengal and Bihar, indicated a lack of public "excitement" over the fast.[76] Linlithgow informed London that he had consulted with Central Intelligence Officers in all Provinces and "all [were] perfectly confident of the ability of the Police to hold the position."[77] The Muslim League, meanwhile, ran articles in *Dawn* ridiculing Gandhi and his fast, which greatly pleased the viceroy.[78] Bengal industrialist (and close friend of Gandhi), G.D. Birla, was pressuring sympathetic members of the Executive Council to resign, but all Members remained in their posts for the time being.[79] Churchill, for his part, remained singularly unimpressed by Gandhi's "fasting antics," and conveyed his suspicion to the viceroy that Gandhi was surely sneaking glucose into his water.[80]

In the next few days Gandhi's physical health began to deteriorate. On the night of the 13 February he had not slept well and his blood pressure stood at 195/104. Nausea on the 14th inhibited his ability to take fluids and acetone was reported to be found in his urine. The viceroy expressed his frustration that Gandhi seemed "insistent on submitting himself to the full rigor of the game."[81] A Congress doctor was transferred from Yeravada Jail to attend Gandhi, and the viceroy telegraphed Churchill on the 15th, informing him that despite repeated entreaties, Gandhi had, in fact, refused to be administered glucose.[82] On the 16th Lumley relayed the surgeon-general's opinion that Gandhi was unlikely to last more than five days more. "There [was] more danger of sudden collapse and death from heart attack," the doctor had informed Lumley, "than of a slow petering out from starvation."[83] Secretary of State Amery, having received the news in London, could only hope for collapse so that "the period of suspense and growing hysteria not be prolonged."[84] He inquired of Linlithgow whether or not flags across the country would be "half-masted" and encouraged the viceroy to write Gandhi's obituary in advance.[85]

On the 17th of February, unnerved by the Surgeon-General's reports, and relenting to the ongoing pressure of Birla and other pro-Gandhi nationalists, three Hindu members of the Viceroy's Executive Council—Homy Mody (Supply), Madhao Aney (Indians Overseas), and Nalini Sarkar (Food)—resigned. Since the fast had begun, Government had been at pains to paint it as a Hindu affair, coding references to support for Gandhi in terms of "Hindu elements."[86] The resignation of Mody, Aney, and Sarkar, fortunately, fit the bill. Muslim, non-League affiliated, Law Member, Sultan Ahmed, and Sikh Health and Lands Member, Jogendra Singh, had wavered but in the end were convinced by the viceroy not to resign.[87] The remaining Indian members of the Executive Council, Dr B.R. Ambedkar (Labour), Sir Mahomed Usman, Sir Firoz Khan and J.P. Srivastava, also stayed put. That the resignations had been thus minimized (and, especially, Hindu-ized) relieved the viceroy. He made plans to "fill the vacancies at leisure," assigned departmental Secretaries to two of the vacant portfolios, and put himself in charge of Food.[88]

Two days after the resignations an ad-hoc "Leaders Conference" was convened in New Delhi to address the situation. With Congress members in jail, and the Muslim League refusing participation, an eclectic patchwork of influential Indians, provincial politicians, businessmen, et al, was organized to draft a resolution addressing Gandhi's fast and imprisonment. Invitations were sent from "Birla House" in Delhi, and a wide variety of prominent Indians attended. At the opening ceremony special mention was made of the Executive Council resignations, and Madhao Aney (the only ex-Member in attendance) received the largest round of ovations from the gathering.[89] Understanding that the viceroy was want to characterize the conference as a "Hindu" concern,[90] the leaders were at pains to enlist a diverse range of participants, including non-League Muslims, Sikhs, and Christians. The resolution that emerged was a tepid appeal, consisting of a total of three sentences urging the immediate and unconditional release of Gandhi "in the interest of the future of India and of international goodwill."[91]

It is interesting (and also a rather sad commentary) that, though Gandhi's correspondences with Linlithgow had been published in the press, and were circulated at the Leaders Conference, no mention at all was made of the "privations of the poor millions" or the "scarcity stalking the land" to which Gandhi had made meaningful reference. In his "welcome speech," C. Rajagopalachari (C.R.) confessed that Gandhi was "a strange man." "What is it that Gandhi wants?" he queried. "The only thing he asks," and the reason for his fast, he went on, "is the right to review the position as a free man."[92] (i.e. Gandhi was simply fasting for his own release.) In his presidential address, moderate/loyalist politician Sir Tej Bahadur Sapru, while distancing himself as far as possible from Congress, rebutted the charges contained in the viceroy's letters, but, again, no mention of Gandhi's references to privation or scarcity was made. Next up to the podium, Bengali Hindu Mahasabha leader, Shyamaprasad Mookerjee, similarly made no reference to Gandhi's concern about deprivations. Informed of the conference afterwards, the viceroy was satisfied: "it [was] not too obvious to anybody for what precisely the old man ha[d] decided to fast."[93] Unsurprisingly the conference had little political impact.[94]

On 21 February Gandhi suffered what the surgeon-general termed a seizure, and his "pulse became nearly imperceptible."[95] The viceroy had already written Gandhi's obituary, made plans for the disposal of his ashes, and broadcast policy on half-masting (negative), and so felt confident that preparations were "well in hand."[96] Later in the day, however, Gandhi had recovered somewhat and was able to ingest fluids. On the 22nd he remained stable and doctors "looked less worried."[97] The doctors' bulletin of the following day was, likewise, encouraging. On the 20th, Horace Alexander of the Friends' Ambulance Unit—in India to aid with cyclone relief work in Midnapore—was allowed to visit Gandhi. Alexander asked Gandhi what he would do if he was released and Gandhi replied that "he would...naturally plunge into the task of bringing relief to those who are suffering from the present scarcity of food and other necessities."[98] The following day doctors reported another "slight improvement," and on the 25th Linlithgow received intelligence that G.D. Birla had received a telephone message from doctors in Poona that Gandhi was out of danger.[99]

Hearing of the likelihood of Gandhi's survival, Winston Churchill again sent a cable to the viceroy to convey his suspicions about the "*bona fides* of Gandhi's fast."[100] The prime minister urged the viceroy to search out and expose any evidence of "fraud." "With all these Congress Hindu doctors around him," Churchill maintained, "it is quite easy to slip glucose or other nourishment into his food."[101]

As it became increasingly apparent, over the next several days, that Gandhi would survive his ordeal, Government in both Delhi and London became increasingly jubilant—as well as denigrating. Linlithgow responded to Churchill that he would not be surprised himself if reports of Gandhi's weakness had been "deliberately cooked."[102] He had long known Gandhi, he told the prime minister, "as the world's most successful humbug," and would not be surprised if the whole affair was revealed to be just another act of "Hindu hocus pocus."[103] Churchill wrote to Field Marshall Smuts that he imagined that Gandhi had "been eating better meals than I have for the last week."[104] On 28 February he also wrote to the viceroy, disgruntled "that the old rascal [would] emerge all the better from his so-called fast."[105] He praised Linlithgow's fortitude and highly recommended the "weapon of ridicule" to further deflate Britain's foe. Linlithgow, in turn, wrote to the Secretary of State for India, "We have exposed the light of Asia—Wardha version—for the fraud it undoubtedly is; blue glass with a tallow candle behind it!"[106] Amery joined in the fun, calling Gandhi a "wooly pacifist, [a] simple…life preacher with no ideas of any particular distinction who has combined a reputation for holiness most successfully with a political dictatorship exercised in a wrecking and negative sense."[107] "Hindu India," he rankled on, would be "immensely relieved that the old fraud's precious life is spared," but, on the whole, Gandhi's "antics" had amounted to nothing.[108]

On 3 March 1943 Gandhi broke his fast. He remained in prison for another fourteen months—as India starved.

De-control

On the 16th of February, the day before newly minted Food Member, Nalini Sarkar, had resigned from the Executive Council, the Government of India sent provincial authorities a memorandum ordering them to fix strict targets for procurement of food grains. Official purchases in Bengal were still faltering and speculators were manipulating the markets. On the 18th of February the Bengal Government abandoned the agency system, and Food Grains Purchasing Officer, A.A. McInnes, was made sole purchaser for the government.[109] According to the viceroy's earlier directive, McInnes employed District Magistrates, Controllers, Civil Supplies officers, and other I.C.S. officials to aid in procurement. Embargoes that had been enforced for the benefit of government-appointed private agents were maintained, and export restrictions continued. Meanwhile, police officers were stationed at all points of entry into Calcutta to ensure that rice was moving only to approved locations.[110] Secret conferences between the Civil Supply Department and "priority" purchasers were held to facilitate procurement, and, again, with government sanction and collaboration, tea gardens and other large employers continued buying in bulk on their own accounts.[111] The aim of procurement initially had been to break the black market by dumping large quantities of rice on the open market, but by this point all shipments were heading directly to large factories and control shops, without regard to effect on prices.[112]

On the 11th of March the Government of Bengal, in fact, decided to abrogate price control entirely. "The Bengal Government," the order read, "in full accord with the Government of India, adhere to a policy of buying as much rice and paddy as possible by free market operations in order to secure the best use of the resources of the province."[113] Towards this end, it was announced, "The Bengal Government declare categorically that there is and will be no statutory maximum price for wholesale transactions in paddy and rice."[114] In some definite sense the black-market had won out. McInnes and the Government of Bengal were now able to report large scale purchases of their own.[115] Within a little more than two weeks after the announcement of the abrogation of all controls, the price of rice, already at more than twice its pre-war index rate in December 1942, had doubled yet again.[116] A few weeks later the Revenue Commissioner of Chittagong reported that "starvation [was] spreading from towns to villages."[117]

Section 93

Meanwhile in administrative circles there were other secret happenings underway. On 16 February the viceroy informed his secretary of state that a "tiresome" and "school-boyish" quarrel had erupted between the elected Chief Minister of Bengal, Fazlul Huq, and Provincial Governor, Jack Herbert. Relations between the governor and the chief minister had been strained to the breaking point at least since the time of "denial." In his letter of 2 August 1942, Huq had detailed at length the extent to which he believed the governor had abrogated his authority on a number of fronts, but had received no reply. In January 1943, Huq had sent another letter to the governor protesting the appointment of Food Grains Control Officer, A.A. McInnes, a man whom Huq knew "nothing about." The duties attached to this office, the chief minister explained, he likewise knew nothing about.[118] This habit of making critical appointments and plans affecting the population deeply without any consultation with the Ministry, Huq charged, had completely undermined the principles of "provincial autonomy." The governor, Huq added, was repeatedly acting as if "the Ministers must be completely eliminated and the Government carried on by you through the various Departments [of the Government of India] as if the constitution did not exist."[119]

Meanwhile, rumors, outrage, and rancor about Government repression in the districts had been rife at least since the time of Hindu nationalist S.P. Mookerjee's resignation from the Assembly over reported police and military atrocities in cyclone- and rebellion-ravaged Midnapore. Since that time, Huq had been under increasing pressure from Mookerjee and his supporters to order an investigation into the brutal suppression of the "Quit India" movement in the district. The Governor was well aware of Mookerjee's campaign, and in the first few weeks of 1943 was pressuring Huq and his cabinet to make an unequivocal statement distancing themselves from the affair. The European Party and Huq's Muslim League opponents joined forces with the Governor to lobby for Huq's compliance. Instead, on 12 February Huq allowed S.P. Mookerjee to make a statement on the floor of the Assembly outlining the circumstances behind his resignation, and the push for an investigation gained steam. On 15 February Huq announced the decision to debate the possibility of an inquiry on the floor of the assembly the next day. Herbert had not been informed before the chief minister had made the announcement to address an inquiry into Midnapore, and now it was Herbert who felt that Huq was stepping on *his* authority.

The governor wrote a sharp letter to his chief minister, reminding him that the issue of an enquiry into atrocities in Midnapore "attract[ed] [his] special responsibilities" and was "undesirable" at best.[120] Herbert ended his letter curtly, informing Huq that he "expected an explanation," in person and by the very next morning. Pushing his autonomy, Huq failed to appear. Instead he responded in writing that he "owed

[Herbert] no explanation whatsoever," and issued a "mild warning that indecorous language such as has been used in [his] letter...should, in future, be avoided in any correspondence between the Governor and his Chief Minister."[121] Huq went on to defend the right of the elected house to establish a committee of enquiry if the majority agreed. This decision, he argued further, most certainly did not "come within the purview of [Herbert's] special responsibilities."[122] In the event that the governor refused the establishment of such a committee, on the other hand, it would be the Legislature who would have "the right to expect sufficient explanation as to why a committee of enquiry [could not] be constituted."[123] Needless to say, Herbert was not pleased.

The budget session in the Bengal Legislative Assembly had begun by early March and the acrimony between Huq and Herbert was complicating an already excruciating process. The governor conveyed his dissatisfaction with Huq to the viceroy, who—annoyed—proposed to let them "fight the battle themselves."[124] Herbert, seeking to rid himself of the chief minister somehow, proposed to the viceroy that Fazlul Huq would be an excellent choice to replace Azizul Haque as high commissioner of India in London. Once Huq was shipped off, Herbert maintained, he would be able to work Muslim League stalwart Hussein Shaheed Suhrawardy into the chair of Chief Minister.[125] The viceroy approved of the idea of a Muslim League Ministry, but had little confidence in Herbert, who he asserted to the secretary of state was the weakest of all his provincial governors.[126] Meanwhile the impasse of a fragmented Assembly wore on the chief minister also, who was under constant attack from the European Party, and obstructionist opposition from the Muslim League. Huq, frustrated with the budget impasse, informed the governor that for the good of Bengal he would be willing to resign if that would facilitate the installation of an all-parties Ministry.[127] Herbert saw his chance. On the eve of the final budget vote he summoned the chief minister to his office where a letter of resignation was already waiting. Huq initially refused to sign, but the governor was persuasive. He assured Huq that the letter would not be registered on the floor of the Assembly. The Governor would only keep it as evidence of Huq's goodwill to all parties, and use it only to lobby support for an all-parties coalition. Huq, however naively, signed the letter. The next morning Fazlul Huq's resignation was already a hot topic on the Assembly floor. The budget session was adjourned immediately and the Ministry fell.

On 31 March, Emergency Rule was declared in Bengal under Section 93 of the Defence of India rules and Governor John Herbert, now with authority uninhibited by democratic process, signed the new budget into effect the next day.

Also in the last week of March 1943, Japan launched daily air raids on the 24 Parganas just south of Calcutta. It was reported that thousands of displaced residents of the district flooded into the city that same week: "their stomachs burning with hunger…dazed and desperate, thinking that if they could just make it to Calcutta, they could find rice to eat…but when they reached Calcutta, their hopes were dashed. They quickly realized that if many residents of the city themselves were unable to secure food supplies, what could they, as outsiders, expect?"[128] Police drove them from street corners and crossroads, and in short order they disappeared into the eclectic chaos of wartime Calcutta, while in the countryside hunger marches drawing thousands of participants were held across the province.[129] For reporting on the same, the Bengali daily *Janayuddha* was fined 1,500 rupees by the Government of Bengal.[130]

The Scramble for Rice

The scramble for rice continued. On 23 April it was announced that all restrictions on river transport throughout the Bengal delta were to be removed in order to accelerate the movement of rice into Calcutta from the countryside.[131] Though the number of boats actually plying had been sharply reduced a year earlier by "denial," the extraction of rice from the countryside remained dependant on river transport, and as such Government gave the "all clear"—even while bombs were actually now falling across the province. A week later another order was issued which removed all restrictions on the movement of rice between districts "except existing restrictions on exports from Calcutta and the industrial area."[132] On the all-India level, Civil Supply Director, L.G. Pinnell, advocated contravention of the "Basic Plan," penning a letter to the Government of India, that in his own words, "virtually demanded" that the Bengal Government and its agents be given sanction to make purchases outside the province to supply Calcutta.[133]

Governor Herbert seconded Pinnell's demand,[134] but was less involved in the deliberations than his robust authority under Section 93 might suggest. The spat with Huq and the unorthodox way that he had ousted the chief minister and dissolved the elected Assembly had not been received well in Delhi or London. The explanations the viceroy had received from Herbert, he wrote to the secretary of state, had been riddled with "a good many inconsistencies," and Herbert's handling of the affair had depleted the viceroy's already wavering confidence in the governor.[135] Linlithgow, dismayed as he was by Herbert's incompetence, however, understood his duty of "protecting [Herbert's] position and saving face."[136] He hoped that Herbert might "get out of it more lightly than he might [have], for the Muslim League detest Huq, and their anxiety to discredit him will divert attention a little from the Governor."[137] The viceroy, himself, was eager to have the Muslim League in power in Bengal, and now feared that Herbert's actions had complicated that eventuality in giving it a colonial taint.[138] The installation of a Muslim League Ministry in such circumstances, cobbled together with support of the European Group and Scheduled Castes, Linlithgow predicted, was sure to inflame "Caste Hindu" opinion, resulting in "an active increase in communal tension with a possible reversion to terrorism."[139]

The governor, in nervous reply, sent off a "personal apologia" to the viceroy, but forged ahead with his efforts to boot-strap Nazimuddin into power. On 13 April he called Nazimuddin to form a Ministry, and in the eleven days that followed, a Ministry consisting largely of the Muslim League, the Bengal Legislative Scheduled Caste Party and the European Group was formed. The new Ministry took office on 24 April.[140] The composition of the new Ministry, and the animosities that it entailed, confirmed the viceroy's forebodings. All Muslim cabinet positions went to League members, and only token Hindus could be persuaded to participate. With the installation of a Muslim League-dominated Ministry, politics in Bengal became increasingly communal, and with starvation mounting across the province, the primary issue at stake from the inception of the League Ministry was the "food situation." That the bare survival of many millions had become a primary administrative concern, lent a certain elemental hue to the acrimonious—and increasingly communalist—political relations that characterized the Muslim League Ministry, promising still darker eventualities to come.

On the day that the Ministry was formed, opposition leaders gathered to address an ad hoc meeting of the "opposition" in the Calcutta Town Hall. Hindu Mahasabha President, Shyama Prasad Mookerjee, issued a stark rebuke to the newly formed government, citing the Ministry as patently illegitimate. "Sir Nazimuddin can never hope," he declared, "to serve Bengal at the head of a Ministry which is opposed by a strong section of Muslims and by the entire Hindu community. The grave problems that confront us, specifically relating to food and internal security, imperatively demand unity of thought and action."[141] Fazlul Huq also spoke and put the new government on notice: the distress prevailing in the rural areas, he warned, was dire, and immediate steps needed to be taken. His own Ministry, he assured another opposition gathering a week later, had "made desperate efforts to avert a crisis," but in vain. The denial policy, exports of rice from the province, de-control, and several successive governmental procurement campaigns had all gone forward without any consultation and had created critical disruptions in rice markets. Now that the crisis was starkly manifest, Huq warned ominously, the new Ministry had the responsibility to cope with the situation post-haste to avoid catastrophe.

Nazimuddin himself was not unaware of the situation that faced his fledgling Ministry. The Civil Supplies Directorate, managed by L.G. Pinnell, had become an independent Department of the Government of Bengal a little more than a week before Huq's resignation. Upon forming his Ministry, Nazimuddin appointed Midnapore native and local Muslim League stalwart Hussein Shaheed Suhrawardy to the critical post of Minister of Civil Supplies. Suhrawardy was a seasoned politician, well versed in the rough and tumble of Bengal politics, who had a particularly colorful history of sparring with Fazlul Huq. Now as Minister of Civil Supplies he addressed Huq's admonitions promptly. He was well aware of the seriousness of the food crisis, he responded in a press note, but could assure the people of Bengal that a solution was in sight. The high price of rice was the result of hoarding by stockists and cultivators alike, and had no relation to any actual shortage, or for that matter, governmental interference. "If only the people had confidence in the future," he lamented, "if only they realized their duties to their more unfortunate neighbors, and if only the hoards in Bengal could be made mobile, the situation could be eased."[142] He warned all "hoarders" to liquidate their stocks at once, or face drastic consequences. He ended his statement with a threat:

> I am determined to use all the powers of Government to see that prices are brought down and see that these hoards are disgorged…I am giving a chance

to the people to do it voluntarily, while I perfect my plans to make them disgorge the hoards. If they do not listen to my warning, let them not think that they can run their hoards underground or that they will be able to succeed in dissipating the hoards.[143]

Suhrawardy's position was, in fact, conspicuously resonant with that of the Government of India. In December when anxieties about the food supply to Calcutta began running high, Linlithgow had written to Amery that "building up of large reserves by middle-class consumers and the tendency on the part of the small subsistence farmer to keep back more of his grain than usual for his own consumption," were primary factors inhibiting the increase of food supplies to Calcutta.[144] In April 1943, the Government of India's Regional Commissioner for Civil Supplies, Mr Justice Braund, made a broadcast over All-India Radio addressing the food situation in similar words. The crisis in Bengal, he assured listeners, was the result of consumers withholding rice from the market and keeping it out of the hands of Government. "Both the cultivators and the householder desire to keep in hand or purchase more food than in normal times," and as a result "there is nervousness and panic which makes a man produce the very scarcity that he dreads."[145] No mention was made of industrial concerns. To these evils, Braund added "the creature who, for sheer greed, grabs and withholds from circulation the food of his fellowmen." He failed to identify this last creature further, but in this instance, at least, the evidence seems to corroborate his assumptions.

Abandoning the Basic Plan

Writing purchases off against the Excess Profit Tax, industrial interests continued bulk purchasing at pace. The British Military also continued purchasing for the direct rations of their troops. From Bengal markets, at the time, these purchases amounted to, per month: 617,712 pounds of beef, 274,221 pounds of fish, 375,890 pounds of goat meat, 623,593 pounds of milk, 1,120,406 pounds of vegetables, 1,213,478 pounds of potatoes, and 185,230 pounds of poultry.[146] These numbers, however substantial they may be, do not include purchases made for private canteens, restaurants, or hotels in and around army encampments, which flourished, particularly in Calcutta. They are also limited to British military purchases at a time when American military engagement in the region was growing, and American soldiers, with their larger paychecks, began extensive participation in the black market.[147] The high demand for ice by military personnel also put a strain on fish markets (which depended on ice for preservation during transport), denying a primary source of protein to middle-class residents of Bengal. In some districts fishermen, already crippled by "boat denial", were forced to throw away as much as a third of their catch due to a lack of ice.[148] The railways were also purchasing "at any price," and had the additional advantage of the ability to move stocks effectively at a time when transportation was scarce and competition for the same was fierce.[149] Both the Railways and Port Trust, it was later revealed, also made arrangements to purchase and move large quantities of rice on the behalf of third parties.[150]

In the second week of May, Azizul Haque, who had been newly named Food Member of the Viceroy's Executive Council and Major General E. Wood, Secretary of the Food Department, visited Calcutta and met with Bengal Civil Supply Minister, Hussein Suhrawardy, in the Writers' Building.[151] The three men held a press conference afterwards and cited "psychological factors" as central to the food crisis in the province. They urged cooperation of the public, politicians, and the press in order to "keep up morale." Haque assured the people of Bengal that the Government of India was prepared to assist the provincial government at some future date, but, in the meantime, Bengal would need to "face the situation [on its own] in a spirit of courage and realism."[152] Major-General Wood produced figures that showed that Bengal had at its command more food grains than it had in 1939, and proposed that Bengal might collect their land revenues in kind, in order to put more of that abundant rice into Government hands.[153] Suhrawardy dismissed Fazlul Huq's contention that "denial" and exports had caused the crisis and reiterated that there was no shortage of rice in Bengal.

The following day, the Civil Supplies Department seized large stocks of rice in Narayangunge, Dinajpur, Bankura, Pabna, and Barisal.[154] The merchants, all modest sized dealers, were reported to have been in breach of the Food Grains Control Order (which had been all but obliterated by "free trade"), having not properly declared their stocks. Suhrawardy promised further action on this front in days to come. The public was shaken. Fazlul Huq, speaking at a meeting in Howrah's Town Hall the next day, noted that "each time Mr. Suhrawardy made a statement, food prices went up."[155] Shyamaprasad Mookerjee, at the same meeting, agreed with Suhrawardy that hoarding was driving prices, but fingered the Government itself as the main culprit. Professor Haricharan Ghosh of Calcutta University said that the statistical figures presented by the government the preceding day were inaccurate and unreliable. A resolution was passed calling for the immediate cessation of exports from Bengal, the import of stocks from surplus provinces, special transport arrangements for food grains to citizens, the establishment of an all-party Food Committee, the immediate release of all Government stocks to the people, and the establishment of a rationing system for the entire population of Bengal. Why these same proposals were not advanced while the petitioners themselves were in control of the Ministry is not a mystery. At that time, they too were similarly preoccupied with maintaining their grip on power and benefiting their better-placed supporters. Concern for the poor of Bengal only seemed to ever emerge as an issue—for either party—when it was recognized as politically expedient.

On 18 May the Government of India, heeding Pinnell's demand, abrogated the "Basic Plan" and all trade barriers between Bengal and its neighboring provinces of Bihar, Orissa, and Assam were abolished overnight. In some sense the order effectively relinquished the last vestige of central authority (or accountability) over the food crisis in India as a whole. The results of the order were predictable. "The introduction of free trade," the Famine Enquiry Commission found, "led immediately to the invasion of the provinces of Bihar, Orissa and Assam by a large army of purchasers from Bengal."[156] Conditions in Bengal were replicated in microcosm, as the mania of bulk purchasing soon destabilized large regions of the peripheral countryside. Prices in Bihar and Orissa shot up immediately, while in Calcutta only a transitory dip in prices was registered. The Government of Bihar lodged an angry protest. "Bengal merchants or their agents," they charged, "went into the interior villages and offered fantastic prices, as a result of which the arrivals of supplies in local markets were extremely poor [and] prices fluctuated almost from hour to hour due to wild speculation."[157] In Orissa the consequences were similar. According to the provincial Government there, "it was undoubtedly the greatest factor in causing high prices, hoarding and the un-availability of food grains to consumers in the latter part of 1943."[158] In short, the Government of India's experiment had confirmed that the policies adopted in Bengal some months earlier, were just as "effective" everywhere. Meanwhile, growing provincial distrust only isolated Bengal further in its plight.

Two days after the inauguration of inter-provincial free trade, the Bengal Ministry announced that it had appointed a sole purchasing agent for the Government of Bengal: Ispahani Limited. The appointment of Ispahani—by a Muslim League-controlled Ministry this time—was a move that greatly inflamed communal sentiment in Bengal and claims and counter claims about the Ispahanis' role in precipitating famine would circulate for many years to come.[159] The Hindu Mahasabha met on 21 May and excoriated the Government of Bengal's food policy, accusing the Ministry of "pro-Pakistan" activities, and again called for an all-parties committee to tackle the food situation.[160] Heated speeches were given condemning the Ministry and a resolution was passed demanding that the League Ministry take immediate action to feed the "thousands of men, women, and children coming from *mofussil* [rural] areas to control shops in Calcutta" where they were gathering to beg.[161]

With other supply concerns taking priority, however, Government instead began shortening the hours that control shops would operate at all. Citing the "hardship" of waiting in long queues in the summer sun for rice at controlled prices, it was announced on 27 May that shops would remain closed in the afternoon forthwith. In an addendum—as if incidental—it was noted: "it has also been decided to limit the sale of rice to one seer per head per day in the interest of maximum equity in distribution."[162]

The question of "equity," however, was again creating conflict. A few days after its Press Note announcing restricted hours at control shops, the government released a second press note saying that it would be establishing one control shop in each approved market exclusively for "local people." The aim was to "facilitate the obtaining of supplies by permanent residents of Calcutta." Residency in Calcutta could be confirmed, the order outlined, by presentation of an A.R.P. "enumeration" slip. Both the A.R.P. and control shops, however, were thought by many, including Muslim League Ministers, to be Hindu enterprises. The A.R.P., Fazlul Huq had also protested, was at least 95 per cent Hindu, which, Huq complained, was clearly the result of discriminatory recruiting policies.[163] "Control shops," which were, in fact, private shops selling essential commodities supplied direct by the Department of Civil

Supplies to the public at controlled rate, were also mostly Hindu-owned. These issues led to increasingly bitter communal relations, which would have disastrous consequences in the years to come.

In the meantime, conditions in the Bengal countryside were rapidly deteriorating and starvation was beginning to truly decimate the province.

4

FAMINE

In May 1943 increasing numbers of deaths from starvation were being reported from Rangpur, Mymensingh, Bakargunj, Chittagong, Noakhali and Tippera districts.[1] The 23 May edition of *Biplabi* from Midnapore recorded five deaths from starvation and eight cases of paddy looting that month. "Driven by the pangs of hunger," it was further reported, "about 600 to 700 people are daily traveling by rail, mostly without tickets, from [Tamluk]…to Orissa in the hopes of procuring rice at a cheaper rate."[2] Others had sold off whatever possessions they still had and were departing for Calcutta in "large numbers."[3] On 25 May a hunger march, comprised of more than a thousand starving men, women and children, entered Tamluk from the surrounding villages. The marchers were turned back by armed police officers and retreated empty handed.[4] Seven individuals including a ten year old were reported to have died of starvation that same week.[5] The writing was on the wall, the journal warned:

> The situation in Chittagong [on the front] is very insecure for the British, who probably have realized they will very quickly have to beat a retreat from Bengal with their tails curled under their bellies. It is for this reason that they are planning, we think, to decamp from this province with whatever booty they can loot—be it bits of straw or hay.[6]

The circulation of such opinions was not entirely arbitrary. In December of 1942 British and Indian troops had launched an ambitious

115

campaign to regain an Allied foothold in Burma, mounting an attack on the Arakan.[7] The operation was launched in secret, but heavy troop movements through Calcutta couldn't be concealed and it was well understood that a major offensive was underway.[8] It was less well known that Japanese troops were creating havoc for Indo-British forces, who suffered from a lack of coordination, poor equipment and training, and endemic malaria. To make matters worse, Indian soldiers also deserted in large numbers, with news of the re-organization of the rebel Indian National Army under the leadership of Subhas Chandra Bose.[9] By the early spring Allied morale was collapsing and the failure of the mission was imminent.[10] Fearful as ever of how defeat would be received in India, the government imposed a news black-out. Word of another defeat at Japanese hands, however, was not easily suppressed. The denial of official information only fostered what *Statesman* Editor Ian Stephens termed a "rumor-breeding silence" in Calcutta. Stephens and his staff could find no justification for the black-out:

> Would the public in any war-theatre, we wondered, have been treated so stupidly? Could one imagine a fortnight's news-blackout in Britain about the ground-fighting during the retreat from Dunkirk or, a year later, the withdrawals in Libya, Greece and Crete? It wasn't as if Calcutta's inhabitants hadn't direct means of gleaning information. 'Security' there was always poor; often the city leaked like a sieve with military data of variable worth; and our own fighting men, Indian as well as British, were now streaming back through it. Their comments on the handling of affairs, with ugly garblings and accretions, were of course widely repeated.[11]

Food Drive

Meanwhile, the rhetoric of "defending" Calcutta only gained steam. In June, the Government of Bengal announced a province-wide "Food Drive." The stated objectives of the "drive" were: "to ascertain the actual statistical position, to locate hoards, to stimulate the flow of grain from agriculturalists to the markets, and to organize the distribution of local surpluses as loans or by sales to those who were in need of foodgrains."[12] No rubric for qualifying the relative "need" of any particular party was established, and in practice the "drive" amounted to just another round of "denial." To achieve the stated objectives a militia of 8,000 government employees, recruited from various governmental departments, was assembled under the authority of the Department of Civil Supplies. In

villages, ad-hoc "food committees" were set up according to the recommendations of local Union Boards.[13] The Home and Civic Guards were
enlisted to enforce "order," and the police, as well as the A.R.P., participated in urban areas outside Calcutta.[14] Calcutta itself was excluded.

The authority to requisition stocks was broad. Any and all stocks of
traders not licensed under the Foodgrains Control Order were to be
confiscated. Any stocks that were deemed to have been inaccurately
declared under the same order were, likewise, subject to requisitioning.
More problematically, any trader, even with correctly declared stocks,
could have his license revoked if he was judged to be "withholding from
the market."[15] Exactly how such judgment would be made was left
vague—presumably refusal to sell to Government agents would constitute "withholding from the market." Once a trader's license was cancelled, his stocks would be undeclared and could be summarily seized.
In some sense, however, these conditions were a moot point. In a second
order District Officers, ultimately, were given authority to requisition,
regardless of the size of the holding, "whatever quantities they considered necessary," as long as they left behind enough for the stock-holder
to remain "self-sufficient."[16]

The environmental complexities of executing such a plan across the
province were formidable. L.G. Pinnell, speaking of the difficulties he
had encountered during "denial," estimated the topographical challenges
of taking a proper inventory of the rice of Bengal prohibitive:

> There [are] no steam launches except one for the use of the District
> Magistrate in each district. There are no mechanically propelled launches in
> the sub-divisions, and none in the *thanas*. You have sub-division which from
> north to south, taking inhabited portions, may be 50 or 60 miles long and
> your only means of getting about is a wooden boat which cannot travel
> against the tide. You can travel when the tide is in your favor, but you cannot
> when it is against you. Similarly for police stations, which are composed of
> large areas; the same kind of transport is there. The whole of this area is a
> network of tidal *khal* running between very big and dangerous rivers and
> your staff consists of the sub-divisional officer, perhaps a couple of Circle
> Officers for an area of 600 square miles, and a *thana* staff of a Sub-Inspector
> with perhaps one assistant for an area of—I would not like to say exactly.
> Under such circumstances, to attempt to visit every village or send people to
> every village in a short period of time [is] quite impossible.[17]

Very little had changed in the year since Pinnell had undertaken to
"deny" the countryside of rice, except that more than half of the country

boats in the province had also been withdrawn from service or destroyed during the same campaign.

The secretary of the Revenue Department explained other difficulties government faced succinctly: "The administrative machinery in Bengal is weak. It is a permanently settled area. We have no revenue staff. The Collector depends for information about agriculture mostly on his circle officers and the District Officer has no grip over the agricultural situation in the district."[18] Meanwhile, district officers now had the authority to confiscate any and all stocks that they thought fit to seize. Unsurprisingly, distrust of the campaign was widespread. The exclusion of Calcutta and its industrial suburbs, in particular, caused popular misgivings. In the wake of a year that had included repeated "procurement schemes," starting with "denial," there were prevalent suspicions that if there were large hoards anywhere, they were certainly to be found in Calcutta. Organizational difficulties were exacerbated by the fact that Union Boards, the most local branch of Provincial Government in rural Bengal, were notoriously rife with factionalism and corruption.[19] In practice there was only a very tenuous adherence to organization in any case.

Boats moving rice from Assam to front-line labor battalions in Chittagong were subject to "over zealous interference" from food drive workers and were forced to turn back.[20] In the Bogra District of Rajshahi, "hoards were unearthed and about ten thousand maunds of rice and paddy were seized."[21] Miscommunications, however, created a very telling reversal. After confiscation, "quantities…had to be released subsequently on the representation of various Government Departments and District Officers that *the seized stocks represented purchases on their behalf by their own dealers.*"[22] In the same district, the end result was "to drive out all hidden stocks to the exporting centers and railway stations where these were immediately snapped up by representatives of big dealers from outside, mainly from Calcutta, and promptly exported out of the district."[23] The fears of many rural Bengalis were being confirmed: large stocks of rice were moving out of the impoverished countryside and into the exempted Calcutta industrial area freely.[24]

Villagers fought back, but were largely powerless. Country boats moving rice from the fertile 24 Parganas to the south of Calcutta (a major supply line) were attacked and paddy looting was "frequent."[25] To address this hazard, the district magistrate "found it necessary to institute a convoy system for rice and paddy boats under armed police guard."[26] To further discourage resistance, collective fines were imposed on villages lining the main waterways if villagers did anything to obstruct the "drive."[27] In the Rajshahi Division there were reports of "considerable opposition to the food census," and rumors spread that "Government were going to take all the rice away."[28] Such rumors were, in fact, circulating throughout Bengal, being reported from almost every district in the province. In Mymensingh there was also panic, with people unaware that they would be allowed to keep any stocks at all.[29]

Public suspicion only escalated further when it was announced on the 17th of June that Field-Marshall Archibald Wavell, Commander-in-Chief of Armed Forces in Asia, had been selected to replace Linlithgow as the next viceroy of India. Some weeks earlier Linlithgow had announced his retirement. Wavell had overseen the defeats in Malaya, Burma and Singapore, and he had only recently suffered yet another humiliating failure in the Arakan. With rumors of military oppression in Midnapore having taken down the elected Ministry in Bengal, and with uniformed agents again beating the bushes for rice, the appointment of Commander-in-Chief Wavell "[came] as a surprise to most people. The average Indian regards it as the prelude to martial law."[30]

By this time, however, a significant portion of the Bengal population was falling well below "average." An incidental result of the Food Drive, with its administrative penetration into the otherwise isolated country-side was a (however reluctant) realization that Bengal was starving. The district magistrate of Faridpur frankly conveyed to the governor that "the drive [had] disclosed a very alarming state of things."[31] The poor were in an "extremely serious position," and starvation was mounting.[32] In Bakargunj the Food Drive had discovered "very little rice," but, "several deaths from starvation [had] been reported, and there must have been many more."[33] Test Works had been opened in Dacca Division and were drawing large numbers (the final indicator of famine according to the Bengal Famine Code),[34] and information was received from Malda that the whole district was "on the verge of starvation."[35] In Nadia and Murshidabad an urgent call for "emergency action to avoid starvation" was issued, and in Pabna fisherman were reported to be starving in numbers. In Chittagong, meanwhile, famine was only continuing to grow more grim. The district magistrate there expressed his concern concisely to the Government of Bengal: "I am referring literally to 'sectional famine' and not to metaphorical talk of starvation which there has been for some months past."[36] The question of how "metaphorical" talk of famine had been previously has already been illustrated.

The despair and trepidation that the march of a uniformed and armed militia, going from door to door in search of rice, must have wrought on an already starving population is difficult to fathom. One is inevitably reminded of W.W. Hunter's description of the 1770 Bengal Famine, when:

> The troops were marched from one famine-stricken part to another, the movement being represented to the king as made for his benefit; and so far from the English administration having laid in a sufficient stock of grain for the army at the commencement of the famine, the peasantry complained that the military wrung from them their last chance of subsistence.[37]

The Bengali journal *Masik Basumati* also made the connection, warning that the entire province would be turned into a graveyard if things continued at the same pace. In 1770, they reminded their readers:

> as much as a third of Bengal had died of famine. The East India Company itself had created that famine. They paid the cultivators whatever trifling price they saw fit to pay, and took away all the crops and hoarded them jealously. And if they sold any back, they sold it back at ten times what they bought it for. Whatever arrived by boat from other provinces, they snatched that up too, while the starving cultivators sold off even their seed crop to survive. But there were also employees of the East India Company itself who protested this unfair situation. Their highest officers [i.e. Hastings & Co.] were found guilty of their sins—what can we expect from our rulers today?[38]

On the 2nd of July Bengal Governor, John Herbert, sent an apologetic letter to the viceroy to convey the inconvenient news. "I am sorry to have to trouble you with so dismal a picture," he wrote, but "Bengal is rapidly approaching starvation."[39] The situation, he informed the viceroy, "could only be described as alarming."[40] Employing the only ever operative "famine code," he warned, "unless we can get in foodgrains on something like the scale originally promised, the law and order...situation will get out of hand."[41] In the margins of Herbert's letter, Linlithgow jotted his own note: "I wonder how far he is right about the Bengal situation."[42] The viceroy's estimation of the governor's competence was low. Earlier that same day he had sent a letter of his own to the governor, sharply reprimanding him for his handling of the Bengal Ministry affair and putting him on official notice.[43] His later response to Herbert's memo on the food situation was similarly terse; he congratulated the governor on the "success" of the Food Drive and noted that the volume of stocks seized during the drive had shown just "how much [rice was] in fact available."[44]

In July the Bengal Legislative Assembly also met for the first time since the Muslim League Ministry had been sworn in. Fazlul Huq addressed the floor with a long statement focusing on the injustices done to his ministry by the governor, and the circumstances that had led to his ouster. He concluded with a stark warning regarding the "serious questions affecting not merely the welfare, but even the *existence* of 60 million people of [the] province."[45] "Famine conditions, which are now raging in Bengal," he attested, "are unprecedented in the annals of [the] province," and could only bring to mind "the great famine of 1770 A.D."[46] Civil Supplies Minister, H.S. Suhrawardy followed Huq and touted the new Ministry's policy, particularly the Food Drive, which, he said, had "restored the confidence of the poor and...transferred the panic to the hoarders."[47] The numbers were difficult to estimate he admitted, but somewhere in the neighborhood of 300,000 tons of rice had been "redistributed." To whom they had been redistributed was a matter of debate. "It is true that millions are starving," Fazlul Huq jibed at a public meeting a few days later, "but there can be no doubt that the food situation has improved a thousand-fold within the last three months—in the homes of certain personages. Sir Nazimuddin is, therefore, partially correct."[48]

Last Ditch Denials

Meanwhile, the poor were on the move by the millions, trudging through the monsoon rains, now half-naked, falling by the wayside and dying, or straggling into urban areas to beg for food. The public health system was in shambles: under-organized, under-staffed and lacking in basic supplies.[49] Public health workers, under-paid as they were themselves, were often enough struggling just to maintain their own existence in impossible times. In all of Bengal, with a population of at least 60 million, there were 4,000 doctors, 2,500 of those working in Calcutta.[50] Even in Calcutta, however, relief for hungry children could not be organized and by July there were reports that infants were dying on the streets for want of milk.[51] In the same months the first outbreaks of famine-related cholera were reported.[52] To make matters worse, during the Food Drive, all of the public health staff of the province had been removed from their posts to participate in the "census."[53] During the same period, however, official priorities remained consistent. The waves of starving people that were moving through Bengal and filtering into its towns and market places, Herbert wrote to the viceroy, were a "particular nuisance" to troops stationed in these same areas, and "a danger to security."[54]

Towards the end of July details of the scheme to round up Calcutta's "beggars" were finalized. On July 30th Governor Herbert promulgated the Bengal Vagrancy Ordinance of 1943. The Ordinance, in its simplest form, "provide[d] for the police to arrest any person who appears to be a vagrant."[55] Though no clear description of what a "vagrant" might look like was offered, begging in public was cited as a primary indicator. It was noted that the Ordinance was "[not] intended in practice to apply to persons who have only recently been reduced to begging by the abnormal rise in the cost of food," but no guidelines were suggested to determine the longevity of any given individual's beggary.[56] Such judgments were left to the discretion of the police or A.R.P. officers on the scene. Those selected would be removed to a "receiving center where the vagrant [would] be medically examined and classified before being sent on to the appropriate Vagrants' Home."[57] Such facilities, however, were still under construction, and so a large warehouse building on the eastern outskirts of Calcutta was commandeered as a temporary site. It was intended "to put 1,000 vagrants at once into this home."[58] The numbers of "beggars" on the streets of Calcutta, however, was steadily on the rise.

On August 4th, Secretary of State Amery, presented an urgent memorandum on the Indian "food situation" to the War Cabinet in London. Heeding Linlithgow's increasingly dire warnings, Amery was forceful and insistent:

> The Indian economy is being strained almost to the breaking point by the enormous demands laid upon it in its dual role as a source of supplies and of men for the Army, and a base for military operations. The large sums of money which have had to be poured into the country, against which there have been no offsetting volume of imports, have created a serious inflationary situation, one of the manifestations of which is a tendency to hold commodities on the part of millions of producers scattered all over the vast countryside. India is essentially a primitive country with only a veneer of developed finance and industry, and the administrative system, although adequate for normal times, is a mere skeleton.[59]

Famine conditions, he noted, had begun to appear and were spreading. Such a state of affairs, he warned, could easily lead to "a marked reduction in the production of munitions and supplies in India…with consequent detriment to the maintenance of the forces in, and drawing their supplies from, India."[60] Furthermore, he cautioned, troops in the British Indian Army could easily fall prey to "subversive activities… if accompanied by reports from home that their families are starving."[61] He asked the War Cabinet to accede to the viceroy's request for the immediate shipment of 500,000 tons of food grains to avoid such eventualities.

Discussion in the War Cabinet on 4 August, Amery wrote in his diary that evening, had begun on the wrong foot, "led off by [Minister of War Transport] Leathers, the Cabinet generally treated the matter as a bluff on India's part."[62] More exasperating still had been the antagonisms of Churchill's personal advisor, Lord Cherwell. Cherwell held no official position in government, but had become ever-closer to Churchill, gaining the prime minister's almost dogged trust and advising him on any and every matter from "de-housing" in Germany, to sterling balances in India.[63] Amery had "fought hard" against the "nonsense talk by Professor Cherwell whom Winston drags in on every subject and who obviously knows nothing of economics, but, like Winston, hates India,"[64] but lost his case. The War Cabinet vetoed the motion, conceding, instead, to a possible portion of 30,000 tons of Australian wheat and a shipment of 100,000 tons of barley from Iraq. Together with 20,000 tons of food grains already scheduled, the cabinet tentatively promised imports amounting to 150,000 tons, concluding "that no further action should be decided on at the present time."[65]

The viceroy, who had already delivered his farewell speech in Delhi, was dismayed by the news from London. The quantity of imports suggested, he informed Amery, would do nothing at all to meet India's "essential demands." As such, he continued, "I cannot be responsible for the stability of India now."[66] Linlithgow was a tired man and wished for a better farewell. The situation in Bengal, he confided to Amery, was spiraling out of control. A few days earlier he had sent off yet another angry telegram to Governor Herbert.[67] He had received reports that the streets of Calcutta had become filthy with the "non-collection of refuse" going entirely unremedied. Revenues in Bengal had been flagging and nothing was being done to collect more. Word had also reached Delhi that "Birla and the Marwaris" were opening relief canteens, upstaging Government's own weak efforts. What were the initiatives being taken by new Director of Civil Supplies, N. M. Ayyar? A rationing advisor, W. H. Kirby, would be sent from Delhi presently to look into the situation. "You will understand," he concluded, "that I am far from happy about the present situation in Bengal."[68]

Herbert, shaken by the viceroy's scolding tone, responded promptly. The clean-up of Calcutta, he promised, was underway. Extra petrol had been sanctioned to the Calcutta Corporation so that its "conservancy" vehicles could ply twice a day, and, more importantly, he assured Linlithgow, "under the Bengal Vagrancy Ordinance, 359 beggars have been rounded up, and further action continues daily. Many others have left the city fearing arrest, and these steps have brought about a welcome change for the better."[69] The governor agreed with the viceroy about the "necessity for additional taxation," and supported a doubling of the sales' tax, as well as the implementation of an additional agricultural tax. As far as the Director of Civil Supplies went, Ayyar was doing a fair job, Herbert reported, though he "should have preferred a European officer for the post."[70] The arrangement of supplying charitable organizations, "including Birla and certain Marwaris," he also assured the viceroy, was taking place under strict official supervision. With Kirby now in Calcutta, Herbert added, a governmental rationing scheme would soon be organized.

Special Rationing Advisor Kirby, however, was meeting with considerable difficulty. He had conferred with Chief Minister Nazimuddin, but had been sorely frustrated. "The general atmosphere in the minister's office," he later testified, "was so difficult that I had to tell [the governor] that I could make no progress."[71] Kirby wanted to utilize existing private shops in order to begin rationing at once, but the chief minister would not hear of it. If rationing were to be introduced, the chief minister argued, it would have to be through government shops, which would be staffed according to a scheme of communal ratios. The problem was, Kirby summarized, "that since 90% of the retailers in Calcutta were Hindus, the Minister very much wanted to encourage the Muslim trader [by utilizing Government shops], and [on the other hand, because] the staff that would be appointed to the Government shops would be mainly Muslim, there were strong protests from the Hindu trading community on that particular point."[72] Rationing was stalled.

Meanwhile Bengal was in freefall. Dire reports of mass starvation were coming in from all over the province, and—more alarming to the colonial state—the spectacle of famine could no longer be contained to the countryside. Starving villagers were continuing to accumulate on the streets of Calcutta and dying there in increasing numbers. On the 8th of August, Ian Stephens, Chief Editor of *The Statesman*, wrote a scathing editorial roundly condemning Government denial. "By mumbling that food shortage did not exist," Stephens charged, "they willed themselves into belief that the dread spectacle would vanish."[73] He urged the Government of India to "take due cognizance of bitter realities in the war-threatened Eastern areas, where what may fairly be called famine prevails."[74] New Delhi took little notice of this first salvo. Azizul Haque, by then the Government of India's Food Member, continued to defend central government efforts and returned the blame to provincial authorities, transportation problems, and environmental difficulties.[75] Meanwhile on the 16th and 17th of August alone, 120 corpses (by official count) were collected from the streets of Calcutta.[76]

Frustrated with the lack of response to earlier warnings, Stephens took the courageous decision to publish a photo-spread of starving Bengalis on the streets of Calcutta. Though any direct reference to the "famine" was officially prohibited, the Emergency Rules were ambiguous regarding photographs. And so, in a single afternoon a crew of photographers sent out by Stephens collected a shocking dossier of famine pictures, some so horrifying that the editor himself found them "utterly unpublishable."[77] Those that were a little less appalling were run in a photo-spread published in the Sunday edition of *The Statesman* on August 22nd 1943— and in some definite sense the event ever since known as the "Bengal Famine of 1943" had been born. *The Statesman* was the most established and well-read newspaper in India. It had a long history of editorial integrity and independence. Though British owned, it was respected as a relatively objective source of information—particularly regarding eastern India and the war front—by Europeans and Indians alike. The publication of famine photographs in August 1943 was regarded by many Bengalis for years to come as a singular act of journalistic courage without which many more lives would have surely been lost.[78]

By Monday morning in Delhi second-hand copies of the paper were selling at several times the news-stand price.[79] The same morning the

Government of India's Chief Press Adviser telephoned *The Statesman* office with indignant reproaches. The Emergency Rules, however, were indeed ambiguous about the publication of photographs, and so no immediate action could be taken. Emboldened by the lack of penalty, Stephens prepared another photo-essay for the following Sunday with an accompanying editorial entitled "All-India Disgrace." In Calcutta, he reported:

> Scores of persons collapsing from under-nourishment are daily picked up from the streets; recorded deaths from starvation cases in hospitals between August 16 and August 29 were 143; 155 dead bodies are known to have been removed from public thoroughfares by the authorities' new Corpse Disposal Squad during the ten days ending on August 24; during the week ending August 21 mortality was 1,129 as against an average of 574 in the corresponding weeks of the previous five years. Cholera, epidemic since June, is again on the increase; there were 140 cases and 74 deaths during the seven days ending on August 21. Typhoid spreads; dysentery is exceptionally prevalent.[80]

However bad conditions had become in Calcutta, Stephens continued, conditions in the *mofussil* were still much worse. He blamed famine directly on "the complacency and misjudgment, greed, myopia and political spite" of the ruling and commercial elite, both Indian and British, and coupled to it a "horrifying catalogue of administrative shortcomings."[81] Remedy, however, was a long way off.

A day before the second *Statesman* photo-essay came out, Herbert wrote to Linlithgow that he was satisfied with the way things were shaping up in Bengal. Despite "unhelpful tales of horror in the Press," he assured the viceroy, "[Government could] claim to have made good progress with [its] plans and organization."[82] Arrangements for the use of A.R.P. shelters for the "detention" of "beggars" had been made, and round-ups were continuing apace.[83] Government "relief" centers had gotten off the ground and firm control over private relief operations had been established. The remaining problems, Herbert complained, were the fault of political intrigue in the Ministry and sensational reports in the press which were only designed to spread "despondency and panic." In a final note to the viceroy, Herbert mentioned that he would be entering the hospital shortly to have his appendix removed and would be out of office for a few days. He never returned.

The true severity of Herbert's illness (which was revealed on his admission to the hospital), the viceroy suggested to the secretary of state, might "prove a blessing in disguise."[84] In Bengal, he noted, "there is a weak Civil Service [I.C.S]; Indianization has further weakened a cadre not too good in any circumstances; the Ministry is not a strong one; the food position is critical; and a pretty firm hand and much experience will be called for."[85] Instead, the Governor of Bihar, Sir Thomas Rutherford, was reluctantly drafted as a temporary replacement when it was revealed that Herbert's condition was terminal. That Rutherford had little executive experience in India may have contradicted the viceroy's preference, but the emergent situation demanded expedient action. Sir Thomas's appointment was signed by the King on 4 September and he assumed office two days later. At the very same time, Linlithgow was pressing his Executive Council to declare a state of emergency in Bengal, dissolve the Ministry and grant the new interim governor Emergency Rule under Section 93 of the Defense of India Rules.

Discussions in the Council broke along communal lines, with Muslim members strongly opposed to deposing the Muslim League Ministry, and Hindu Members arguing for just such an intervention. At length the acrimony of the debate discouraged the viceroy from proceeding along strictly constitutional lines. Instead, he informed Amery, the path to Emergency Rule might be paved by more coercive means. In particular, the Central Government might:

> impose requirements on Ministerial Government in Bengal of such a nature either (a) that no self respecting Government could or would carry on consistently with them since they would represent such an interference with that Government's responsibility or (b) that e.g. the Nazimuddin Government would lose its Hindu supporters and might no longer have the requisite majority in the House.[86]

But this move would be time consuming and tricky, particularly as communal sentiment in Bengal was becoming increasingly embittered in the context of famine. In fact, the viceroy noted to Amery, the entire issue of Bengal's "food situation" was rapidly entrenching communal animosities even at the central governmental level and the matter needed to be handled "with extreme care."[87] In the interim the viceroy entrusted to his new governor the responsibility of getting Bengal "around the corner."[88]

In the meantime Amery returned to the plea for immediate imports. With former Field Marshall Wavell as the incoming viceroy, efforts were made to enlist high ranking military officers to back the case. Commander-in-Chief of the Indian Army, Claude Auchinleck, convinced of the urgency of the situation, telegrammed the Chief of the Imperial General Staff, Field Marshall Alan Brooke to join the cause. "So far as shipping is concerned," Auchinleck assured Brooke, "the import of food is to my mind just as if not more important than the imports of munitions."[89] Brooke had been briefed on the severity of the situation and offered his support. Together with the other Chiefs of Staff he presented a memorandum to the War Cabinet warning that "unless the necessary steps are taken to rectify the [food] situation, the efficient prosecution of the war against Japan by forces based in India will be gravely jeopardized and may well prove impossible."[90] Amery also authored his own report. "The fact is to be faced," he urged, "that there are famine conditions in some Eastern Districts and that in Calcutta hundreds are dying of starvation…the conditions so described are becoming a menace to supply operations and…the sight of famine conditions cannot but cause distress to the European troops."[91]

The War Cabinet met two days later, and with Winston Churchill as Chair, decided against the viceroy's request. Churchill, for his part, made the point that "the starvation of anyhow under-fed Bengalis is less serious than [that of] sturdy Greeks."[92] Of the 150,000 tons promised on the 4th of August, only 30,000 tons of Australian wheat had reached India. The 100,000 tons of barley promised from Iraq had not yet been shipped and a further 20,000 of scheduled imports had been similarly delayed. At length the War Cabinet agreed to add an additional 50,000 tons of food grains which, together with the 120,000 tons outstanding from the War Cabinet's decision of 4 August, would be delivered some time "by the end of 1943."[93]

Starvation

At the point of starvation, a body does not simply wither up and die. Rather, starvation is a complex battle of forces that excoriate, deform and eventually annihilate the bodies and minds that it is allowed to prey upon. It is a humiliating, indecent and relentless *process* of deterioration and eventual demise. The body becomes weakened to the point of complex breakdown, with organs failing one by one, a host of opportunistic diseases taking root, and madness often accompanying. As the official surgeon-general's report on the Bengal Famine concluded, "[though] very few patients suffered from starvation alone…this does not mean, however, that starvation was not the predominant feature…and it was often starvation which was the ultimate cause of death."[94] In acute form those starving were "mere skin and bone, dehydrated, with dry furred tongues, sores on lips, staring eyes, usually with…sores, or ulcers, frequently passing involuntary stools."[95] Scabies was a ubiquitous problem, with as many as 90 per cent of victims covered from head to toe in ulcerous wounds. Acute edema of the limbs was also a common factor, and anemia was universal.

They wandered the streets, the surgeon-general wrote, "clad in filthy rags, and a peculiar body odor emanating from them was often noticed. They were apathetic, oblivious of their surroundings or cleanliness and sometimes unconscious; the pulse was rapid and feeble, and temperature subnormal."[96] Meanwhile, within the body a battle to the death was raging. The following description contained in the surgeon-general's report, sketches the havoc in process in medical terms:

> Cloudy swelling of the liver and kidneys is a common finding. Congestion of a marked degree is met with in sections of the lungs and the kidneys. In addition, in some of the cases, the lung alveoli present evidence of exudate, chiefly composed of mononuclear cells. The intestinal mucosa shows denudation of epithelium, particularly over the villi. The villi themselves are implicated with mononuclear cells to an abnormal extent. It appears that the cholesterol contents of the suprarenals diminish, as the usual vacuated appearance in the appearance of the cells of the cortex is not conspicuous. Liver and spleen show evidence of congestion and in cases where malaria [is] consistent, deposits of haemozine pigments are also found in the cells of the reticula endothelial system.[97]

Malaria was, more often then not, consistent, as were several other fevers and pulmonary diseases. A condition known as "famine diarrhea," which proved extremely difficult to treat, was likewise endemic. Hookworms, round worms, and other intestinal parasites, played their role in further devitalizing emaciated bodies. Cholera, and—increasingly—smallpox, also found the famine-stricken exceedingly easy prey.

Mental disorder and madness was yet another nagging and widespread symptom of starvation. "One of the most distressing features of the famine," the surgeon-general's office noted in retrospect, "was the mental attitude of the more advanced cases of starvation."[98] The report continues:

> The more desperate cases of hunger became childish in mind, wandering from place to place in search of food, ransacking rubbish heaps, and sometimes absconding from hospital where food and relative comfort and security

were obtainable…these unfortunates seemed to be guided by an instinct compelling them to move on in fruitless and erratic attempts to find food. Irritable and unreasonable, childish and apathetic, difficult to nurse and filthy in habit, the starving sometimes cried for food even when food was before them. In one destitute hospital an emaciated man was observed to be crying and snarling like an animal. He was sitting on a hospital bed with a brimming plate of rice and curry in front of him, making no attempt to eat. Enquiries revealed that he was crying for food. He could not realize that there was already ample food to eat in front of him and his instincts compelled him to cry for more and more food. Oblivious to his surroundings and more animal than human, emaciated, dry lips drawn back over decayed and septic teeth, coated tongue, uttering inhuman cries, filthy and scabrous, he represented the nadir of human misery and the epitome of famine.[99]

A report by the Calcutta University Anthropology Department released towards the end of September confirmed the now starkly manifest disintegration of the entire social fabric of Bengal due to famine as well. Across the province, a team of researchers had found, "husbands have driven away wives and wives have deserted ailing husbands; children have forsaken aged and disabled parents and parents have also left home in despair; brothers have turned deaf ears to the entreaties of hungry sisters, and widowed sisters, maintained for years together by their brothers, have departed at the time of direct need."[100] In Malda a scene, the likes of which was becoming increasingly common by mid-September, was reported in the *Amrita Bazar Patrika*:

> One Bhogurdi Mandal of Lahapur, P.S. Nawabgunj, Malda, was charged under Sec. 302 I.P.C. for murdering his only son Mozaffar, aged about three years on September 16 on the ground of his inability to feed him and other members of the family, who, it is reported, had no food for 3 or 4 days. The accused was tried by District and Sessions Judge, Malda, and was found guilty by the jurors. He was sentenced to transportation for life but having regard to the tragic circumstances of the case the Judge recommended to the Government to exercise their prerogative of mercy.[101]

On 12 September an assistant inspector of police in Faridpur was brutally murdered by a mob when he tried to enforce a new (and again, ad hoc) Control Order.[102] The General Head-Quarters' own Weekly Intelligence Report had earlier confirmed that "cholera, small-pox and starvation are causing hundreds of deaths daily [in and around Dacca] and similar conditions prevail over a large area of East Bengal, and have given rise to widespread incidence of thefts and dacoities. Suicides and child-selling have also been reported."[103] On 15 September the United States Council General in Calcutta cabled to the U.S. Secretary of State in Washington. He wrote:

> I would suggest to high-placed officials in Delhi, who deprecate the over-dramatization of the sufferings of the people of Bengal to pay a visit to the province…at one of the kitchens in Faridpur I noticed a man lapping up gruel like a dog. I saw abandoned children in the last stages of emaciation… a man vainly wandering for food collapsed on the doorsteps of the Collector's court room. As the body was being removed, a woman huddled in a corner thrust out a bundle and cried "take that also." It was her dead child…[104]

Throughout the countryside corpses were piling up too fast to dispose of or even count. In September, the District Relief Committee in Noakhali reported, "Men women and children are dying daily in great numbers, some on roads and at other public places. Disposal of the dead bodies has become a problem with the living. Sometimes dead bodies are thrown into the river instead of being properly buried or cremated."[105] In Dacca, the Associated Press reported, "cremation of Hindu dead bodies has become quite a problem for want of fuel. Dead bodies of destitute persons are often thrown into the river or buried."[106] In Midnapore a worker for the Friends' Ambulance Unit described the situation in mid-September vividly:

> During the last fortnight there has not been a morning on which I have not seen, as I went out of the town on my jobs, dead bodies by the roadside. A fight between vultures and dogs is not a rare sight…disposal of dead bodies has become a problem. In the villages the affairs are worse; people are dying in large numbers of malaria and starvation. There are not enough able-bodied men to burn the dead, which often are just pushed into the nearest canal. If you go down the canal from Contai to Panipia, you will feel sick; for the bloated dead bodies you will see will be numerous.[107]

"Sick Destitutes"

The image of Calcutta, however, remained of critical importance. The spectacle of famine could not continue to play out on center stage. Calcutta was now one of the most important supply-fronts in the entire Allied war effort, accounting for as much as 80 per cent of the armament, textile and heavy machinery production used in the Asian theater. Hundreds of thousands of Allied troops were moving through the city to the front, and returning there on leave, fueling a thriving "rest and recreation" industry that included dance halls, restaurants, bars, and a mushrooming prostitution industry. Huge profits were being made and the city was, in fact, more cosmopolitan than ever before. By 1943, in Ian Stephens's words, Calcutta:

> was a great war-base…a vortex of humanity into which men doing war-jobs from all over the world, uniformed or not, were being sucked…American forces started arriving; and with their high living standards and total ignorance of India probably felt most alien of all. There were Chinese troops, some 30,000 or so, who had passed through the Bengal-Assam hills on their retreat from Burma…and Chinese merchant seaman, some thousands too… there were Australian, New Zealand, and Canadian Air Force types…[and] coal-black troops from West Africa under British officers…and, of course, masses of young men from Britain of every social class…and (also) Indians, mostly from the subcontinent's North-West or South and therefore feeling almost as foreign in Bengal as the so-called white men.[108]

Famine-stricken bodies on the city's streets came as a dreadful inconvenience.

Rutherford, on his arrival in Calcutta as the interim governor, found the scenes in Calcutta "ghastly"—with good cause. The A.R.P. air-raid shelters, which were being used now for famine relief, were filthy and ill-prepared.[109] More than half of the tube wells sunk in 1941 for "emergency measures" were out of order and cholera was running rampant.[110] Sweepers, amongst the lowest of the social groups in Bengal, were themselves unable to obtain sufficient food and were dying and deserting from their posts in numbers. *Doms*, the caste whose traditional role was the handling of corpses, were similarly (if ironically) rendered destitute, and were found to be in increasingly short supply.[111] Meanwhile, that there were so many corpses piling up in Britain's "second city" was a diplomatic nightmare. Neither the police nor the A.R.P. could cope.

Consequently, towards the end of August, two private organizations, the Hindu Satkar Samiti and the Anjuman Mofidul Islam,[112] were contracted to dispose of corpses according to religious affiliation. Hindu corpses were taken to the burning ghats and Muslim bodies taken to the burial grounds. How distinctions between "Hindus" and "Muslims" were made—particularly given the abject condition of the bodies at the time of death—is extremely difficult to comprehend.[113] Though in life these victims had been deprived of the barest means of survival or dignity—

stripped of all local affiliation, dispossessed of all lands and possessions, and, indeed, due to a crippling shortage of cloth, mostly naked as well— in death they were still "Hindu" or "Muslim." All that was left of the dead, at least by official account then, was this one, presumably inextinguishable marker that somehow was understood to adhere to the body itself.

Aside from material difficulties with corpses, the sheer numbers of the dead created great administrative anxiety. On 9 September Government decided it would henceforth withhold all official death statistics from the press. Such numbers, they argued, could serve no particular purpose and, with an acute paper shortage prevailing, newspapers might even "welcome" the opportunity to save space on their front pages for more important stories.[114] Due to quick protest from the press the order was repealed after only two days. The statistics reported after the stop-order, however, were of a different kind. In all official reports, in the place of any term such as "starvation victims" or "famine sufferers," the term "sick destitutes" had been substituted. Furthermore, the number of "sick destitutes" who had died on the streets of Calcutta, in these new reports, was accompanied by an attachment that assigned various causes of death to the corpses collected. A large majority of deaths were now euphemistically attributed to "chronic ailments, neglected in the past."[115] This presumably did not refer to the long and brutal trajectory of starvation.

Those still living on the streets of Calcutta posed an even more complicated problem. On 28 September the Bengal Council (the governor's advisory committee) passed yet another Vagrants Bill, giving Government sweeping powers to round up "sick destitutes" in Calcutta. The Council urged that the A.R.P. and Civic Guards be used energetically in the campaign.[116] In a related effort, Mr O.M. Martin, I.C.S., the newly appointed Relief Commissioner (though no famine had been declared or officially mentioned) issued an appeal on 1 October requesting "legitimate" residents of Calcutta to "refrain from indiscriminate charity" that would only encourage the "sick destitutes." Poor houses outside the city, he assured "priority" Calcuttans, were being rushed into operation, and relief kitchens in the city, in the meantime, were more than sufficient. "These unfortunates," Martin suggested, "are now more in want of shelter than food." "As poor houses are established, one after another," he added, "it will be advisable to curtail the number of food kitchens so that vagrants may become accustomed to look for relief in the poor houses rather than in other places."[117]

Outside the city famine deaths were becoming too numerous to count. Newspapers reported deaths from starvation in 25 of the 27 districts in Bengal through the 11th of October.[118] Rice had all but vanished from local markets and villages in many districts had become hollowed out by famine. On October first the Associated Press reported from a village in the Dacca Division:

> An unclaimed dead body of a Hindu boy of about 12 years partly devoured by jackals and vultures was found yesterday morning lying in front of the Government Grain Shop near Chashara Police Outpost at Narayangunge. It is suspected that the boy was molested by jackals and vultures in the preceding night when he was in a precarious condition owing to starvation.[119]

In Burdwan a similar scene was reported by the United Press, "the dead body of a famished man was found almost entirely eaten up by vultures and lying by the side of Banisagar tank…the body was removed by police to the burning ghat."[120] In Faridpur, the new District Magistrate, F. A. Karim, had arrived to find the streets "absolutely choked with famine-stricken people." On one street corner an old man had collapsed. Karim approached and looked into the man's glazed eyes sadly, while all around him "people were laughing and saying 'The old fellow is dying! The old fellow is dying!'"[121] Death had become a public spectacle, and little more. *Biplabi* reported from Midnapore that on 10 October "a man driven by hunger was eating foodgrains scattered along the railway track…seeing this members of the railway police started pelting him with stones. The man started running and fell into a ditch alongside the track where he died."[122]

Meanwhile Linlithgow was making preparation for his departure from Delhi after his seven and a half year tenure as viceroy of India. In a desultory report to Amery on 14 October he looked forward to seeing the secretary of state in person in London. "Then…I shall not propose to weary you," he wrote, "with arguments or representations on any aspect of the Indian problem; for I shall be *functus*, and it will be for my successor to carry the burden. But broadly speaking, I can feel as I lay down this great charge that I leave the country in pretty good trim."[123]

Round-ups and Resistance

On the 27th of October interim Governor of Bengal Thomas Rutherford promulgated the Bengal Destitute Persons (Repatriation and Relief)

Ordinance. This new ordinance empowered "any officer authorized by Government to apprehend any person who, in the opinion of such officer, is a destitute, and detain him or her in a place provided for the purpose until the person is repatriated."[124] Temporary collecting centers could house up to 8,000 people, and a more permanent facility north of Calcutta had been prepared for the immediate uptake of 4,000 more. In the next three days the police, aided by A.R.P. officers—and other deputized agents of the state[125]—rounded up as many as 3,000 "destitutes" from the streets of Calcutta and moved them to these newly inaugurated Government "reception centers."[126] But with an estimated 150,000 "sick destitutes" clogging the thoroughfares and by-lanes of Calcutta the pace of removal needed to be vastly accelerated.[127] Difficulties with the round-ups, however, continued.

The chief problem, Relief Commissioner O.M. Martin explained, was that "people did not want to go into shelters."[128] Though they had been "rescued" by the government and taken to "poor houses" where "they got two good meals a day and also got clothes…they kept running away."[129] That people so thoroughly depleted by the ravages of hunger, having traveled a deathly journey in search of bare existence, and having watched so many die along the way, were able, with the last of their energy, to resist the authority of the state by such measures, is an important counter-point to all studies that have asserted the passivity with which famine sufferers in Bengal perished.[130] Government food kitchens in the "repatriation camps" were, in fact, severely under-staffed and ill-equipped. The rations given amounted to approximately 800 calories per day—a quantity far from sufficient, or even humane.[131] "You pretend to keep people alive by subsisting on that ration," T. G. Davies of the Friends Ambulance Unit decried, "but all the time [you are] slowly starving [them] to extinction."[132] In this light, escape from such facilities surely saved lives.

In the first few days following the order's promulgation, the police, with the assistance of the A.R.P., tried to use "persuasion" with reluctant destitutes, but after five more days they had only managed to round up an additional 7,000 "sick destitutes." Consequently, on 5 November the Bengal Government announced that, of necessity, stricter measures would be adopted. Efforts so far had "produced negligible results" and "sick destitutes" continued to resist. Persuasion, in other words, was failing and so stricter measures would have to be used for collection and detention. Blame for the resistance was allotted to opponents of the government, who were organizing to "defeat Government's policy of persuading destitutes to leave the streets, by spreading canards among them," and the objectives of these "designing persons," it was further claimed, was that "of keeping Calcutta streets full of destitutes so that the situation may be exploited for political and other purposes."[133] With this new policy outlined, "destitute repatriation" took on the aspect of aggressive round-ups of famine-stricken men, women and children, by police, civil defense, and military personnel, who roamed the streets of Calcutta in official vans and lorries in broad daylight, often chasing down their sick and destitute prey through alleyways and by-lanes and loading them onto removal vehicles by main force.

B. K. Guha, Relief Co-ordination Officer in charge of collecting destitutes, like others, was having a hard time convincing the starving, half-naked, and diseased wretches that he was assigned to round-up that Government was operating in their best interest. When an orphanage for famine refugees had been set up outside Calcutta, it fell to Guha to find orphans to occupy it. From Calcutta he was expected to send only eight or ten children. After three or four days, however, he became increasingly frustrated: "at first some of the orphans were persuaded to agree, but thereafter they would not go and when we inquired what was the reason, we were told that they had been told that they were being sent to Asansol and if they went they would be killed."[134] For adults, Guha sadly informed the Famine Enquiry Commission, suspicions were equally hard to suppress. Many of the "sick destitutes" had fixed on the idea, he lamented, that "Government [would] take you to these centers and from there send you to Arakan or Assam [the war front]…and you would be sacrificed there."[135] When asked who could have been spreading these ideas, Guha confessed that he could not be sure, but the rumors were prevalent. To some extent these apprehensions, however, seem to have been based on fact.

Royal Engineer, Alan Shaw, stationed with 345 Company Command, was working on the Imphal Road in the vicinity of Assam. He remembers that during the famine:

the streets of Calcutta were cleared of starving men who were formed into labor battalions and sent up the Line of Control. About two hundred of these unfortunates were placed under 345 Company command and occupied additional bamboo huts in our lines. We were ordered to use them for clearing jungle instead of the usual teams of Indian Tea Association laborers of which there was a battalion of one thousand every ten miles along the Imphal Road, each commanded by an ex tea planter Indian Army Captain. The "refugees" were accommodated in bamboo huts separate from our troop lines, but benefiting from the same carefully chlorinated drinking water and sanitary arrangements. At first they were pathetic sights, too weak with starvation to do useful work. But even after months of proper feeding most had little inclination to work, were a potential threat to military discipline, and required more supervision than we could afford.[136]

On the open streets of Calcutta, Guha suffered similar disciplinary challenges. There was reluctance on the part of the destitutes to go to the poor houses, he told the Famine Enquiry Commission, and "when we used to come with police lorries, they used to get frightened—the mother would run in one direction and the child in another."[137] Such scenes created an outcry, but as Relief Commissioner O. M. Martin testified, such dislocations were all but inevitable: "when we picked up people under compulsion it very often happened that some persons were separated from their families…if anybody on the street said that his daughter or wife was lost, he was told to go to a particular poor house and find her out."[138] At length Guha discovered that the "dispersal of families" was particularly bad public relations; and so his organization changed tactics and began operating under the cover of night. In this way, he remembered, "sometimes we found them sleeping together and then we could collect the whole family."[139]

In order to demonstrate that undue force was *not* used during the round-ups, Guha related the following rather revealing, if disjointed, story to the Famine Enquiry Commission:

> I had information that a large number of destitutes had collected in South Calcutta, and I was asked to take charge of them because they had gathered in the portico of a retired government official and made the place filthy. He could not drive them out. The destitutes consisted of mother, children and grown up girls. On seeing us in the police lorry, they all dispersed and raised a hue and cry. I was surprised at this. I tried my best to collect them. They ran into an adjoining house. I approached the lady of the house and explained my mission to her. She persuaded them to board our lorry. While in the lorry they shouted and cried and actually created a scene. They were shouting that they were being killed. As a matter of fact, if any criminal charges were to be laid, it should be against me personally.[140]

Once in the poor houses, the destitutes continued to create scenes: refusing food, resisting regimens, stealing blankets and other items, and continuously trying to escape. As Martin explained, there was a certain "mental demoralization…that made [the] problem very difficult." The situation may have been worst of all with children:

> The wandering habit amongst the children was difficult to be stopped. Famine orphanages had to have prison rooms. Children—skin and bone— had got into the habit of feeding like dogs. You tried to give them a decent meal, but they would break away and start wandering about and eat filth. You had to lock them up in a special room…they [had] developed the mentality of wandering. People got awfully cruel.[141]

Imagination fails when attempting to fill in the silence between the penultimate period and the last and chilling sentence of unspecified "awful cruelty" with which O. M. Martin concluded his testimony before the Famine Enquiry Commission.

In the context of famine, establishing a "right" to remain in Calcutta often meant the difference between life and death. A right to Calcutta meant a territorial claim. The round up and removal of "sick destitutes" from the streets was, in this sense, only a more stark and authoritarian means of establishing "priority." Questions of who "belonged" in Calcutta and who did not, who was to be granted residence and who removed, who was "essential" and who disposable, had all been central to patrolling the urban space of Calcutta at least since the onset of the war. Famine only heightened the stakes and ensured that these same questions would continue to breed contention and violence for many years to come.

Bengal in Ruins

"Repatriation," in any case, was a fantasy. By November of 1943 much of the countryside of Bengal lay in ruins. There was very little to go back *to*. Deaths and desertions had emptied out entire regions. The low-paid village *chowkidars* who kept vital statistics in villages during normal times, themselves had died or deserted in numbers.[142] No accurate statistics of deaths were available, but mortality figures compiled later confirmed that mortality during this period was immense.[143] Where rice was now available at all, its price was out of reach of the majority of the population. Starvation had already claimed many hundreds of thousands of lives, and malaria and cholera were running rampant, wiping out those who had so far survived starvation.

A special correspondent from *The Statesman* went on a tour of the 24 Parganas south of Calcutta. He found the region starkly depopulated. "The countryside at present," he wrote, "tells a strange story of desertion and despair."[144] The long-awaited *aman* crop was ripening, he wrote, "but who will harvest it?" The peasant who in normal times would be looking forward to the harvest, the correspondent wrote, "sits on his doorstep, bewailing his lost family, and in many cases is too tired and too disease-ridden to take courage and hope out of the fast-ripening paddy."[145] In a typical village the reporter found, "all the members of families lying ill with malaria or dysentery and no one to tend them," while he found other houses "lying desolate as all the occupants had died."[146]

Scenes in Midnapore were similar. In November the artist Chitta-prosad made his epic journey through the district, composing sketches of famine victims that were to become iconic. Chittaprosad, hailing from Chittagong, had been contributing pen and ink drawings to the Bengali Communist weekly *Janayuddha* for some time. During the early months of 1943 he began focusing his attention on the food administra-tion in Bengal, composing satirical sketches of the nexus between gov-ernment employees, control shops and black marketeers. As conditions in the province continued to deteriorate, his sketches turned towards depicting the sufferings of famine victims. In his journey through Midnapore Chittaprosad, like *The Statesman* correspondent, found vil-lage after village depopulated. In Midnapore town he found a small family who had abandoned their village in June. When asked when they would go back, they told the artist,

> To speak the truth, babu, with what hopes can we go back to our village? Last year's harvest was not poor, yet we couldn't get food in our own village. Two days after harvesting, the paddy disappeared. When we say we *will* go back to our village, it is because we are afraid of the military. No one knows where they will send us or the children if they catch us. What use is it to us if they send us back to our village?[147]

Chittaprosad published this and other accounts, together with his sketches from his tour of Midnapore, in a book entitled *Hungry Bengal* shortly after his return from the district. The book was quickly banned and 5,000 copies were confiscated and destroyed.[148]

In the worse-hit districts of eastern Bengal, where mortality was still higher, the scenes were still more desolate. In certain sub-divisions in Barisal, Tippera, Faridpur and Chittagong, a careful study by the Indian

Statistical Institute estimated that close to or above 10 per cent of the population had been entirely wiped out in 1943 alone.[149] The Institute's estimates were that across the province 2 million people had died of famine in 1943, most in just a few short months.[150] Noted Bengali social reformer, Jnananjan Niyogi, surveyed the grim landscape and lamented:

> Gone are the cultivators, gone are the householders, rice is gone from the houses. There are no longer cows to give milk. The deities are starving, for there is no worshipful service. The cultivators have sold their draft cattle for the sake of subsistence and somehow manage to survive, yet even they don't understand how to carry on. The ponds have dried up, turning to mud. Water is scarce and pure water completely lacking. Numerous diseases have broken out, and the former spontaneous joy of the Bengalis is absolutely ruined…the noose of poverty has entangled them body and soul, and they have become paralyzed.[151]

The Good Viceroy

Substantial help, no matter how late and how insufficient relative to the immensity of catastrophe, was on its way. Archibald Wavell was sworn in as Viceroy on the 20th of October 1943, and set to work on the famine situation at once. He, like Linlithgow, judged clearing Calcutta to be of primary importance, but he also seems to have been the first British official to view the loss of innocent life in Bengal as a moving priority as well. He set up a Distress Relief Fund within days of assuming office and, whereas Linlithgow had failed to visit Bengal himself since December 1942, Wavell was "off to Calcutta" within a week to assess the situation first hand.[152]

He landed in Calcutta on the afternoon of 26 October and began an "incognito" tour of the city that same evening. He met with "sick destitutes" himself and despite the disguise, some were "scared by the visit, and ran away…others, including those in very bad condition, were indifferent."[153] The next day, again traveling "incognito," he flew out to Midnapore to survey relief centers, emergency hospitals and general conditions there. On the following day, shaken by what he had seen, the new viceroy announced that full use of military resources would be expended to mobilize immediate and extensive famine relief efforts in Bengal.[154] The very day he returned from Bengal, he telegraphed the commander-in-chief for India and requested immediate and substantial military assistance to cope with the famine in Bengal. His request was granted without hesitation. Commander in Charge of the Eastern Command, General Mosley Mayne was put in general charge of military aid to Bengal and Major-General A.V. T. Wakely was put in command of the all-important movement of supplies. At their disposal was a full division of British troops, comprised of 15,000 soldiers. Military lorries, priority rail arrangements, and the Royal Air Force, all of which were already in the region, were also to be deployed in relief efforts immediately.

Only three days after his return to Delhi, Wavell could inform London that troops were being located throughout the hardest hit districts and supplies were moving out of Calcutta and into the countryside at pace. Additionally, arrangements were being made for large-scale medical relief, and materials for temporary shelters for the homeless were being sent. The alacrity with which Wavell organized these relief efforts was, at once, a testimony to his own initiative, as well as a very troubling contrast to the apathy and indifference with which at least a million people had already been left to starve. In the end, there is no question that Wavell's prompt and comprehensive engagement saved an inestimable number of lives, but the situation in Bengal had been allowed to deteriorate to such a degree that the relief initiated in November 1943, for many, was far too little and far too late. The cards were also still stacked against Wavell's sense of purpose.

The War Cabinet again met on 10 November, with "The Bengal Famine" now an international sensation. Very little of that famous Iraqi barley had made its way to Bengal, and because hostilities in the Middle East had taken a turn for the worse, the remainder of the shipment was doubtful.[155] The secretary of state asked for commitment of 50,000 tons of food grains per month for the forthcoming year, together with an additional 50,000 tons from Australia for immediate shipment. When the War Cabinet met, however, with the prime minister, again "in the Chair," Churchill broke into "a preliminary flourish on Indians breeding like rabbits"[156] and, in the end, the Minister of War Transport, Lord Leathers, found Amery's request for immediate shipments "impracticable."[157]

At the same meeting, a Canadian offer for the immediate shipment of 100,000 tons of wheat to India was considered. Canadian Prime Minister, McKenzie King, had informed Amery that the wheat was available and the ship was all ready to be loaded and could depart on 12 November.[158] The trouble was, Amery wrote in his journal, "that

Winston so dislikes India and all to do with it that he can see nothing but waste of shipping space."[159] Leathers concurred with Churchill that Canadian shipping could be utilized to better affect and the War Cabinet "invited" the prime minister to send Prime Minister King an immediate telegram "deprecating the proposed allocation of a Canadian ship."[160] King, receiving the same, promptly cancelled the shipment.

Meanwhile, Amery was making the best of Wavell's decisive action. On 11 November he informed the House of Commons that the "military machinery for detailed distribution [was] already working," and surmised that "there [was] good reason to be satisfied with the progress made."[161] Military relief programs were operating efficiently and aid was getting into the far reaches of the Bengal countryside. Even mules were being used to pack rice into remote villages.[162] Just as importantly, the *aman* crop was fast ripening and it looked to promise an abundant harvest. Amery reported to Wavell that his efforts had made an excellent impression in England.[163] To the viceroy, the secretary of state penned an optimistic letter:

> It is true that you draw a pretty disquieting picture of the Bengal food situation, of the epidemics that may follow, of Rutherford's fade-out, and of the hopeless corruption and inefficiency of the Bengal administration at large, but I do feel that you are really taking hold and that your initiative, both through the Army and through the Governors, will get things into ship-shape condition before it is too late.[164]

At what point the situation might have been understood as "too late" is anybody's guess. Disease was running rampant, quinine, for treating malaria, was extremely scarce, cholera was epidemic, the public health administration was in shambles, the price of rice was still highly elevated, hundreds of thousand, if not millions had already died, millions more had been weakened by hunger to the point of collapse, the Bengal Ministry was still entangled in embittered debate, no rationing scheme had yet been established, starvation was still claiming thousands of lives, and the "cloth famine" had practically denuded the entire suffering population while the cold season was on its way. But by the first week of December Calcutta had been largely cleared of "sick destitutes" and the Secretary of State for India was assuring the House of Commons that progress was being made. Major-General D. Stuart, who had been put in charge of famine relief, announced on 4 December that, due to Government's efforts, there was now "no shortage of food in the majority of the famine areas."[165] In official imagination the Bengal Famine was all-but over. On the ground in Bengal, however, imagination could only go so far.

Then on 5 December 1943 war again took center stage.

5

JAPAN ATTACKS

The Forgotten Chapter

Analysis of the social, economic and political impact of World War II on India, as Indivar Kamtekar has rightly pointed out,[1] has often been relegated to footnotes in the history of modern India. With attention more frequently focused on the macro-politics of nationalism, the Pakistan movement, and negotiations for self-rule, the extent to which war shaped priorities, national alliances, and imperial policy in India during the 1940s has been largely overlooked. And yet, whatever were the concerns, contentions, or calamities that confronted the Indian population during the period, the imperatives of the colonial state remained deeply enmeshed in a calculus of Total War. Defence, mobilization, security, and morale remained the primary mantras of authority in India—and particularly in Bengal—throughout the first half of the decade, and the exigencies of war allowed an authoritarian resolve that served to accentuate and, in fact, accelerate the entrenched predatory dynamics of colonial rule—even as Empire itself was crumbling. In this sense, and as Kamtekar has argued, "the state's new burst of energy and activity [with the outbreak of war] provides a flare of light enabling us to see its features more clearly."[2]

The spotlight of war was nowhere in India as bright as it was in Bengal. Since the onset of war—and even before—governmental priori-

145

ties in the province were consistently established in direct relation to overarching concerns of "defense." After the fall of Burma in the spring of 1942, Bengal became the front in the Allied war against Japan, and Calcutta became the primary staging ground for the push east against a formidable enemy. By 1943, as many as 300,000 Bengalis had been recruited into the A.R.P., the Civic Guards and the Home Guards, to form an ad hoc provincial native police force under the ambiguous banner of "national defense." In the disastrous scorched earth policy—officially known as "The Denial Policy"—transportation facilities throughout the delta had been destroyed, and all stores of putatively "excess" food grains had been seized. Colonial manipulation of provincial politics had destabilized the organs of self-rule, and commercial firms, reaping record profits in war-related industries, continued to scour the countryside to appropriate supplies of rice, both as speculative commodity and as "dearness allowance" to conciliate restive workers. And, finally, famine had arisen out of the mix of wartime inflation, commercial and governmental myopia, and administrative chaos—devastating the province and creating social, political, and economic ruin that would haunt Bengal for generations to come.

It was under this dark cloud of famine, on 5 December 1943, with hunger-stricken bodies still accumulating on Calcutta's streets, that the city's dock complex at Kidderpore was bombed in broad daylight by two consecutive waves of Japanese aircraft. I have found nothing in my extensive historical research on the period that mentions the Calcutta bombings as anything but peripheral. Yet, as I will illustrate below, it was an extensive attack that caused considerable material and economic damage. It was also a uniquely revealing "flare of light" shone on the nature of administration in Bengal at that time. Much of the prejudice, indifference, and dehumanization that lay at the foundation of colonial ideology was crystallized, in microcosm, during this particular calamity, and much of the rhetoric of concern for Indian welfare and security, which had justified an intensified authoritarianism in British India, was revealed as entirely shallow. In this sense the realities of war in Bengal are related, on a deep structural level, to both the famine that preceded it and the continuing violence that followed.

The Port of Calcutta

The Calcutta docks are situated on the east side of the Hooghly River little more than a mile downstream from the city center and 100 nautical miles upstream from the mouth of the river at the Bay of Bengal. Established in 1780, the docks at Kidderpore were the first deep water docks in British India, built to accommodate the East India Company's fast-growing trade in Bengal. Throughout the nineteenth century, however, as Bengal was increasingly de-industrialized, and the extraction of large quantities of raw materials—particularly opium, cotton, coal, jute, indigo, oilseeds, and tea—became the economic engine that fueled colonial profit, the dock capacity at Kidderpore was proving insufficient. In 1870 a Board of Port Commissioners was appointed to oversee the development of the docks to meet increased needs. Locks at the mouth of a greatly expanded basin to protect the inland dock area from tidal fluctuations, and an extensive network of storage sheds, mechanical cranes, and twenty-seven deepwater berths were added to accommodate larger seagoing vessels. The King George Docks at Garden Reach, with ten more deep sea berths, three dry docks, and heavy cranes serving another enhanced complex of warehouses were added in 1929, and the Port of Calcutta was now on par with any other dock system in the world. Ten years later, on the cusp of World War II, shipping traffic through the Calcutta Port amounted to nearly 10 million tons a year.[3]

As the docks grew, the area around them developed into a thriving commercial/industrial hub, with textile factories, jute and cotton mills, coal depots, iron works, and tea warehouses lining the banks of the river around the port, and Calcutta's expanded "docklands"[4] had developed into a sprawling industrial quarter of the city. The adjacent, densely populated neighborhoods of Kidderpore, Watganj, Mommenpur and Metiabruz became thriving, if poor—and mostly Muslim—residential districts. The Hooghly River, to the north of the docks, had extensive moorings and remained lined with ships waiting to enter the locks at Kidderpore all year round. To the south, a channel led out to "Tolly's Nullah," linking the docks to an extensive canal system that connected the port to the rice- and jute-rich regions of eastern Bengal along 1,127 miles of navigable waterways. The docks of Calcutta, in this sense, were also a critical strategic target for Japan.

During the war labourers associated with the docks, in particular—as of labour in Calcutta more generally—were officially understood as "essential,"[5] and as such, were—ostensibly—both protected and provisioned by numerous wartime acts.[6] Rhetoric about the welfare of the industrial labour-force in Calcutta was, in fact, central to an ideology that justified various schemes of appropriation and differential distribution of rice, which, in turn, contributed significantly to the acute impoverishment of the Bengal countryside, and ultimately famine.

But, as the bombings make clear, the "priority" associated with labour during the war proved to be highly contingent. Just who was, in the last analysis, "essential," and who disposable, was often a matter of expediency rather than principle. In the end the fate of poor, disenfranchised, and ultimately replaceable dock labourers meant very little, indeed, to a colonial administration at war. Even the exact numbers of labourers associated with the docks is not easy to ascertain with any degree of certainty. The Bengal Chamber of Commerce, for one, in its report on the bombings put the number of dock labourers at 11,000,[7] while Port Commissioner, Sir Thomas Elderton (I.C.S.), in his separate report, put the number at 18,000.[8] This discrepancy is puzzling, but more puzzling is that Elderton himself subsequently informed the Governor of Bengal that as many as *"30,000* workers enter the dock area every day."[9] To make matters still more complicated, eminent historian Suranjan Das, in his analysis based on Intelligence Branch records notes that in December of 1942 there were 60,000 dock labourers in Kidderpore.[10]

It seems then that very many workers on the docks were contract labourers, or "coolies "—low-paid, unskilled, mostly immigrant workers who toiled long hours, sometimes in intense heat or driving monsoon rain, for poor wages. Many were without any provision for housing or messing, uncounted for by the Chambers of Commerce and unrecognized by the colonial state: without, in short, any of the wartime "priority" cited by governmental and industrial interests to rationalize their relentless campaigns to appropriate rice in the countryside, putatively to feed industrial Calcutta. J.W. Stanworth, of the British Merchant Navy, passed through the Kidderpore Docks during the war and witnessed a typical sight. His vessel was sent to load 10,000 tons of coal for export from Bengal to Shanghai. He recounts:

> This was all loaded by hand. Long planks of timber were placed from the quay to the deck of the ship and an endless belt of human misery ran up one plank with a basket of coal, threw the coal down the ship's hold and ran down the other plank. Some people were filling the baskets and partners of

two lifted the baskets on the shoulders of the endless belt of men. It was stifling hot on the ship as the port holes had to be closed to keep the coal dust out as much as possible. No one could sleep as the coal was being loaded 24 hours a day, non-stop, so after consultation we were taken to the Seamen's Club where we could bathe and sleep in cool rooms.[11]

Labor conditions even for those who enjoyed company "benefits" as permanent employees, were anything but luxurious. Working hours were long, environmental conditions harsh and housing arrangements insufficient. Of the regular workers, only 39 per cent were provided with housing at all.[12] The vast majority of dock laborers—both regular and contract—lived in the "coolie lines"—privately constructed, congested, slum-like encampments, with rows of corrugated tin or bamboo-mat shacks built haphazardly in empty lots close to the factory doors. They were notorious for their poor ventilation, lack of clean drinking water, insufficient sanitary arrangements, and dangerously cramped quarters.[13] These encampments were also often run by unscrupulous local strong-men, who demanded exorbitant rents, and lent money to the perenni-ally indebted "coolies" at similarly extortionate rates. Furthermore, even while industries were logging record profits,[14] due to wartime inflation the real wages of already severely impoverished[15] industrial workers *fell* by as much as 30 per cent.[16]

Obviously the hardships on contract laborers—who comprised a majority of the urban labor population—were the most difficult of all. Along with unskilled factory and dock workers, several other groups of workers fell into the same category. Particularly noteworthy in relation to an analysis of the bombings, are the *khalasis*, a caste of itinerant Muslim seamen, hailing mostly from the Chittagong and Noakhali dis-tricts of eastern Bengal. *Khalasis* were renowned throughout the region for their sailing skills, and were an essential element in the riverine com-mercial networks of Bengal and beyond. They not only plied country-boats through the inland passages of the province, consisting of a myriad of tidal inlets and dangerous and unpredictable rivers, but also manned small ocean-going vessels that worked the coast between Bengal and Burma. Like itinerant boat people in many places in the world, they were known to be tough and resilient. Though "denial" policy had amounted to a wholesale attack on their livelihood, some 20,000 coun-try-boats had managed to evade the Government scheme. The majority of *khalasis*, however, were driven to Calcutta. In and around Calcutta they worked the docks and jetties, transporting commodities, raw materials, and food supplies from import wharfs to markets, and from factories to the docks for export. They were, however, mostly employed on a contract basis that afforded them little security in perilous times. The Bengal Steamer Khalasis Bill of 1943, brought before the Legislative Assembly in January, called for the recognition of *khalasis* directly by companies, which would afford them the protection of "priority" status. The bill was defeated, however, by opposition from assembly members affiliated with the Bengal Chamber of Commerce. As such, the *khalasis* remained unprotected throughout the vicissitudes of war and famine.[17]

Apart from the laborers who inhabited the docklands, there were now Allied soldiers of every stripe. With major operations planned in Southeast Asia, the American presence, in particular, was mounting throughout the autumn of 1943. A large American Army depot had been constructed, and heavy mechanical cranes added to the docks at Garden Reach. The British Army had a depot of its own on the docks, and barracks for soldiers of both nations, as well as those of many other Allied nations, were scattered throughout the area. As a member of the Calcutta Police who was stationed in the area remembers:

> the docks boiled with activity (and crime) as vast amounts of military ordinance poured in, and the Burma front and Nationalist China (via the Ledo Road) were kept supplied by troop and 'military special' trains through the Herculean efforts of the East Bengal and Assam-Bengal Railways. Soldiers, sailors and airmen from all the Allied nations wandered the streets in search of "rest & recreation" which usually consisted of a feed, a fight and sex (in any order) inevitably necessitating much police intervention.[18]

Japan Attacks

On Sunday 5 December 1943 Calcutta awakened to its ongoing tribulation of famine. Three of the six A.R.P. "corpse disposal" vans, originally commissioned by the Government of Bengal for air raid casualties, were making their rounds collecting "sick destitutes" in various stages of starvation from the streets of Calcutta and removing them to "repatriation camps" outside the city.[19] The irony of removing the *dying* from the streets of Calcutta in vehicles commissioned for the removal of the dead is telling. That tools allocated to deal with war were busy with famine "relief," is similarly instructive. Two more of these vans were with the

Hindu Satkar Samiti and the Anjuman Mofidul Islam for the removal of Hindu and Muslim famine corpses, respectively. The sixth van, in a state of disrepair, was with the Calcutta Corporation awaiting re-commissioning. In the face of famine, disease and despair—as well as profit, political intrigue and indifference—the war with Japan had faded into the background, both in popular and official imagination. Nearly a year had elapsed since Calcutta had last been bombed, and the momentous events of that year had greatly attenuated popular concerns about Britain's war.

Calcutta was still, however, very much critical to its pursuance—even if the actual defense of Calcutta had failed to become a real priority. The Indian Command had been requesting better equipment to defend the city for some time, but military preparations had evolved little since 1941.[20] After the first bombings of Calcutta, elite "Beaufighters" had been rushed in from the Middle East, and as recently as November 1943, three squadrons of highly effective "Spitfires" had also been sent to the region. But by mid-1943 both the Spitfire and Beaufighter squadrons had been shifted to advanced positions for offensive maneuvers, and Calcutta was left defended by nothing more than a handful of obsolete "Hurricanes," together with a few batteries of equally out-of-date anti-aircraft guns.[21] Meanwhile, the Allied war in Europe was going well, and with increased American involvement in Southeast Asia optimism was running high.

When the air raid sirens began to wail at 11:15 A.M., there was little excitement. Interrupted from his morning work, *Statesman* Editor, Ian Stephens, remembers feeling "no more than a vague annoyance."[22] A.R.P. drills were still a regular part of life—however insignificant the war seemed in relation to the monstrous difficulties Bengal faced. Moreover, the possibility of Japan mustering the audacity to launch a daylight raid seemed remote. At 11:27 AM, however, the sirens began to sound the "red alert," which meant that an attack was imminent. Within 20 minutes the sky filled with the rumble of Japanese bombers; as many as 250 planes in all, stepped up at three levels and descending from a cruising height of 20,000 feet down unto the docks of Calcutta.[23] The bombers had launched from central Burma and had angled south across the Bay of Bengal, completely avoiding Allied defenses, which were bunched along the Burmese front at Chittagong and Shillong. By 11:45, out of a clear blue sky, a massive, broad-daylight attack on Calcutta was underway.[24]

The Japanese bombers, meeting no opposition, streaked in low and picked targets at will and heavy explosive and anti-personnel bombs began pounding the docks. A series of heavy explosive bombs hit the coaling berths on the western edge of the south basin of the Kidderpore docks, igniting the coal and turning the wharf into a blazing inferno, which spread to the adjacent goods' sheds rapidly. The concussions from the heavy explosive bombs, which left impact craters 12 feet wide and 6 feet deep, also blew out the overhead electric lines and disabled communications. A second primary target, the Bengal Nagpur Railway depot, a few hundred yards north of the coaling berths, was also under heavy attack. Anti-personnel bombs—which burst into high velocity fragments of steel and shrapnel immediately on impact with the ground—rained down on the depot, piercing steel rail webs at ranges of up to 30 feet and destroying the railway's mainline. Fifty railway wagons, one engine and the goods yard were struck and partially or totally destroyed—as was the quarters of the "lower paid staff" of the railway. A heavy explosive bomb was also dropped on the offices of Bird and Company, sandwiched between the coal berths and the railway depot. The Hooghly Jute Mill was hit by seven bombs and suffered extensive damage. Barges waiting to load or unload, anchored in the dock basin, were targeted as well, with the resulting fires jumping from barge to barge quickly. By 11:57—only twelve minutes after the bombing had begun—at least eleven barges were "blazing furiously" on the water.

Anti-personnel bombs were also raining down on the "coolie lines," and the fires from the coaling berths and goods sheds spread throughout the workers' hostels. The sweepers' quarter of the Bengal Nagpur Railway was demolished, and the river dock of the Government Timber Depot was destroyed. Damage from anti-personnel fragments spread out in a 300 yard radius from the site of the bomb blasts, and as such shops, private residences, and small factories outside the dock gates suffered collateral damage, or were struck directly by misguided bombs. The Clive Jute Mill in Garden Reach was also hit and heavy explosive bombs fell in residential areas of Watganj and Kidderpore. A petrol pump, the A.R.P. barracks, a "coolie market," the Tramway Depot Drivers' Quarters, and a ration shop were also directly hit. Bombs also fell outside the general dock vicinity, with reports of heavy explosions in Bhawanipur and Alipore, more than a mile away.

Along the docks and in the attached Bengal-Nagpur Railway yard, "coolies" took cover wherever they could find it, many going "to ground in or under any form of structure which had the effect of hiding them from overhead. Corrugated iron sheds, wagons and latrines were all used and were, of course, entirely useless."[25] Anti-personal bomb fragments ripped through the walls of these same structures killing many instantly. In its A.R.P. report, however, the Railway noted that those who died without sufficient shelter were, in fact, "mainly non-B.N.R. employees." The difficulty in the dock area, the report cited "was that there was not always shelter for the *outsiders* who were present in the goods yard."[26] At the Hooghly Jute Mill, immediately adjacent to the main dock, the shelters provided by the company were "extremely defective," lacking any proper covering wall, and even inside these shelters, workers were killed by flying fragments.[27]

The luckiest of the workers, perhaps, were those who successfully escaped the dock area once the shelling began. These laborers, it seems, may have been following the lead of military personnel in the area, who made great haste for the dock gates when the bombs began to fall. The Commissioners for the Port of Calcutta penned a complaining note to P. D. Martyn, Secretary of the Government of Bengal, a few days after the bombings, testily requesting that "orders be issued that soldiers working in the Dock area must take cover in the Dock area. We want coolies to do this," he added, "but they certainly will not as long as men in uniform rush for the gates immediately when they hear sirens." The "behavior of the American Negro troops," the Commissioners noted in particular, "was disgraceful."[28] The report of a Kidderpore Fire Brigade worker, stationed near the dock gates, was careful to assign blame to American troops more generally:

> While reporting to control on the siren from the chummery, I happened to be near the above entrance. There was in front of me a jeep and American truck proceeding towards the dock. As soon as the dock siren was audible the truck immediately stopped and turned in the opposite direction, away from the dock, and in turning I went passed and saw a man lying in a precarious condition on the road, where the truck had backed and turned.[29]

British soldiers appear to have "stood to" with more fortitude, but contributed considerably to the panic. A Military Police security control officer on the spot describes the scene near the coaling docks as chaotic. Military lorries, parked too close together relayed the coal berth fires across to the warehouse sheds. Other lorries had flat tires and blocked emergency vehicles from entering the area. Troops poured in from ships and adjacent areas and "using their own stretchers, gathered the casualties together, sending them off to Hospital in army lorries."[30] In other places British soldiers "seized Port A.R.P. stretchers, vehicles, etc., blocked roads by parking vehicles haphazardly, and generally speaking made it impossible for the Port A.R.P. to function in an organized fashion."[31] Both the Port A.R.P. Controller and the 24 Parganas Controller also complained that the military had grossly interfered with their operations.

This subordination of the A.R.P to military personnel during the bombing—after four years of training, exercises and pay-rolling—is a telling demonstration of the true level of confidence that had been invested in this organization of local loyalists. The A.R.P. had been widely utilized by Government as a vehicle of propaganda, co-opting influential Hindu citizens into the "war effort." Their "drills" had been planned to instill a sense of "emergency" in the population. They had been used to police the urban populations of Bengal during disturbances and they had been posted in front of control shops to "keep the peace" when citizens of the city were clamoring for rice. During the "food drive," they had been deputized to seize supplies of rice from private citizens, and once famine victims began to fill the streets of Calcutta, they were sent out to round them up, by force if necessary, or to cart off their dead bodies to the nearest crematorium or burial ground. Now that bombs were falling and decimating the docks, however, the Air Raid Precautions services were unceremoniously pushed aside. In what would become a highly controversial report a Military Police control officer stationed on the docks observed that civilian civil defense workers were nowhere to be seen and that soldiers in uniform had had to step in to fight fires and treat the wounded.[32] I will return to these charges, contained in paragraph seven of the M.P.'s report below.

Finally, at 1 P.M., after two waves of heavy bombings, the All-Clear signal was sounded and the docks lay in almost total ruins. The coal berths had been razed by fire, along with as many as fifteen of the twenty-nine storage sheds lining the perimeter. The Bengal-Nagpur Railways yard had suffered extensive damage, with at least fifty wagons and one engine destroyed in the attacks, and the tracks leading out from the yard had been heavily damaged by anti-personal shrapnel and heavy explosive bombs. In the basin the burned out hulks of eleven barges, three ships (the SS Matheson, SS Nauchung and the SS Irtria), one dredger, and four tug boats smoldered on the water, and large sections of the "coolie lines" along the Eastern Boundary Road had been devastated by fire. The area was also strewn with hundreds of corpses—human and animal—untended and unclaimed, that had already begun to rot in the afternoon sun. To make matters worse, the gates of the docks remained unmanned and hundreds of curious on-lookers entered the area to survey the damage and collect "souvenirs," with "crowds… allowed to collect around the [dead] bodies, resulting in very exaggerated rumors."[33] Confusion, chaos, and disorganization, as well as an administratively expedient rewriting of events, continued for many days to come.

At the same time, a steady flow of traffic away from the docks and industrial areas was picking up pace. Along Garden Reach Road, the main axial roadway running through dockland, a column of approximately 7,000 workers was reported moving towards points unknown. Along the Grand Trunk Road, the main highway into the surrounding districts, another group of an estimated 2,000 "coolies," with bullock carts loaded down with personal belongings, was fleeing the city. From Bird and Company's dock complex as many as 10,000 contract laborers "absconded immediately after the raid," leaving the firm with less than half of its force, and workers employed by the Port Commission also fled in large numbers, with only 1,800 of the enumerated 11,000 laborers remaining. From the Hooghly Jute Mill, 80 per cent of workers quickly decamped or otherwise "disappeared," and the survivors of the B.N.R.'s heavily bombed sweepers' quarters also "ran away" en masse. What percentage of these same workers had actually been killed in the bombing is a question that is extremely difficult to answer.

For those that remained, "morale" was carefully monitored and engineered, by force where necessary. The post-raid A.R.P. report from the Bengal-Nagpur Railway noted that "an attempted exodus on the part of *outsiders* by the Shalimar Ferry [which would have taken them across the river to relative safety] was checked."[34] Under what authority and by what means the B.N.R. was able to arrest the movement of laborers who were not in their direct employment is not specified. Nor is it mentioned by what means and under what conditions these same workers were detained within the dock complex. The Port A.R.P., for its part, noted that stevedores and other essential dock hands were being "housed in camps under military control."[35] In this context a note from the Port Commission that several hundred of its own "essential labor" had been "accommodated in a warehouse shelter as a measure to instill confidence,"[36] also hints at a rather coercive "accommodation."

If the living remained of certain concern, however, the dead did not. As night fell corpses still littered the docks, unclaimed, unidentified and untended. Within a few hours the crowds of "sightseers" were replaced by crowds of looters who stepped over the dead bodies to ransack the docks for any unburned coal or other commodities left behind by the bombs and fires.[37]

Damage Control

In the morning many of the corpses still remained where they had fallen, while front page headlines in *The Statesman* relayed the official report from the Government of India that "a number of bombs" had been dropped on "the Calcutta area," but that the damage had been "slight."[38] The scenario may have been much more grim, the government communiqué went on, had the defense of the city not been so stalwart: "Our fighters intercepted the enemy aircraft and a heavy and effective a-a [anti-aircraft] barrage was put up."[39] No further information was given. The report was, in fact, an exemplary model of succinct vaguery and misleading understatement—in close keeping with official orders. In April 1943, after the earlier air-raids on Calcutta, a Defense Circular was sent to all Provincial Governments outlining the official protocol for reporting on raids, stressing "the vital necessity for the most careful wording [of post-raid reports]."[40] No mention should be made of the specific target of the bombing, instead, the circular read, "this will be in general terms, i.e. 'Calcutta area,'—not 'Docks of Calcutta.'"[41] The extent of the destruction should also be left indefinite: "where necessary to publish any mention of damage the general terms 'slight,' 'moderate,' and 'heavy' or synonyms of these will be used. *These terms will have no relation to any specific numbers of casualties.*"[42] As to the number of casualties, the instruction went on, "an underestimate is better."[43]

Such obfuscation, however, failed its first test. The discrepancy between the information officially and unofficially circulated created resentment and only served to heighten local anxieties. Rumors quickly began to spread about extensive damage to the docks and heavy casualties. Dock workers were in a state of "extreme nervousness as a result of the casualties which took place among them,"[44] and the fear that they carried with them out of the docks was contagious. It was well known, moreover, that damage to the dock area had been anything but "slight," with plumes of smoke and ash from the attack being seen as much as two miles away.[45] Additionally, the hundreds of "sightseers" and looters who had surveyed the wreckage and seen corpses still littering the docks had carried these impressions back home with them. Even labor managers complained of an "almost complete lack of [accurate] authoritative information," which made it impossible to rally "morale."[46]

The claim that the attack had been effectively countered by the Royal Air Force (R.A.F.) and anti-aircraft fire also rang extremely hollow. In none of the A.R.P. reports had this been mentioned. Rather, the report from the Bengal-Nagpur Railway was typical in citing consternation at the fact that "so many planes were allowed to fly over targets in perfect formation and drop bombs with no apparent opposition."[47] *The Statesman* accused the armed forces of complacency and speculated that perhaps "the well known British disposition for relaxation over the week-end" (the attack had come on a Sunday) might explain the manifest lack of opposition with which the Japanese attack was met.[48] The Calcutta A.R.P. report outlined more general sentiments:

> Indian opinion is strongly critical of the R.A.F.'s failure to protect Calcutta; the success of the raid has caused some to think that the stories of R.A.F. successes elsewhere are exaggerated; others think that the British cannot defend Calcutta from air-attack. British opinion is even more strongly critical and is indignant that Calcutta, stacked with war materials, its docks full of ships, should be left unprotected.[49]

Boosting morale was a hard sell. On the third day after the bombing, less than 20 per cent of the dock labor showed up for work. The attack had been devastating; very little warning had been given, no defense had been mounted, shelter had been inadequate, the official line on the attack had been patently specious, rumors were spreading unabated, and, to make matters worse, dead bodies, uncollected and unidentified, still littered the docks—even on the third day—decomposing in the December sun.[50]

Bodies

In an ancient—but still popular—Indian folk tale, "The King and the Corpse," a famous and powerful king becomes indebted to a wandering beggar who has paid him unexpected tribute. For the riches that the beggar has bestowed on the king, the sovereign agrees to do the beggar a favor. The favor that the beggar asks of the king is for him to bring a corpse to the burning ground, where the mendicant, who is also a sorcerer, will perform certain rites on the corpse to enrich his own power. The king dutifully goes to a site in the forest where the corpse is hanging from a tree, cuts down the corpse, heaves it over his shoulder, and begins his long march to the funeral ground. The corpse, however, is possessed by a spirit that awakens when it is slung over the king's shoulder. As the king proceeds, the spirit quizzes him with a series of morality tales, in the form of riddles, that test the king's enlightenment. With each correct answer, the corpse slips from the king's grasp and returns to the tree from which it was originally found hanging. Each time the king, again, cuts down the corpse, heaves it over his shoulder and heads off to the cremation ground to meet the beggar. But each time, again, the corpse tests the king and, again, ends up slipping from his grasp. The tale can be interpreted in a number of ways, but here I reference it only to point out the relationship between sovereign power and the corpse. That the idea of the corpse as the king's recurrent burden and moral interrogator is well entrenched in Indian literature is interesting—and is of special relevance to this analysis.

In many ways, 1943 could be considered the "year of the corpse" in Bengal. In the latter half of the year, in particular, the corpse had become a ubiquitous and material "social fact." That there were as many as 1.5 million lives lost to famine in 1943, also meant that there were as many as 1.5 million corpses that remained behind and had to be dealt with—or not. The tremendous weight—in both material and socio-political terms—of these corpses put an enormous strain on Bengal society and administration. The management of corpses represented a recurrent moral riddle that had to be solved. Some famine corpses had been retained in "constructive possession" of the state, others had been turned over to religious organizations for removal, and still others had been unceremoniously tossed into rivers and canals. Many others remained untouched where they had fallen and became a feast for wild dogs and vultures. Overall, the relationship of the corpse to "the king" during famine was dependent on its differential relation to power. Corpses that proved compromising to colonial power—primarily those in Calcutta—were "unclean" and had to be removed promptly and through official channels. Corpses that did not impinge on the functioning of the state were left to fate.

The treatment of the corpse, in this sense, provides a clue to the value attributed, by the state, to the life that once resided in it. Because the corpse consists of only the material aspect of being, without the contingency of agentive contradiction or contest, it is a kind of *tabula rasa* upon which the script of power is most clearly inscribed. The corpse, in this regard, represents the limits of essentialism: a stark and eerie ideological map to the psychological terrain of power.

The removal of air raid corpses was understood to be a central responsibility of the Civil Defense Services. The A.R.P., first of all, had its own corpse disposal squads, which had been drilled and trained in accordance with the A.R.P. Services Ordinance of 1941.[51] These teams had gained extensive experience removing corpses from the streets of Calcutta during famine. Their lorries, in fact, were still removing starvation victims from the city's streets when the 5 December bombing took place. The A.R.P. also had hundreds of beds in local hospitals reserved exclusively for air raid casualties.[52] When the bombing actually took place, however, it appears that neither the A.R.P. corpse disposal squads, nor the A.R.P. hospitals served their prescribed purpose. Instead, the earliest reports from the A.R.P. Controllers of the Port and the B.N.R. noted that the R.A.F. interceded in casualty recovery efforts at every juncture, and began loading bodies onto *military* transport vehicles, almost immediately, and removing them to unknown destinations.[53] Seth Drucquer, the officer-in-charge of the Post Raid Information Services (P.R.I.S.), responsible for gathering casualty statistics, noted on 6 December that the removal of "large numbers" of casualties by military personnel to *military hospitals* had severely hampered efforts to count the dead and injured. Bodies had also been shifted to several other non-A.R.P. hospitals, and had even been moved between unauthorized medical facilities without explanation or official documentation.[54]

When Drucquer received word through unofficial channels that bodies had been taken to the Indian Military Hospital, he visited the hospital to collect statistics. There he found only considerable "irregularities in the situation."[55] No list of persons admitted had been kept, no record of treatments administered was existent, and no attempt to identify the casualties had been made. The deputy supervisor of the port precinct also visited the Indian Military Hospital and reported that the military officer in charge could not even tell him of the exact number of casualties brought in, nor how many were dead or alive. The treatment given to the injured was also rudimentary, "nothing but tincture iodine being applied in many cases."[56] Many were housed outside the hospital in army tents, and held throughout the cold December night "without adequate clothing or blankets." They had not been given food and no proper sanitation facilities had been arranged. In effect, conditions starkly analogous to those prevailing throughout the famine-stricken province were recreated in microcosm at the Indian Military Hospital. The evidence pertaining to casualties of the raids taken to the British Military Hospital is still less documented. When Drucquer paid a visit to this hospital he was simply "refused admittance." At the private Campbell Hospital, Civil Defence Information Office staff were similarly denied access and hospital administrators "refused to give any details regarding the dead bodies collected there."[57]

Those bodies not taken into military custody were the subject of considerable uncertainty as well. Concerning these corpses, confusion reigned between the police, the A.R.P., and the Calcutta Corporation as to their "respective responsibilities."[58] The Bengal Nagpur Railways A.R.P. Controller, in his report, complained that no clear instructions on removing dead bodies had been given. The Port A.R.P., for its part, followed the famine model, making over bodies to the Hindu Satkar Samiti and the Anjuman Mofidul Islam, ensuring proper funeral rites to the dead according to perceived religious community. The B.N.R. A.R.P. also recorded the religious community of the dead that were collected under its auspices, but little else. In his initial report, the A.R.P. Controller for the B.N.R. noted that A.R.P. "sanitation sweepers" had assisted R.A.F. personnel and "other European officers" lifting bodies onto R.A.F. lorries, but admitted later that it had lost track of many casualties in the process.[59] The police, for their part, removed an unspecified number of corpses to the nearby Mommenpur morgue, where the bodies lay for several days in tight "files," again without identification or enumeration.

Obviously, under such conditions, even a rough estimate of the number killed during the bombing of 5 December 1943 becomes extremely difficult. In his final report, Drucquer—on a line penciled in and rough with erasure marks—reported the total number of dead, "as revealed," at 335. (To put this in perspective, during the first air attack by the German Luftwaffe on England during the "blitz," 436 Londoners were killed, and it was considered a catastrophic event.) The number killed on the docks, however, remains highly inconclusive. The Secretary to the Home Department of the Government of Bengal remained skeptical, reporting to the General Secretary that the Port A.R.P numbers were "very doubtful," and warned that government would have to "explain that the removal of large numbers of casualties to a military hospital had made the compilation of accurate statistics virtually impossible."[60] The Secretary replied that he would issue the necessary caveat about the dead removed to military hospitals, and also noted that a "considerable number of casualties…occurred on board ships and on freighters and barges,"[61] though their numbers, as well, were unknown. Similarly, there was little attempt made to enumerate those bodies that had been consumed by fire. Fires in the congested "coolie lines," in particular, raged unabated for several hours and large portions of the encampments lay in complete ruins by late afternoon. A military security control officer had noted in his report that during the bombings he had seen "*nothing* being done by Civil Defence Services [in regards to fires in the coolie lines]. It is understood," he continued, "that the firefighting services were busy elsewhere, but the coolies, who were a high percentage of the casualties, received no help from First Aid, Rescue, or Ambulance Squads until after the 'All Clear.'"[62]

The pervasive disregard, disrespect, and even disgust, with which the bodies of these (poor) laborers were treated reveals important aspects of the colonial mindset at the time—aspects which contributed significantly to the mentality of debasement, erasure and *de*-prioritization that led to famine. While these bodies served any economic or political purpose, they were touted "essential." Once their utility had been negated—as corpses—they became a "security risk," endangering the war effort (by registering the success of Japan's attack), encumbering the administration (by the awkward materiality of their corpses), and generating rumors (that threatened efforts at damage control). Their bodies, for the most part, had to be whisked from public sight, denied, obscured, and, ultimately, forgotten. Far from being protected or prioritized, they had been defiled, degraded, or entirely neglected once their utility had been—violently—revoked. This fact exposes the myth of patriarchal concern for the industrial labor of Calcutta that consecutive programs of appropriation, "denial," and militarization all banked on, and reveals the emptiness of the rhetoric that justified much of the official policy that precipitated mass starvation in Bengal. Ultimately, during the air-raid, these "essential workers" fared little better than poor villagers during famine. Their violent deaths, except for the risks to "security" that were entailed, meant next to nothing to the colonial state. Despite claims to the contrary, they were expendable, insignificant, and very easily dehumanized.

Of the 335 corpses officially counted in the Post Raid Information Service's Final Report, 260 were thus recorded as "unidentified." Seth Drucquer, in his report, attributed this shortcoming to several different causes. Non-A.R.P. hospitals, he complained, had made no attempt to gather information on the bodies brought to them, and the police had not gained access to many of the bodies until several days after the raids. Although "there [was] a provision for the Police to photograph unidentified dead bodies after raids," he noted, "by the time the Police arrived, they were too much decomposed for such photographs to be of any value."[63] In a hand written and parenthetical addendum Drucquer added that "probably the Police, like the P.R.I.S., were not informed of the whereabouts of casualties until it was too late."[64] The Police Commissioner himself defended the record, reporting that their primary concern had been solely "to have the dead bodies removed from sight as early as possible."

Although the corpses accounted for were thus disposed of without name, physical description, or any personalized record that would facilitate future identification, there was, in the last analysis, one single mark of classification assigned to most of the bodies. Given that these same bodies had been left to rot, had been denied care, and had been all but systematically denied; the trace of "identification" that *was* recorded has to be understood as the state's most "essential" distinction of all—one that would adhere to even an anonymous body, deprived of all social connection, dignity or recognition. That last trace, interestingly enough, was religious affiliation. Like in the case of famine victims, how exactly such a determination was made, particularly of bodies in advanced stages of decomposition, is difficult to fathom. The Officer-in-Charge of the Post Raid Information Service remained frustrated. In his Final Report to Government, he explained:

> The labels which the Police tie on to unidentified dead bodies and of which a copy is given to P.R.I.S. contain a column for marks of identification on the body. A very large number of labels received did not have this column

filled up, only one words being entered, such as; "Muslim," or "Hindu." This is of no use at all in establishing identification subsequently.

As during famine then, the sole distinction made by the state often enough was whether the corpse was to be understood as "Hindu" or "Muslim." This simplistic binary distinction had become so ingrained in administrative thought that it was understood, by this time, as the only necessary categorization—for even a corpse. The colonial state was, in this sense, reifying religious affiliation, by means of corpses, that would parallel the political distinction that was being used to "divide and rule." The idea that Hindu-ness or Muslim-ness adhered to the very body of the population, moreover, was a subtle license to violence against the *bodies* of the "other." The way that bodies were handled during and after the air raids was both an example of all that had been learned during the famine—and was also a template for what was to come. It is a chilling fact that in the dehumanizing darkness of war and famine, this one simple and explosive distinction was all that was required any longer in demarcating the disposable citizens of Calcutta. It is furthermore, a similarly telling and chilling foreshadowing of the darkness still to come.

Settling Accounts

The Essential Services [Maintenance] Ordinance of 1941 had made it a criminal offence for any worker engaged in "essential" war-related industries and enterprises from abandoning their station of employment without "reasonable excuse," under penalty of imprisonment. "The fact that a person apprehends that by continuing in his employment he will be exposed to increased physical danger," it was noted, "does not constitute a reasonable excuse."[65] The threat of imprisonment it was understood, however, would do little to assuage the fears of current workers and might actually discourage labor recruitment. The War Injuries Insurance Ordinance, promulgated in the same year, was, in effect, a companion—and counterbalance—to the Essential Services Ordinance. Under the War Injuries Ordinance any individual "gainfully occupied" in war-related industries was entitled to compensation in the case of injury "caused by the impact on any person or property [by] any enemy aircraft."[66] Reparation was to be worked out in accordance with the Workers' Compensation Act of 1923, and as such, the risks of war were associated with the occupational risks of employment. In the case of death, compensation would be made to the next of kin according to the same payment scheme. The War Injuries (Compensation Insurance) Act of 1943 reinforced the provisions of the earlier ordinance, clarifying that the liability of compensation was to rest on employers, who were subsequently to be reimbursed under the provision of the (mandatory) War Risks Insurance Ordinance.

In the days following the 5 December air raid, both the central and sub-area offices of the Post Raid Information Service were swamped with relatives of dock workers who had gone "missing" during the attack. The agency, however, was only able to satisfy a "very limited number of enquiries…owing to the large number of unidentified cases."[67] Applicants missing relatives had come not only to locate the whereabouts of their kin for sentimental reasons, but also to file insurance claims against the deaths of their family members—in extremely hard times. It was the responsibility of the Post Raid Information Service to assist "relatives of persons killed in filling up forms for claims under the War Injuries Scheme."[68] However, its chief officer informed his superiors, the lack of identification of the majority of corpses had made it "impossible to enable claims to be filed."[69] It is likely that this state of affairs saved the capital interests operating in the dock area the inconvenience of having to formally declare that the enumerated dead found on their premises after the raids, were, in fact, "outsiders."

The exculpation of the Civil Defense Services from charges of inaction was a much more delicate bureaucratic affair. A memo by one particular Military Police Security Control Officer, forwarded to the chief of the general staff, stated in paragraph 7 that, "during the period between the first bomb and the all clear, Civil Defense Departments were conspicuous by their absence—the entire fire-fighting, first aid and rescue work being done by the fighting services."[70] This memo created quite a stir. The Chairman of the Port Commissioners, Sir Thomas Elderton—a well connected man and also the A.R.P. Controller for the port—took sharp issue with the charges made by the military officer. He wrote an indignant memo to the Bengal Secretariat deploring the accusations, and assuring the secretary that Civil Defense forces in the port had acted swiftly and courageously. The Bengal Secretariat, in turn, issued a note to the central Civil Defense Department of the Government of India, "to record its most profound disapproval of the action of the Military Security Control Officer."[71] The additional secretary to the Government of India assured the Bengal Secretariat that "suitable steps [would be] taken to impress on the officer concerned the unfortunate repercussions which may result from derogatory comments on the Civil Services."[72] The officer concerned, however, put it on record that his report had been "based entirely on personal experience," and, as such, could not be retracted. In the end, however, the now infamous paragraph 7 of his report was changed to read: "During the period between the first bomb and the all clear there was delay in getting the Civil Defence Services into operation in some areas. When they started to function, however, they worked satisfactorily." E. R. Kitchin of the Bengal Secretariat sent an apology to Sir Thomas for the "injustices of the M.P.S.C.O.'s comments," and Elderton sent him back an appreciation for his good work, noting that "anyhow the man who made the mis-statements is no longer here."[73]

The question of the removal of bodies by British military personnel— rather than the A.R.P.—was similarly tricky to resolve. The same Military Police Security Control Officer had alleged in his controversial memo that "not one Indian civilian gave help or dared to touch a casualty," and that the R.A.F. had done all the removal of bodies themselves. Alone this allegation may have been dealt with similar to the first. However, both the B.N.R. and Port A.R.P. reports had complained of military interference with the removal of bodies, suggesting that their stretchers and ambulances had been commandeered by the military. Of special concern was the B.N.R.'s response to question 15 (i) on the A.R.P.'s "First Report" form: "Who did the actual handling and removal of corpses?" The—perhaps at the time, seemingly innocuous—answer was initially given: "R.A.F. and other European Officers volunteered to lift and remove bodies to mortuary in a lorry loaded by the R.A.F."[74] In subsequent days, with the number of "unidentified" bodies generating public and administrative unease, and reports of military interference with Civil Defense operations causing consternation, the question of corpse removal simmered. Finally, more than two weeks after the bombing, the record was summarily "clarified." The A.R.P. Controller for the Railways sent a memo asking the Home Department to "kindly correct" query 15 (i)— in answer to who had moved corpses—to read: "Volunteers from among the B.N.R. officials, and Indians, including a Sikh, 2 Brahmins, and Indian Christians of the B.N.R. Sanitary Staff…with the help of a lorry provided by No. 978 Squadron R.A.F." Nothing remained of the R.A.F. but the lorry, and in the place of their personnel, now sat this somewhat comical "rainbow coalition" of colonial Indian cooperation.

Meanwhile, the R.A.F. had accounts to settle of its own. Reports in *The Statesman* and other media outlets that Calcutta had been left wholly unprotected rankled the forces. Leslie Chippett of the R.A.F. remembers the accusation and its aftermath colorfully. Chippett's squadron had just returned to Calcutta from Chittagong, less than twenty-four hours before the bombing, and "although far from prepared [had] struggled to get some [obsolete] Hurricanes into the air." To no effect.

> Imagine the anger of the squadron from CO to the lowest [rank] when on the following Monday the Calcutta newspaper was very scathing, "Where was the RAF, do they have the weekend off?" It was decided to show these critics [who] sat at home with their gins that the RAF did exist. On the following weekend a particularly important race meeting was to be held at Calcutta racecourse. Imagine the members chagrin when as the race commenced Hurricanes appeared at naught feet "beating up" the racecourse. Horses went everywhere and I believe the race was concluded in the slowest time on record. I saw no further criticisms of 67 or any other squadrons. Further to this there is a story about a camera gun, film or lack of it, and discrepancies regarding a "kill" made in that raid, but I'll leave that for another time.[75]

Imagine, also, the effect on an already traumatized population of such hi-jinx.

In fact, apart from patently specious official assurances printed in newspapers, little was actually done to boost the all-important "morale" of the Indian population. A concerned business owner in the area posted a letter of protest on 10 January 1944, in which he wrote:

> Over one month has elapsed since the air raid on December 5th, and in the vicinity of our factory on Hide Road [Kidderpore], the only repairs which have been carried out appear to be those undertaken by the Calcutta Electric Supply Co. to their substation…all the small shops and *bustees* still remain exactly as they were a few hours after the raid. The ruins of a Key-man shelter which was destroyed in the Port Commissioners' Depot have not been cleared away and is not exactly a good advertisement for Air Raid Precautions. It occurs to us that at very small cost, and bearing in mind that in the War Risks Insurance Fund there is a sum of about 9 crores (900 million) rupees at the moment, all the necessary repairs to shops, buildings and dwelling houses in the area can be fully restored. The effect on morale and the propaganda which would be possible as a result needs no further elaboration.[76]

The Bengal Minister of Commerce, Labor and Industry investigated the situation and found that the War Risks Insurance Fund did not apply. "Repairs to shops, buildings and dwelling houses damaged by air raids cannot be helped from this fund," he wrote, "a scheme for insurance against war damage to immovable property not covered by the [War Risks Insurance Fund] has been considered and rejected."[77] By the end of the war, the War Risks Insurance scheme had collected 4.2 billion rupees through mandated enlistment, but had paid out less than 5 million.[78] The Secretary of the Home Department was disappointed. "The wording of the Metal Box Company's letter may [have been] unsuitable," he responded, "but there is something in what they say, viz: that air-raid damage should not be left just as it is indefinitely for all to see…this is not very satisfactory; i.e. a general denial of responsibility all around."[79]

Air Raid Damage

The house that my father grew up in, on Mommenpur Road, was one of those dwellings that had been damaged in the raid, and was never made whole again. Apart from the cracks in the foundation that had resulted from close proximity to the bomb blasts on the docks, there was also unseen damage that seemed to linger on indefinitely. My father carried with him, for the rest of his life, a profound and deep seated terror and anxiety that had been imprinted on him by this attack. Our family's connection to the docks and to the air raids themselves had been, to be sure, uncommonly extensive. His father, a retired policeman with dwindling accounts, had property along the docks in the *bustee* settlements of migrant laborers, whom he shook down for rent on most weekends. My father's older brother—who even at this time was more or less the head of the household at 24 years of age—was an A.R.P. warden in Mommenpur. Under his jurisdiction the morgue, less than a mile from the house, also fell. The neighborhood itself was inhabited mostly by underemployed and impoverished laborers associated with the docks and its concomitant factories, warehouses and workshops, and had been swamped after the bombing with terrified dock laborers "lying up" in its by-lanes and bazaars. Flocks of "sightseers" had also moved through the area to observe the damage—and had moved back out bearing witness. Nowhere in Calcutta, in fact, could the "rumors," panic, and trepidation have been more pronounced.

Surely the complex of factors involved must have impacted my father's young mind profoundly. But it was simply, in fact, the actual visceral, terrifying and apocalyptic sound and magnitude of the blasts that had shattered his nerves and continued to haunt him throughout his life. He had already lived in midst of famine, with bodies pilling up on the streets day by day. And he would live through, after only a very short interval, events that one would imagine would be even more deeply traumatic But, perhaps because of his age at the time, or perhaps because of his temperament, the impression left on him by the bombing of the docks was the deepest and most nagging of all. He never described (and possibly could not have even processed at such an age) the details of the event. In fact, from listening to his stories, I was under the impression that Calcutta had been bombed almost every night—as perhaps he was. He only referred to the bombings as the shattering of windows, the cracking of the foundation, and the repeated ear splitting reports that made him feel that the world itself was coming to an end. It was a story without beginning or end. No time frame or outline of events seemed to punctuate his memories and make them chronological. The bombings, in this sense, were memory without context.

Several accounts that I have heard or read from people who were children in 1943 are similar in this way. Though the bombings of Calcutta have been an almost unnoticed chapter in the modern history of India, or even Bengal, they do seem to hold a particularly prominent place in the memories of the children who lived through them. To give one example, below is the memory of one child at the time:

> I remember as a little girl aged 8 years old living in Calcutta during WW2 in our extended family. *The Japanese bombed the city every night* at that time as it was an important city and capital of the British Raj. As it was getting dark the air raid siren used to start and we all had to go into our basement room for safety. We often had to stay for two hours or more until the all clear was sounded. We used to have our dinner early to eat before the air raids. As a little girl I used to always get very frightened during the bombing.[80]

The idea that the bombings took place "every night," although Calcutta suffered nothing of the sort, may, indeed, have more to do with "always being frightened" by the bombings that did occur, than with the frequency of the actual bombings. Undoubtedly there is a whole body of scholarship on the progress of post-traumatic stress in children, but that is beyond the scope of this present analysis. Suffice it to say that every time a city is bombed in recent times, and its citizens are "shocked and awed" by the impact of weapons far more powerful than those that were in use in 1943, and I reflect that in that city (of perhaps millions) there is a large proportion of children, I think of my father—and also of my mother, who wore a pin in the 1970s, that read: *"war is not healthy for children and other living things."*

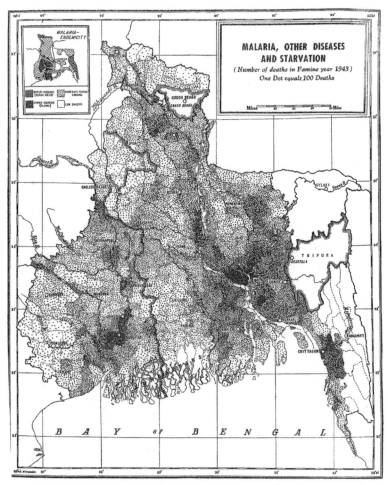

3. Famine distribution in Bengal districts

6

SECOND FAMINE

Once famine had become an international news story, reporters flocked to Bengal to bear witness. T. G. Narayan of the Madras-based newspaper, *The Hindu*, arrived in September 1943 and toured the famine-stricken districts of the province for several months. He compiled his observations in a book, *Famine Over Bengal*, published in the early months of 1944. His tour ended in the district of Barisal at the end of December, by which time Narayan had seen enough. "There was too much misery around," he wrote, "the air was thick, heavy and foul with unrelieved distress, disease and degradation. The famine had been more or less driven out of urban areas, but it was still there in the country-side."[1] Disheartened, Narayan retreated to Calcutta to recuperate and compile his findings. In the city, however, he found little respite from the anxiety that his journey had spawned:

The city had had a [bombing] raid—its heaviest—while I was away, and the air was heavy with talk about it. My heart and mind were elsewhere. I remembered the sights I had seen of human misery…and with a heavy heart I set to work…It was not easy. It was not pleasant. Ten days' effort on the typewriter brought me to the previous chapter. Thoroughly flagged out, I pushed away the typewriter, switched off the lights and got out onto the Maidan for a long walk by myself to collect my thoughts. It was pitch dark, except for occasional flashes of light from the overhead power-lines as the tram-cars' guide pulleys rolled along their joints. The stars looked down on a sleeping world and everything seemed still in sleep. But far out in the remote villages of Bengal,

171

I knew, men, women and children were not sleeping the sleep that came to those who had a full meal after the day's toil. Many of them were fever-stricken, hunger-stricken, and would have no sleep.

I asked myself what chances they had of being relieved in the present and of being saved in the months to come…with the promise of a bountiful harvest was Bengal to turn the corner, and did she see ahead of her the prospect of safety? Or was there danger lurking in the dark future, hatching in the womb of time, ready to descend on a hapless people and smite them again? Would there be a repetition in 1944 of the holocaust of 1943? Would Bengal's countryside be once again laid waste and strewn with the wrecks of her children…? Were the people again going to die like trapped rats…? I found no hopeful answer. The night air was crisp, but it failed to refresh my weary spirit and I turned for home. It was very still and even the traffic had gone off the roads. The stars had disappeared behind banks of clouds and, as I stumbled in and out of the baffle walls, the night *chowkidar* flashed his torch, stirred himself and said goodnight. As a sign of recognition, he added, "It is a very dark night, *Huzzoor*, the Japanese won't come." Not wholly awake to what he said, I answered, "Yes, it is a very black night, but there are many hours to go before it will be dawn."[2]

Ending Famine

By November of 1943 the new Viceroy, Archibald Wavell, had managed to implement an extensive military relief operation that was moving large quantities of rice into the country-side from Calcutta. Major-General Stuart (in over-all charge of military assistance) had at his command twelve to fifteen thousand British troops, and Major-General Wakely (in charge of movements) was given significant priority in respect to transportation to get rice where it was most needed. In addition—although the official line was still that famine had been precipitated by the hoarding of *cultivators*—orders were issued that seemed to belie a less perfunctory understanding of famine in Bengal: the export of rice and paddy from the province was prohibited,[3] direct purchasing in the country-side by large industrial firms was banned,[4] a moratorium on the movement of rice and paddy out of twelve principle rice-growing districts was enacted, and, perhaps most importantly, the Government of India committed itself to feeding the city of Calcutta through direct imports from outside Bengal in order to alleviate the drain on the decimated country-side.[5] With these several measures enacted by the end of 1943, the government switched gears and began arguing for an "end" of famine in Bengal.

In the last week of December Viceroy Wavell made a second trip to Bengal to monitor the progress of relief. On that occasion, in his first public speech as Governor-General of India, he encouraged members of the combined Chambers of Commerce in Calcutta to forget about the past and begin thinking about the future: "I do not propose here to enter into long consideration of how we reached our present difficulties," he assured the gathering, "our business is not to look back but to look ahead."[6] The Food Member of the Viceroy's Executive Council, Sir Jwala Prasad Srivastava, also in Bengal, met with prominent citizens in Dacca, and—despite complaints about shortages of rice in both the city and the districts[7]—he too waxed optimistic: "we are now faced with the problem of the future," he informed the gathering, "the food crisis is probably over and I wish and pray that it may never occur again."[8]

On 12 January 1944, in an effort to further administrative closure to the spectacle of starvation in British India, Wavell telegraphed Secretary of State Amery to suggest the prompt organization of a Famine Enquiry Commission, designed—ostensibly—"to investigate and report to the Governor-General in Council upon the causes of widespread distress, starvation and disease in Bengal in the year of 1943."[9] Following the official rhetorical trend, he also assured the secretary of state that the enquiry would "be concerned with the future rather than with the past."[10] The "terms of reference" were, accordingly, delimited. The commission would be tasked to report on: "(a) the possibility of improving the diet of the people and the variety and yield of food crops, (b) the possibility of increasing the administrative system, particularly in the districts, and (c) the need for better provision for medical relief and public health."[11] The proceedings, the viceroy suggested, should take the form of a Royal Commission, which, he noted, could be organized "almost immediately."[12] Such a program of enquiry, Wavell knew, would be an essential step towards putting an "end" to famine in Bengal. Even *The Statesman* got into the mood of closure, publishing a "Famine Retrospect" early in January.[13] The "Bengal Famine of 1943"—as it has been known ever since—was officially becoming a thing of the past.

But the view from Calcutta—or for that matter from Delhi—as T.G. Narayan had pointed out, was deceptive. Freda Bedi, a reporter for the Punjab *Tribune*, like Narayan, was sent on assignment to document famine in Bengal. She arrived in Calcutta in January 1944 to begin her tour of the province. The city, she reported, was "full of busy life…there are soldiers everywhere, and the restaurants are bursting with food and music and merry-makers."[14]

> But look into the faces of the middle-class and the poor. Some of them have got a haunted look. They are thinner. 'Tell me,' I said [to one], 'is the famine over—at least the worst of it?' 'Good God, no' was the reply. 'They have only made Calcutta more comfortable for the rich to live in: they have pushed the inconvenient sights back into the villages.'[15]

In these same villages, Bedi herself found "stark hunger...everywhere." In one particular village near Dacca, she happened on a hunger-bent young woman, cooking what little rice her destitute family could afford out in the open-air:

> ...her shoulders were heaving as she stirred it. She covered her face, for strangers had come. I went up to her and looked in her eyes: they were full of tears. Tears were falling into the rice. It was a bare half-*seer* floating in the water. "For seven people," her husband said in a low voice. In how many villages, I wondered, are the poor eating their bare handful of rice slop salted with a woman's tears?[16]

At Government "free kitchens" many of Bengal's poor fared little better. The doles of "gruel" handed out were radically insufficient, amounting to 800 calories a day—less than a third of the ration mandated by the (neglected) Bengal Famine Code.[17] The deputy surgeon-general of Bengal, himself, was confounded; "it was incredible," he admitted, "that they could have lived on [such rations]...particularly considering that many people who attended the kitchens had to walk a mile or two to get it."[18] Graft, he added, was wide-spread, with much of the food going to "the man running the kitchen...local headmen of the villages, schoolmasters and other similar types of men."[19] Malaria, cholera, and, with increasing virulence, smallpox, were also sweeping through the hunger-stricken population unabated. Weakened bodies succumbed within hours of the onset of disease. Official medical relief had begun only in December and remained grossly inadequate. Quinine for treating malaria was the new black-market craze and an acute scarcity of cloth had left millions half or fully naked throughout the winter months. In December Army Relief Headquarters was fielding cries of distress from several districts "saying that people were dying, not on account of lack of food, but on account of the weather because they had nothing to put on, no blankets and no clothes."[20]

The official line that famine was over, however, continued to pervade all political and administrative thinking. An early "end" to famine in Bengal first and foremost served certain instrumental purposes for the British. Relations with the United States, in particular, were at a critical juncture in the context of wartime cooperation and sharp criticism of British colonial rule in India represented a sore spot in diplomatic relations. The conclusion of famine in Bengal would be one less open wound. The end of famine would also forestall further criticism of the Government of India domestically, particularly after the failure of the Cripps Mission, little progress on the constitutional front, and the bulk of Indian Congress leaders still in jail. On the even more charged and divisive provincial level the idea that famine was "over" also served certain political purposes. For the Muslim League an end to famine would avert condemnation of failure and shore up its beleaguered authority by lending it the credibility of having contained disaster. Likewise, the opposition willingly adopted the rhetoric of the "end" of famine instrumentally. With the "Bengal Famine of 1943" officially in the box, the specter of a looming "Second Famine"[21] could be used to chip away at the Nazimuddin Ministry. The Muslim League thus found itself in the untenable position of having to defend the rhetoric that famine had ended, while having to deflect predictions of a "second famine"—which, in truth, could have been declared at any given moment.

Whose Famine?

The ascension of a Muslim League-controlled Ministry in early 1943 had served—as the viceroy had predicted—to exacerbate already strained communal relations in Bengal. With Congress outlawed after the upheaval of 1942, "opposition" or "allegiance" during the Nazimuddin Ministry increasingly became synonymous with "Hindu" vs. "Muslim" interests. The dire impact of famine served to galvanize these animosities still further, congealing communal rhetoric into material claims and counter-claims concerning the means of bare existence. Economic collapse, wide-spread destitution, despair, and ultimately mass death provided a grim bio-political substrate upon which the most virulent strains of communal ideology flourished. As famine deaths mounted and the calamity of starvation in Bengal became increasingly central to political debate, communal resentments became leaden with the weight of hundreds of thousands of corpses—as well as the care of millions more who hovered on the verge of death. Famine, in this sense, lent a dark and elemental tone to an already acrimonious debate—not least of all in relation to relief efforts.

Because official relief operations were extremely belated and grossly inadequate, private organization had gained disproportionate importance from early on. With Congress leaders jailed and the organization in shambles, the Hindu Mahasabha, in particular, was able to gain a popular foothold in Bengal that had eluded them electorally. In order to extend its own banned authority, "Congress, which had obvious difficulties in organizing country-wide relief owing to its entire machinery having been declared illegal, decided to accord Dr [Shyama Prasad] Mookerjee [President of the Provincial Hindu Mahasabha] every possible support and co-operation."[22] Under this arrangement the communalist ideologies that the Hindu Mahasabha represented also became increasingly entangled in provincial politics. Mookerjee made energetic use of famine to discredit the Muslim League, rally Hindu opposition, and lobby for an executive abrogation of the Ministry (Section 93). Under his auspices the Bengal Relief Committee (BRC) was set up, becoming the umbrella organization for a large contingent of private relief efforts whose primary objective was aid to "middle-class Bengalis."[23] For many, "middle-class Bengalis" were simply code words for *Hindu*. Lending credence to such anxieties amongst the Muslim poor, the organization set up most of its relief centers in villages and wards where Hindus were in the vast majority.[24]

Mookerjee himself was an extremely divisive figure and accusations of communal bias in the Mahasabha's implementation of relief were rife. When journalist T. G. Narayan visited a Hindu Mahasabha hospital in Midnapore he found, much to his surprise, that fifteen out of forty beds were empty. Apart from so few patients, he found, however, that "every room in the hospital had a picture of Dr Shyama Prasad Mookerjee. I don't know what therapeutic effect that had…[but] it would have been much better to have filled up the hospital with dying patients."[25] The Revenue Department of the Government of Bengal, in charge of local governmental relief operations, also fielded complaints that the Mahasabha was only giving relief to Hindus and issued a sharp warning to the BRC that Government would cut off its supplies if the practice continued.[26] Members of the Mahasabha admitted that they had given differential relief to Muslims—uncooked rather than cooked grains—but denied observing any other "consideration of caste or creed."[27] They also countered that Government relief centers mostly employed Muslim cooks, which made it altogether "impossible" for Hindus to take food at many Government "gruel kitchens."[28]

Nevertheless, government food establishments also served as an avowal of the Muslim League's concern. Though the inadequacy of relief drew sustained criticism, the scope and visibility of government relief kitchens made a good impression on the (mostly Muslim) poor, bolstering the popularity of the Food Minister, Hussein Shaheed Suhrawardy in particular.[29] The Muslim League itself opted against organizing any relief operations under its direct control, in order, League officials said, not to "give those people [the Mahasabha] a chance of making accusations against us only to justify themselves."[30] Instead the Muslim League channeled its privately garnered resources through the Muslim Chamber of Commerce, hoping to avoid any charges of a conflict of interest. When word got out, however, that Muhammad Ali Jinnah had sent a check to the Chambers Relief Fund with money stipulated specifically for "Muslim relief," bitter controversy ensued and the matter quickly became an all-India scandal.

Hindu nationalist and ardent Mahasabha activist, Vinayak Savarkar, in "retaliation" against Jinnah and the Muslim League called for "every Hindu organization and individual to follow the brave lead of the Bombay Provincial and some other Hindu Sabhas [and] send all help to rescue, clothe and shelter Hindu sufferers alone."[31] Savarkar went further still and accused Muslim organizations in Bengal of withholding relief from Hindus unless they agreed to convert to Islam.[32] Chief Minister Nazimuddin defended the record acerbically at the Muslim League's All-India conference in Karachi, deploring Savarkar's accusations and categorically denying that "conversions of starving Hindus had taken place."[33] The Muslim Chamber of Commerce also argued that while approximately 5 per cent of the donations it received were for Muslim relief only, it had not earmarked these same funds since more than 5 per cent of the recipients of Chamber relief were Muslims in any case. But such arguments had very short legs in the political climate of famine and antagonisms became only further entrenched.

With London's continued refusal of imports, a promising *aman* harvest, above all else, was being counted on to relieve famine, but the

Government's *aman* procurement scheme—of central importance to relief—was also being hampered by political division which broke along communal lines. In the Bengal countryside the ghastly depredations of famine had depopulated whole villages and had left an entire society numbed and traumatized. Scarcity, homelessness, hunger, and disease continued to reign, and hundreds of thousands of corpse were still accumulating in the countryside. Millions more teetered on the brink of extinction. The suspicion that governmental manipulations and impunity had been at the root of the misery of Bengal was widespread. Such a context was ripe for the "opposition." The Hindu Mahasabha began an energetic and highly effective campaign against procurement, encouraging Hindu citizens to offer "stubborn resistance" to all government efforts to purchase rice.[34] Due in large part to these efforts, by March the Government of Bengal had been able to acquire less than 15 per cent of its target of 1.15 million tons of rice and paddy, straining Government efforts to control both prices and supplies.[35]

Once again Bengal politics reverberated on a national scale. The Food Member of the Government of India, Cawnpore industrialist J. P. Srivastava—himself an active member of the Hindu Mahasabha—criticized the Muslim League Ministry's procurement plans stridently in the Executive Council, decrying its poor organization and biased objectives. His criticism drew predictable ire from the joint secretaries of the Muslim League Ministry, who in response denounced the viceroy's food member himself, "whose attitude to the Bengal Ministry's food administration," they noted, "has been so surprisingly similar to that of the [Hindu] Opposition elements in the province."[36] A statement issued by the Ministry condemned Srivastava's meddling as divisive propaganda designed only to "give the Bengal Ministry a bad name."[37] On this count they accused the Food Member of "import(ing) politics into food questions"[38] and demanded his resignation from the Viceroy's Council. Secretary of State for India, Leopold Amery, brushed off the controversy breezily: "I am afraid this is typical of the way in which the communal question enters into everything," he wrote to the viceroy, "I am not sure that you will not have to end up by composing your Executive entirely of Indian Christians or by inventing a new official religion to which all Government Servants and Ministers should be bound to subscribe!"[39]

The implementation of rationing in Calcutta, which would also be a crucial step in controlling prices throughout Bengal, became similarly entangled in communal acrimony. The Ministry was pushing hard to open government shops that would be staffed according to legislated communal ratios (which mandated parity for Muslims), while interested Hindu parties lobbied vigorously for a system run through existing trade channels—which were Hindu-dominated.[40] The Government of India had sent their Special Rationing Advisor, W.H. Kirby to Calcutta several times in the summer of 1943, but he had made little progress. Towards the end of 1943, the viceroy, frustrated by the communally-charged standoff, invoked central authority under Section 126-A of the Government of India Act and testily ordered the Ministry to "establish a specific number of shops and to include a specified number of trade as well as Government shops," immediately.[41] This, in some sense, was understood as a communal compromise. The ministry reported back that it would arrange for 1,000 ration shops to be opened by 31 January 1944, of which 55 per cent would be private retail shops (read: "Hindu") and 45 per cent would be government shops (read: "Muslim.")

Food Member J.P. Srivastava again mounted an attack, charging that the Bengal Ministry's only concern was to "admit more Muslims into the grain trade."[42] He also noted that a lack of grain reserves in Bengal, in any case, would doom the scheme to failure. The Joint Secretaries of the Government of Bengal responded pointedly that "the inclusion of even a few Muslim shops [was] too much for the Hindu Mahasabha representatives at New Delhi."[43] They also pointed out that the central government had agreed to supply Calcutta with imports from outside the province and as such grain reserves in Bengal had little bearing on the city's ration scheme. The expediently organized "Central Rationing Committee" of the Bengal Hindu Mahasabha responded, issuing a veiled threat to the Ministry to double the number of private shops in order to "ensure smooth working and efficient distribution of food-stuffs."[44] The Government of Bengal replied to this attack in a curt press release. They would "value co-operation and even healthy criticism" with ration planning the memo read, but were prepared to take immediate and decisive measures against "any attempt to sabotage it."[45]

Criticisms of the amount of the projected daily ration also stirred up communal sentiments. The proposed plan to allot only three and a half *seers*[46] of rice per person, per week was little more than two-thirds of the ration outlined in the Bengal Famine Code. In response to a quick out-cry, Government agreed to increase the weekly ration to 4 *seers* per week and also promised to arrange for supplementary provisions for "heavy workers" at cooked-food canteens.[47] Members of the Hindu community took immediate issue with this solution. Hindu workers, it was suggested, could not be expected to take cooked food from government canteens where ritual purity could not be ensured. The Hindu-dominated Calcutta Corporation took up the cause, passing a resolution that stated, "in view of the fact that it is impossible for Hindus to have cooked food in canteens, Government [is] requested to increase the quota of [uncooked] rice to one *seer* per day to [Hindu] heavy workers..."[48] In the same resolution the Corporation also petitioned for an additional ration to be allowed to Hindus for religious worship, particularly in regards to *bhog*, or the "feeding of the deities." Food Minister, H. S. Suhrawardy, rejected the claim, noting that in Bombay no such provisions had been made in the rationing scheme already underway and the gods had survived.[49] The issue simmered for many weeks to come.

Despite ongoing contentions, however, rationing got underway in Calcutta on 31 January 1944. By most accounts, and contrary to grave predictions from the opposition, the logistical arrangements proved adequate. Complaints were received from many quarters, however, that the quality of rice being distributed at ration shops was extremely poor; some of it entirely rotten and some contaminated with dirt and other filler. At an emergency meeting of the Calcutta Corporation a moldering and stinking sample was presented to the Director of Public Health and held up to his nose. "He reacted to it violently. He was shocked at the sight it presented and turned up his nose against it."[50] As pitiable as it might be to feed starving people rotten food, the likely explanation for such is darker still. As milled rice can be stored for up to one year (and paddy up to three) without significant deterioration, it is likely that the rice now being distributed to ration shops had been in the possession of Government and/or its corporate clients for *more than one year*. Though Famine Enquiry findings on hoarding were inconclusive, that vast stores of now rotten rice were being unloaded on the market in the first months of 1944 is damning evidence that rice was, in fact, rotting in government and corporate warehouses as millions starved.

The quality of foodstuffs being fed to the still starving masses in the countryside was still worse. In Murshidabad a sub-divisional officer at Lalbagh had found stocks of wheat sold to his precinct entirely "unwholesome." The district magistrate suggested that it might at least be sold to local farmers as fodder for cattle. The government's Veterinary Surgeon, however, upon inspection found the grain unfit, even, for animal consumption. Rejected as cattle feed, this same rice was then "reconditioned" and returned to local markets—where it was sold for human consumption.[51] In many places a very coarse grain called *bajra*, more commonly eaten in upper India, was also being fed to "sick destitutes" who had never before eaten it. As Major-General Stuart later reported, for many eating *bajra* "led to diarrhea for about three days; after that they apparently became accustomed to it...but cholera was present at the time [and] they were frightened that it might be cholera."[52] The starving were known to have delicate stomachs. In Faridpur the District Magistrate reported that "in the gruel kitchens just one kind of food was being served out irrespective of the condition of destitutes. The result was that in one case the entrails of a destitute came out soon after his taking the gruel and he died."[53]

Governing Bengal

Given the severity of the situation in Bengal, the viceroy's patience for the constitutional arrangements of "provincial autonomy" was thin. Like his predecessor, Wavell had little faith in the elected government of Bengal and was particularly alarmed by "the reckless way in which political capital [was being] made of the Bengal trouble."[54] He found Chief Minister, Kwaja Nazimuddin, "honest but weak,"[55] and he estimated the much more formidable Food Minister, Hussein Suhrawardy, "all big talk and small action."[56] What Bengal needed, Wavell thought, was "inspiring leadership" with a broad *central* mandate. The only way to realize this necessity, he concluded, was to abolish the provincial government and grant the governor, under direct authority of the viceroy, emergency rule in Bengal (Section 93). The procedure of superceding provincial autonomy and enforcing autocratic white-rule in Bengal, however, would be difficult to execute. As the viceroy recognized, the Ministry in Bengal commanded a substantial majority in the Legislature and the abrogation of its authority would create considerable animosity with the Muslim League and perhaps among Muslims more generally.[57] The move might additionally only encourage Hindu nationalists in the province, who had been lobbying for the dissolution of the League Ministry since its inception. From a legal angle, as well, Section 93 would technically only be applicable in the advent of an actual break-down in the functioning of the provincial legislature, which was not yet the case in Bengal. The *resignation* of the Ministry, on the other hand, would dampen the impression of heavy-handedness and possibly ameliorate the rancor that dismissal would entail. A possible route to Section 93 by resignation had already been laid out by the former viceroy. Under Sections 52-(I) (a) and 126A of the Government of India Act, the governor could claim extraordinary powers in any province where "peace and tranquility" were under threat. These powers might be used to issue directives that "no self-respecting Government" could or would agree to, bringing about a resignation.[58]

When presented with this option, however, the acting Governor balked, wishing to avoid such extraordinary means—and responsibilities. Wavell, frustrated, wrote to Amery that he wished for a permanent governor "who [did] not worry too much about constitutional form and [was] determined to get things done."[59]

Given the recent history of governorship in Bengal, Wavell's call for Governor's Rule in the province was, to say the least, ironic. Sir John Herbert had caused Linlithgow considerable consternation and grief, and then just a few days before *The Statesman* had published its pictures of famine, he had been removed to the hospital for an "appendix operation"—from which he never returned. Hearing the news of Herbert's rapid decline, Linlithgow had grown superstitious, "Government House, Calcutta, continues to add to its lamentable reputation," he wrote to the secretary of state, "you will remember that not only did poor Brabourne collapse there after one of these internal operations, but his acting successor, Reid, then had a serious appendix…and now Jack Herbert."[60] In Herbert's stead Rutherford (then Governor of Bihar) had only reluctantly agreed to serve in Bengal until a permanent replacement could be found. After his first meeting with Sir Thomas, the new viceroy had confided to Amery that he found the acting governor "second-class" and without "fire in his belly."[61] Major-General Mayne also expressed his "gravest doubts" to Wavell about Rutherford's competence, while Rutherford, in turn, "expressed surprise at Mayne's anxiety about the general situation, and said he thought much too much was being made of it. Shortly thereafter he retired to Darjeeling for rest."[62] A few weeks later Amery reported to Churchill: "Rutherford is not in good health and I have no confidence in his capacity to deal with the situation."[63] A salary of Rs. 10,000 each was now being paid to two ill and incompetent governor's of Bengal—in the darkest midst of famine.[64]

Herbert died on 11 December 1943 and a memorial was given at St. John's Cathedral in Calcutta. Wavell attended and later that afternoon met with Mayne, Wakely, and several senior civil servicemen, "none of them optimistic about the future of the food problem in Bengal."[65] Not only was Rutherford complaining of ill-health and seemed to have "lost-heart," but "his senior officials such as Williams, Chief Secretary, and Stevens, the Food Commissioner, [were] lacking in energy, and there [were] signs that they [were] not cooperating with the Army."[66] What was desperately needed, the viceroy informed London again, was a "first-class man who is ready to sacrifice his immediate prospects to do work of the highest importance to the prosecution of the war."[67] Churchill approached Richard Casey, an Australian Parliamentarian who had been drafted into British Civil Service as minister of state in the Middle East in 1942. The prime minister promised Casey that if he accepted the governorship of starving Bengal he would submit his name to the King for a "peerage of the United Kingdom."[68] Casey declined the full offer, citing his intention to run for office in Australia in the elections of 1946, but agreed to serve a truncated term—without knighthood, which might damage his prospects at home.[69]

Hearing that he was getting a "first-class" man for Bengal at last, Wavell redoubled his efforts for Section 93, turning to the secretary of state to have emergency rule authorized by the War Cabinet in London. Amery sympathized with Wavell's desire to circumvent protocol. "Acts," he assured the viceroy, "were meant to be evaded or overridden if necessity is great enough."[70] The secretary of state prepared an extensive brief for the War Cabinet, who met on 11 January and rejected the viceroy's bid. Members worried that if Section 93 was introduced under such circumstances "the Hindus would be delighted," and Muslims might become "actively hostile."[71] If the Government of India, moreover, became responsible for the momentous problems of Bengal, they themselves might be stranded on "very insecure ground."[72] Wavell was severely disappointed with the decision and reminded Amery that in such matters it was really incumbent upon the Cabinet to trust his judgment.[73] Amery, seeking to hearten Wavell, responded that at least a "man of Casey's experience and personality had been appointed."[74]

The mood on the ground in Bengal was less celebratory. When news of Casey's appointment reached long-suffering Midnapore, the reaction in the local journal, *Biplabi*, was caustic:

Following the death of Sir John the big bosses (Churchill, Amery, Wavell and Co.) spent much effort searching the forests and jungles of Australia and suddenly chanced upon a comparatively civilized animal by the name of Mr. Casey; in an announcement they broadcast their intention of making him the ruler of Bengal. There must be some secret reason why Churchill, Amery and Co. awarded the honor…to the land of the kangaroos…a certain class of animals…that are famous for their ability to jump considerable distances with the help of their tails and hind legs…Is it to be tolerated that we will be ruled by an inhabitant of Australia, where Indians cannot exercise any right?[75]

Richard Casey was sworn-in as Governor of Bengal in the Throne Room of Government House, Calcutta on 22 January 1944. After the oaths had been read, a seventeen gun salute was issued from the ramparts of Fort William, and Casey, accompanied by his wife, "left the Throne Room in procession."[76] Erstwhile Acting Governor, Sir Thomas Rutherford, was supposed to return to his post in Bihar, but was granted leave out of India, effective immediately, on health grounds. He had had enough. Casey, on the other hand, had his work cut-out for him, and set diligently to work, sorting through the tortured intricacies of administration in Bengal. He worked hard for a few days, meeting with ministers and secretaries, commissioners and commanders, but did not make it to the end of his second week. On 28 January he ended his diary entry despondently: "I developed a fever and had to go to bed this afternoon. Lieutenant-Colonel Denham White is looking after me."[77] He was incapacitated for several weeks to come—while Bengal continued to starve.

Imports

As Amartya Sen's study of famine mortality in Bengal has confirmed, "very substantially more than half the deaths attributable to the famine of 1943 took place after 1943."[78] In the first half of 1944, the Bengal Famine Enquiry Commission's report recorded, districts which had not been "severely affected" in 1943 saw "a general rise in the death rates" in early 1944, and in districts where starvation had been most prevalent mortality "continued on a high level."[79] A study done by the Calcutta University Department of Anthropology early in 1944 also estimated that two-thirds of the province—more than 20 million people—had been "severely affected" by famine.[80] 25–30 per cent of cultivators with small holdings had lost their land,[81] and landless agricultural laborers, fisherman, skilled artisans, and transportation workers had been rendered homeless and destitute in high numbers—their families fragmented by death and disease, their means of livelihoods bartered for survival, and their communities shattered.[82]

Wavell knew that the only real remedy was to import large quantities of food grains and stabilize prices. The viceroy wrote a sharp telegram to London in the last week of December, warning that the immediate import off 1 million tons of food grains into India was imperative to ward of impending nation-wide catastrophe.[83] The War Cabinet met on 7 February to consider the viceroy's demand. Churchill questioned the statistical basis of the Government of India's request and showed himself "gravely concerned…that shipping…should be used on a major scale to import food into India."[84] The Minister for War Transport, Lord Leathers, concurred. The Cabinet furthermore emphasized that if there was any shortage at all in Bengal, it was statistically insignificant. It was also noted that in Bengal shortage was, in any case, "political in character," being caused by "Marwari supporters of Congress in an effort to embarrass the existing Muslim Government of Bengal, the Government of India and His Majesty's Government."[85] No imports were granted. To appease the viceroy, however, a separate Food Grains Committee was established, consisting of the secretary of state, the minister for war transport, the food minister, and Churchill's closest advisor, now Paymaster-General, Lord Cherwell—who, Amery had noted in his diary, "like Winston, hates India."[86]

When Wavell received news that his request had been denied, he was incensed. The Bengal Famine, he reminded London, "was one of the greatest disasters that [had] befallen any people under British rule and damage to our reputation…is incalculable."[87] The statistics reported, he admitted, had been defective, but had been based on the best estimates available. A "rigid statistical approach," he added, was, in any case, "futile."[88] He had personally discussed the supply situation with all provincial governors and had visited, in person, seven of the eleven provinces. The reality of shortage and the threat of an even more massive, nation-wide famine was manifest. He ended his telegram bluntly: "I warn His Majesty's Government with all seriousness that if they refuse our demands they are risking a catastrophe far greater than the Bengal famine that will have irretrievable effect on their position both at home and abroad. They must either trust the opinion of the man they have appointed to advise them on Indian affairs or replace him."[89]

He was persuaded to remain, but continued his campaign. "This [is] a matter of life and death for hundreds of thousands of Indians," he reminded Amery, "and one by which our good name in the world for justice and kindliness may be irretrievably ruined."[90] Wavell tailored the original request for 1.5 million tons down to 500,000 and requested that a deputation be sent to the United States to ask for help with shipping. In the event that these efforts failed, he also requested permission for India to apply to the newly formed United Nations Relief and Rehabilitation Administration (UNRRA) for aid. In the meantime he recruited the assistance of the Commander-in-Chief for India, General Sir Claude Auchinleck, and the Supreme Commander South-East Asia, Admiral Lord Louis Mountbatten. Both Commanders sent telegrams to the chiefs of staff conveying their conviction that it was "an urgent military necessity for food to be imported into [India.]"[91] The coupling of food imports with war requirements was the only hopeful approach. That hundreds of thousands were continuing to die remained a non-starter.

The War Cabinet met to consider the viceroy's "counter-offensive" on 21 February.[92] They had before them his series of forceful telegrams, together with those of Mountbatten and Auchinleck, and also the Food Grain Committee's anemic report. After short deliberation it was agreed that little could be done. The minister of war transport suggested that the 50,000 tons of Iraqi barley promised would be replaced by 50,000 tons of wheat—at some future date—but the shipment of another 50,000 tons already *en route* to India from Australia would have to be cancelled and redirected to the Balkans. In all a total net loss of 100,000 tons was incurred. A telegram to the viceroy was sent conveying these conclusions and also noting that the minister of war transport was "fully satisfied that [the] United States have no shipping." An appeal to UNRRA, Lord Leathers added, was, likewise, pointless, as they had no shipping of their own.

On receiving this news, Wavell cabled to Amery angrily: "To expect me to hold the critical food situation here with empty hands is stupid and shortsighted."[93] Once again, the hand of Churchill's confident and chief council, Lord Cherwell, was deplored. "I see from your letter," Wavell added, "that that old menace and fraud the Professor was called in to advise against me. The fact is that the P.M. has calculated his war plans without any consideration at all of India's needs."[94] The viceroy sent telegrams to Auchinleck and Mountbatten with the request that they might arrange, on their own, for the replacement of military cargo with food grain imports for India. They responded that they could, and petitioned their chiefs of staff to endorse the practice. The chiefs of staff met on 18 March and wrote a brief advocating the immediate import of at least 200,000 tons of wheat to India, the allocation of 10 per cent of cargo space on military vessels, and an approach to America for help with additional shipping. The War Cabinet convened the following day and agreed only to the import of 200,000 tons of grain to India in the coming six months.[95] In its conclusion it was stipulated, however, that there would be "no prospect" of additional imports in 1944 and the allocation of 10 per cent of military shipping for food was found unfeasible. Lord Leathers also again expressed his aversion to any approach to the U.S. for assistance.

Wavell was shocked and in a terse reply noted that the import of 200,000 tons was a mere one-sixth of India's present needs.[96] Procurement in Bengal had continued to be moribund and crop damages were being reported from several other provinces. In the third week of April he again approached Amery for further action. Taking a novel approach, this time he informed Amery that "the promised import of 200 [thousand tons] just balances civil position with nothing (repeat nothing) to meet defense requirements of 724 [thousand tons] for 12 months...I am informing Supreme Commander and Commander-in-Chief of [our] inability to meet service requirement."[97] The viceroy's telegram came as a "great shock" to London.[98] Meanwhile, at a recent meeting of the Indian Food Grains Committee, Lord Cherwell, "The Professor," had suggested that "a certain number of wealthy Indians should be hanged," and that this might solve the crisis.[99] The secretary of state was of the mind that the import of food grains might be a better measure. But at a meeting on 24 April, the War Cabinet again concluded that nothing could be done—neither hanging nor imports. Churchill was "truculent" as ever, "and came very near saying that we could not let Indian starvation interfere with operations."[100] A telegram to Washington was, however, reluctantly agreed to.[101]

In the telegram mention was made of Wavell's "gravest warnings," and also of the "grievous famine" of 1943. But mention was also made of the "good crop of rice" in Bengal and no specific information of the extent of shortfall that the viceroy anticipated was included. His Majesty's Government had done its honest best, Churchill assured his counterpart. "I have been able to arrange for 350,000 tons of wheat to be shipped to India from Australia during the first nine months of 1944. I cannot see how we could do more."[102] When Wavell received a draft of the telegram he responded wryly to the secretary of state, "I see that the Prime Minster speaks of having made *350,000* tons of wheat available—which apparently means a promise to us of another 150,000 tons over what has already been promised."[103] Amery assured the viceroy that that was not the case: "Leathers put it that way in order to make it clear to the President that we had done our best."[104] President Roosevelt, apparently, felt that that was good enough. More than one month later he cabled back to express his "utmost sympathy," but reported that he would be "unable on military grounds to consent to the diversion of shipping."[105]

Receiving the news of Roosevelt's refusal, Wavell was despondent. "There has been dangerous, and as I think, *deliberate* procrastination. I have never believed that the tonnage required to enable me to deal properly with our food problem would make any real difference to [military] operations in the West or here."[106]

Famine Enquiry

A short time later, according to the officially compiled *Medical History of the Bengal Famine*, on the morning of 10 July 1944, a 32 year-old, "male Hindu," identified only as "Netai," was picked up from the streets of Calcutta and removed in an Air Raid Precaution lorry to the Campbell Medical Hospital Calcutta.[107] Netai had been starving for at least six months and was weak and emaciated on admittance. He had a history of intermittent fever for two months, but tested negative for malaria. His fever may have been the result of *kala-azar* (black fever) or it may have resulted from pulmonary infection or other organ failure. His left lung had impaired resonance, fine crepitus, and his breathing was diminished. It is possible that he, like millions of others, had spent the winter without shelter or clothing, which, combined with starvation, had left him with chronic pneumonia. The hospital had no reagents to run a sputum test to confirm or contradict a diagnosis of tuberculosis, which was also a distinct possibility. High levels of phosphate in his urine suggested kidney dysfunction. He also had acute edema in his feet and hands, and like all patients in his sample group, severe anemia. His blood sugar was also far below normal and he was suffering from diarrhea. The diarrhea may have been from any number of infectious diseases such as para-sprue or it may have been a "specific type of diarrhea found in starving individuals which is not infective in origin and may be called 'famine diarrhea.'"[108] He was spoon fed barley water and was administered sub-coetaneous saline. On 18 July his condition was still deteriorating; his pulse was feeble and his respiration hurried. He died on 20 July 1944 in bed 20A at Calcutta's Campbell hospital. His body was claimed by relatives the same day. No post mortem was done.

Eleven days later, on 31 July, the "Royal Commission to Enquire into the Bengal Famine of 1943" convened in Delhi under the chairmanship of I.C.S. Officer, Sir John Woodhead. Woodhead, a white British citizen, had been appointed by the India Office in London despite protests in India that an Indian should preside over proceedings.[109] In keeping with current colonial policy, one Hindu representative, S.V. Ramamurthy, and one Muslim representative, Afzal Hussain, were also included as examiners. The panel was rounded off by an expert on public health, Dr W.R. Aykroyd, and a representative member of the Indian business community, Manilal Nanavati. The terms of reference were to be, as already mentioned, future-oriented. Care was to be taken so that "officials giving evidence [would be] assured of complete immunity of victimization,"[110] and the entire proceedings were to be held *in camera*, as "it would be most embarrassing if officials were examined in public."[111] Witnesses were called to testify from the Government of India, the Government of Bengal, military and private relief organizations, and commercial interests involved in the rice trade. No testimony was given by any representative of the India Office or His Majesty's Government in London.

The Famine Enquiry Commission was, in some sense and as already mentioned, primarily an effort to punctuate the "Bengal Famine of 1943." It was also, however, a fairly thorough examination of the economic, political, and social context of famine in Bengal. As such, the full transcript of the proceedings provides an extensive record of the events, personalities, and forces that characterized famine in Bengal. The Commission's *Report on Bengal*, published in 1945, was, on the other hand, a relatively brief narrative summary of the information gathered, edited to conform to the "terms of reference" which had been outlined beforehand. The full proceedings were never published, but remain in the public record at the National Archives of India in New Delhi. The wealth of information that is contained there-in has been used extensively throughout this study. Here, certain items of testimony given at the Famine Enquiry Commission will be examined in an effort to foreground the context in which the proceedings actually took place.

On 14 August 1944, Mr. Justice Braund, Regional Food Commissioner, Eastern India, testified before the Woodhead Commission. As food commissioner since March 1943, Braund had intimate knowledge of the food supply and distribution system in Bengal. He was also intricately involved with the *aman* procurement scheme of 1944. In his testimony Braund gave a frank and unflattering picture of the state of affairs in the province. Mill capacity was wholly inadequate, the lack of storage facilities was a serious problem, transportation services were extremely deficient, and the staff of the Civil Supplies Department was still in a state of chaos.[112] The high price of rice had been caused by a systemic breakdown involving all of these factors—none of which had yet been remedied. The current price of rice, he noted, was still more than four times higher than in early 1942. After hearing the grim picture that Braund sketched, Nanavati asked whether or not rice was yet within the reach of the poor in Bengal. "No, it is not always," Braund replied. Lieutenant-Colonel K.S. Fitch, Deputy Surgeon General of Bengal, confirmed Braund's surmise admitting that, "generally…there is still a lot of underfeeding."[113]

The honorary secretary of the British Indian Association drew the implicit conclusion that neither Braund nor Fitch had ventured: "the continuation of famine conditions," he testified, "may be said to be persisting."[114] Mr Barman, of the Calcutta Corporation, also explained to the Commission excitedly on 13 September 1944, "there are yet famine deaths. I can cite a famine case examined by Dr Roy, just at the junction of Howrah. He died only yesterday being famine-stricken." Nanavati rejoined perplexed, "Is it happening here?" Dr Ahmed of the Corporation responded in Barman's stead, "Yes, there are quite a lot of people dying even now."[115] Members of the Provincial Kisan Sabha, a peasant rights organization with the closest links of any to the rural poor, described conditions as "a complete crack-up of rural life—rural economy, rural society and rural humanity—this is the reality of 1944. The village artisans; weavers, fishermen, boatmen, black-smiths—all have been ruined. Fishermen have no fishing nets, boatmen have no boats, weavers get no yarn, black-smiths get no iron or steel."[116] According to their estimates 10 million had been forced from their homes by hunger. Three and a half million had died. "The remaining six and a half million—homeless, landless, and denuded of all that is human, are moving about in the 90,000 villages of Bengal…[but] let nobody think that famine has ended with this toll."[117]

Pervasive ruin of society, dislocation of economic life, and the continuing hardships of scarcity, inflation, hunger, and disease were endemic facts of life for the majority of the population of the province. The mostly Hindu, "middle-class," though surviving better than the (mostly Muslim) rural poor, were not immune. By April 1944 the prices of a wide array of essential commodities in Bengal had risen by an average of more than 250 per cent in just three years.[118] The price of lentils, a primary supplement to a rice diet for those who could afford them, had more than tripled, and eggs were three and a half times more dear. Fish, which was the most important source of protein for the middle-class, had also more than tripled in price, due to a stubborn scarcity of ice for preservation. Coal and kerosene prices were likewise grossly inflated and long queues led to daily scenes of frustration and turmoil at control shops throughout Bengal. Even with fuel for cooking, matches were at times unavailable, and cooking oil prices had risen nearly 400 per cent. Government had commandeered a full 70 per cent of the country's supply of paper at the beginning of the war, which created a paper shortage that crippled publishing, small businesses, and educational enterprises central to the middle-class economy and culture.[119] Lead pencils had increased in price by 1,500 per cent and the acute scarcity of cloth was causing indignity for the poor and middle-class alike.[120] In conclusion to his testimony before the Famine Enquiry Commission, the District Magistrate of Faridpur noted, "it is now people with fixed incomes, middle-classes, lower middle-classes, who are gradually getting impoverished, both financially and in health."[121]

Politics

If, as Sugata Bose has argued, class conflict in Bengal "did not, without external influence, flow easily into the communal mould,"[122] the devastations of famine provided a unique and exceptional circumstance for just such an eventuality. Survival in the midst of death by deprivation was a double-edged sword: it could only be exacted at the price of the death of others. Callousness and self-interest thrived. Charity became extremely strained and society became mean and chary in the furnace of want. The director-general of food for the Government of India, identified these psychological factors as part and parcel of famine: "Public confidence," he testified before the Enquiry Commission, "was so undermined and people felt so insecure that everyone tried to keep what he had in his own hands."[123] Those able to make do, he continued, "were simply callous to the suffering of fellow-villagers and the civic spirit was entirely absent."[124] Corruption thrived, and "honesty," representatives of the Provincial Kisan Sabha attested, had been "eliminated." The famine of food, they asserted, had engendered a "moral famine" of equally disturbing proportions.[125] Religious bigotry under such circumstances, it is no stretch to conclude, can be understood as yet another pernicious disease that thrived in the wake of famine.

By the autumn of 1944, the Muslim League's call for a separate state of Pakistan had become increasingly vociferous and now represented the most pressing "national" dilemma of all—not least of all because of famine itself. The question of Muslim freedom from Hindu economic dominance had long been a primary concern of the Muslim elite who formed the backbone of the All-India Muslim League.[126] Catastrophic economic failure, leading to acute scarcity, despair, and ultimately mass death from starvation, only accentuated the urgency of the issue, providing a stark backdrop upon which the idyll of Pakistan could be sketched. At the All-India Muslim League's Council meeting in 1943, Bengal's Chief Minister, Khwaja Nazimuddin, argued that famine had clearly shown that Pakistan was a necessity for the poor Muslim masses. The famine had demonstrated, he declared, "that situations like the present cannot be tackled by a Central Government and in the future no Central or Federal scheme for India can ever hope to meet a situation like this."[127] Meanwhile, at the same meeting, "a uniform food policy for all Muslim majority provinces" was outlined by Jinnah.[128] The idea was, in some sense, a test run of "Pakistan," an exercise organized to presage the benefits of Muslim political solidarity and economic independence.

"Pakistan" was fast becoming an issue the Congress could not ignore. By the middle of 1944 a new scheme for a final "communal settlement" was advanced by ex-Congress faithful, and close confidant to Gandhi, C.R. Rajagopalachari. The "Rajagopalachari Formula," as it came to be known, represented what Secretary of State Amery termed a "conditional and partial concession of 'Pakistan.'"[129] The formula advanced a plan for the Muslim League and Congress to work together towards self-rule while deferring the question of a fully separate Muslim state until after the war. At that time, according to the "formula" district-by-district plebiscites in Muslim-majority provinces would be taken to decide the terms of a possible division of India—with an ambiguous caveat for "mutual agreements" in relation to defense, commerce and other "essential purposes in the event of partition."[130] Such a program, it was well understood, would guarantee the partition of the provinces of Bengal and the Punjab—two extremely important Muslim-majority provinces—along communal lines. The likely division of Bengal and the Punjab and even the hint of a central administrative apparatus were deeply antithetical to the Muslim League's professed main-line, but Gandhi's acceptance of the scheme lent it enticing relevance.[131]

Many Congress followers also supported the overture, but acceptance was far from universal. The Hindu Mahasabha, in particular, was vehemently opposed to any detente with the Muslim League and was especially hostile to even the mention of "Pakistan" in national debate. To Hindu Nationalists, Gandhi's support of the plan amounted to a reckless betrayal of Hindu interests. S.P. Mookerjee, who had once declared that "the indivisibility of India was his God,"[132] was shouted down at a Mahasabha rally in Calcutta for his suggestion that the Mahasabha might support the "Rajagopalachari Formula" along with Congress.[133] In August he had traveled to Delhi to discuss the particulars with Gandhi and it was reported that he had left "much encouraged." It is entirely likely, however, that his own ministerial aspirations in Bengal were at least as influential as Gandhi's arguments. When the Jinnah-Gandhi negotiations proved abortive, and sentiments between the Muslim League and Congress hardened, S.P. Mookerjee ventured to broker no further compromise with the League and again retreated into bitter opposition.

Meanwhile, disruptions and deadlock in the Bengal Assembly had all but halted provincial administrative machinery. Governor Casey visited the chamber during a debate on the Secondary Education Bill[134] and found the proceedings "perfectly disgraceful."[135] The "Hindus in the Opposition" he wrote, gave a "splendid example of intolerance," shutting down all debate and holding the floor by main force. When the governor argued for the immediate removal of the speaker, Nazimuddin warned him that he was unable to do so "for fear of riot in the house, which would be followed by communal disturbances in Bengal generally."[136] Meanwhile, the detente between the Congress and the Muslim League at the center had facilitated the possibility of an otherwise highly unlikely alliance between Mookerjee and H.S. Suhrawardy. The Muslim League in Bengal was, at this time, becoming increasingly divided, with Chief Minister Nazimuddin seen to represent non-Bengali, elite Muslim interests, and Food Minister and Midnapore native, H.S. Suhrawardy, representing the Bengali rural and urban poor.[137] A short time after the near "riot in the house" the opposition, led by Mookerjee, approached Suhrawardy to suggest a coup against Nazimuddin.[138] Suhrawardy approached the governor in a quandary and Casey warned the food minister against a plot "clearly designed to split and confuse the Muslim League forces still further."[139] Suhrawardy heeded his advice for the time being.

Meanwhile, conditions on the ground in Bengal continued to be extremely grim. Malaria hit its peak in November 1944, with as many as 51.7 per cent of blood samples examined at Calcutta hospitals testing positive for parasites.[140] Cholera and smallpox were still decimating the countryside,[141] and the price of rice still remained beyond the reach of millions.[142] Rationing had been operating in Calcutta and Dacca, but the rest of the province was still without. Even in Calcutta, where famine was officially a thing of the past, the urban poor lived on the absolute margins of life and death. Governor Casey toured the slums of the city in December 1944 and was shocked: "I have seen something of the way that hundreds of thousands of the citizens of Calcutta are obliged to live," he reported, "[and] I have been horrified."[143] The myth of Calcutta's relative prosperity had been belied. "Human beings cannot let other human being exist under these conditions," the governor opined—but help was still a long time coming.

Wavell, meanwhile, had maintained his crusade for food imports and by the end of 1944 had managed to wrangle 1 million tons out of

London. On New Year's Eve he sat at his desk and mused: "So ends 1944. On the whole not a bad year for India…"[144] Richard Casey, on the ground in Bengal, shared none of the viceroy's optimism. On 1 March 1945, after thirteen months on the job as governor, he drafted a frank and gloomy report to the viceroy. "The Empire has cause for shame," he wrote, "in fact…after a century and a half of British rule, we can point to no achievement worth the name in any direction."[145] He continued,

> What stands out principally in my mind is the pitiful inadequacy of the administration of the province. Judged by any standards which I am acquainted with or which I can imagine, the administration is of a very low order. On these standards Bengal has, practically speaking, no irrigation or drainage, a medieval system of agriculture, no roads, no education, no cottage industries, completely inadequate hospitals, no effective health services, and no adequate machinery to cope with distress. There are not even plans to make good these deficiencies—and even if there were, it would be quite impossible to pay for them, as things are.[146]

The I.C.S. ranks, in particular were of extremely low caliber and their numbers "grossly inadequate to the barest needs of a modern administration on the most elementary schedule."[147] Little help had been given him from the Government of India or His Majesty's Government, and little light was on the horizon. "In short," he concluded, "I believe that unless I am given more active assistance, I will have to discuss with you whether or not it is worth while my remaining here."[148]

A few weeks later the Ministry in Bengal collapsed. The virulence of attacks by the opposition, together with the forces of division inside the Muslim League, had weakened Nazimuddin's regime to the breaking point. The end came on the 28th of March 1945: two years to the day after Fazlul Huq had been unceremoniously removed from power. Behind the scenes Nazimuddin had been attempting an alliance with Kiran Sankar Roy of the "orthodox" Congress, which would have given him the leverage to remain in power despite routine defections by the Suhrawardy faction, who now frequently crossed lines to vote with the opposition.[149] Negotiations between Nazimuddin and Roy broke down, however, and on 28 March a trap was laid for the chief minister. An almost incidental Agricultural Grant Bill came to the floor and was defeated when eighteen members of the ruling party crossed over to the opposition. Failure to pass the Agricultural Grant tied up the budget bill and failure to pass the budget amounted to a no-confidence vote in the

Ministry. The Bengal Ministry was disbanded on 29 March and Section 93 was declared in Bengal, with Governor Casey, a disillusioned and interim executive, gaining extensive emergency powers to govern the province without democratic interference.

The Lean Season

By this time allied forces in Europe and Asia were moving from victory to victory and the end of the war was now well within sight. Japanese and Indian National Army troops had been successfully fought back from the boundary regions of British India by the autumn of 1944. They retreated to Mandalay in Burma, which in turn fell to Allied advance in March 1945. On 2 May, Rangoon was recaptured and the Japanese threat to India had been all but extinguished. Less than a week later, on 8 May, Nazi Germany unconditionally surrendered to the Allies and the streets of London and New York were mobbed by victory celebrations. On the very same day, the Famine Enquiry Commission's *Report on Bengal* was published. Although the report detailed the pervasive failure of the colonial administrative apparatus in India, as publication had coincided with V-E Day the viceroy noted, "the impact [was] considerably lessened!"[150] The collateral damage of famine could hardly take headlines on such a historic day. Governor Casey, however, remained reflective. "There does not seem to be much doubt," he jotted in his diary that evening, "but that India represents an administrative and governmental failure on a scale that fortunately is not common in the world…It all makes one very ashamed."[151]

Wavell, also skeptical of the merits of empire, had been pushing for a resumption of negotiations for self-rule in India since the beginning of his viceregal tenure. Churchill had been foremost in opposition to resuming the process and no moves at all had been made since the failed Cripps Mission. With the war in Europe now over and elections in Britain scheduled for July 1945, however, the prime minister gave the viceroy permission to revive the political process. The Congress Working Committee was released from detention on 15 June and a conference was scheduled at Simla towards the end of the month. The proposal to be presented by the viceroy differed little from that rejected by Congress at the time of the Cripps Mission, but Allied progress in the war now made the prospect of provisional "Indianization" with the promise of more comprehensive independence after the war much more enticing. In the first few days of the conference there was considerable optimism, but negotiations broke down when Jinnah refused to allow any party but the Muslim League to appoint Muslim representatives to sit on the Viceroy's Executive Council. The Muslim League, Jinnah contended, should be the sole representative body of Muslims in India, and Jinnah its "sole spokesman." This idea proved wholly unacceptable to Congress, whose President, Maulana Azad, was himself a Muslim. The viceroy, siding this time with Congress, was dismayed by Jinnah's "arrogance and intransigence."[152] Negotiations fell apart.

General elections had meanwhile taken place in the United Kingdom and much to the shock of Conservatives, they and their heroic wartime leader, Winston Churchill, were swept from power by the Labour Party in a landslide victory. Clement Attlee replaced Churchill as prime minister and Lord Pethick-Lawrence replaced Leopold Amery as secretary of state for India. The Labour party was assumed to advocate Indian independence, and despite the failure of the Simla Conference there was anticipation that the new government would move in a "liberal" direction. Wavell traveled to London towards the end of August to meet the new leadership and though he found the leadership paying certain lip service to Indian independence, he found that "the rank and file of the Labour party and the country at large take little interest in India."[153] He returned to the sub-continent with little more to report than that elections to the General Assembly and provincial legislatures would be held—for the first time since 1937—in the coming months. The viceroy wrote to Pethick-Lawrence just a few days after he returned to inform the secretary of state that "serious scarcity of rice in Bengal" was anticipated.[154]

It was the end of summer and once again the province was approaching its lean season when local reserves were perennially running low, prices were rising, and anticipation of the coming *aman* crop was all that kept many of the province's poor from absolute despair—even in a normal year. In 1945, however, it was being predicted that the *aman* harvest was likely to be just 65 per cent of average.[155] The monsoon rains had failed, drought conditions were prevailing, the province was still being devastated by disease, and by August fears were rising that Bengal was facing imminent starvation on a large scale once again. Military medical and food relief had been withdrawn in late 1944 and little had been done by the provincial government to replace the loss. Casey had initiated an ambitious program to re-build country boats in order to reha-bilitate the dismantled transportation infrastructure, but the scheme was riddled with corruption and was flagging badly.[156] An increasingly acute coal shortage was crippling rail movements throughout the country and the transport of food remained a low priority.[157] Land rehabilitation schemes were entangled in political maneuvering and millions in Bengal remained homeless. Calcutta itself was now fully rationed, but the rest of Bengal, with the exception of Dacca and Narayangunge, were with-out any rationing scheme at all. Meanwhile, supplies as well as prices were still subject to the vicissitudes of the "free market."[158] And perhaps most alarming of all, the supply of industrial Calcutta, which was widely understood to have been deeply implicated in the calamity of 1943, had been removed from Government of India responsibility and the city would, once again, be dependent on rice from the country-side.

Victory over Japan under these circumstances meant little in Bengal. Repressive wartime controls remained in effect and hunger continued to be the order of the day throughout the districts. In August 1945 Fazlul Huq was on the stump at Calcutta University, thrashing the Muslim League and warning that their policies imperiled Bengal with the threat of an even greater famine than the "last." Casey called on Huq and scolded him for his "exploitation of the food situation for political ends."[159] The speech, he chided the ex-chief minister, had been a "naughty one" that the governor could not tolerate. Shortly thereafter the governor summoned the editors of all the major newspapers in the province and implored them, as well, "to desist from crying 'famine.'"[160] S.P. Mookerjee was, meanwhile, maintaining his attacks, warning of an impending "second famine" and reminding his audiences that an "Anglo-Muslim League conspiracy" had been responsible for the greatest catastrophe in living memory. The same, he added, provided "a bitter foretaste of Pakistan rule in Bengal kept in power by the British bayo-nets."[161] He also reminded his gatherings of the singular relief work that the Mahasabha had done and assured them that they would continue the fight to make "famine's recurrence impossible."[162] H.S. Suhrawardy was, at the same time, reinforcing his own public image, expanding the connections and influence that he had accrued as food minister, particu-larly with the increasingly active Muslim student community who had earned important political capital in voluntary service at government "gruel kitchens" during relief efforts.[163]

For the poor of Bengal, however, the autumn of 1945 proved yet another act in the ongoing script of dislocation, hunger, disease, and unmitigated despair. The continuing "cloth famine," in particular, was becoming increasingly acute. Governor Casey while on a visit to New Delhi approached the Government of India's Department of Civil Supplies about "the nakedness of Bengal," but was able to move "hardly a *dhoti*" out of the Central Government.[164] As the cold weather approached the situation become only more dire. Relief agencies operating in the districts were compelled by law to accept shipments of cloth from warehouses in Calcutta, regardless of quality. The district magistrate in Jessore, for one, complained bitterly about this, noting that "some of the cloth sent [was] reported…to be so moth-eaten or so rotten that it cannot stand the slightest strain. This is grossly unfair on our local handling agents who have to pay the Calcutta agent irrespective of the quality delivered… and also on the public, especially the poor folk who have to pay hard-earned rupees for bad stuff."[165] The dead, as of autumn 1945, faired only a little better. Protests had been raised about the lack of cloth, even, to cover the deceased, and special provisions were made to ration whole cloth for corpses. Following standard procedures related to the dead in general, however, rations for mortuary cloth were allocated according to religious community, with yardage figured according to respective Hindu, Muslim or Christian needs.[166]

Meanwhile, grim prospects for the rice harvest continued to unsettle prices and the black market was again holding sway.[167] By September the chief secretary was reporting "appreciable demand for rice from Government stocks for the districts."[168] At the same time, rations in factories were being reduced and the quality of rice being doled out was still extremely poor.[169] By November "steps [were being] taken to reinforce Calcutta's stocks by [again] moving stocks from the districts."[170] Massive retrenchment in war-related industries had also left hundreds of thousands unemployed and the general mood in the city was growing increasingly restive. Strikes for "victory bonuses" were widespread and at General Electric's Garden Reach factory "there was a riot…on account of bad rice supplied to the workers and the Manager was assaulted."[171] In the countryside, as winter approached, conditions deteriorated further. In Bankura district there was "agitation over distress" and reports of death from starvation.[172] In the districts of Midnapore, Khulna, Dacca and Bankura "Test Works" were opened (the final measure of determining famine according to the Bengal Famine Code)—all drawing tens of thousands of "volunteers."[173]

Disturbances

On 21 November 1945—amidst such bad news from every quarter—Calcutta erupted into violence. The trouble began when a large crowd of students gathered to protest the trials of Indian National Army soldiers captured by British authorities on the defeat of Japan in Burma.[174] After a rally at Wellington Square in downtown Calcutta, a procession began towards Government headquarters at Dalhousie. The meeting itself had been authorized, but when the crowd approached Dharmatala Street they were met by a cordon of police constables and a tense standoff ensued. The confrontation grew more heated in the early evening and by morning there were reports that shots had been fired and at least three student demonstrators had been killed. By the afternoon of 22 November rioting was widespread with outbreaks becoming "steadily more violent in character."[175] Student demonstrators by this time had been joined by a diverse contingent of urban residents including taxi drivers, "up country" laborers, Bengali factory workers, and, according to the governor, "the hooligan element [more] generally."[176] Running battles between rioting crowds and the police and military were fought throughout the city. After four days of violence at least thirty-three people had been killed, with another 400 seriously injured, including 200 police, fire brigade workers, and military personnel.

The activities of the students on the 21 November, Governor Casey informed Wavell, could not explain the amplification and diversification of violence that rocked the city. The disorder, in this sense, "was not the result of a widespread conspiracy to plunge Calcutta into anarchy."[177] Rather the violence emerged spontaneously and could only be understood to represent a diverse range of animosities, grievances, and anxieties. It also exampled an unprecedented sense of desperation. "Both in North and South Calcutta," Casey reported, "a feature of the disturbances comparatively new to Bengal was that crowds when fired on largely stood their ground or at most receded a little, to return again to attack."[178] The targets of the crowds included police installations, public transport facilities, symbols of governmental authority, and military vehicles and personnel. In a telling and highly significant sign of the times, attacks were also made on government ration shops and private retail outlets were forced to shuttered their establishments by angry mobs.[179] Department of Civil Supply lorries were also targeted, some being attacked and burned and as many as six going completely "missing" during the disorder.[180] The Calcutta Rationing Department issued a press release on 24 November. "It is in the interest of the people themselves," the publication read, "to see that Food Rationing lorries are enabled to work so that people may be fed."[181]

That the citizens of Calcutta were acting contrary to their own interests was a viewpoint also held by all the major political parties. On 21 November protestors had tied together Muslim League, Congress, and Communist Party flags in a rare gesture of political unity.[182] The parties themselves, however, quickly denied involvement, making claims and counter-claims implicating rival organizations. Muslim League representatives rushed to the Governor's office on the 22nd to assure Casey that the League "deplored the present disturbances and disowned any responsibility for them."[183] They, in turn, fingered Sarat Bose, leader of the Bengal Congress. Bose also unequivocally denied involvement and went so far as to issue a "frantic appeal" to residents of Calcutta, urging them to remain "disciplined" to Congress directives.[184] Bose subsequently put blame for the disturbances on the communist party,[185] with whom Congress was recently having very bitter differences.[186] The Communist Party, though involved in the initial protest through their students' wing, was, by 23 November, touring the affected areas in "propaganda cars…dissuading students from further participation."[187] After three days, the lack of support from organized political parties precipitated a "sudden collapse of the trouble and the speedy return to normal conditions."[188]

"Normal conditions" in the autumn of 1945, however, and as detailed above, were a grind of poverty, ill-health, and acute anxiety. That this popular "disturbance" was short-circuited by lack of institutional support is a sad and telling commentary on the disconnect between party and popular interests in Bengal. After several long years of colossal calamity, suffering, and insecurity, and with the specter of acute food shortage again looming on the immediate horizon, the desperate measures that characterized the November disturbances in Calcutta can, and should, be understood as a revolution denied. "The most significant feature of the disturbances," writes historian Pranab Kumar Chatterjee, "was absence of communal strife…no trace of mutual rancor between the communities was evident all through the November episode."[189] That communal rancor was, on the other hand, becoming increasingly enmeshed in party politics, particularly with elections scheduled for the coming months, is significant. The emergence of unified rebellion in November 1945 is testimony to a sense of solidarity with which the population of Calcutta understood their highly uncertain collective fate. The political elite, on the other hand, continued to channel the anxieties and frustrations of the masses into an entirely more sectarian mold.

In February 1946, disturbances again broke out in Calcutta that mirrored the November model. The flashpoint was again the trial of INA soldiers, but, again, the "disorder" that ensued belied the deep and pervasive anxieties of a population under siege. Demonstrators fought pitched battles with police and military forces across the city, burned government transport, looted shops, and, again, stood their ground against police and military firings. "As in November," historian Sumit Sarkar notes, "there quickly developed a remarkable unity in the streets between students and workers, Muslims and Hindus."[190] Governor Casey, whose bags were already packed for Australia, met with Muslim League stalwart Hussein Suhrawardy concluding that the day's activities "show[ed] quite clearly that [he had] no recognized authority over his followers."[191] Sarat Bose again disassociated Congress from the disturbances as well.[192] After two days of clashes, eighty-four people were dead and more than 300 injured.[193] Meanwhile, the incoming Governor, Sir Fredrick Burrows, was scheduled to arrive in Calcutta on 13 February to assume Emergency Rule in Bengal. Because of the disturbances Casey had to telephone the viceroy to advise delay. Transporting Burrows from the airport would "take a great many police (who [were] being sorely tried) away from much more important tasks."[194]

"The Almost Revolution"[195] of February 1946 was the last of its kind in colonial Calcutta. The conflagrations that Burrows would have to deal with in the coming months were of a much different, and darker, nature.

Second Famine

The viceroy informed London on 1 January 1946 that the food situation in India was critical. If Congress called for a mass movement, Wavell warned, food shortage would surely intensify the response.[196] "To have another disastrous famine within the space of three years," he cautioned further, "would afflict the conscience of the world."[197] He lobbied for immediate and substantial imports, but, yet again, received less than satisfactory replies. "India's need is unquestionable," the Labour Party's secretary of state responded, "but...it would be foolish to raise false expectations of greatly increased imports."[198] Perhaps, the secretary of state added, a cut in rations could save the situation.[199] Wavell found the suggestion that rations in India should be reduced to 12 oz. per day deplorable. He pointed out that a 12 oz. ration amounted to only 1,200 calories, "which any health expert [would] admit is a hopelessly inadequate diet."[200] He also puzzled at the audacity of the India Office in London. "I cannot believe," he bristled, "that anyone will contemplate keeping such a large population on the edge of starvation for the whole of this critical year."[201]

With few other options, however, Wavell contemplated this exact course. He met with his Executive Council and found them, somewhat surprisingly, amenable to the idea of a ration cut. A few weeks later he met with Congress President, Maulana Azad, and even more surprisingly, found Azad agreeable to a reduction of rations as well. In a press statement Azad explained that Congress was "essentially a political organization based on the will and aspirations of the people...fully alive to the urgency of the new spirit and to the impatience of the younger generation. But we are equally conscious of our heavy responsibility at this critical time."[202] Part and parcel of that responsibility was to urge the public to co-operate with India's current colonial caretakers, which meant accepting Government expediencies. In this context, he reasoned, the cut in rations was "a far-sighted measure for saving millions of lives."[203] The leadership of the Muslim League similarly complied with the necessity of reducing rations and pushing the masses of India further towards "the edge of starvation."[204]

In the winter elections the Congress and the Muslim League had been established as the overwhelmingly dominant players on the national scene. Congress had commandeered a majority in the Central Assembly, winning fifty-seven out of a total of 102 seats and earning 91.3 per cent of the non-Muslim vote.[205] The Muslim League scored a parallel victory, winning all thirty Assembly seats reserved for Muslims after garnering 86.6 per cent of the Muslim vote. The fact that franchise was extremely limited—less than 1 per cent for the Central Assembly elections—did little to curtail the enthusiasm with which each party now claimed broad and sweeping representation. The election results also served to reify the rivalry between the League and Congress, centralizing the over-determining issue of contention between them, namely Pakistan. A high level Cabinet Mission was organized by Wavell in conjunction with the India Office in London in order to hammer out a final resolution that would determine the terms of a transfer of power. The "Cabinet Mission," as it was called, traveled to India and commenced its work in March 1946. By 16 May the Mission had come up with a plan that won tentative agreement from both parties.

The May 16th plan involved a three-tiered federation, with a weak central authority that would remain in control of defense, foreign affairs and communications. Provinces would be "grouped" according to majority religious communities, with Group A comprised of Hindu majority provinces in south and central India, and Groups B and C consisting of the four Muslim majority provinces: Punjab and the North Western Frontier Province in the west; Bengal and Assam in the east. Each grouping would be given wide-ranging governmental autonomy and the minority community in any of the three groupings would be guaranteed a measure of equity by the balance of power in the groupings where they maintained majority status. This plan, it was thought, would give Jinnah and the Muslim League a very close approximation of the "Pakistan" that was central to their demands—particularly in establishing the entire provinces of Bengal and Punjab under Muslim control—as well as placating Congress with the promise of a unified central authority. Though they had given provisional approval to the scheme in May, however, the Congress leadership began to back-pedal quickly, most conspicuously on whether groupings were to be understood as compulsory or based on plebiscites. Further acrimony mounted in June as the Congress leadership became ever-more equivocal, with leading industrialists lobbying for a stronger central government that would guarantee their economic primacy over the sub-continent as a whole.[206] Around this particular issue Congress support for the negotiations finally collapsed.

Equally rancorous dispute surrounded the composition of an Interim Government, which would oversee the constitutional and administrative processes in the lead-up to independence. The Muslim League demanded parity with Congress in any provisional government and again stipulated that only they should be allowed to appoint Muslim representatives to the Interim Council. The Cabinet Mission conceded to these demands, but Congress remained vehemently opposed to the monopoly on Muslim representation proposed by the League. In turn, the Muslim League argued that if Congress was unwilling to participate in the Interim Government proposed by the Cabinet Mission, it was incumbent upon the viceroy to move ahead with the formation of a provisional government without them. Members of the Cabinet Mission, however, fearing a mass movement if Congress was excluded, rejected Jinnah's insistence and on 26 June the viceroy announced that while constitutional negotiations would continue, the formation of an Interim Government would not be presently possible. Three days later the Cabinet Mission left India.

The viceroy, for his part, felt that, "however absorbed [Government] may [have been] in the constitutional problems, the food situation [was] even more urgent."[207] Promises of imports from the U.S. had proved hollow, and London had little more to suggest than that India might be able to work a deal for sixty large tractors which were for sale at the American Air Depot at Agra.[208] Meanwhile, Wavell complained, the Muslim League and Congress were content to "pay lip service to the idea that the food crisis should not be a matter of party politics, but in the end they will not forgo party advantage even in the face of famine."[209] Animosities were nowhere higher than in Bengal. The Muslim League, campaigning on the "single issue of Pakistan,"[210] won a substantial victory in provincial elections, registering 93 per cent of the Muslim vote, and in April consummate Bengali political strongman, Hussein Shaheed Suhrawardy, formed "an almost purely Muslim Ministry...with an almost purely Hindu opposition."[211] Franchise had been no more than 10 per cent of the population,[212] however, and it is entirely unclear to what extent the majority of the population remained interested in the ongoing Ministerial morass. The insufficient *aman* crop was now in and the province was careening towards the lean months with few solutions to an impending disaster. Reports from most districts in Bengal indicated that acute distress was imminent.[213]

Wavell discussed the possibility of cutting rations still further with his Executive Council, but it was concluded that any further cut might "create very serious labor trouble and by affecting confidence would probably doom the prospects of procurement so as to leave us even worse off than before."[214] Towards the end of June there were demonstrations in Calcutta, orchestrated by provincial Kisan Sabhas, demanding immediate arrangements for the movement of at least 200,000 tons of rice to distressed districts and the immediate constitution of a Food Advisory Council.[215] Government gave in to the latter demand, organizing an all-parties Council to advise government on procurement, storage, and distribution of food grains, but no measures were taken for the movement of food relief to deficit areas.[216] While reports of starvation were filling the newspapers and famine was again becoming headline news, the viceroy called on Maulana Azad to dissuade the Bengal press from fomenting "alarm about the food situation."[217]

At the same time a "U.S. Famine Mission" arrived in Calcutta to tour Bengal in order to gauge levels of distress and make recommendations to the U.S. Government.[218] The Mission visited deficit districts and studied distribution, rationing arrangements, and over-all health conditions.[219] When asked to comment on their conclusions, members of the Mission suggested that Bengal's problems were "too big and too complex" to make any statement presently. On 10 July *The Statesman* reported that mortality rates in Calcutta had risen more than 15 per cent over the previous week,[220] and on 16 July the Government of India's food adviser warned that the rationing system in Bengal was highly inefficient and the province again "might face famine."[221] On 25 July Congress representatives tabled an adjournment in the Bengal Council that focused on the "acute distress prevailing in different parts of the province because of the government's failure to reduce prices and to maintain an adequate supply of rice," and warned that "starvation on a wide scale [had] already begun."[222] The dreaded "second famine" had finally arrived and Congress laid the blame squarely at the Muslim League's door. Muslim League representatives retorted that the Ministry was "being attacked for an offence that was not committed by them. It was the Section 93 Administration which should have been the subject matter for discussion as the food policy pursued by that regime was responsible for the present situation."[223]

On the 2nd of August a banner headline in *The Statesman* read: "Millions to Die of Starvation." The Famine Mission had completed its investigations and had issued its report, and in conclusion, the article read, the United States Department of Agriculture, "feared a serious famine was developing in Bengal."

Meanwhile the Cabinet Mission had completely broken down and the impasse between the Muslim League and Congress at the center had become intractable. On July 10th Nehru gave a speech unequivocally rejecting the May 16th plan, asserting that the Indian National Congress would not agree to mandatory groupings. The All-India Muslim League, bitterly disillusioned with both Congress and Britain, convened a three-day meeting at the end of July. At this meeting two resolutions were passed: one rejecting the Cabinet delegation's plan for Indian independence; and a second calling for "direct action" for the achievement of Pakistan. The 16th of August was designated "Direct Action Day," and Muslims across India were called on to observe a *hartal* (general strike), and to conduct public meetings and rallies throughout the country in support of Pakistan. On 4 August it was added that Direct Action would also include a no-tax campaign, "particularly in respect of taxes levied by the Central Government."[224] The primary objective of the announced program was to show the collective strength of the "Muslim Nation" and to demonstrate that they, like Congress, could organize a program of mass disobedience to express their political will. Furthermore, and rather importantly, the intended target of "direct action" was to be the British as least as much is it was Congress—or for that matter "Hindus," more generally.[225]

In the mix of what was to come, famine in Bengal was again forgotten.

RIOTS

Direct Action

The central platform of Direct Action in Calcutta, as elsewhere across India, was the call for a city-wide *hartal* on the 16th of August. The use of *hartal*, a mass civil disobedience tactic amounting to a general strike, had gained popular currency as a potent form of anti-colonial protest, employed, in particular, by the Indian National Congress. In this regard the Muslim League's call for Direct Action was aimed at proving that it too could get people out into the streets in large numbers in support of its own political agenda. Primary on that agenda was to demonstrate for the establishment of Pakistan. Worrying that violence would tar the political legitimacy of the League's demand, Bengal Chief Minister, H. S. Suhrawardy, released a statement to the press on 7 August calling on Muslims to ensure that Direct Action Day in Bengal would be observed peacefully. "This is the first step we are taking in pursuance of our new policy," he reminded followers, "let us show to the world that we can perform our task with complete discipline and that we have sufficient self-control and control over our people."[1]

A few days later the Suhrawardy Ministry declared the 16th of August a public holiday, arguing that this was in the interest of public order and would "minimize chances of conflict."[2] This move, however, was also essentially a governmental endorsement of the Muslim League's call for

"Direct Action." Predictably, when the holiday was announced in the bitterly divided Bengal Legislative Assembly, acrimony erupted. Deploring the exercise of "Government in using their authority to give [official] effect to a communal party's decision,"[3] Congress representatives tabled a motion to overturn the public holiday ruling. The motion was promptly, and without debate, thrown out by the (Muslim League) Deputy Speaker. After angry protests, heckling, and rancorous dispute, Congress Party representatives stormed off the floor and took the debate into the streets. At a public meeting of the Provincial Congress Committee in south Calcutta the League's plan was denounced, with the leader of the Bengal Congress urging "the public to perform their normal duties on August 16th."[4] A movement to thwart the League's call to popular action took hold, and in the days that followed political rancor escalated dangerously as Direct Action Day approached.

Apart from the city-wide *hartal*, a mass rally on Calcutta's broad central park, the Maidan, scheduled for three-o'clock in the afternoon, was the central component of the League's plan in the city. Accordingly, starting early in the morning on the 16th of August, Muslims from every corner of Calcutta and its industrial suburbs began to travel, mostly on foot, to the center of the city to assemble for the demonstration. With the lanes and by-lanes of Calcutta becoming thoroughfares for Muslim processionists in the early hours, reports of trouble began filtering into police headquarters by 7:30 A.M. Armed Muslim processionists on their way to the Maidan were attempting to force Hindu shops to close, and bricks and other projectiles were being thrown from Hindu rooftops onto passing Muslim processionists below.[5] Looting and violent confrontations between large mobs were reported a short time later, and by 9:30 serious disturbances had erupted in north Calcutta.[6] Also around 9:30, casualties began filtering into Calcutta Medical College hospitals.[7] By noon, thirty-seven arson fires had been reported and violent clashes had broken out all over central Calcutta.[8] By this time also, police were fighting running battles with rioters in the streets and resorting to tear-gas and *lathi*-charges to deter rioting mobs—who at times were attacking them directly.[9] At 2:30 P.M. the police commissioner telephoned the governor to inform him that the situation was rapidly deteriorating and that he and the chief minister were both of the opinion that the military should be called in immediately to quell the disorder.[10]

Despite the ongoing violence, the rally on the Maidan began at 4 P.M. It was attended by at least 100,000 Muslims from all over the city and its industrial suburbs.[11] At the gathering, rumors were rife that Muslims had been attacked and killed in many quarters of the city on their way to the Maidan. The crowd was already highly excitable, and these rumors served to increase the collective anxiety precipitously. The keynote speakers were the former and current Chief Ministers of Bengal, Kwaja Nazimuddin and H. S. Suhrawardy. Nazimuddin, according to the Governor's report, "in a wooly speech, on the whole preached peacefulness and restraint, but rather spoilt the effect by asserting that till 11:00 that morning all the injured persons were Muslims."[12] Suhrawardy also gave a half-hearted and unremarkable speech, but is reported to have assured the crowd that the police in Calcutta had been "restrained"— though no transcript of his speech exists.[13] Meanwhile, even during the speeches, violence was continuing to spread throughout central and north Calcutta. Clashes had also erupted in Tollygunge and Bhawanipur in the south, as well as in the industrial "docklands" of Kidderpore, Mommenpur and Garden Reach. When the demonstration at the Maidan ended, there was massive looting along the central business corridor, and as congregants fanned back out into the city, violence across Calcutta escalated further. A curfew was imposed at 6 P.M. and military troops were dispatched from Sealdah sometime around midnight, but by this time the violence had already spiraled out of control and neither the police nor the military could do much to contain the situation.

After five days of largely unrestrained murder, looting, arson, mutilation, torture, and dislocation, much of the city lay in ruins. A British journalist present on the scene reported:

> A sense of desolation hung over the native bazaars. In street after street rows of shops had been stripped to the walls. Tenements and business buildings were burnt out, and their unconsumed innards strewn over the pavements. Smashed furniture cluttered the roads, along with concrete blocks, brick, glass, iron rods, machine tools—anything that the mob had been able to tear loose but did not want to carry off. Fountains gushed from broken water mains. Burnt-out automobiles stood across traffic lanes. A pall of smoke hung over many blocks, and buzzards sailed in great, leisurely circles. Most overwhelming, however, were the neglected human casualties: fresh bodies, bodies grotesquely bloated in the tropical heat, slashed bodies, bodies bludgeoned to death, bodies piled on push carts, bodies caught in drains, bodies stacked high in vacant lots, bodies, bodies.[14]

Nothing approaching the carnage that had taken place in Calcutta between the 16th and 20th of August had ever before taken place in the history of modern India. Estimates of from 4,000 to 5,000 killed have been advanced,[15] but the true number of dead is impossible to ascertain. An unknown number of bodies were burnt in fires, stuffed into sewers, dumped into rivers, or otherwise disposed of without account. Close to 200,000 people were in need of immediate relief, with at least 100,000 homeless. The Calcutta riots also left deep psychological scars, both individually and collectively. Relations between Hindu and Muslim religious communities suffered an irreparable shock that would greatly accelerate the push towards the partition of India—which took place exactly one year later. The violence in Calcutta precipitated riots in Noakhali in east Bengal in October, and the violence in Noakhali (and Calcutta) reverberated in Bihar a month later. These several riots, in turn, set the tempo and tone for the catastrophic violence across India that accompanied partition in 1947. In this sense, it can be said, Calcutta provided the spark that ignited the conflagration of violence which would leave at least 1 million people dead and more than 10 million people dispossessed and dislocated.

Despite the significance of the Calcutta Riots in the lead-up to partition, they have received extremely limited analysis. In most historical works, the riots are recognized as a crucial juncture in Hindu/Muslim relations, but to the extent that they are explained at all, they are rather uncritically linked to the Muslim League's call for Direct Action to attain Pakistan. In one of the few more thorough examinations of the riots, historian Suranjan Das expands on this same logic to conclude that the Calcutta riots "were organized and overtly communal—religious and political."[16] In this sense, existing scholarship on the Great Calcutta Killings consistently revolves around a top-down explanation that hinges on a claim of political instigation. In what follows I will take a much more focused look at specific enactments of violence during the riots in order to demonstrate that the Calcutta riots were far more complex than explanations which focus on either narrowly "political" or broadly "religious" factors suggest.

Specifically, I will first investigate the extent to which these riots can be understood as a pitched battle for *territory* in Calcutta—at a time when gaining a secure foothold in the city remained key to survival for many millions. Second, I will analyze the unrestrained looting that took place during the riots, in an effort to identify the various motivations and objectives behind participation in this defining aspect of the riots.

In the third section I will investigate two large massacres that took place, highlighting class and labor relations as they were relevant to these incidents. Next I will turn the lens on the functioning of the colonial state during the riots, underscoring, in particular, the extent to which the priorities and prerogatives that constituted governance in Bengal during war and famine informed attitudes toward the riots. In the fourth section I will again look at the treatment of the dead, exploring what the abject dehumanization of bodies during the riots reveals about state and society in Bengal in the wake of six years of famine and war.

Territory

The demographic pressures on Calcutta, throughout the 1940s, were intense and unremitting. According to census numbers, in 1931 the city of Calcutta had a population of approximately 1.2 million people.[17] By 1941, as a result of economic flight from the impoverished countryside and migration related to war-time industrial production, the population of Calcutta had increased to nearly 2.1 million.[18] By 1945, due to the ramping-up of war-related industrial production and various other dislocations wrought by the years of war and famine in Bengal, the population of the city had doubled again to more than 4 million.[19] This last number does not include "outsiders," who were unable to confirm legitimate residence according to A.R.P. enumeration practices, on the basis of which rationing privileges were also determined. Nor does it include the large number of military troops still stationed in Calcutta at the time. Housing in the city, meanwhile, had long been insufficient, with more than sixteen residents per household recorded in 1931.[20] By 1941 that number had increased to 27.5 heads (and stomachs) per household and was steadily rising throughout the decade. The conditions in the slums of Calcutta were especially deplorable, with over-crowding to the point of suffocation in many of the city's *bustees.*

Meanwhile, summary eviction of residents of Calcutta and the seizure of their property in the name of war had given official sanction to the idea that civilian property ownership in the city was entirely contingent on martial priority.[21] Under the Defence of India Rules during the war close to a thousand homes had been requisitioned for military purposes[22] and few additional houses had been built, which led to increased rents and a further intensification of overcrowding in existing quarters.[23]

When put to question on the floor of the Bengal Assembly just three days before the riots broke out, the secretary to the governor confirmed that there was an "acute shortage of residential accommodation in Calcutta," and admitted that only 200 of the 985 civilian residencies occupied by American and British troops had been de-requisitioned since the end of the war.[24] With an average occupancy of 27.5 people per household (by the conservative 1941 numbers), this would have meant that of the nearly 30,000 people dislocated by the military in Calcutta alone, more than 20,000 were still dispossessed. To the south of Calcutta entire villages had also been "evacuated" by the military, de-housing an additional 30,000 people many of whom had filtered into the city in search of provisional accommodation and subsistence.

During the height of famine, the city came under only increasing and, at times, extremely volatile, demographic pressure. Starting in the early months of 1943, waves of "destitute" villagers began pouring into the city in various stages of starvation and collapse and occupied the city's public spaces and back alleys: begging for rice-water, and dying on the open streets in large numbers. Fearing diplomatic censure over the spectacle of famine in the heart of empire, as we have seen, one of the first measures of "famine relief" was to collect the tens of thousands of famine victims from the streets of Calcutta and forcibly remove them to "rehabilitation camps" outside the city. The treatment of famine refugees, in this sense, demonstrated that, if necessary, force was a legitimate means of clearing the city of those who did not "belong," or were otherwise considered a threat. The ration system, established in early 1944, followed this same logic, with "outsiders" excluded from the guarantee of subsidized access to foodstuffs—even while the countryside remained un-rationed and starving. As might be expected, those who could claim authorized residency in Calcutta clung to their territorial claim jealously and tenaciously. Then, in the summer of 1946, with the food situation again rapidly deteriorating, "starving destitutes" were, again, being removed by force in large numbers.[25] The question of who belonged to Calcutta and who should be "removed" was again becoming paramount. During the riots that decision would be taken into unofficial hands.

The earliest violence reported on the 16th of August seems to have erupted, above all else, in relation to the perceived territorial specificity of the *para*—tightly knit neighborhoods that were popularly recognized as discrete and cohesive demographic and territorial entities.[26] From early in the morning, Muslims from all parts of the city traveled in processions to the Maidan and along the way had to move through many Hindu-majority neighborhoods of the city. As Muslims processionists waving flags and chanting slogans passed through Hindu *paras* in crowded north Calcutta, trouble arose. Bricks and other projectiles, which had been stockpiled on local rooftops by Hindu residents, where hurled down onto the Muslim processionists below, while in other neighborhoods Muslim processionists, some of them armed with *lathis* and other weapons, attempted to force Hindu shops and bazaars to close. Violent skirmishes erupted and some of these skirmishes quickly developed into the first large-scale clashes of the riots. In this regard, it can be said, the earliest conflicts of the Calcutta riots erupted over very specific and identifiable *territorial* tensions that developed, in particular, in relation to local Hindu perceptions that their territory and economic freedom were being "invaded" by unruly and threatening Muslim processionists. The extent to which famine and war had aggravated and complicated the significance of territorial rights in Calcutta, in this regard, cannot be overlooked.

Years of famine and war had also rendered the right of access to public spaces in Calcutta a matter of contest and contingency. Since the beginning of the war, access to public space in Calcutta had been increasingly restricted and policed, most clearly during air-raid drills and "blackouts." During famine the right to occupy public space in the city at any time of the day or night became increasingly qualified. Those who were starving, understood officially as "sick destitutes," could be removed from the streets and parks—without notice and by main force as necessary. The jewel of all public space in Calcutta was the Maidan—Calcutta's Central Park.[27] The "occupation" of Calcutta's most conspicuous public space by many tens of thousand of Muslims on the 16th of August was already a highly charged and symbolic spectacle. The governor of Bengal, in his report to the viceroy, noted that an estimate of 30,000 in attendance had been supplied by a Central Intelligence officer, "a Hindu," while a much higher number—500,000—had been provided by the Special Branch inspector, "a Muslim."[28] The commissioner of police, a European, estimated the crowd to number at least 100,000.[29]

For the minority Muslims of Calcutta, many coming from the overcrowded and squalid slums of the city's industrial wards, to physically occupy the city's most hallowed civic space, en masse, was a bold expression of corporate power. The rhetoric of a unified political agenda advanced by the Muslim League leaders who spoke at the rally seems to have meant something less. Golam Kibria, a Muslim coal seller from Park Circus, had made the journey to the Maidan with the local Muslims of his neighborhood sometime in the early afternoon. He remembers thousands of people, waving flags and shouting slogans, and also remembers rumors swirling of Hindu attacks on Muslim processionists in Kalighat and Bhawanipur, but remembers nothing of the speeches made.[30] The crowd seemed to have an energy of its own, quite divorced from what was transpiring on the podium or over the weak sound system. When the rally broke up, there was widespread looting along the business corridor adjacent to the Maidan, and increasingly violent clashes erupted as Muslims passed back through Hindu *paras* on their way back home. By 7 P.M., violence was endemic across Calcutta, with arson, looting, and murder being reported from numerous areas of the city. Much of the violence continued to have a certain undeniable territorial logic about it that had been years in the making.

The Sen family, who I interviewed in 2003, lived in a two story house in a narrow, self-contained alley of Ananda Palit: a small Hindu neighborhood sandwiched in the heart of Muslim Calcutta, with Park Circus to the south, Motijil to the north, and Taltala to the west.[31] To the east there is a local railway line that runs goods from the 24 Parganas south of Calcutta to Sealdah Station, a mile north of Ananda Palit. In the early afternoon of the 16th of August, from the rooftop of the family house, Soumesh Sen recalls seeing a gang of armed Muslim men, "two to three hundred strong," making their way north from Park Circus along the elevated railway tracks towards Ananda Palit. Shouts of *"Allahu Akbar!"* and *"Larke lenge Pakistan!"*[32] filled the air. Sensing trouble, a contingent of Hindu men was quickly organized from the neighboring houses to head-off the mob before it crossed into the *para*. A skirmish ensued by the tracks and, according to Soumesh, one of the Muslim interlopers was struck across the wrist by a large knife and the mob fled, retreating back down the tracks towards Park Circus.

That night a second crowd attacked the *para* from the north, crossing the small bridge that spans a transport canal separating Ananda Palit from Motijil. Again chants of *"Allahu Akbar!"*[33] rent the air—this time answered by a thin but defiant call of *"Bande Matram!"*[34] From their window, the Sens could see that all the Hindu houses along the main road of Ananda Palit had been set on fire and were burning unchecked. A resident of one of the houses was later reported to have approached the arsonists and demanded to know what the purpose behind the attack was. He was stabbed to death on the spot—and the mob quickly retreated.

The next morning, again, Muslims from Motijil crossed the bridge and entered Ananda Palit. There was more arson, and some looting, but no fatalities. Meanwhile, a group of men from the *para* had organized for battle, assembling phosphorous bombs and gathering knives and lathis to ward off attack. Together they were able to drive the Muslim attackers back across the bridge by midday. That night, again, the neighborhood was encircled and chants of *"Allahu Akbar"* could be heard from all four directions, but no attack was launched. From 18 August, efforts to defend the neighborhood were further organized; guns were fashioned out of pipes and other weapons were amassed from local resources. Stray attacks and counter-attacks continued for two weeks, during which time the Sens were prisoners in their house, subsisting on figs from a tree in the courtyard.

It had been a terrifying ordeal, but "during the fighting," Soumesh Sen noted, "very few people were killed." This last fact is somewhat unique perhaps, but in other aspects, this recollected story of Ananda Palit is typical of many incidents that took place during the Calcutta riots. Attacks on minority enclaves within "opposing" community majority wards were extremely common. In the case of Ananda Palit, the primary focus of attack was the actual physical dwelling space of the Hindus of the *para*. The objective was to drive them out of "Muslim Calcutta." The battle was fought, in many respects, like an ordinary turf war. Both the railroad tracks and the bridge served as putative boundary lines, and the conflict unfolded based on an identifiable logic of territorial incursion and defense. Though there is an obvious "communal" aspect to these battles, the prevailing demographic and socio-economic pressures that had reached a critical point in Calcutta by this time remain extremely relevant. Efforts to purge majority neighborhoods of minority communities—"outsiders" so to speak—during the riots have to be understood also from within the purview of the overcrowding, scarcity, and stratified "prioritization" that war and famine had visited on the city.

On the other hand, while it is true that many of the Muslim combatants rallied to the cry, *"Larke Lenge Pakistan,"* the call for a Muslim "homeland" can not be understood as sufficient cause for the scale of violence. Hindus formed a significant majority of the population of Calcutta and few Muslims could have imagined that open warfare in the streets would alter the city's composition in any way profound enough to transform the demographic equation. Furthermore, if the leadership of the Muslim League themselves were uncertain about the geographic specificity of an eventual Pakistan, how much more so the poor and disenfranchised Muslim masses of Calcutta who participated and suffered in the riots? The promise of "Pakistan" was, indeed, used to instigate attacks on Hindu neighborhoods, but in many instances it seems to have been denuded of any practical content. Souresh Sen notes that "leaders of the Muslims...told them that this area will be yours—so go on rioting. Because this is a small area, if they take it into their Pakistan then they will be very happy." In this example, "Pakistan" is only a somewhat provisional *casus belli* in a highly contentious socio-political context characterized by a multitude of anxieties and motivations. Above all else, this context was constructed in relation to differential access to scarce resources based on claims of rootedness to the city. The riots, in this light, are understood not as a nationalist battle for the promised land of Pakistan—which would be home to India's 100 million Muslims—but as a much more specific, localized battle for the control of city blocks, alleyways, and neighborhoods in Calcutta, the city of survival.

The prevailing territorial dynamic of *local* dominance was, in fact, so deeply entrenched in the unfolding logic of the riots that it could scarcely be obscured. Many newspapers in the city quickly stopped printing the religious affiliation of victims in their reports, fearing that the news of the killings of members of one community would lead to reprisal attacks by the other. Little specification of victims was, however, necessary. As Soumesh Sen noted, "in Hindu areas, Muslims were being attacked, and in Muslim areas Hindus were being attacked...if you knew so many people were killed in Entally, you must know that they were Hindus and if you knew so many people were killed in Beliaghata, you knew that they must be Muslims."[35] In this sense, much of the violence amounted to purges of "enemy" communities from specific localities, not wholesale and gratuitous killings of Muslims by Hindus, and visa-versa. *Paras* were also quickly militarized to protect against incursion and, as in Ananda Pali, pickets of civilians were posted to keep guard of local territorial boundaries. In other parts of the city, road barriers were erected to inhibit infiltration by "outsiders," as was the case in Park Circus, were the main roads of entry were barricaded with barbed wire.[36]

The violation of neighborhoods by rival communities was, moreover, persistent and complex. In the many interviews that I have conducted, it was most often the *sound* of the riots that had remained lodged in survivors' memories. As in the case of Ananda Palit, actual infiltration of neighborhoods by riotous crowds was routinely preceded by *acoustic* penetration. Enervating choruses of "*Allahu Akbar!*" by Muslim combatants, and "*Bande Matram!*" by Hindus, were remembered by almost everyone I have interviewed as terrifying incantations that portended imminent peril to persons and property. Though at a semantic level neither invocation carries any explicit threat, both served as ominous and alarming indications of being surrounded by a hostile enemy. In this way neighborhoods could be besieged and their residents' sense of territorial security undermined even without physical incursion. Soumesh Sen remarks that even after the Hindu *para* of Ananda Palit had been secured by local armed guard, and Muslims no longer dared to attack, "every night there was still the *sound: 'Allahu Akbar! Allahu Akbar! Allahu Akbar!'*—and with those sounds only, we were getting frightened." Because sound is able to cross boundaries—even those that have been secured against physical attack—it seems to have been a constant reminder of the fragility of territorial sovereignty. That it was the *sound* of the riot that haunted so many who I interviewed for many years to come, again, bears a distinct correlation to famine, during which time it was the plaintive *voice* of "sick destitutes" that so many Calcuttans remember as representing the horror of that time.[37]

The physical destruction of homes of the "opposite" community represents a far less abstract example of territorial warfare. Arson was extremely widespread and has to be understood as a systemic effort to "de-house"[38] an enemy sector of the population, rather than, for instance, simply an expression of political or cultural animosity against a rival community. Given the arcane, and in many places, ad-hoc nature of property laws in Calcutta, the destruction of homes by means of arson amounted to a violent revocation of thousands of territorial claims—which depended more on perpetual habitation than official sanction. Though no reliable tally of the destruction of homes can be ventured,[39] the toll on residential properties was immense. "Calcutta," it was noted in the *Statesman* on 20 August, "is like a town that has just known a heavy air-raid."[40] In the first three days of rioting, the Calcutta Fire Brigade reported more than 1,200 calls, with each call representing an average of four fires burning in that locality.[41] Given the average occupancy of houses utilized above, this number represents the dispossession and dislocation of at least 130,000 residents of Calcutta—and this only derived from calls to fires that could be (and were) reported. The number of Calcutta's poor who lost their homes—as well as their lives—in overcrowded *bustees*, which were also a primary target of arson,[42] is even less well documented.

In so far as there was a concerted effort to deracinate members of rival communities from distinct areas of the city, it was an effort that was quickly showing results. On 20 August the commissioner of civil supplies reported:

> By Sunday, the 18th of August, large streams of refugees from affected areas were collecting at various centers, mostly operated under the auspices of non-official relief organizations or ad-hoc non-official bodies set up for the occasion. Large exchanges of population took place within 48 hours as a result of persons of one community leaving their homes where there was a preponderance of the other community.[43]

Also on 18 August, the governor, with assistance from the military and police, initiated "Operation St. Bernard," an effort to move minority communities from areas where they were under threat, to rescue camps set up on the Maidan and elsewhere.[44] By the next day as many as 10,000 people had been removed from their homes under police and military escort. Operation St. Bernard, under the directorship of "denial" mastermind L.G. Pinnell, continued for the next ten days to come. Such an operation, it might be suggested, while undoubtedly valuable for families under armed attack, ironically (or not) gave official sanction to the inclination of the rioting mobs to "relocate" populations.

The work done by the rioters, however, was on a far greater scale. On 28 August, the Relief Department reported that there were 189,015 riot refugees being cared for in 307 quasi-official camps supplied by the Civil Supplies Department.[45] This number, approaching 5 per cent of the city's population, does not include those who had fled one area of the city and were sheltering with friends or family members in another part, nor does it include those who had fled the city altogether. As to the latter ranks, some approximation of their numbers can be had in relation to the fact that by 23 August, 110,000 people were reported to have departed the city by train since the beginning of the violence.[46] This number does not take into account those who fled on foot or by other means. If account is taken of these refugees as well, it is easy to draw the conclusion that as much as 10 per cent of the city's population was dislocated by the riots—which would represent the largest displacement of an urban population in the history of colonial India until that time.

While "de-housing" on this scale could not have possibly been foreseen and would have been impossible to plan, it is, nevertheless, a fact that the riots resulted in a massive dislocation of people, the reduction of Calcutta's population by many tens—if not hundreds—of thousands, and the "purification" of entire wards of the city by brute force. The deaths, dislocations, relocations, and exchanges of populations that occurred during the Calcutta riots were, in this sense, an eerie foreshadowing of things to come across India. However, it is extremely important to understand that the Calcutta riots were not a *merely* communal affair; rather, they were just as importantly the catastrophic culmination of underlying tensions related to territory, belonging, and residency in Calcutta that were many years (and lives) in the making.

Loot

In a similar sense, the extent to which unrestrained looting characterized the Calcutta riots cannot be viewed through the exclusive lens of political instigation or communal animosity. By the summer of 1946, a steady rise in prices coupled with cuts in rations had already precipitated considerable labor unrest, with as many as 242 industrial strikes occurring in Bengal in the first six months of the year.[47] On 11 July the postal workers union had also resorted to a strike over dearness allowances and job security, effectively cutting Calcutta off from the rest of India in the weeks preceding the riots. Rice was, again, in increasingly short supply and the "position" of mustard oil, kerosene, and seed potatoes had also become "chronic" by the beginning of 1946.[48] In the winter months cloth shortages had reached a critical stage and were breeding deep anxieties and resentment. Even wealthier residents of Calcutta were having difficulty finding sufficient yardage to maintain their sense of dignity and station.[49] For the poor, things were considerably more desperate.

Hand loom weavers throughout the province complained of an acute shortage of yarn, and a thriving black market in piece goods was keeping prices artificially high and supplies short.[50] The fact that the war had ended and residents of Bengal were still hungry and threadbare was extremely galling. Levels of theft in Bengal had soared since the beginnings of famine,[51] and with reports of difficult times ahead, crime statistics were again on the rise in late 1945.[52]

This context is important background to include before investigating the widespread looting which—from the earliest reports of trouble on the 16th of August—was noted as an endemic feature of the Calcutta riots. No estimate of the total value of commodities looted from private residences, businesses, and governmental warehouses has been ventured in any quarter, but the scale of looting was immense. Tellingly, when asked to which community—Hindu or Muslim—most of the looted items recovered by the police belonged, the Deputy Commissioner of Police confessed, "It is very difficult [to tell.] The quantities are very huge. Practically the whole of the Indian museum was used for display of the articles recovered."[53] Although some historians have sought to fold even the looting committed during the riots into a strictly communal explanation,[54] once again, more detailed, and less Manichean, analysis is needed. In the highly fluid and explosive situation on the streets of Calcutta in August 1946, specific enactments of "loot" were complex, participation was variously motivated, and, very often, an instrumental opportunism governed the transgression of looting more than any other single factor.

In the early afternoon of August 16th, Muslims from Howrah, the industrial suburb just across the river from central Calcutta, were crossing the Howrah Bridge on their way to the scheduled meeting at the Maidan. Like Muslim processionists from other areas of greater Calcutta, they carried flags and shouted slogans, stopped traffic and broke into scuffles with shopkeepers who had not closed to business for the day. The situation, however, remained relatively under control. Sometime in the early afternoon, however, according to the Police Inspector's report, "a large number of processionists *who had already crossed the bridge* were suddenly found rushing back to Howrah, shouting "Luto Howrah!"[55] From that point on the situation in Howrah deteriorated, with twenty-eight incidents reported by nightfall. Of these twenty-eight incidents, nineteen involved looting, with the most common articles looted being cash, cloth, and gold jewelry. Many of the reports listed the community of the owner of the shop looted, but not that of the looters. Thus a typical entry reads, "24.) A cloth shop belonging to a Muslim at 62 Grand Trunk Road was looted," or, "27.) Cash and gold were looted from a Hindu shop at 5/B Maidan Road."[56]

That Muslim processionists from Howrah, on their way to the meeting at the Maidan, turned *back* from their intended destination in order to loot Howrah is extremely telling. To skip the main event at the Maidan—an assembly organized to demonstrate for Pakistan—in order to ransack the commercial district of Howrah, would suggest a rather tepid dedication to the cause of the day. Moreover, it was not to loot *Hindus* that the crowd turned back, but, demonstrably, to loot *Howrah*. What seems to have gripped the crowd was not a politically motivated will to wreak "communal" havoc in the streets, but rather a more mundane and spontaneous inspiration to take part in a free-for-all for personal gain. That, in a majority of cases reported on the day, the religious affiliation of the looted party is given, but not that of the looters, throws communal explanations into further doubt. The report that a "country liquor shop at 542 Grand Trunk Road belonging to a Hindu"[57] was looted, for instance, remains inconclusive in regards to the affiliation of the looters, except that they were likely drinkers. By the 17th of August, the police blotter was a bit more suppositional, the typical report reading, "a stationary shop of a Muslim at 70 Circular Road was looted by some unknown men—probably Hindu."[58] Given the endemic poverty and prevailing hardships of life in Bengal at the time, however, any statement about perpetrators of such property crimes, without further evidence, remains inconclusive at best.

Even in regard to the most famous case of looting during the Calcutta riots—where the perpetrators where identifiably Muslim and the shop undoubtedly Hindu—there also may yet have been discriminatory factors at work, apart from the communal affiliation of the parties involved. At approximately 4:30 P.M. on the 16th of August, while the meeting on the Maidan across the street was just underway, a gun shop on the corner of Chowringhee and Dharmatala was broken into and looted by a Muslim mob. To understand this one event, which is the most often referenced incident of loot during the riots, as primarily a "Muslim" attack on (specifically) "Hindu" commercial property, would be rather simplistic. To think that this gun shop was looted not because it had guns, but because the owner of the gun shop was a Hindu, would be extremely naive. Calcutta, at this time, was already exploding, and it is much more likely that it was the content of the shop that attracted looters, rather than the community of its owner.

About less renowned incidents of loot it can also be also said that there were discriminatory aspects at work other than communal calculation. Scarcity of cloth had been a factor in several prior riots in Bengal,[59] and in the riots of 1946, with cloth scarcer than ever, tailor shops, cloth warehouses, and textile piece goods stores were, again, singled out for attack. Golam Kutubuddin's family had been in the cloth business for several generations by 1946. They had four clothing retail shops in Howrah and a cloth wholesale warehouse in Burabazar. Their primary residence, in a Hindu neighborhood in south Calcutta, was besieged during the riot and the family took shelter in the American military barracks by the lake. The family survived, but was economically ruined. All four shops in Howrah and the warehouse in Burabazar were looted and burned to the ground. It was not discovered who had looted their businesses and no arrests were made. Golam Kutubuddin's father, after surviving the riots, died a short time later of a heart attack brought on by economic ruin.[60] Whether or not the perpetrators of each attack were Hindu, does not limit the range of possibility as far as motivation. That all five shops, in different locations, were separately looted and destroyed, demonstrates a particular focus of the looting crowds that was seen in many areas of the city.

The Deputy Commissioner of Police, H.N. Sircar, on patrol throughout Calcutta, came across several scenes of cloth looting in the first two days of the riot as well. On Chitpur Road in central Calcutta, he witnessed a "big crowd" breaking into a cloth shop. The officers with him *lathi*-charged the crowd and it was quickly dispersed. No mention is made of the religious affiliation of the looters or the owner of the shop, which doesn't seem to have been of any significance to the Commissioner. In the dock area, at Kidderpore, a few hours later, he again came across a large crowd looting a cloth shop. Eight rounds were fired by the police and three men were wounded. The men were arrested and "a handcart which had been loaded up with looted cloth was deposited at the police station." Again no specifics were given about the communal affiliation of the victims or perpetrators. Shortly thereafter, also in Kidderpore, Sircar again came across a lorry full of cloth moving down

the road. About this incident there is a better indication of the participants. The lorry was stopped and it was found that the occupants were
all uniformed police constables. They told the Deputy Commissioner
that they were on official business, but when Sircar began to ask for
names and badge numbers, they fled away.[61]

Calcutta was an anarchic and permissive city, and there were tremendous anxieties and socio-economic uncertainties just below the surface.
Police constables were poorly paid, struggling to get by, and morale in
the force was extremely low.[62] In the College Street area several more
lorries of cloth were looted from the Dalia Tailoring Shop, a large retailer
dealing in fine Benarasi silks. The shop was completely emptied out and
gutted, and, again, police constables were implicated.[63] The Commissioner of Police, Donald Hardwick was not, himself, aware of this particular incident, but testified later that he had investigated several other
very similar cases involving constables.[64] The Sen Law and Co. liquor
store in north Calcutta was also looted, this time by a "large number" of
Anglo-Indians and police sergeants.[65] Also in north Calcutta, two
inspectors and a sergeant showed up at a "European" locksmith shop
with a large iron safe. They explained to the proprietor that the safe
belonged to one officer's wife. It was later discovered, however, that the
safe had been looted from a civilian's house earlier in the day.[66] In central
Calcutta three other constables on patrol were arrested for participating in the loot of a second gun shop in Dharmatala. One of them, quite
embarrassingly, was discovered to be the orderly of the Deputy Commissioner of Police, Philip Norton-Jones.[67]

Even children, it would seem, were taking part in the free-for-all. While
passing the Kamalaya stores in central Calcutta on the 16th of August,
Deputy Commissioner H. N. Sircar found "some *chokras* were bringing
out articles through the glass panes which had been smashed."[68] *Chokras*,
the Deputy Commissioner explained to the Enquiry Commission, are
servant boys, usually between the age of ten and fourteen. Their designation as *chokras*, moreover, seems to have been more relevant to the report
of the incident than the religious affiliation of the boys. What Sircar
would appear to be attempting to convey is that all order had been lost,
and *even chokras* were looting upscale shops in broad daylight.

The choice of targets also varied widely. When the meeting on the
Maidan let out and looting quickly spread down the upscale Chowringhee commercial district, several European shops and businesses were

looted, including the Enfield motorcycle showroom on Park Street.[69] The Statesman House (the large complex of buildings where the newspaper's offices are housed) was also surrounded by rioters who attempted to enter, breaking windows and setting fire to the doors, before being chased off by the police.[70] The Grand Hotel also came under attack, before being taken under police protection.[71] Across the river at Howrah, the next day, a large mob attempted to loot the Bengal Central Bank, but this attack was, likewise, repelled by swift police intervention. The police similarly broke up a mob looting the Bata Shoe shop (a Czechoslovakian concern) in Dharamtolla on the same day. That each of these locations was protected by prompt police action—even while in the alleys and bazaars of Calcutta looting was going on unabated and on a fantastic scale—is extremely telling, and is something to which I will return.

The Civil Supplies Department, which handled the movement of foodstuffs to ration shops and its industrial clients, well understood that it too needed protection—particularly in the context of famine, past and present. The depots of Civil Supplies were kept locked and heavily guarded due to the very real likelihood "of depots being subject to mob attack."[72] No Civil Supplies lorries moved until the 19th of August, and began plying then only on a limited scale and under close military escort. The Relief Department, both during and after the riots, similarly moved rice around the city only under heavy armed guard.[73] Official reports released by the Civil Supply Department confirmed, however, that despite these measures, at least 32 ration shops had been attacked and looted.[74] When rationing was resumed on the 20th of August only 430 out of 1,288 shops opened for business.[75] In addition to the food shops looted, the Civil Supplies Department reported "a number of cloth, kerosene, and mustard oil rationing shops were also looted, but details are not yet to hand."[76] The Burabazar rationing offices were also attacked and looted, and a Civil Supplies warehouse in Kidderpore was looted and burned to the ground.[77]

Also confirming the distinct socio-economic nature of looting which took place during the riots is that much of the loot recovered by the police in the days following the riots was found in the *bustees* of the city.[78] In the *bustees* lived Calcutta poorest and most marginal residents, many of whom were immigrants from outside Bengal, and all of whom lived in acute deprivation, ill-health and adversity. Most worked as contract employees or casual laborers, eking out livings as porters, carters (*coolies*), doormen (*durwans*), sweepers, rickshaw pullers, cow-tenders (*goalas*), butchers (*kasais*), blacksmiths, masons, or dock workers (*khalasis*). Of the population of Calcutta they had suffered the brunt of famine and disease—without any of the benefits given to "priority" workers in the city. They also composed the bulk of the victims during the riots, as well as a significant proportion of the perpetrators. Many *bustees* were the scenes of large massacres and many others were completely burned to the ground.[79] How many had died, killed, looted, been dislocated, maimed, lost loved ones, or simply—living without the barest means of protection—been terrified to the point of madness, is impossible to know. To write off their involvement, however, as a narrowly cultural, or macro-politically inspired phenomenon, without reference to the specifics of their socio-economic situation, is to reveal very little about the Calcutta riots.

Labor

The Muslim *khalasis* of eastern Bengal, as has been noted earlier,[80] were itinerant and expert boat-men, renowned for their knowledge of the complex and dangerous inland waterways of Bengal. From the early days of the colonial enterprise, *khalasis* had been drafted in large number into British mercantile firms as ship hands. Though many continued to earn their livings traditionally, working the tidal delta in local country-boats, by 1930 there were at least 130,000 *khalasis* "belonging" to shipping and industrial firms in Calcutta.[81] The terms of their employment were highly exploitative. They were often contracted into service as children, forced to work long hours, and insufficiently sheltered and fed. As Ravi Ahuja has found, *khalasi* "employment relations were structurally more akin to those of plantation laborers whose 'indenture' contracts subordinated them under their employer as persons for the whole duration of their contract."[82] Unemployment among *khalasis* was often high, and, if idle, they remained under contract without pay. Provisions made for compensation in the case of disability were also tenuous, and during World War I their status as contract laborers made it difficult for families to draw from the War Risks Compensation scheme in the case of injury or death.[83]

Even in relation to these pre-existing conditions, the 1940s were an extremely difficult decade for *khalasis*. In particular, "boat denial" had deprived them of the capacity to earn a relatively independent living on local boats, driving more and more into the clutches of the large trading and shipping concerns of Calcutta—European and Indian alike. The owners of country boats received full compensation for the loss of their vessels during denial, but the workers of those boats (i.e. *khalasis*) received only three months' wages. With inflation pushing Bengal to the point of economic collapse, this arrangement left them especially vulnerable to the predations of famine and disease. Their plight was desperate. In 1943, the Bengal Steamer Khalasis Bill was drafted to establish *khalasis* as recognized employees of industrial firms, which would have given them preferential access to subsidized foodstuffs and other priority benefits granted to "essential" laborers during war. The bill was defeated, however, by the big-business lobby in the Bengal Legislature. Among the most influential members of this group were Jeremy Benthall—Member of the Viceroy's Executive Council and managing director of Bird and Co.; and G.D. Birla—Marwari industrial magnate whose textile and jute interests in Calcutta were unrivalled in India. Having failed to establish any legal normalization of their labor status, it is also entirely likely that *khalasis* comprised a large number of the "outsiders" who were killed in the Japanese bombing of the Kidderpore docks in December 1943.[84] Given the various circumstances compounding their already long-standing economic hardships, *khalasis* seem often to have found themselves in the crosshairs of the structural and direct violence of war-time Bengal. The Calcutta riots proved no different.

On the morning of 17th of August, while Calcutta was still reeling from its first long night of arson, looting, and murder, approximately 500 *khalasis* left their quarters in a "coolie" *bustee* of Benthall's firm Bird and Company in Howrah, commandeered a number of boats and steamers, and headed down and across the Hooghly River towards the Calcutta docks. They landed at Bichali Ghat in Metiabruz, which served the surrounding factories—most notably G.D. Birla's Kesoram Cotton Mills and the Kesoram Tent Factory—and proceeded to loot and set fire to the warehouses along the river. They then turned on several goods boats anchored near the jetty and set them on fire as well. Fifteen boats, each manned by four boatmen, were destroyed. "The attack was sudden," the official report noted, "and it was apprehended that most of the boatmen lost their lives being unable to escape." A "vigorous search" was made for the men who were on the boats, but no bodies were retrieved from the scorched hulks. Some bodies were later found floating in the shallow water near the bank. These bodies—"Hindu" bodies—were collected and "disposed of" by the Hindu Satkar Samiti.[85]

What stands out in this case is not necessarily the fact that the boat-men killed on the water were "Hindu"—rather, that they *were not* kha-lasis may be more material. That the *khalasis* first attacked the ware-houses before attacking the boats is also significant. Although it is not certain from the record, it can be fairly well assumed that the warehouses and the boats were commercially related. What seems just as likely is that the raid had been planned beforehand, as it would not be easy to coordinate an attack by 500 men on a single location without premedi-tation, and that they traveled some distance to strike at this particular location would also tend to imply a more calculated intent. In this con-text, it is entirely likely that the *khalasis* chose their target in relation to a specific grievance, and that this grievance was most likely against the owners of the warehouses and boats. That the *khalasis* first attacked the warehouses and then burned the boats would also indicate that the pri-mary motive was the loot and destruction of the targeted party's prop-erty. The men who died on the boats, in this sense, were apparently not the primary target of attack, but, instead, represented the "collateral damage" of a raid on property. It also seems likely that the destruction of the boats had something to do with the fact that no *khalasis*, who formed the bulk of dock and boat labor pool in Calcutta, were on the boats. In this incident, in other words, there are very clear undertones of an attack on a specific industrial/trade interest that likely involved perceived discriminatory labor practices, and perhaps other *particular* grievances, harbored against a known "enemy."

I begin this section on labor with the *khalasis* because their involve-ment has been noted in several accounts of the riots, but little back-ground information or analysis has been forthcoming.[86] The *khalasis*, themselves, also came under attack by both "up-country Hindus" and Sikhs in the B.N.R. railway yard at Kidderpore. Attacks and counter-attacks between *khalasis* and Hindu and Sikh laborers proliferated on 18 and 19 August, resulting in many deaths and much bitterness.[87] How many *khalasis* were killed during the riots, as during the bombings, is not clear. What is clearer is that the *khalasis'* experience of violence (both as perpetrators and victims) had consequences far beyond what might be imagined from their demeaned social status. Having fled Calcutta in mass after the riots, many *khalasis* returned to Noakhali in eastern Bengal, with stories of atrocities to tell. Subsequently, the *khalasis* of Calcutta have been directly implicated in the Noakhali riots, where the Hindu minority was the primary target of attack.[88] These riots, in October 1946, were the first reverberation of the Calcutta riots, and the next step on the road to the even greater communal violence that wracked India for the next year in the lead-up to partition. In as much as the circle that connects the violence in Calcutta to its first reverberation in Noakhali runs through *khalasis*, then, understanding something of their motivations and experiences is especially important.

In the official record of the river incident during the Calcutta riots, the ownership of the warehouses and boats is not specified. The question is therefore open to speculation. Given that there was a high concentration of Marwari capital in the area, particularly with the Birla mills close by, it is not unreasonable to surmise that the warehouses and boats that were destroyed were related to these interests. Relations between the Marwari community and Muslim laborers in Calcutta were historically tense, and had erupted into violence several times over the years. Marwaris in Calcutta had made fortunes in the jute, textile, and coal industries, and by the mid-twentieth century were the scions of Indian capitalism. Many families of the rich Marwari trading community had built their palatial homes, in fact, on land from which poor Muslim tenants had been "cleared."[89] Tensions between Marwaris and Muslims in the early twentieth century had also resulted in Marwaris refusing to rent houses to Muslim tenants.[90] In addition, Marwaris had long been popularly understood to engage in unfair trade practices such as commodity speculation and hoarding, which caused inflation and ultimately scarcity.[91] In the mid-twentieth century, price manipulations in the raw jute market—of which Marwari traders comprised 75–80 per cent of dealers[92]—had disastrous consequence for the Muslim cultivators of eastern Bengal, in particular, who then suffered disproportionately from starvation and disease in the 1940s.[93] Marwari speculation in and hoarding of rice during the war was also widely suspected to have been a direct contributing factor in bringing about famine.[94] Marwari monopolistic control of the cloth industry, coupled with a reputation for hoarding, was also deeply resented and was even indexed in popular culture by a rhyme.[95]

More importantly for the analysis to follow, perhaps, were Marwari industrial labor practices in war-time Bengal. The mills and factories of

Calcutta were turning record profits throughout the war and in this context needed to guarantee a certain "priority" status for their regular workers to kept production running. Consequently, while millions across the region were starving, essential employees at Calcutta's bigger mills and factories were granted preferential access to subsidized food grains that very easily could mean the difference between life and death. On the other hand, that mills and factories hired very many laborers on a contract basis, without the "priority" benefits given to a select group of regular employees, caused tremendous bitterness. Refusal to hire laborers because of their religious affiliation, understandably, fostered even deeper animosity. Discriminatory labor practices of Marwari industrialists, which disadvantaged Muslim laborers, in particular, created abiding acrimony.[96] It is in this context that one of the most notorious massacres that took place during the Calcutta riots has to be examined.

Metiabruz, a heavily Muslim-majority area in Calcutta's "docklands," was home to the Kesoram Cotton Mills and the Kesoram Tent Factories, both G.D. Birla concerns. Close around the factories were several workers' *bustees*, inhabited both by the many Muslims who worked as coolies and contract laborers in the general vicinity, as well as by the core of Birla's recognized and "regular" workforce, which was comprised of Hindu laborers many recruited by the mill from one particular small locality in the neighboring province of Orissa.

At 10:30 in the morning on August 17th, Muslim laborers of Metiabruz began a brutal and relentless attack on Birla's Oriya workers. In the first assault—on Litchi Bagan, a Hindu *bustee* adjoining the Kesoram Cotton Mill—fifty Oriyas were killed, 250 were severely injured, and it was reported that at least sixty women were raped and brutalized.[97] In a neighboring Hindu *bustee* at least fifty more Oriya laborers were slaughtered at around the same time. Houses were looted and set on fire and several local temples were desecrated. There was also an attack by Muslims of the locality in the *bustee* adjoining the Kesoram Tent factory, which was set on fire, resulting in the death of an additional fifteen Hindu workers. A short time later the factory barracks themselves were attacked and another "50 Oriyas were done to death and about 100 more were injured." Kesoram Cotton Mill authorities quickly began rescue missions in Litchi Bagan, ferrying their priority workers into the factory buildings where they could be protected from Muslim attack. Nevertheless, at 11:00 the next morning, there was yet another attack on Oriya workers near the mill, and another 40 laborers were killed.

By nightfall on the 18th of August, several thousand Hindu workers were sheltering in the Birla factory. They were protected by armed police guard and "special arrangements" with Civil Supplies were made to feed them. There were as many as a thousand who were injured, some mutilated to the extent that "the mill doctor at Kesoram fainted when the injured were brought in." The violence, however, had not yet come to a close. On the afternoon of August 19th, an armed mob of Muslims broke into the mill itself, but were turned back by police fire.[98] In all, 129 arrests were made in connection with the incident, and the mill remained shut for many days to come. Shortly after the massacres, the chief minister of Orissa visited the mills personally to inquire into the condition of the Oriya laborers, lending national scope to this particular incident. The Hindu nationalist media, meanwhile, made hay of the event, running exaggerated stories of the already spectacularly ghastly event to demonstrate Muslim barbarity.[99] From the Muslim perspective, things obviously looked different. On the 22nd of August, relief authorities held a meeting to assess the situation. At the gathering, according to the District Magistrate, "most inflammatory speeches were made, chiefly by the Muslims present, in which they appeared to blame Marwari cotton mill authorities for causing the riots by not employing a sufficient number of Muslims."[100]

Undoubtedly there are many factors beneath the surface that go unexplained by the existing record of this incident, but it can somewhat safely be ventured that it cannot be very well explained by "Direct Action." The tenacity and single mindedness with which the Oriya factory workers were attacked speaks of a more complex motivation than political rhetoric can account for. In this context, the representation of Muslim labor grievance as a causal factor, particularly given the long history of Marwari-Muslim relations, cannot be easily dismissed. It is significant, in this regard, that facilities of the mills were themselves entered, and in the case of the Kesoram Tent factory, attacked directly. It is also significant that the Muslim mobs did not go on a killing spree of "Hindus" in general, but that their choice of targets was entirely specific, and was inexorably linked to the Birla mills. In some definite sense, this attack of Oriya (Hindu) workers at a Marwari (Hindu) industrial plant, by disadvantaged (Bengali) Muslim laborers, would be wrongly categorize under the broad (and all-too-simplistic) heading of "Hindu-Muslim violence." The particularity in this case—as well as in many others—is far too important to be dismissed in favor of a resort to an argument of simple "communal hatred."

The extent to which famine paradigms can be traced through the entire course of the events at Metiabruz is also worth noting. That the territory of the mill itself, in several instances, became a battleground, is significant. Competition to be *in* the mill had become especially fierce during famine, at which time "essential" employment meant material survival. During the riots the mill was, once again, a protected space from the misfortunes reigning "outside." The mill, even in the heat of this unprecedented breakdown of order, was still granted "priority" status; protected by armed police guard and able to make "special arrangements" with Civil Supplies for food—even while many in Calcutta lived on whatever bare stocks they had at home for several weeks to come. In short, those sheltered in the mill during the riots were granted a secure space. Also similar to the famine paradigm, however, was that, in truth, consideration as to the fate of even "priority" workers remained secondary at best. Writing to Stanford Cripps several weeks after the riots, G.D. Birla spoke nothing of the massacre of his own workers, noting instead that the riots had been a "mixed evil" in that, even if many thousands had been killed in Calcutta, the Muslim League had been chastened by the fury that they (in Birla's estimation) had released.[101]

Both of the cases that I have looked at above involve Muslims attacking Hindus, but the number of Muslim *bustees* across the city in which massacres took place is far larger. In Shampukur, northern Calcutta, there was an "extensive massacre" of Muslims on the night of August 16th.[102] No report of the incident was received, however, until the governor himself, on tour of Calcutta on August 17th, came across a "number of corpses on the road." The Karamtolli *bustee* near Chitpur Road was also the scene of a massacre, as was the Sahib Bagan *bustee* in Kalighat.[103] In Nakasipara, on the eastern side of Upper Circular Road, "most of the Muslims in that *bustee* were absolutely wiped out."[104] And in Bhawanipur, "Muslims were murdered and killed in hundreds."[105] Perhaps because of the very same structural mechanisms that led to the exclusion of the victims of these massacres from any security at the time, very few specifics are to be found in the existent record of any of these incidents—whereas the two incidents that I have detailed more thoroughly above involve commercial interests and, as such, some record was maintained. Given the lack of information on these other incidents, it would not be wise to speculate on the causes, motivations and variables that defined violence in these *bustees*, but undoubtedly there were complexities to these attacks, as well, that betray simplistic explanation. It is enough to say, without further information, however, that these victims in Muslim *bustees* were poor laborers who, as in the case of famine and war, were, again, rendered most vulnerable to violence in the permissiveness and ferocity that defined the Calcutta riots.

Anti-Colonialism and Administrative Collapse

In November 1945, as detailed in chapter six, there was a massive and relatively spontaneous anti-colonial uprising in Calcutta which was put down with swift and comprehensive martial force. The extent of the repression which was necessary to quell the disturbances had greatly troubled then Governor of Bengal, Richard Casey. Speaking with General Auchinlek after the rebellion, he expressed his conscience on the matter, admitting that he "had [General] Dyer and Amritsar constantly on [his] mind in the last few days."[106] In his own diary he worried, "I do not want to kill these poor misguided creatures—I only want to frighten them and stop them doing the stupidities that the rabble-rousing politicians have driven them to."[107] Although Governor Casey's sentiments might be imagined admirable, there is also something disingenuous about his logic. As the governor well knew, both the Congress and the Muslim League had expressed themselves unequivocally *against* this popular, and remarkably non-partisan, expression of anti-colonial anger.[108] Even Gandhi, when he met with Casey shortly after the outbreak, told the Governor that "no good purpose could be served in having a public enquiry into the recent disturbances."[109] Subsequent disturbances in February 1946 followed an extremely similar pattern, both in terms of the outbreak of popular unrest, and the response—both governmental and political.

These two popular and decidedly anti-communal demonstrations which were directed against the power structure were met, on the one hand, by the prohibitive violence of the colonial state, and on the other, by disapproval and disavowal of the national Indian leadership. In both cases, the audacity of the demonstrators—even in the face of armed assault by the police and military—had shocked both the government and the political parties. The magnitude of these spontaneous eruptions served as a barometer of the pent up frustrations and anxieties of a society that had been pushed to the wall by war, famine and administrative failure. Heeding this troubling indicator of popular discontent, Government had established an "Emergency Action Scheme" to deal with future disturbances against the state. The Emergency Action Scheme revolved around protecting (only) government and corporate interests from attack in the event of further disturbances in Calcutta. Leaders of the national political factions, meanwhile, engaged in self-aggrandizing political showmanship aimed at diverting attention away from the colonial state and towards their own domestic political enemies. What these measures, together, managed to achieve, was to flatten the violence of the masses, which had been recently expressed upwards, onto a horizontal plane. That is: the anger, frustration and violence of the people, which had just recently come to a head in united violence against the state, twice repressed and twice disavowed, exploded laterally—in civil war.

From his earliest report to the viceroy on the 16th of August, Governor Burrows warned that events in Calcutta were serious, but reassured Delhi that the "disturbances have so far been markedly communal and not—repeat not—in any way anti-British or Anti-Government."[110] In his final report of 22 August, he similarly celebrated the fact that "though 'Direct Action Day' was intended to be a gesture against the British," the violence had remained entirely "communal."[111] This same contention has been echoed in all subsequent scholarship on the Calcutta riots in a rather uncomplicated fashion. It is, however, a contention that does not live up to historical scrutiny. As has been already mentioned, Calcutta during the riots was an extremely permissive space and enactments of violence were highly diverse, multifaceted, and complex. As has also already been noted, there *were* attacks on European, governmental and quasi-governmental targets such as ration shops, Civil Supplies warehouses, the Bengal Central Bank, the Statesman House, the Grand Hotel, and the property of large industrial firms—who since the beginning of the war had been granted *de facto* "governmental" status. These attacks, however, were all promptly and decisively addressed and the violence contained—as per the Emergency Action Scheme.

Attacks on the police were also widespread, and were also dealt with on a priority basis. At 11:00 A.M. on the 16th of August, the Deputy

Inspector of Police, H.N. Sircar, received word that the Burtolla police station near Hatibagan in north Calcutta was under attack. The second officer in charge of the station explained that he was unable to hold the situation without armed reinforcement. A Riot Squad was quickly dispatched and the offending mob dispersed.[112] At 11:30, on Chitpur Road the police were having similar difficulties—the crowd there "was truculent…and attacked the police with brickbats." A call was made and "reinforcements from Lal Bazar soon arrived."[113] In central Calcutta, on Chittaranjan Avenue, police were fighting a hit and run battle with an angry mob that fell back when tear-gassed, but advanced again when the gas had dissipated. "The crowd was then dispersed by force."[114] Shortly thereafter the headquarters of the North District Police was itself attacked by a mob, and the deputy commissioner of police, north district, was called in from field operations to address the situation.[115] The damage to high profile targets was thus being contained—the "Emergency Action Scheme" was working. That the native bazaars, *bustees* and by-lanes were seething with arson, loot and murder did not alter that success; the Scheme had been designed to protect colonial interests, and nothing more. Nevertheless, Calcutta was sinking further into mayhem.

By as early 3 P.M. on the 16th (even before the Maidan rally) the situation had deteriorated to the point that the Commissioner of Police made the request for immediate military assistance. "We could not hold out indefinitely," he testified later, "we were being attacked."[116] Military intervention it was thought, however, might yet divert the rioting crowds to colonial targets. Brigadier E.K.G. Sixsmith, for one, feared that the "premature use of military might have turned these crowds… [and] we knew the situation on the 16th might have developed into anti-Government riots."[117] The Brigadier's delicacy here is extremely significant. As has been seen, whenever a European or governmental target was attacked, there was a swift dispatch of auxiliary force from Police Central Command that was able to defuse the situation before any serious damage had been done. Civil Supplies depots and vehicles, as well as important commercial interests, were also under armed guard. But the Emergency Action Scheme could not hold back the reigning chaos indefinitely. Throughout the evening the violence continued to escalate. The military was finally deployed shortly after midnight.

While the Emergency Action Scheme may have been something of a provisional success, the most significant aspect of the colonial state in relation to the riots, was its abject dysfunction.

During the riots Bengal Chief Minister, H. S. Suhrawardy, was, throughout, in the police "Control Room," frantically scribbling notes to the commissioner of police, advising him on how and where to allocate police "pickets," and worrying incessantly about fellow Muslims in the city. Since that time, and for this reason, he has been imagined by some historians (as well as many Hindu residents of Calcutta) to have been directing the riots from this remove by clever deployment of available forces to strategic locations that would protect the Muslim community.[118] But, in fact, it was the sheer ineffectiveness of the entire administrative apparatus to demonstrate *any* control over the situation that is most pronounced throughout the riots, and Suhrawardy was no exception. Even by 3:00 in the afternoon on the 16th of August, the chief minister was himself joining the appeal for the military to be called out.[119] In reality, the kind of "order" that is conferred on the Calcutta riots by explanations of instigation or governmental conspiracy was simply in very scarce supply during the riots. There may have been disproportionate agencies that influenced specific and limited events, but it is very difficult to argue that there were significant mechanisms of "control."

In fact, even in the Control Room itself, chaos reigned. By early afternoon on the 16th, the "Incident Board," which had been developed in relation to the Emergency Action Scheme, had broken down completely and had to be abandoned.[120] Calls were pouring in from every corner of Calcutta and no response could be mounted.[121] Undermanned and under attack, police presence quickly became increasingly futile. Years of endemic poverty, high crime, and the duty of "removing" starving destitutes, had also strained police morale to the breaking point and corruption in the ranks was "rife."[122] Even while Suhrawardy was in the Control Room advising the commissioner, ordinary policemen were out in the streets looting lorries full of cloth and handcarts full of liquor. In the volatile neighborhood of Kidderpore police had insufficient ammunition to mount any kind of effective intervention,[123] and in the Jorabagan police station there was panic and fear.[124] The police headquarters at Lal Bazar was itself choked with thousands of refugees, which only added to the prevailing confusion. A substantial massacre of several hundred *bustee* dwellers took place only 200 yards from the gates of Lal Bazar and the officers inside were none the wiser.[125] Fire brigade workers also came under attack, which prevented them from answering many calls.[126] In addition, the city's water supply system broke down, further hampering fire-fighting efforts.[127] Telephone exchanges also went out of order,[128] and hospitals could not cope with admissions. "By Sunday," a British nurse working with one ambulance crew reported, "every city hospital was hanging signs of refusal outside its gates."[129] The Calcutta Corporation's sanitation services also ceased to function, and garbage and corpses, both human and animal, rotted on the streets for days to come.[130] And—maybe most troubling of all for survivors—the city's rationing system collapsed.

Without the necessary wherewithal to deal with the deteriorating situation, the city's administration fell back, again, on its tired implements developed in relation to war and famine. Refugees were removed from Lal Bazar and other police compounds where they had collected, and carried in police lorries to famine camps operated by the Relief Department.[131] These relief camps, however, soon filled up with panicked and desperate refugees and additional provisions needed to be made. Subsequently, the horse stables at the Calcutta Turf Club were selected as a suitable place to warehouse those who had been driven from their homes by mob violence and could not be accommodated in existing famine camps. Within a short time, the stables were fitted out with supplies gathered from A.R.P. air-raid shelters and were opened to additional refugees. The Civil Supplies Department, also established during famine, meanwhile cut off all its deliveries except to "priority" sites, namely: hospitals, relief camps, and facilities for "essential" personnel, such as the Kesoram mills.[132] This, again, resurrected war-time prerogatives. "Regular rationing to the public," it was decided at a closed-door meeting at Civil Supplies headquarters on the 18th of August, "would be a sheer impossibility until confidence was restored."[133] In the meantime, as in the case of famine, private relief organizations did the bulk of the heavy lifting, sheltering and feeding the vast majority of the nearly 200,000 people dislocated.[134]

The Publicity Department, established in the earliest days of the war, was also pressed into service. But, as the Director of Publicity—one P.S. Mathur—complained in his report, "the Publicity Department was never asked to keep itself ready for communal disturbances."[135] All the department had at its disposal were a sheaf of "health leaflets" to be distributed in times of "emergency," and eight "propaganda vans" which had made the rounds during A.R.P. drills, and during famine, to educate the public in civic responsibility. The vehicles were in a dilapidated condition, "very worn out…and far from being 'trouble free.'" Of the loud-speakers with which they had been fitted-out, "one was condemned outright, four were in working condition but could not bear much strain, and three others needed major repairs and were in the work-shop."[136] Yet, dutiful to a fault, the director of publicity went off to work in the governmental office complex on August 16th, only to find, "there was no other officer in the Writer's Buildings as far as he could see." He went home that same afternoon after a few lonely hours in the office, only to find that "a pitched battle was going on just in front of his own house…and it was only with great difficulty that he could enter." After another futile day at the office on the 17th, the director of publicity was summoned to Lal Bazar and told in no uncertain terms by the deputy commissioner of police to get his propaganda vans in working order and out on the roads. "But propaganda vans," the director noted petulantly in his report, "though quite suitable for fighting panic and guiding law abiding citizens, are of no avail where mobs and organized groups of hooligans are concerned." Nevertheless, after much inconvenience and jerry-rigging he was able to get three of the eight vans running and fitted out with loud speakers, found some drivers, and headed out on the roads at 9 P.M. on the 18th. But with the publicity director's further thoughts on this matter, it is easy to agree: "when there is fighting on every street and every road, when the trouble is so wide-spread, when clashes take place between armed groups of hooligans and angry mobs, publicity vans can be of little avail."[137]

Bodies

Throughout the chapters on war and famine I have argued that how a society and government deal with their dead is of great importance in understanding the value that is accorded to the living of that society as well. Since the height of famine, beginning in early 1943, until the riots broke out, Bengal was confronted with many millions of excess corpses in every corner of the province. These corpses represented an over-whelming material predicament for both government and society. Throughout the period cremation facilities and burial grounds worked overtime, but corpses only continued to pile up. Faced with the sheer enormity of the weight of these bodies, as has been seen in chapter four, indifference to the fate of the dead began to reign. The majority of those killed by famine across Bengal's countryside were left to rot out in the open sun on roadsides or in fallow fields. Tens of thousands more were tossed unceremoniously into rivers and canals throughout the province. Bodies in all states of decay and putrification—and even in the last stages of life—were also torn apart by vultures where they had fallen, or dragged through the lanes of abandoned villages by hungry jackals. The Bengal countryside had become a vast charnel house, and the land itself did most of the work of digesting the millions of discarded bodies.

Unlike in the countryside, the stacks of corpse that began accumulating on the streets and by-lanes of Calcutta by the summer of 1943 represented an acute embarrassment to empire and, as such, needed to be dealt with in a more efficient manner. The dead who had breathed their last on the streets of Britain's "Second City," were thus put under the "protective custody" of the state: loaded up, *en masse*, onto military and police lorries; enumerated, labeled, and disposed of in relatively orderly fashion. To achieve this end, two private organizations, the Hindu Satkar Samiti and the Anjuman Mofidul Islam were utilized to dispose of corpses according to "community." That bodies, deprived of any sense of decency or human value, were yet assigned this one last measure of classification, can be understood as the height of essentialism. That it was the state, moreover, that sanctioned this final distinction on corpses is both striking and disconcerting. Because any and all social value of these individuals had been violently revoked, the labeling of corpses, "Hindu" or "Muslim," amounts to biological distinction that was imagined to have adhered to the very bodies themselves. In the total absence of any other social value, that sole label was still imagined to *matter* to the state.

The violence in the streets of Calcutta in August 1946 was, in some definite sense, a very gruesome echo of the official truism, propagated in relation to famine and war, that bodies themselves—even corpses—should be understood as either "Hindu" or "Muslim." In other words it might also be said that famine and war had introduced the idea that the mass annihilation of *bodies* could be understood as a "communal" phenomenon.

During the Calcutta riots, corpses, yet again, became a prevailing and ubiquitous social reality. The streets and alleys of the city were, in fact, littered with corpses in all sorts of "grotesque attitudes."[138] Mutilated bodies, bodies defiled, bodies hacked to pieces, half-burnt, bludgeoned, stabbed, crushed, disfigured, discarded, and decaying, defied all previous imagination. Bodies floated in the river and choked the city's sewers. Bodies lay about in unmanned hand-carts and were heaped with other mountains of trash in the ruined streets. Bodies lay beneath the rubble of burnt-out buildings and hung from ceilings by their hair in looted houses.[139] A *Statesman* reporter, on 21 August, reported that in an open plot in Shampukur he had come across a pile of about fifty bodies "that had been thrown haphazardly in two heaps and were being devoured by vultures."[140] In Park Circus "beside the burnt and looted remains of a two storied house lay the bodies of two men and a dog. Vultures had attacked the former, leaving the dog alone."[141] In Howrah, "a Muslim was found sitting on the dead body of a Hindu who had been stabbed to death." As police approached, there he remained, until he was arrested.[142] Kim Christen, working for Friends' Ambulance Service, came across a wheelbarrow full of bodies on Chittaranjan Avenue. Among the corpses she found a boy with a pulse. Before she could revive him, however, he expired and was left in the barrow, as it was not her mission to administer to the dead.[143]

Government, on the other hand, had no choice but to administer. It was a mammoth task for an administration in collapse. The cast of characters involved was, accordingly, immense. At least seven I.C.S. officers oversaw a process that involved, also, several ranking members of the Department of Public Health as well as the Geographical Institute. The fire brigade lent assistance, as did the deputy secretary of the development board, the assistant secretary to the governor, three judges from the Calcutta High Court, an official of the Bengal-Assam Railroad, and, of course, the Hindu Satkar Samiti and the Anjuman Mofidul Islam.[144] But these actors represented only the organizational apparatus. The dirty work, the actual lifting, shifting, and handling of bodies was done by several hundred *doms* and Anglo-Indians—*doms* because this was understood to be within their caste distinction, and Anglo-Indians because, as Christians, they were thought to be outside the parameters of the "communal" fray. The military also lent its services, providing lorries and light engineering troops, or "pioneers," who dug trenches to receive the dead. Burial operations however did not go as smoothly as the extensive and varied personnel expended on the job might imply.

On the afternoon of the 18th of August, authorities contacted the secretary of the Mohammedan Burial Board to ask for his assistance with burial space. He informed the Public Health Department that they had room at the Bagmari Burial Ground in Maniktola for the intern- ment of several hundred corpses. A few military "pioneers" and a bull- dozer were sent to the grounds to dig open pits to receive bodies, and the military lent lorries with armed escort for the work of collecting corpses from the streets. All was ready, except for the *doms*, who were proving exceedingly reluctant to be, again, pressed into government's grisly business of ridding the streets of Calcutta of its rotting and man- gled corpses. Two days had elapsed since the riots had begun, and the work was "unimaginably foul." At length, the deputy commissioner of police was enlisted and he managed to wrangle up a contingent of six- teen *doms*. Four corpse-removal parties, under I.C.S. leadership, with four *doms* each, went out onto the streets in military lorries to collect the dead. When the 3-ton lorries, loaded down with bodies, began to arrive at Bagmari, however, it was found that they could not fit through the cemetery gates. *Doms* were thus engaged, with handcarts, to off-load the corpses from these lorries and wheel them a quarter-mile through the monsoon mud up to the pits were the bodies were haphazardly dumped. After several hours of such work, the *doms* refused to labor any longer and operations were called off for the day. In the meantime, the gates of the cemetery had been removed and several lorries of dead—which had been arriving all the while—were parked up "hard by the graves"—yet to be unloaded.

The next morning, the team of *doms* who had worked on the 18th, failed to show up for service, and replacements were difficult to locate. By the time a new party of *doms* had been arranged, the scene at Bagmari was even more chaotic. More than ten military lorries filled with hun- dreds of corpses had joined those of the Public Health Department and were in queue to deposit their payloads into the open pits. However, the bulldozer, which was in use digging pits, was bogged down in mud, and the "pioneers," meanwhile, had dug more trenches, which made the grounds impassible to the lorries. "Despite continued showers and a marked reluctance on the part of the doms to get to work," five of the lorries were somehow unloaded. The military pioneers, however—and for unspecified reasons—refused to "earth the graves," angrily departing *en masse* and leaving behind only a few hand spades. This created further difficulties, as "Doms are not grave diggers, and were not familiar with the spades, and the attempt to employ a section of them to shovel earth over the graves was abandoned when (only) half a trench had been filled." By this time it was after 9 P.M. and the *doms* again struck work, "being tired wet, thirsty and apprehensive of the curfew." The remaining lorries, stacked with corpses, were left behind and operations were suspended for the day. In the night, twenty-two other *doms* were rounded up "following the clues furnished by an Executive Engineer of the (Calcutta) Corporation," in anticipation that those used on 19 August would not show up the next morning.

On the following day, again, an additional nine lorries had been brought in by the military before government workers had arrived. The pre-existing, unloaded lorries, however, had blocked access to the graves, and so the military lorries were again left at a distance. The fresh crew of *doms* was pressed into hard service to clear the queue quickly, but by 8 A.M. refused to work any further. The military, who had brought their own *doms*, thus dumped the bodies that they had brought at the gates of the cemetery and headed back out into the streets to collect more. A small contingent of *doms* was left behind. They unloaded two more trucks "and left the bodies lying on the grass." In the meantime, fifteen additional *doms* were squeezed out of the Calcutta Corporation, and the corpses that had been left lying immediately outside the graves were interred. These *doms*, however, having had no food, demanded breakfast, but then were not willing to be fed the "famine gruel" supplied by the Relief Department. They also demanded a steady supply of "*pagalpani*" (literally "crazy water")—"the only stimulant that will make doms work"—but, in the midst of the riots, none could be found. Only "with difficulty," therefore, "were they induced to inter the bodies near the graves." Those that had been dumped at the gates by the military were loaded back onto lorries by the remaining *doms* and dumped again nearer the graves. At this time, however, these *doms*, too, refused to work any further and walked off the job. The Bagmari Burial Ground was thus left with bodies scattered everywhere, open graves full of bodies un-earthed, and little space left for more bodies to be brought in. A deal was struck with the secretary of the Mohammedan Burial Board that "on supply of transport and escort," the remaining bodies would be buried and the pits filled in by Burial Board workers. This work was reported to have been completed only a week later, on August 26th.

Having thus closed operations at Bagmari, it was decided to "open" the A.R.P. burial pits at Gobra, which had been dug in anticipation of air-raid casualties during the war. Open pits were available to receive approximately 1,000 bodies, but other pits were filled up with water, which had to be pumped out by the Fire Brigade to clear them for more. A whole "colony" of *doms* was "fortunately" located near Hazra Road and a "steady supply" of lorries began bringing corpses to the A.R.P. pits at Gobra. The Hazra *doms* too proved unreliable and obstinate, however, and they too struck work after just a few hours. Frustrated, the organizers of the burials contacted the Anglo-Indian Civic Union, who agreed to send a battalion of Anglo-Indian workers to handle the corpses, on payment. "These proved, from the 22nd onwards, a valuable supplement."

All the while, bodies kept arriving at Gobra and the work there proceeded at an increasingly chaotic pace. "Bodies were frequently unloaded at Gobra hurriedly, by night, and the tendency was to tip them, without arrangement, round about the pits." This created extra work during the day, at which time corpses needed to be assembled in a more orderly fashion inside the pits. "This work was nauseating and picked men were necessary to take charge of it." How men were "picked" is not mentioned. The work at Gobra continued for the next six days, at which time the Anjuman Mofidul Islam, together with the Mohammedan Burial Board, were employed to "tidy up and fill the pits." The operation had been extremely trying for all those involved. It had only been held together, in fact, by the begrudging co-operation of the always difficult *doms* and sheer dumb perseverance. It had also been "dependent on military transport and escort," as well as on "gunny (for carrying bodies hammock-wise), pagalpani (for doms), beer (for Anglo-Indians), stench-masks, *kodalis* [something like a garden hoe], and quicklime." By official count, and in such a fashion, 3,468 copses were disposed of in the mass graves at Bagmari and Gobra.

What stands out most starkly in this account is not just the reckless, ad-hoc and debasing manner in which these bodies were managed—though it does provide an illuminating insight into the workings of the colonial state at this time—it is perhaps more interesting that, even after taking such care during famine and war to categorize bodies by religious affiliation, in the context of the riots this practice was totally abandoned and the neat system of demarcation and disposal broke down. Unclassified bodies were dumped into mass graves without distinction and bulldozed over in monsoon mud. The Calcutta Corporation gave orders to burning ghats to burn all corpses irrespective of community, and the Anjuman Mofidul Islam, likewise, labored under directions to "keep no separate count." In short: the riots had done the work of final identification, no further assignment was needed. The administrative task of distinguishing Muslim bodies from Hindus bodies had been accomplished, instead, by a violence that, beforehand, had marked these bodies as "communal." The Calcutta riots had, in this sense, concretized a bureaucratic distinction that now could be left unreported.

In addition to those bodies collected and disposed of by the state, there were countless other bodies that went completely unrecorded. The exact toll of the Calcutta riots therefore cannot be known. It was likely, however, many times the official figure. How many bodies were burnt in the thousands of fires that gutted the city, how many were dumped into rivers and canals, and how many were disposed of by family members in private ceremonies at burning ghats and burial grounds, is completely unknown. Even the official numbers reported are extremely unlikely to represent the total number of bodies disposed of through state auspices alone given the disarray of the official operations at Bagmari and Gobra.

A great number of bodies were also stuffed into the city's manholes and sewers. In Ballygunge, Mintu Dutto witnessed corpses arriving by train from many other parts of the city. The bodies were unloaded from the train by Sikhs, who had sided with Hindus during the riots, and heaped indiscriminately onto pushcarts, by which means they were transported to the main sewer opening and crammed inside. This procedure went on most of the day, disappearing an untold number of bodies into the sewage system.[145] On the night of 20 August a report was received by the Public Health Department that "3 or 4 bodies" were stuck in the sewers at Ballygunge and it was feared that they might float over the grating at the pumping station and jam the pumps.[146] A party of *doms* was assembled and an operation was undertaken to clear the lines. The *doms* were paid the special rate of 12 rupees per body to dangle by ropes into the open sewer and fish out bodies from a depth of 14 to 20 feet. In this fashion, 110 bodies were retrieved from the sewers of Ballygunge, though it is unclear how many more were simply flushed through the system and out into the river. Miraculously a Muslim boy who had been "killed" in Park Circus on the 16th of August was rescued alive during this operation on the 25th—nine days later.[147] That he had been beaten and left for dead in Park Circus, more than a mile away, would confirm that bodies were transported to different parts of the city for secret—if production-line—disposal.

A similar retrieval operation was undertaken at the Mommenpur pumping station, which was also choked with corpses. By official account, twenty bodies were retrieved. But this number, too, is perhaps arbitrary. Narendra Krishna Mukherjee attended the operations at the Mommenpur pumping station in hopes of identifying his brother in-law who had been killed on August 17th, but whose body had not been found. No identification was possible, however, as the sewer was congested not with bodies, but with body parts. The corpses had been hacked to pieces in order to fit into the tight opening of the sewer. N. K. Mukherjee found a hand that he believed to be his brother-in-law's, but was never sure.[148]

In north Calcutta there were also widespread reports of bodies having been stuffed into manholes and sewer openings. No retrieval operations were undertaken, but a *Statesman* reporter toured many parts of north Calcutta, and while there were no bodies left in the open streets, he "was greeted with an overpowering stench in many localities (that) seemed to confirm (his) information that numberless bodies (had) been pushed into the city's sewers through manholes."[149] In fact, there had been a noticeable and nagging drop in the water pressure in many parts of the city, which frustrated Corporation officials and hampered firefighting efforts. At first it was thought that open hydrants had caused the drop, but it was later discovered that at the pumping stations pressure was maximal. This indicated to Corporation engineers that there were blockages in the main lines and a "choking" of pipes in the entire system. The water mains were accordingly "regularly and systematically flushed" for the next several days, and the problem was resolved.[150] Calcutta had digested its dead.

These are not the signs of a society driven to madness by political rhetoric—these are the signs of a society de-humanized by abounding violence, death, and impunity. These are the signs of an *already* tortured society.

Communalism

What may appear absent to some readers from the foregoing analysis is the omission of any sustained analysis of the "communal" nature of the riots. My intention has not been to deny the prevalence of this particular aspect of the Calcutta riots, but to demonstrate, by concrete example, that the riots were not merely communal. By 1946, Bengal had long been a society under siege. Fear, uncertainty, oppression, and ultimately death on a monumental scale, had frayed the psychological, administrative and moral fiber of society until, in August of 1946, Calcutta became completely unraveled. The riots were, in many respects, a free-for-all in which any number of grievances, anxieties, and animosities could find uninhibited expression. All of these expressions—the sum total of the highly variegated violence that took place—are what comprise the event called the Calcutta riots. Underlying much of the violence, and many of the trends that characterized the riots, were anxieties that were many years in the making. There was also a tremendous amount of communal enmity that was unleashed—which, itself had been cultured in the petri-dish of war and famine.

In most cases the looting, arson, and murder that took place was, indeed, directed violence, with Hindus targeting Muslims, and Muslims targeting Hindus. As I have argued, however, in many cases, there were often variables and particulars that confound the conclusion that communalism alone can explain the violence. In other cases, a very base and uncomplicated hatred of the "enemy" community does appear to have been primary. Many victims of both communities were randomly stabbed to death in the streets with no other motivation than the murder of the "other." Temples and mosques were desecrated and the property of the rival community destroyed without any logic other than to cause economic damage to a hated adversary. In north Calcutta a group of Hindu women were raped, slaughtered and hung from the ceiling by their hair.[151] In Beliaghata, the severed heads of Muslims impaled on spikes were paraded through the streets.[152] In Sovabazar, a group of terrified Muslim men, women, and children ran to a five-story roof top to escape a Hindu mob. The assailants, rather than chasing their prey, set fire to the building and the heat from below caused the roof to collapse. All sixty-odd of the victims fell to their deaths and their bodies were consumed in the fire.[153] In Mommenpur, a Hindu family was attacked by a local mob of Muslims and all the male members of the household were executed, one by one, while the women and the children were made to watch.[154]

The list could go on, but there is no need. About naked hatred and senseless murder there is very little that is interesting. What is more interesting is that this descent into carnage and communal blood-lust did not occur in a vacuum. It emerged in the context of a collective madness that had seized Calcutta, erupting on the day of a political demonstration. This demonstration and the politics behind it have already been detailed in some depth. Neither the demonstration itself, nor the politics behind it, can account for the carnage that ensued. The over-determining factor, even in politics, and more specifically in communalist politics, leading up to this event was famine. Politics had become deeply enmeshed in society's grief, and its attempt to come to grips with the avoidable death of at least 3 million of its citizens. It is one thing when an opposing party is accused of kick-backs or catering to its own constituency; it is another when they are accused of being responsible for the death of millions. Famine hardened the political discourse to a dangerous extent. It also hardened society at large. Scarcity, uncertainty, and fear of destitution were for many years the prevailing social realities for a large sector of the population. That it was this same sector of the population that constituted the primary aggressors, as well as victims, during the Calcutta riots is no coincidence. Issues of belonging, of claiming space, of commandeering resources, of eliminating economic competition, and of defending entitlements, were at least as important to the course of the riots, as were issues of politics or religion. The historical record very much confirms this argument.

In some sense, the Calcutta riots became a far more nakedly "communal" conflict only *after* they had been declared "over." By August 22nd, there were 45,000 troops in the streets of Calcutta, which, as during famine, meant that the riots were officially "over." But killings, evictions, and generalized uncertainty still prevailed. Many of the people I have interviewed have said that the riots continued for many weeks or months to come, and do not adhere to the official "five day" line. Once the din of unbridled violence had receded, however, the shallow rhetoric could start again. The enormous complexity of the riots could be elided in favor of political explanations that privileged, again, the powerful as representatives of the weak. This, in some sense, was only a further dehumanization of the (mostly poor) victims. The tensions, anxieties, and apprehensions that underpinned the violence would not be addressed, and the idea that the riots *also* represented an expression of material grievance could simply be ignored. Moreover, any admission of the participants acting in relation to their own consciousness could be denied. They had merely been automatons of "communalism."

The only official investigation into the riots, the Calcutta Disturbances Enquiry Commission, followed this same logic. The proceedings
took the form of a court trial, rather than a hearing. The majority of
witnesses called were police officers and military personnel. They were
confronted by a Hindu advocate who often questioned them in hostile
and leading terms, and by a Muslim advocate, who tried to demonstrate
that the atrocities of Hindus were that much more fierce. The proceedings began in November 1946, and muddled along in this blame game
for the next several months. Finally, in July 1947, with independence—
and partition—pending, and without ever reaching a conclusion, the
commission was closed. A presiding member explained:

> Your Lordships might remember that during the last session we had com-
> municated with our Lordships that it would serve no useful purpose by
> continuing this Enquiry. We sincerely feel that the sooner we forget about
> the Great Calcutta Killing the better it is for all of us. The bitter memory of
> those days, 16th to 20th August 1946 might jeopardize the smooth working
> of a plan which has been accepted by the major political parties, and we
> think it should not be adjourned, but the whole proceeding should be
> dropped.[155]

The president of the commission and all presiding members concurred. Since that time few have taken up the case.

By the time the Commission closed, India was a sea of dislocation,
massacre and despair. The greatest "exchange of populations" in recorded
history was underway. Independence from colonial rule was within
reach, but the partition of India was excoriating the human landscape.
In 1946, following close on the heels—and in direct relation to—the
Calcutta riots, there had been riots in Noakhali, Bihar, and the United
Provinces. Communal hatred only gelled further in the oven of these
outbreaks, feeding a pernicious dynamic that made hatred and revenge
ever-more central in each echo of violence. The Punjab, in the west of
India, erupted into pandemonium in 1947, and communal carnage
there scarred the population for generations to come. When all was said
and done, as many as a million people had been killed and at least
10 million had been permanently "de-territorialized."

Though the Calcutta riots were the spark that ignited the conflagration, they have received little scholarly attention. They deserve attention
and they deserve explanation. That explanation rests in the truly devastating, unremitting and calamitous violence that preceded the riots. The

profound and pervasive links between war, famine and riot are tortured and complex, but they are also manifest. They are, moreover, far from uncommon. Whenever there is civil war, ethnic violence, communal riots, or any other type of horizontal violence—particularly in the Global South—look for the hunger that preceded it, and it is more often than not very easily found.

CONCLUSION

In this account I have attempted a stark deconstruction of the anatomy of structural violence in Bengal during the 1940s. My objective has been to give a frank catalogue of the political, economic, psychological and social forces that precipitated famine, and to further demonstrate the complex ways that famine impacted the political and communal landscape of India in the lead-up to independence and partition. In this effort I have sought to clearly outline, in plain language, the ways that the intimately entwined ideologies of war, colonialism and capital exacerbated long-standing inequalities, resulting in a multifaceted breakdown of the economic, political, and moral order of the province. It is a massive affair to kill off 3–5 million people in the period of a few short years, but—as I have tried to demonstrate—it is not a mystery as to how or why that happened. Furthermore, understanding the mechanics of how and why famine came to pass in the 1940s in Bengal goes a long way towards understanding the larger power dynamics of the time, including the tone of national discourse and the descent into civil violence that began in Calcutta in 1946 and culminated in the mass dislocations and carnage of partition. In this sense, analysis of the political economy of famine not only can provide a key towards understanding the nature of starvation and death in Bengal in the 1940s, it can also illuminate very critical aspects of the prevailing social and political order in colonial India on the eve of independence, which, in turn, is a critical contribution to the larger history of global empire and war.

In the context of Britain's war in Asia, the Bengal Famine cannot be understood merely as the story of a particularly grotesque form of "col-

251

lateral damage" (as it sometimes has been); it must also be understood, less euphemistically, as the direct outcome of intentional policies and priorities that many, including high officials in the colonial government, fully recognized would bring dire hardship (and even starvation) to the people of India. In their fight against imperial Japan, Britain and its allies were willing to sacrifice Bengal in order to pursue war elsewhere, as well as to regain their lost supremacy in Asia. There is a long record that supports this blunt conclusion. The Bengal famine was no "accident" of war-time "bungling", but rather was the direct product of colonial and war-time ideologies and calculations that (knowingly) exposed the poor of Bengal to annihilation through deprivation.

Those who were operating industrial firms in and around Calcutta— both British and Indian alike—made similar "cost-benefit" analyses based on war and (record) profits that factored in Bengal's poor as the losers. Throughout the entire period they continued to target the countryside's agricultural production with relentless insistence, despite all indications that their efforts were throwing the province's economic order into total disarray. Meanwhile, the national leadership, ever-leery of agrarian unrest which might unhinge their claims to be the sole legitimate representatives of the Indian people, themselves hid behind the ideological insistence of war, adopting the prize of their participation in the war-effort as a bargaining chip that might be used to leverage their "inevitable" ascent to power. As negotiations "at the top" scrabbled forward, the national leadership circled around the pie of independence, failing even to notice that large sectors of the population in Bengal were beginning to starve. That many of these leaders—in both the Congress and the Muslim League—had intimate economic, social and political ties to Calcutta's industrial production (and the record profits that firms were tallying at the expense of the rural population) makes their blindness to famine appear less innocent than it at first might seem. Even as the death toll continued to mount, attentions remained focused on increasingly contentious claims to power rather than the welfare of a population buckling under the material hardships of collapsing colonialism and total war.

At the same time, the correspondingly divisive gentry of Bengal's provincial political establishment were becoming deadlocked in bitter rivalry. With on-going material deprivation and death in the province being used as a tool in the acrimonious debate, concern for famine victims was increasingly partitioned along lines of identity and belonging. That none of the parties wielding power at any level made any concerted argument against famine *before* it erupted into public view, was not so much the result of an oversight, as it was a matter of willed ignorance and studied indifference. The mounting tribulations of the wretched masses of Bengal—and India as a whole—were on few minds in Calcutta, Delhi, or London. Famine, "when it came", created something of a scandal and embarrassment for the brokers of power—locally, nationally and internationally—but even then, reassessment of the deathly structures of inequality that had led to mass starvation were not forthcoming. Britain wanted to call a quick "end" to famine, and most parties, for varying reasons of self-interest, were happy to get in line.

Famine, however, did not simply slip into its cave like some sad dragon, but continued to take its toll: hammering a devitalized population deeper and deeper into uncharted despair. Death and dislocation by hunger had altered the very demographics of the province, with whole villages wiped out or abandoned, and many millions on the move. On the ghostly stage of Bengal, meanwhile, other dramas were being acted out, and the moans and meanderings of the devastated underclasses failed to move the leadership to remedial action. Instead, famine, in the abstract now (as catastrophe survived), was bandied about for political gain, ladening an already rancorous debate with the weight of several million destroyed bodies. Even the flag of a "Second Famine" was hoisted, without the least sense of irony in light of the fact that the "first" famine continued to decimate the province.

For the middling populations, sandwiched precariously somewhere between those who were damned and those who sat in privileged denial, life was harrowing, anxious and uncertain. "Below" them was a mass of wretched misery, and "above" them were competing cabals of self-serving patricians. They clung to what they held—in terms of resources, influence, and "priority"—with a sometimes ruthless resolve, while crippling scarcity continued to make life bitter well into 1946 (and beyond). The dual struggle for survival and dignity for these middle classes was a torturous affair. Many, it has to be admitted, had to sacrifice the latter to the former, which led to a steady unravelling of the moral fabric of Bengal, and a concomitant hardening of oppositional social identifications at this level of society as well. Almost by definition, to survive in Calcutta, meant to watch (and hear) other people die. Bengal had a certain sense of collective pride that was undoubtedly itself a victim of famine, with fears for survival becoming entangled in a kind of "survivor's guilt" that sunk into the collective consciousness. When one sector of a society dies of the torture of hunger—in plain view, and with unending pleas for redress—the very food that sustains the more fortunate sectors of that same society must surely "taste" somewhat different.

That in the congested and contested urban core of Bengal, further violence—anarchic and annihilating—finally exploded, should be less of a surprise than it is commonly understood to be. From where did all that sudden, life-annihilating hatred come? It is far too short-sighted, and far too ill-conceived to end the conversation talking about "Hindu" and "Muslim" sensibilities, or instigations. The Calcutta riots, although distinct from the annihilating violence out of which they emerged (particularly in their participatory nature), have to be read from within the context of a *cumulative* violence that began with chronic, multi-generational poverty, was compounded by war, and brought to a catastrophic head in devastating famine. The ruin of Bengal was not simply about material conditions and mortality, it was a ruin of compassion and tolerance as well. The riots in Calcutta refracted the complex ruin of Bengal in violent colors and with novel forms of cruelty, self-interest and heartlessness. They did not emerge out of the thin blue sky of "communalism".

When examined closely, there is something insidiously tautological about annihilating violence—the violence of genocide, famine, "total war", and communal butchery. The first condition of such violence is that its victims must be understood as something radically different from its perpetrators; they must be construed as something savage, dangerous, bestial, or otherwise not quite human. The violence done to them subsequently, then, does not just feed off these arguments of "difference", it actually justifies them in real time, making whole sectors of the population, indeed, appear grotesque, frightening and foul. Through violence, the Other is successfully degraded, physically disfigured, mentally deranged, spiritually bereft, or otherwise noticeably de-humanized. In the process, the "argument" of difference has gotten that much easier to make, and as such, continuing violence that much easier to digest and dole out. Now they are visible wretches, with visible axes to grind, half-mad, bedraggled and calling for blood—we told you! Savages! More violence will be necessary. Their very existence has become a threat to the moral order. And this next round of violence will, again, make them "less human", more desperate, and, again, that much easier a "target" for hungry power. It is a vicious feedback loop that can be seen across the planet even today.

In this cycle of violence, there is perhaps no more relentless means of degradation, and no more punishing form of systematic violence, than the protracted, multidimensional and cross-generational disfigurement of bodies, minds and communities through chronic material depriva-tion. Famine represents its most ideal form. To make the Other resemble something truly less than human—a walking apparition, a death before the fact, a skeletal zombie, crazed by hunger, grief, incapacity, collapse— may even, on some deep level, be connected to the very psychology of power itself. When we look at famine victims, we are always shocked— they don't even look quite human! Stick figures etched in relief against a barren stretch of earth. Famine is the representation in relief of power at its fiercest. (And that is why every act of resistance, however seemingly insignificant or doomed, must be understood as a tremendous tribute to dignity deferred, and retrieved as such.) It is to make of human beings mere insects, crushed beneath the boot of power. Moreover, the de-humanization that famine achieves is pervasive and extends beyond the direct victims themselves. Society itself goes gaunt. Compassion withers. Unheeded pleas echo in dreams and waking gestures. Survival bears guilt, guilt breeds contempt, and so: more violence. Famine defines a class against whom all comers can do violence, and so generates a hier-archy of violence from that starting point. The number of stories that I have come across of relatively random acts of violence committed against the most wretched of Bengal's population is truly astounding, and deeply disturbing. Man-made famine is a sort of eerie missive from power that announces a suspension of humanity and a revocation of the social contract.

The ramifications of this train of events in Bengal proved to be immense. In the preceding chapters, I have attempted to demonstrate just how deeply engrained famine became in the political, social and psychological landscape of the times, and have also mentioned the incen-diary role that the Calcutta riots played in communal relations in India as a whole. The impacts of the injustice and violence that characterized Bengal in the 1940s hardly ends there. While the nationalist clouds were rumbling above, and scalpels were being sharpened for the vivisection of the sub-content, an armed agrarian uprising, the Tebhaga Movement, was unfolding across still-undivided Bengal. "At the bottom" the primary concern was neither partition nor independence, it was economic justice. Sharecroppers, a group decimated by famine throughout the preceding years, were burning down their landlords' threshing houses, seizing crops, and demanding a fairer share of the fruits of their own labor. There could not have been one amongst the *bargadars* who had not been touched by famine, and all had watched thousands of those around them perish of starvation and disease. One of the first actions of state by the newly minted governments of *both* India and Pakistan was to violently suppress this movement on both sides of the border of divided Bengal. The movement was crushed, but simmered below the surface for decades to come, energizing the Communist Party's rise to power in West Bengal three decades later. In some sense, the resistance movement germinated in the petri dish of famine, had remained coiled at the heart of politics in Bengal all that time.

On the other end of the spectrum, the consolidation of capital, and the boom in industry that accompanied war—and which was so funda-mental to the policies that engendered famine—also resulted in lasting political and economic formations that would impact the history of South Asia for decades to come. The exact extent of profits made, and the relation of these profits to the immiseration of Bengal is a topic for further research. It is safe to say, however, that fortunes were made, and these fortunes were funneled into, and became the backbone of, the nationalist movement. With this confluence of political and economic purposes came certain ideologies and configurations of influence that have remained central to the Indian power structure until today. In some definite sense, the rise to power of this class of industrialists, and their influence in Delhi, were also concocted in the crucible of famine. The claim of "priority"—in the face of war—both granted to and appro-priated by the mill owners and commodity moguls of Calcutta was directly linked to the the hunger, dispossession and despair of the coun-tryside. The exact relationship between these capital interests and the Congress leadership, in particular, is, again, worthy of further research.

Apart from such structural and political considerations, the extent to which famine impacted Bengali collective self-understandings and popular culture is a subject for study that may well be inexhaustible. In the years that followed the events detailed in this book, famine became a sort of self-conscious banner of the whole of Bengal for generations to come—a "sign" under which the province has long labored. I find it just remarkable the alacrity with which youth in Bengal, even today—70 years later—take to conversations about the Bengal famine. Few of them have not heard, and many of them have a fair understanding of the event, and will speak about it with a passion and indignation that keeps famine always fresh and relevant in modern Bengal. It is obvious that they have learned about famine, probably from as early as they can remember; at the foot of some auntie, or grandfather, or parent, or neighborhood teller; but also from movies, popular reference, music and art. The means and modes of the transmission of famine, and the ways that famine continued to impact individuals and communities, as well as political, cultural and economic understandings, well into the late twentieth century is ground for much further investigation.

The decades following the famine and riots, and then partition, were a period of intensive change and struggle, and memories of famine, and its myriad entailments, remained deeply lodged in Bengali hearts and minds. Artists of famine like Chittaprosad, Somnath Hore, Gopen Roy, Ramkinkar, Atul Bose, Gobardhan Ash and Zainul Abedin (to name just a few), became icons of the post-colonial era, and, even by 1944, the Indian People's Theater Association was touring villages and towns staging trenchant dramas (like Bijon Bhattacharya's *Nabanna* [New Harvest]) that portrayed the despair and injustice that had wracked "Hungry Bengal". Famine and hunger, in fact, were central motifs around which creative thought constellated for generations to come. "Hungry Bengal"—the title of Chittoprasad's compilation of sketches and essays of famine-ravaged Midnapore (after which this book is also titled)—became the label chosen by the next generation of writers, painters and poets who, in the 50s, 60s and 70s, continued struggling to come to grips with the enormity of the tragedy that had enfolded in the 40s. The names of many of these artists are as ubiquitous in Bengali households as are the individual stories, passed down by grandmothers and grandfathers, and now great grandmothers and great grandfathers, which have illustrated the landscape of famine more intimately to ensuing generations. Famine has written a rich text into the culture of Bengal, and continues to do so until today.

But, despite both the political resistance of the Tebhaga movement and the effervescence of creativity that referenced famine and infused great grief with profound meaning, for the poor of the province material conditions continued to be brutal and unremitting. Hunger and despair remained the status quo for many millions—and remains so today. Prevailing socio-economic conditions have been the only prompt needed to "remind" the poor of famine. While researching in Calcutta, steeped as I was in the history of famine and riots, I often stepped out of the archives and into the streets with a disorienting sense of simultaneity between the city before me and the history of it that I was delving into. When I travelled into the countryside, that sensibility only redoubled. Hunger seemed still everywhere—haunting the shadows, moaning in dingy corners, written on the faces of young children on street corners, gnawing at the spines of middle aged sweepers, and silently ravaging the collective consciousness of society at large—an ongoing instigation to yet further violence, yet further indifference, yet further merciless competition for resources, for space, for human dignity. At length there arose a burning question in my mind—which still burns today—did the Bengal Famine ever really come to an "end"? Film-maker Mrinal Sen has begun an answer in his film *Akaler Sandhane* [In Search of Famine]. In this work Sen creatively depicts the way that famine continues to poke through the thin skin of "prosperity" in modern-day Bengal, forever reasserting its "lost" contemporaneity. *A ghost never quite dead.*

Mysterious as it now sometimes seems, famine also managed to find me, some 8,000 miles away from Bengal, even before I could speak a word of Bengali or had the faintest idea of Bengal's history—apart from bombings, famine and riots. It had been fleeting images of these three events, based on decontextualized, late night stories, that came close to comprising the entirety of my knowledge of all things Indian, no less Bengali, until well past my own childhood. My father had left Bengal in 1957. He had never really gone back, and there was very little of what he had left behind that he chose to impart to his three American children. He was a gentle man, and a quiet man. He worked extremely hard, and was proud of the life that he had forged in the absence of history. His was the model of a certain brand of post-war "modernity", typical of many immigrants from the Global South at that time: the indeterminate atom-self who joins the faceless millions like him, to lay claim to a certain "floating identity", extracted from the historical continuum, by means of an entirely anonymous self-representation. For most of his life, the tightrope walk that such representation demanded was handled with grace and agility. But there was a sorrow deep within that always gave the lie to my father's performance. For many years I had assumed that it was simply a part of his character, that it stemmed from his passive nature, or perhaps from the sadness of some youthful dream deferred. But at length, as I began to understand both he and myself better, I realized that it must be connected to those scattered memories of his boyhood that he would relay on certain, infrequent, evenings. The bombings, the famine, the riots. And I also began to realize that the dreams that mattered in this regard, were the nightmares that would fill the house with guttural moans of inexplicable dread on certain New York nights. Late in his life, when I asked him about those dreams, he would tell me that it was an abstract impression of a tremendous weight pushing down on his chest, a weight that he felt would crush him alive.

That weight, I came to realize, was the weight of a very profound sorrow, a sorrow that knew few bounds. My father was a boy when the events charted in this book took place, born in 1932. In my extensive interviews with other survivors of that time, the year of his birth has taken on some significance. In my work, I have interviewed some who were born a good deal earlier than my father (as early as 1915) and some born a few or several years later (as late as 1937). After some weeks, and then months, of talking with people in these general age groups, I was able to guess with a surprising degree of accuracy just what year any of my contacts were born. Those of the slightly older generation had the most detailed memories, of course, but they also had the most cogent explanations. They may have been 20 years old during the famine, and then 23 during the riots. They had watched with a discerning eye, and they had listened closely to those around them. The years of war and famine had left deep impressions on them, and they spoke about those years with indignation and pointed purpose. They had distinct under-standings of why things had happened the way they did, and I learned a tremendous amount from them that is reflected in this work. Those in the youngest category, on the other hand, had no such purchase on the course of events. Most of them, in fact, remembered very little. They had been afraid. The adults had been panicked. It was a terrible time. Details were few and the sequence of events vague. Finally, those my father's age were somewhere in between: they could remember a fair amount and in fairly vivid detail, but they could not explain. They had been stunned into a kind of metaphysical silence by visions and happen-ings that had remained just beyond their level of comprehension intellectually, but perhaps not so emotionally. They had been damaged in a different way, and a sort of placid, but extremely deep sorrow seemed to be their lot in life. It is that sorrow, I have realized more and more, which has informed this work above all else. Though my tone may be angry, and the prose may be clinical, it is the sorrow of my father and his generation that I have been at great pains to redeem in these words. I have been searching for a ray of understanding to offset that bewildered sorrow with explanation. I hope I have managed to achieve this goal in some small measure.

Without question, the realities of the times that I have lived through while completing this book have also left their impression on this work. In short, they have been years of perpetual war in the United States, with mantras of "patriotism" and "security" monopolizing all airwaves. Again, I have often been left with an eerie feeling of simultaneity between my historical work on war in Bengal and the clamor of war that has surrounded me over these many years. More and more in my research I have come to understand the extent to which famine in Bengal was really a direct and inextricable product of war, not just in terms of the inflation that war unleashed and the hierarchies of social, political and economic "priority" that war enforced, but just as importantly in terms of the deafening din that war created: a roar of manic purpose that blotted out any other rival claims of purpose. War cast the poor of Bengal in a deep shadow, in the darkness of which they could be sacrificed without ceremony. Unless and until they could produce something useful to the war machine, their fate as human beings would cease to register on the radar, and their voices of distress would be rendered unintelligible by the megaphone of power. Only when their starvation was interpreted as a threat to the war effort, was it recognized. War bred fear, it bred authoritarianism, and it bred economic dislocation. In the name of war, opposition was stomped out, democratic process was suspended and discourse was monopolized. In the thicket of war, inequality and injustice were buried, and "marginal" voices were silenced. Under this cover of silence, a grievous crime was committed, in broad daylight, and scarcely anyone present rang the alarm.

When great powers understand themselves to be—or at least declare themselves to be—in dire existential crisis in regards to some external "threat", the demand for attendance to their particular "emergency" (war) becomes totalizing. Consequently, the trumpeted exigencies of war blot out all other rival concerns, such as voices demanding social or economic justice domestically. War masks poverty. War masks injustice. Common cause must be made or there will be hell to pay. War masks hunger and environmental disaster. Whatever bodies are annihilated, and whatever earth is scorched, destruction will cloak itself in necessity. War masks economic crime. If nothing else obtains to victory, either at home or abroad, the economy of war, at least, will win out. War masks authoritarianism. Because the masters of war are those with the most power, and the most might, it is always their call (to arms!) that must be heard. All other cries of emergency, or existential alarm, will be silenced—by force if need be—so that the clarion call of war can be heard: a trumpet flourish, imagined by the arrogance of power to reach down to (and even move) the lowest of the low. Their concern is "our" concern. The great power is calling for the physical annihilation of an implacable and barbaric "enemy"; all other claims towards justice must first assume subservience to that call. War demands discipline. Sacrifice will be necessary, and belts will tighten. Calls for economic justice that go against the flow of the war economy will be silenced. Any further accusations of injustice against the great power will be grouped in the ever-expanding category of "threat". The next step is "enemy", and enemies will be destroyed, burnt alive if necessary. War masks sanity. One will not even be allowed to stand apart—"you are either with us or against us." War masks calls for equality, making of them the insignificant carping of a discontented class. War masks individuality. The counting of bodies becomes monotonous. Put them all together in a single pit. War masks beauty. Although they say that flowers grow—even in the fields of Hungry Bengal.

EPILOGUE

"When an old person dies, a library burns to the ground."

African proverb

When I first began researching the 1940s in Bengal, the *living* memory of war, famine and riots was still very much present in Bengali culture. It seemed that in any house I visited in Calcutta (which the city was still called at that time) there were members of the household who could recall, from personal experience, the turmoil of war, the depredations of famine and the terror of communal violence. Memories, of more than fifty years prior, were sharp and insistent. Even on buses and street corners, I would happen upon elderly denizens of the city, who, when they discovered my purpose, were eager to *talk*. The cataclysmic history that they had borne witness to seemed to be bottled up inside them and needed to get out. Often enough our discussions ended with profuse gratitude that I had come to *listen*. For so many years, already, they had been telling their tales, to children, and then grandchildren, and even great-grandchildren, but who could really understand the gravity of those memories and their importance? What did they *mean*?

In these more than twenty years since that time, the experiential threads of war, famine and riots in Bengal have become increasingly attenuated. As I mention in the dedication, most of those closest to me, those upon whom I relied for direction and moral support in this work, have died. And so it is across Bengal, now more than seventy-five years since the events catalogued in this work. Even the intergenerational transmission of the first-hand memory of these times has atrophied.

263

Young people, now several generations removed, have heard—but are increasingly removed from the webs of memory that kept these events still breathing—the often hoarse, sometimes ponderous, predictably outraged, sorrow-tinged voices that told of these impossible times. Those voices stayed with me throughout my years of research, and also became interwoven with my own voice in this book. But even for me, time has reduced those voices to a whisper—ghosts, now, reminding me of the promises I had made a long time ago to tell the story.

One of the most ubiquitous refrains I heard in those early days of research, was that the famine of 1943, that inhuman spectacle that each and every elderly person I interviewed had witnessed, was "man-made." And so, the emphasis of my own work has been less on the pathos of starvation than on the architectures of power and disempowerment that brought it to pass. Colonialism, it is abundantly evident, was perhaps the *necessary* condition of famine in mid-twentieth-century Bengal, and so, much of this work is about tracing the sclerotic and deathly hand of empire in the manufacture of famine. Which policies, enacted according to which ideologies, can be identified as primary causes? And, just as importantly, who were the chief architects of famine? These were my starting questions. But as my research deepened, I came to fully recognize that colonialism itself is not a monolith, and the enactments and agencies that precipitated starvation in Bengal are complex. Who collaborated with the colonial state in its predatory policies that left a whole province reeling in starvation? And what did *they* have to gain? And, just as importantly, what were the socio-political ramifications of starvation on such a scale? How did this economically driven catastrophe impact society, and how were those impacts indexed in the context of 1940s Bengal?

A second all but ubiquitous trace of memory that I encountered in my rounds was an aural fragment repeated by so many whom I interviewed: "*Phan dao! Phan dao! Bachao ma, phan dao!*" It is the sound of begging in the streets of Calcutta during famine: "Give us the starch water from your cooked rice, Mother! Save us! Give us the run-off from your rice pot!" It is the voice of starving villagers who flooded the streets and by-lanes of Calcutta, wretched and skeletal, covered in sores, many dying within days of arrival, or being rounded up and disappeared by authorities in the dead of night. I have heard their voices, over and over again, theatrically enacted by the dozens of middle-class survivors of famine that I have spoken to about those days in Calcutta. Questions concerning the manufacture of famine are essentially empirical questions. The questions that this second trace of memory elicit are, if anything, more complex. Why did these starving and wretched villagers, dying on the streets of Calcutta, *only* beg for starch water? And why is this particular aural fragment so embedded in the collective memory of famine in Bengal?

In established households of Calcutta, in solid brick-built homes, there were, indeed, stockpiles of rice. That category includes the vast majority of those survivors from the 1940s whom I have spoken to. As noted in chapter two, when the Government of India advised the Bengal Chamber of Commerce in early 1942 to inform its members to begin stockpiling at least three months' worth of foodstuffs for all its employees, there was panic. The edict was quickly broadened to include the "general public," and a scramble for rice at every local level in Calcutta ensued. Only in established households in Calcutta were there the kinds of connections and resources necessary to make large purchases of food stores. In many houses there were stocks sufficient for six months and more.[1] What does it mean to be asked for *only* rice water when you're sitting on small mountains of rice? To what extent does your own fear for survival *inform* that wretched, minimalist plea?

In a number of the interviews I conducted, people recounted very individualized depictions of death by starvation, day by day. A wretched woman to whom one's *father* had given cooked food only the day before she died. (Did they only beg for *phan* because that is all that *women* could give, overseeing the cooking, but certainly not the supplies?) What does it mean to *live out* your survival in face-to-face confrontation with the fact that it is directly contrasted with this other person's annihilation? In the pathos with which that phrase is recanted by survivors of the 40s in Calcutta, is there also the sadness of an unspeakable guilt and helplessness? Bombs were falling on the city; anything could have happened. Had fear throttled charity to the extent that nothing more could be *expected* beside *phan*? These are, in a definite sense, moral questions.

In recent years, the question of the Bengal famine being "man-made" has gained increasing academic and public attention. Interpretations of this now long past historical event have also become increasingly embedded in political alignments, most notably hinging on questions regarding the role of Winston Churchill in relation to the famine. In the summer of 2020, during the global Black Lives Matter upheavals, his historical legacy came under direct fire, not least of all because of his well-documented role in the manufacture of famine in Bengal. Rather than give my opinion on that one particular aspect of the larger story, I will say here that I am happy to have written this work, anatomizing the complex mechanics of power implicated in the Bengal famine. I am wary of historical simplification, behind which some form of nationalism or another always seems to be lurking. I have done my best in this work to relay the complexities of mass death and structural violence in mid-twentieth-century Bengal. Working, as I have already said, primarily from the clues and prompts that I was able to gather in conversation with survivors from the 1940s, I did feel an urgent need to detail the mechanics of power and disempowerment in as much depth as I was capable. This effort, it seemed to me, was a sort of moral *duty*, to repay the warmth and cooperation with which I had been received by them.

In that sense, just as those living threads of inspiration and guidance have become attenuated, so too has the meaning of this work changed. What is its core value now? Although I do believe in the historical imperatives of this story in its own right, the urgency of this research has become less historically situated. It has become less grounded in living history. The last several years, in India and Bengal, as well as globally, have themselves been years of turmoil, dislocation, polarization and, also, pervasive despair for many millions. The December 2018 move towards "demonetization" in India, which perilously dislocated market relations and economic confidence across the country; the more recent Covid-19 "lockdown," which amounted to a state of martial law, pushing the poor of Bengal closer to the economic abyss of the 1940s than I ever expected to see in my life; and, of course, the rise of communalism, and the increasing imbrication of toxic identity politics and the daily life of India—what is the *living* purpose of the history I have outlined here in this present context?

It might be that the sort of historical analysis that I have attempted here, in relation to the war years in Bengal, can provide some template for understanding the structures of power today, which do seem distinctly analogous. Power continues to operate in deathly ways, the lineaments of which are identifiable. Issues of environmental degradation and climate change are rendering the socio-economic landscape of the planet at large increasingly unstable. Large geo-political manipulations of "great powers" are shaking fragile foundations of local life, just as distant thunder clouds, heard but not seen, might shake the earth. Economic dislocations follow, one after the other, while political rhetoric chases jealously behind, making little more than hay out of acute human suffering and cynically fomented fear. Uncertainty abounds, frays solidarities and constrains associations, as horizons narrow and hunger proliferates. And, yet again, enormous profits are being made, in direct, if hidden, relation to the deepening deprivation—to the point of annihilation—of the planet's poor. It is my hope that this work can, in some small way, contribute to a more critical analysis of the times we are living through. Perhaps that is its core meaning now—at least to me.

But in the present times, the focus of my thoughts turns more and more to that other historical thread that remained so consistent in my interviews—that fragment of sound, and the moral riddle that it has always held for me. "*Phan dao! Phan dao! Bachao ma, phan dao!*" That plaintive echo, emanating from skeletal bodies that rent the air with sorrow and distress. Is it not some sort of miracle that, while the bodies of those who issued those pleas have so long ago been annihilated, their voices have spanned generations? What should we make of them now? In all the uncertainty and turmoil of our present condition, with the shibboleths of authoritarianism, war and social division being worshipped with manic insistence, in this all but deafening cacophony of present-day life, could these thin voices from a distant past, echoing across decades, have anything at all to say? Maybe it is that we are not alone. Maybe it is that we are all connected, no matter how profound the cleavages of privilege and power. If we give nothing but thin gruel in response to great need, will we too be haunted by voices until the end of our days? It is entirely likely that not a soul who is reading this epilogue now will go hungry tonight. In these present times, questions about privilege and disempowerment, and how they interface, are perhaps *still* the most critical of all. Why did they only beg for *phan*? And why did the pleading voices of those who died in that holocaust of hunger remain so stubbornly embedded in the memories of those who survived the Bengal famine, for so long? It does make one wonder…

Toronto, January 2023

NOTES

INTRODUCTION: IN SEARCH OF FAMINE

1. Sen (1981), p. 1.
2. What this exploration will further illustrate is that the factors that Sen identifies do not operate in isolation, but rather describe something of a feedback loop, fueling each other and thereby creating a deepening of the crisis over time. That is: the existential uncertainties of war created panic buying (by individuals, government, and industrial concerns alike), which put pressure on prices; the pressure on prices created a speculative bubble, which led to the withdrawal of more grains from the open market, further escalating prices, which led, in turn, to further panicked purchasing, which created further psychological trepidation, that led to increased hoarding, which again sent prices higher, leading to further commodity speculation, hoarding, uncertainty, etc. The administration of Bengal, already thrown into acute disarray by the advent of war, attempted one "solution" after another, advancing *ad hoc* measures, that created further uncertainty, which it then attempted to reign in by additional new measures, that led to further chaos in implementation, which led to a new docket of interventions, which generated greater distrust, that led to further price volatility, etc. Similarly with regulation: throughout the period one regulatory (or anti-regulatory) regime after another was explored, which only fed both the market instability and administrative chaos, etc.
3. See, in particular, Chapter Three and the section on Gandhi's fast.
4. Davis, p. 21.
5. *Report on Bengal*, p. 1.
6. Greenough, p. 96.
7. Letter from Fazlul Huq to Governor Jack Herbert, August 2, 1942, reprinted in: Shila Sen, p. 273

8. Ibid, p. 13.

9. *The Statesman*, 18 December 1943.

10. Sen (1981), p. 215.

11. Ibid, p. 202.

12. Ibid, p. 200–1.

13. Bose (1986), p. 96.

14. Greenough (1982), p. 265.

15. See Guha (1983) and Bhadra (1985). Also Scott (1985).

16. A tern used by Suranjan Das to describe the psychological effects of famine on the people of Bengal. In Das (1991), p. 162.

17. Jalal, p. 223.

18. Ibid, p. 216.

19. See, for instance: Sumit Sarkar (1983), or Bose and Jalal (1998).

20. On 19 August–, Wavell wrote to Pethwick-Lawrence, "the present estimate is that appreciably more Muslims than Hindus were killed." (T.O.P. Vol. VIII, p. 274.) Vallabhbhai Patel, in a letter to Stanford Cripps in October also suggested that "in Calcutta the Hindus had the best of it. (T.O.P. Vol. VIII, p. 750.)

21. Das (1991), p. 74.

22. Ibid, p. 59.

23. Ibid, p. 6.

24. Ibid, p. 310 (emphasis added).

25. Ibid, p. 170.

26. Ibid, p. 162.

27. This passage is extracted from the Bengali monthly children's magazine, *Rangmashaal*. The magazine was published bi-monthly according to the Bengali calendar. Magh 1348, corresponds to January 1942 by the Gregorian calendar. The section "letter box," from which this passage is taken, was a regular feature. *Didi-bhai* means "big sister." No other reference was given to determine who *Didi-bhai* was. This section begins every issue with a communication to "my dear little brothers and sisters," relates the news of the day, and then goes on to answer questions sent in by readers the previous month. (The translation is mine.)

Chapter One: War

1. *Amrita Bazar Patrika*, "Air Raid Precaution," 24 December 1940.

2. Ibid.

3. WBSA, Intelligence Branch, W-72/41

4. Ibid.

5. Ibid.

6. Ibid.
7. Ibid.
8. Ibid.
9. Ibid.
10. Baker (2008), p. 2.
11. Ibid., p. 280.
12. Quoted in Zweiniger-Bargielowska, p. 16.
13. Zweiniger-Bargielowska quoting Board of Trade, *Report*, 1937, p. 14
14. Zweiniger-Bargielowska, p. 14
15. Ibid.
16. Zweiniger-Bargielowska (2000), p. 16.
17. Ibid., p. 14.
18. Ibid.
19. Ibid., p. 33.
20. Ibid, p. 12 (emphasis mine),
21. Quoted in Zweiniger-Bargielowska (2000), p. 44.
22. Ibid., p. 36 (from 22 million to 11 million tons).
23. Ibid., p. 53.
24. See W.W. Hunter (1883), also Nand (2007) and Kali Charan Ghosh (1987).
25. Hunter, pp. 19–20.
26. Quoted in Kali Charan Ghosh (1987), p. 4.
27. Hunter, pp. 26–27.
28. Ibid., p. 39.
29. Ibid., p. 40.
30. Ibid., p. 34–35.
31. Ibid., p. 23.
32. Ibid.
33. Hunter, p. 33.
34. In his *Rule for Property on Bengal*, Ranajit Guha traces the earliest impetus for a Permanent Settlement in Bengal to the 1770 famine. "The first two advocates of Permanent Settlement both regarded the famine as the most conclusive evidence of the worthlessness of the existing economic policies and the best reason that could be there for seeking an alternative in terms of a more stable and comprehensive land settlement." p. 16.
35. See Nand's appendix "Famines in Colonial India, 1750–1947", p. 60–4
36. Brewis (2010).
37. *Bengal Famine Code, Revised Edition of 1905*, p. 54.
38. Ibid, p. 12.
39. MLA—Member of the Legislative Assembly. The Legislative Assembly in New Delhi was the national Indian governmental body. It worked in con-

sultation with the Viceroy of India, the king's representative, whose authority necessarily accedes that of the Legislative Assembly.

40. Testimony of K.C. Neogy in *Nanavati Papers*, p. 1287

41. Ibid.

42. Ibid. The Government of India Act of 1935 had—ostensibly—established
a devolution of the central (colonial) government's power in a policy know
as Provincial Autonomy

43. Bengal was broken up into twenty-some larger Divisions, Division were
divided into Districts, Districts into Sub-divisions, and Sub-divisions into
Thanas, or police districts. At a very local level, there were also Union Boards.

44. The administrative body of "self-rule" in the city, established by the Calcutta
Municipal Act of 1923.

45. Chatterjee, Pranab Kumar (1991), p. 104.

46. Ibid.

47. Sen, P.K. (1945), p. 4.

48. Ibid.

49. Ibid.

50. Casey Diaries, 9 February 1944.

51. WBSA, Home Confidential, Confidential Fortnightly Report on Bengal,
Second Half December, 1945.

52. Bayly and Harper (2005), p. 72.

53. All information following is taken from WBSA, Home Confidential,
W-551/41.

54. WBSA, Home Confidential, W-351/46.

55. *A.R.P. Handbook*, WBSA, Home Political, W-551/41.

56. Ibid.

57. WBSA, Home Confidential W-477/42.

58. *Amrita Bazar Patrika*, 1 November, 1940.

59. Ibid.

60. Ibid.

61. Ibid.

62. WBSA, Home Confidential, W-77/42 (emphasis mine).

63. *Casey Diaries*, May 7th, 1944.

64. From this "infinite variety" Sugata Bose is able, however, to construct a
working typology of agrarian patterns of land use in his *Agrarian Bengal*.

65. Guha (1963), p. 13. Guha traces the difficulties that company revenue officials had in sorting out the heterogeneous nature of Bengal's rural land relations based on "tradition recorded only in memory and customs embedded in a variety of local usages [which] wielded an authority equal to that
of any written code."

66. WBSA, Home Confidential, W-477/42.

67. Ibid.
68. Ibid.
69. Bayly and Harper (2005), p. 17.
70. *The Leo Amery Diaries*, p. 606.
71. Ibid, pp. 605–6.
72. Ibid, p. 621.
73. Henry Hodson's Autobiography at: http://www.athelstane.co.uk/hvhodson/hvhbiogr/biogr09.htm (last accessed 1/20/10, 1:02 PM), Chapter IX, p. 1.
74. Middle-class, educated "gentlefolk".
75. Menials.
76. Ibid.
77. WBSA, Home Confidential, W-477/42.
78. All the following from WBSA, Intelligence Branch, file #250–40. Translated from Bengali in file.
79. Ibid.
80. See Kamtekar (2002), p. 199: "The Indian public showed no desire whatsoever to contribute to the state's finances."
81. Of the many Bengali people surviving from these times that I have interviewed, all remember this rhyme gleefully. It is interesting, moreover, that the *next* generation, those born after the war, also know this rhyme and can recite it—with similar satisfaction.
82. Tagore, preface to Mitter (1934).
83. Mitter (1934), p. 42.
84. Ibid., p. 5.
85. Ibid.
86. Ibid., p. 23.
87. Ibid., p. 13.
88. Ibid., p. 31.
89. Bose (1986), p. 102.
90. In Bengal, the rural gentry were mostly Hindu landlords, while the majority of the cultivators were Muslim. There were historic tensions between these groups revolving around rents, credit relations and shares of crops that could break along communal lines during periods of economic hardship. See chapter six in Bose (1986), "Agrarian Class Conflict, Nationalism and Communalism in East Bengal," for a closer look at this dynamic.
91. Ibid., p. 111.
92. Ibid., p. 125.
93. Ibid., p. 140.
94. Ibid., p. 88.
95. *Amrita Bazar Patrika*, 27 October 1940.

96. Ibid.

97. Bose (1986), p. 214.

98. "War Diary, Aug.–Oct. 1941," WBSA, Home Confidential, W-60/41.

99. Quoted in Bose (1986), p. 214. A "Goonda" is something like a "thug," "goondaism" is something of a code word during the entire period to refer to demonstrations and/or violence perpetrated against the government, local authority, or military.

100. Bose (1986), p. 215.

101. Ibid.

102. Ibid., p. 261.

103. "War Diary, Aug.–Oct. 1941," WBSA, Home Confidential, W-60/41.

104. Ibid.

105. Ibid.

106. Bhattacharya, Sanjoy, p. 75.

107. *Casey Diaries*, 27 January 1944.

108. Quoted by Bose (1986), p. 262.

109. "Distant Thunder".

110. Midnapore is a district 100 miles southwest of Calcutta, often and again, the center of anti-British "terrorist" activity in Bengal.

111. Government subsidized shops for rice and other essential commodities.

112. Chakrabarty (1989), p. 105. Actual numbers for jute mill workers' place of origin, 1940: 11.6% Bengal, 43.1% Bihar, 36.4% U.P., 3.4% Orissa, 2.4% other.

113. As operations got underway in the Middle East and North Africa, India was supplying as much as 1.2 *billion* yards of cloth per year. See Kamtekar (2002a), p. 195.

114. Chakrabarty (1989) p. 9.

115. Chatterjee, Pranab Kumar (1991), p. 84.

116. Ibid., p. 77.

117. Bhattacharya (2000), p. 85.

118. Quoted from Home Political Files, GOI 218/42 in Bhattacharya (2000), p. 41.

119. During the war the Government of India established a "Priorities Committees" along with organizations like the War Transport Boards that would work out special schemes for provisioning "priority" workers in war time industries. The best current work on the various schemes of legislation and administration in war-time Bengal is Sanjoy Bhattacharya's *Propaganda and Information in Eastern India, 1939–45.*

120. *Official History of the Indian Armed Forces in the Second World War*, p. 145.

121. Bhattacharya (2000), p. 19.

122. Bayly and Harper (2005), p. 72.

123. Ibid., p. 106.
124. Ibid.
125. *The Leo Amery Diaries*, p. 722.
126. Ibid.
127. Bayly and Harper (2005), p. 116.
128. Winston Churchill, *Complete Speeches*, p. 6532.
129. Bayly and Harper (2005), p. 120.
130. Ibid.
131. Ibid., p. 142.
132. Ibid., p. 143.
133. From Dorman-Smith Memoirs, quoted in Bayly and Harper, p. 86.
134. Ibid. With colonialism had come a large immigrant population of Indians, who served at the lowest and highest levels of society. From Bengal and Orissa, waves of mostly Muslim immigrants had come to find work as sweepers and "coolie" laborers. Upper caste Hindu Bengalis were imported to serve as functionaries in the colonial bureaucracy. And from trading communities in the Punjab and Gujarat, Marwari and Chetiar business-men had come to turn profits in lucrative agricultural and piece goods markets. The success of these immigrant populations created considerable resentment among the Burmese population. Throughout the 1930s Burma had seen anti-Indian riots and pogroms that left simmering ethnic tensions in their wake.
135. Ibid., p. 158.
136. Ibid.
137. From Dorman-Smith Memoirs, quoted in Bayly and Harper, p. 163.
138. 'Report on the Burma Campaign' in Dorman-Smith Papers, quoted by Bayly and Harper, p. 162.
139. Tinker, pp. 1–15.
140. Bayly and Harper, p. 183.
141. Tinker, p. 12.
142. Ibid., p. 13–14.
143. Chakrabarty (1989), p. 9.
144. Ibid, p. 50.
145. See Chapter 4 of Ann Hardgrove (2002), and Chakrabarty (1989), pp. 53–60.
146. Chatterjee, Pranab Kumar, p. 105.
147. Bayly and Harper (2005), p. 193.
148. Chatterjee, Pranab Kumar, p. 105.
149. Kamtekar (2002b), p. 87.
150. Nanavati Papers, Testimony of L.G. Pinnell, p. 547.
151. Kar, pp. 94–5 (translation mine).

152. Bose (1986), p. 202.
153. Sen, Shila (2001), p. 80.
154. Quote from a campaign speech printed in *Amrita Bazar Patrika*, 16 December 1936.
155. Sen, Shila (2001), p. 85.
156. Ibid., pp. 88–89.
157. Sen, Shila (2001), pp. 126–27.
158. Ibid., p. 127, footnote 1.
159. In the Government of Bengal's "War Diary" for August—October 1941, it is noted: "Muslim reaction to campaign in Iran were undoubtedly uneasy…an undercurrent of dissatisfaction and distrust which principally takes the form of criticizing Great Britain for actions which, in its methods, is represented as being exactly like that of Nazi Germany." WBSA Home Political File W-60/41.
160. Ibid., p. 127, footnote 2.
161. Fazlul Huq's letter to Liaquat Ali Khan, 8 September 1941. Printed in Sen, Shila (2001), Appendix IV, p. 265.
162. Ibid., p. 267.

Chapter Two: Denial

1. Appendix IV of the Famine Enquiry Commission's *Report on Bengal*, p. 217, indicates that the price index for rice, pegged at 100 for the week ending 19 August 1939, reached 172 in December 1941.
2. *Report on Bengal*, p. 28.
3. Knight (1954), p. 47.
4. Ibid, p. 49.
5. Nanavati Papers, Testimony of Major General E. Wood, p. 503.
6. Ibid.
7. Nanavati Papers, Testimony of Mr. Barman of the Calcutta Corporation, p. 1276.
8. See Chatterjee, P.K. (1991), p. 84.
9. Nanavati Papers, Testimony of Representatives of the Bengal Chamber of Commerce, p. 1404.
10. Nanavati Papers, Memo of the Calcutta Municipal Corporation, p. 197.
11. Ibid.
12. Nanavati Papers, Testimony of Azizul Haque, p. 435.
13. Greenough (1982), p. 102.
14. Congress demanded immediate concessions towards self-government in exchange for backing the war effort, and colonial representatives promised independence only after the war—if Congress agreed to cooperate in the meantime.

15. Henry Hodson's Autobiography at: http://www.athelstane.co.uk/hvhodson/hvhbiogr/biogr09.htm (Last accessed 1/20/10, 1:15 PM) Chapter IX, p. 3.

16. Ibid., Chapter XII, p. 5.

17. Ibid., Chapter IX, p. 4.

18. In his testimony before the Famine Enquiry Commission, Special Officer L.G. Pinnell, in charge of denial policy, suggests: "I don't think anybody has been able to explain why the Japanese did not invade us…there was nothing whatsoever to prevent the Japanese from coming whenever they wanted." Nanavati Papers, p. 544.

19. Nanavati Papers, Testimony of M. K. Kirpalani, p. 779.

20. M.A. Ispahani's testimony: "When I met the Commerce Secretary he said that they found it difficult to remove rice and paddy from the coastal area to about 200 to 300 miles in the interior." Nanavati Papers, p. 631.

21. Both Mirza Ahem (M. A.) Ispahani and his brother and partner at Ispahani Limited, Mirza Abol Hassan (M. A. H.) Ispahani, were established members and staunch defenders of the All-India Muslim League, with intimate ties to its leader, Mohammad Ali Jinnah. M. A. H. Ispahani and Jinnah carried on a long and genial correspondence throughout the period, with Ispahani reporting to Jinnah on the divisive, and at times fractious, workings of the provincial Bengal Muslim League.

21. The firm itself, M. M. Ispahani Limited, was a well established trading company, with extensive connections to sub-agents and purchasers across the Eastern Region.

22. Nanavati Papers, Testimony of M.A. Ispahani, p. 631.

23. In his letter of 2 August 1942 to Governor Herbert, Fazlul Huq wrote: "The Joint Secretary says that when he was arranging to carry out your orders, you grew impatient and gave him definite directions to arrange for removal of excess rice from three districts within 24 hours…The Joint Secretary, in his haste and hurry to oblige you, advanced twenty lakhs of rupees to a nominee of a friend to begin the work." Huq's letter was widely circulated and the allegations here never denied by either Herbert or Kirpalani, which tends to lend them credence. The letter itself is reprinted in the Nanavati Papers, p. 743.

24. Ibid.

25. Nanavati Papers, Testimony of M. K. Kirpalani, p. 780.

26. Ibid.

27. Three of the agents (Poddar, Dutta, and Khan) had no experience at all in the rice business. See: Nanavati Papers, Testimony of representative of the Bengal Rice Mills Association, p. 1211.

28. Harris-White (2008), p. 5.

29. Nanavati Papers, Testimony of M.A. Ispahani, p. 639.

30. Nanavati Papers, Memorandum of the Bengal Rice Mills Association, p. 179.

31. Ibid.

32. Ibid.

33. Ibid.

34. Nanavati Papers, Testimony of L.G. Pinnell, p. 545.

35. Ibid, p. 566.

36. Ibid, p. 569.

37. Pinnell notes elsewhere: "We told the Government of India in one of our messages that people were reluctant to move rice because there was looting." Nanavati Papers, Testimony of L.G. Pinnell, p. 569.

38. Ibid.

39. *Report on Bengal*, p. 25.

40. Nanavati Papers, Memorandum of the Bengal National Chamber of Commerce, p. 35.

41. In his analysis of charges of corruption during "rice denial" Paul Greenough, for instance, in his *Prosperity and Misery in Modern Bengal*, concludes that the nature of the appointments and the government cover granted to agents, make is seem "more than likely that the popular suspicion of fraud and rapacity was correct." p. 95.

42. Nanavati Papers, Testimony of Nawab Habibullah Bahadur of Dacca, p. 914.

43. Nanavati Papers, Testimony of representatives of the Bengal Rice Mills Association, p. 1211.

44. Nanavati Papers, Memorandum of the Bengal National Chamber of Commerce, p. 44.

45. *Report on Bengal*, p. 25.

46. Pinnell, in his testimony before the Famine Enquiry Commission: "while I was touring the denial districts, the steamer agent at Chanpur in East Bengal told me that some big Bombay firm had just bought up a whole lot of rice at Chanpur, and significantly added that somehow the Bombay firm had managed to get transport to move the whole lot of rice to Bombay— and that in the middle of a war situation!" Nanavati Papers, p. 551.

47. WBSA, Home Confidential, file W-493/42.

48. Ibid.

49. Quoted in Ghosh, Kali Charan (1944), p. 52.

50. Ibid.

51. Huq's letter to Herbert of 2 August 1942. Nanavati Papers, p. 742.

52. Nanavati Papers, Testimony of L. G. Pinnell, p. 545.

53. Ibid.

54. Ibid.
55. Ibid.
56. "Army Proposal of 23 April submitted to Chief Civil Defense Commissioner, Bengal" in *Pinnell Papers*, p. 5. Quoted in Greenough (1982), p. 89.
57. *Report on Bengal*, p. 26.
58. Nanavati Papers, Testimony of L. G. Pinnell, p. 543.
59. Nanavati Papers, Testimony of Lieut. Col. Cotter, Public Health Commissioner of the Government of India, p. 382.
60. WBSA, Home Confidential, "War Diary for May–June 1942," file W-77/42.
61. Nanavati Papers, Testimony of P. N. Banerjee, p. 868.
62. Ibid.
63. In the Famine Enquiry Commission, after its extensive work, was unable to determine the "complete number of the numbers of persons affected…" *Report on Bengal*, p. 27.
64. Ibid.
65. WBSA, Home Political, "The Movement of Troops and Behavior of the Public," file W-249/42.
66. Ibid.
67. Ibid.
68. Nanavati Papers, Letter from Huq to Herbert, p. 743.
69. *Harijan*, 22 March 1942, p. 3.
70. Ibid.
71. *Harijan*, 19 April 1942, p. 1.
72. *Harijan*, 3 May 1942, p. 4.
73. Ibid.
74. WBSA, Home Political, "War Diary: May–June 1942," file W-77/42.
75. WBSA, Home Political, "War Diary: May–June 1942," file W-77/42.
76. Linlithgow adopted this terminology to refer to the July 10th resolution. See, for instance, Linlithgow to Amery, T.O.P. Volume II, p. 382.
77. T.O.P. Volume II, Linlithgow to Amery, p. 363.
78. T.O.P. Volume II, Amery to Linlithgow, p. 374.
79. Ibid.
80. T.O.P. Volume II, Amery to Churchill, p. 376.
81. T.O.P. Volume II, War Cabinet 91st Conclusions, pp. 377–8.
82. T.O.P. Volume II, Linlithgow to Amery, p. 382.
83. T.O.P. Volume II, Amery to Linlithgow, p. 390.
84. Ibid.
85. The text of this resolution is reprinted in T.O.P. Volume II, pp. 385–7. All quotes are from this reprinting.
86. T.O.P. Volume II, Amery to Linlithgow, p. 393.
87. T.O.P. Volume II, Linlithgow to Amery, p. 394.

88. T.O.P. Volume II, Linlithgow to Amery, p. 398.

89. Linlithgow to Herbert, July 16, 1942. Telegram 2109-S, MSS.EUR.F. 125/42.

90. T.O.P. Volume II, Herbert to Linlithgow, p. 440.

91. T.O.P. Volume II, Linlithgow to Amery, p. 448.

92. This plan is outlined in: Government of India, Home Department to Secretary of State, 24 July 1942. T.O.P. Volume II, pp. 447–50.

93. Churchill's Complete Speeches, 18 March 1931. (Winston Churchill (1874–1965), British statesman, writer. Speech, March 18, 1931, Royal Albert Hall, London. "On India," Maxims and Reflections, ed. Colin Coote (1947).)

94. *The Leo Amery Diaries*, p. 734.

95. Ibid., p. 832.

96. Azad calls the 14 July resolution a "first draft" of the 8 August resolution, Ibid., p. 78.

97. Azad, p. 84.

98. Sumit Sarkar, p. 391. For a more complete treatment of the extent, spread, and nature of the Quit India movement, see the same, pp. 388–404.

99. T.O.P. Volume II, p. 96.

100. In his book *Event, Metaphor, Memory: Chauri Chaura, 1922–1992*, Shahid Amin, traces the interesting and innovative manner in which Gandhi, as national icon, came to influence the popular uprising of 1922 in contradictory, contingent and colorful ways. A similar argument could be made for the ways that Gandhi as a socio-political *symbol* shaped the 'Quit India' movement of 1942.

101. T.O.P. Volume II, Linlithgow to Amery, p. 708.

102. T.O.P. Volume II, Linlithgow to Churchill, p. 853.

103. Chatterjee, P.K., p. 115.

104. Ibid., p. 125.

105. In his introduction to *Biplabi: A Journal of the 1942 Open Rebellion*, Bidyut Chakrabarty argues that local leaders of the movement in Midnapore were particularly adept at converting "suffering into political support." Introduction to *Biplabi* p. 2.

106. Nanavati Papers, Memorandum of the Bengal Rice Mills Association, p. 182.

107. Nanavati Papers, Testimony of D. L. Mazumdar, p. 522.

108. Ibid., p. 523.

109. Nanavati Papers, Testimony of L. G. Pinnell, p. 549.

110. Ibid., p. 549.

111. Nanavati Papers, Memorandum of the Bengal Rice Mills Association, p. 182.

112. WBSA, Govt. of Bengal Record of War Activities, File W-77/42.

113. *Biplabi*, p. 27.

114. Bose (1986), p. 262.

115. Ibid. Bose quotes from the District Officer's Chronicles: "the chief grievance of the mob appeared to be the scarcity of paddy in this locality."

116. Nanavati Papers, included in Testimony of C. J. Minister, p. 1092.

117. WBSA, Hone Confidential, "Action Under Ordinances other than Defense of India Act," file W-77/42.

118. Apart from the economic hardship that such fines entailed, they also created further communal disharmony. Muslims appealed to the government to be relieved of collective fines, arguing that 'Quit India' was a Hindu phenomenon, and were granted reprieve. See: WBSA file W-77/42

119. WBSA, Intelligence Branch, file # 573/42.

120. Ibid.

121. See Kamtekar (2002) pp. 199–201; also Roy (1944), pp. 24–35

122. *The Leo Amery Diaries*, p. 833.

123. Ibid., p. 836.

124. Ibid.

125. *Biplabi*, p. 33. CLARIFY: the journal, or Chakravarty?

126. Ibid., p. 35

127. Ibid.

128. Stephens, p. 71.

129. All numbers used here, unless otherwise noted, are taken from Greenough (1982), pp. 92–97.

130. Nanavati Papers, Memorandum of the Bengal Rice Mills Association, p. 182.

131. Greenough (1982), p. 93.

132. Nanavati Papers, Testimony of B. R. Sen, p. 441.

133. India Office, L/I/1/1106, Telegram no. 8953 (emphasis added).

134. See, for instance, the Communist Party's weekly, *Janayuddha*, 28 October 1942, "Sara Banglay Khadda Sanket" (trans.: "Food Crisis Grips All of Bengal"). This article, alone (printed before news of the cyclone leaked out), reports cases of death by starvation in Faridpur, Mymensingh and Jalpaiguri.

135. T.O.P. Volume III, Linlithgow to Amery, p. 518.

136. Ibid.

137. T.O.P. Volume III, Linlithgow to Amery, p. 358.

138. *The Statesman*, 13 December 1942, "Rice Scarcity".

139. *The Statesman*, 15 December 1942, "Food Shortage in Calcutta".

140. *The Statesman*, 17 December 1942, "Rise in Price of Rice".

141. *The Statesman*, 19 December 1942, "Employers in Conference".

142. Ibid.

143. A somewhat odd term for the scarcity of cloth that plagued Bengal through-out the war period, "cloth famine" is the term widely used by survivors from this time. The cloth famine reached its height in the mid-forties, at which time even the middle-classes were complaining of the indignities of threadbare clothing and a lack of even rags. I thank Bengali historian Gautam Bhadra who encouraged me to pursue the thread of "cloth famine" during this period.

144. *The Statesman*, 21 December 1942, "Food Situation Discussed: Mr. Huq Meets Traders and Mill Owners".

145. *The Statesman*, 13 December 1942, "Rice Position".

146. Harry Hodson's Autobiography, Chapter VIII, p. 4 at (http://www.athelstane.co.uk/hvhodson/hvhbiogr/biogr08.htm).

147. T.O.P. Volume III, Linlithgow to Amery, p. 410.

148. Ibid.

149. It was reported in *The Statesman*, 22 December 1942, that "many lights" were not extinguished and that police would take "drastic measures" in the future to deal with non-compliance to "black-outs."

150. Stephens, p. 82,

151. *The Statesman*, 22 December 1942, "Calcutta's First Raid".

152. Stephens, p. 82.

153. Nanavati Papers, Testimony of P. N. Banerjee, p. 285.

154. Ibid., p 80.

155. Nanavati Papers, Testimony of Reps. of the BCC, p. 1404.

156. Ibid.

157. Stephens, p. 83.

158. *The Statesman*, 22 December 1942, "Viceroy's Message to Calcutta".

159. Stephens, p. 82.

160. Ibid.

161. *The Statesman*, 27 December 1942, "Remedy Needed".

162. Ibid.

Chapter Three: Priorities

1. *The Statesman*, 31 December 1942, "Control of Stores in Calcutta,".

2. Ibid.

3. Nanavati Papers, Testimony of L. G. Pinnell, p. 553.

4. Nanavati Papers, Memorandum of the Bengal Rice Mills Association, p. 184.

5. Nanavati Papers, Testimony of Bengal Rice Mills Association, p. 1226.

6. *Report on Bengal*, p. 34.

7. Knight, p. 83.

8. Nanavati Papers, Memorandum of the Bengal Rice Mills Association, p. 183.

9. Ibid.

10. With the advent of "provincial autonomy" the Indian Civil Service officers were ostensibly responsible to provincial ministries, but during the period under consideration the I.C.S. became increasingly instrumental to the *circumvention* of self-rule in Bengal.

11. See Ewing (1984).

12. Nanavati Papers, Testimony of A.A. McInnes, p. 647.

13. Ibid., p. 658.

14. Nanavati Papers, Testimony of L.G. Pinnell, p. 558.

15. Ibid.

16. Ibid, p. 556.

17. *Report on Bengal*, p. 37.

18. Nanavati Papers, Memorandum of the Bengal Rice Mills Association, p. 184. The text reads: "practically all purchases made by the F.G.P.O. went to feed what were called the essential industries and essential priority consumers."

19. See: Nanavati Papers, Testimony of the Marwari Chamber of Commerce, p. 1446, Testimony of Bengal Chamber of Commerce, p. 1406, Testimony of Ashutosh Bhattacharjee, p. 1468.

20. Nanavati Papers, Testimony of L.G. Pinnell, p. 564.

21. *Janayuddha*, 17 February 1942, "Banglar Grame Grame Khadya-Samasya".

22. Ibid.

23. *Janayuddha*, 20 January 1942, "Garhi Garhi Atta Pacharer Chesta".

24. *The Statesman*, 7 January 1942, "Cheap Meals for Citizens".

25. *The Statesman*, 10 January 1942, "No Supplies".

26. *The Statesman*, 11 January 1942, "Letter to the Editor".

27. *The Statesman*, 22 January 1942, "Beggar Problem in Calcutta: Government Action".

28. Ibid.

29. Ibid.

30. *The Statesman*, 24 January 1943.

31. T.O.P. Volume III, Govt. of India Food Dept. to Secretary of State, 9 December 1942.

32. Ibid.

33. Ibid.

34. T.O.P. Volume III, Secretary of State to Govt. of India Food Dept, 15 December 1942 (emphasis mine).

35. T.O.P. Volume III, Linlithgow to Amery, DATE? and subsequent p. 396.

36. T.O.P. Volume III, Amery to Linlithgow, p. 413.

37. T.O.P. Volume III, Linlithgow to Amery, p. 455.

38. T.O.P. Volume III, Memorandum by Mr. Amery, p. 474

39. T.O.P. Volume III, Amery to Linlithgow, p. 520.

40. T.O.P. Volume III, Linlithgow to Amery, p. 544.

41. T.O.P. Volume III, Linlithgow to Provincial Governors, p. 580.

42. Ibid.

43. T.O.P. Volume II, Government of India, Home to Secretary of State, p. 535.

44. T.O.P. Vol. II, War Cabinet W.M. (42) 105th Conclusion, p. 588.

45. Ibid., p. 587.

46. T.O.P. Vol. III, Gandhi to Linlithgow, p. 518 (emphasis mine).

47. T.O.P. Vol. III, Lumley to Linlithgow, 22 October 1942.

48. T.O.P. Vol. III, War Cabinet Paper W.P. (43), p. 452.

49. Quoted in Baker, p. 23.

50. *Leo Amery's Diaries*, p. 867.

51. Ibid.

52. T.O.P. Vol. III, Linlithgow to Amery (text of letter to Gandhi), p. 463.

53. T.O.P. Vol. III, Amery to Linlithgow, p. 510.

54. See: T.O.P. Vol. III, Amery to Linlithgow, p. 513.

55. T.O.P. Vol. III, Gandhi to Linlithgow, pp. 517–9.

56. Ibid., p. 518.

57. T.O.P. Vol. III, Linlithgow to Gandhi, p. 536.

58. T.O.P. Vol. III, Linlithgow to Amery, p. 540.

59. T.O.P. Vol. III, Amery to Linlithgow, p. 557.

60. T.O.P. Vol. III, Gandhi to Linlithgow, p. 558.

61. Ibid., p. 559.

62. T.O.P. Vol. III, Linlithgow to Amery, p. 565.

63. Ibid., p. 570.

64. War Transport Member, Edward Benthall, had extensive connections in Calcutta industries. Appointed to the Executive Council in July 1942, he was the long-time Chairman and Senior Partner of Bird & Co., the largest European industrial firm operating in and around Calcutta. Bird & Co had made its name in Bengal's booming jute industry during World War I, but had diversified into coal and paper by the 1940s and remained a formidable presence in all three industries. He was also well schooled in the rough and tumble of Bengal politics: the influence peddling on which it revolved, and the systems of patronage which were necessary to grease the wheels. For European firms, manipulations within the Bengal Legislative Assembly depended on the influential European Group of legislators, with whom Benthall was quite well acquainted. Even in the late 1930s, when profits were still moribund, Benthall could brag of the powerful position he and Bird & Co. exercised in the Bengal Legislature. "In fact," he remarked to an associate, "if we work things rightly I believe they would adopt any policy that we liked to press on them." Between Benthall and Congress

Nationalists there was little love lost. Disruptions to transportation during the "Quit India" unrest had hampered war production in Bengal significantly. In a time when paper shortages were an increasing concern, Bird & Co. continued supplying paper at cost to the Muslim League's local organ, *The Star of India*. Moreover, Bird & Co.'s primary competitor in Bengal had been, for many years, Marwari business mogul, and unabashed Indian nationalist, G.D. Birla—Gandhi's close friend and ally. Having muscled his way into the European boys club of the Bengal jute industry in the 1920's, Birla had established a foothold in the jute business that posed a direct threat to Bird & Co.'s supremacy. Based on success in the jute industry, the Birla family had subsequently branched out into coal, paper, and cotton, thus contesting Bird & Co. on several fronts. In 1943, as leading industrialists in a highly profitable market, however, both firms had a vested interest in maintaining order in industrial Calcutta, as did another Member of the Viceroy's Executive Council, Nalini Sarkar. Sarkar, like Benthall (and Birla), had deep roots in Bengal's industrial infrastructure. Sarkar's experience included terms as President of the Federation of Indian Chamber of Commerce & Industry and, later, the Bengal National Chamber of Commerce and Industry, as well as Commissioner of Calcutta Port Trust. He also had his own jute mills and his expertise in the notoriously "irregular" workings of the Bengal Legislature was, like Benthall's, formidable.

65. Ibid.
66. Ibid.
67. *Leo Amery's Diaries*, p. 871.
68. Ibid., p. 872.
69. Ibid.
70. Ibid.
71. T.O.P. Vol. III, Linlithgow to Amery, p. 643.
72. *Leo Amery's Diaries*, p. 873.
73. Ibid.
74. T.O.P. Vol. III, Linlithgow to Churchill, p. 650.
75. Ibid. ("Hopie" is short for Victor Hope, the Marquess of Linlithgow's given name).
76. T.O.P. Vol. III, # 473, Lumley (Bombay) to Linlithgow, # 475, Rutherford (Bihar) to Linlithgow, # 518 Herbert (Bengal) to Linlithgow.
77. T.O.P. Vol. III, Linlithgow to Amery, p. 657.
78. Ibid., p. 667.
79. Ibid., p. 652.
80. T.O.P. Vol. III, Churchill to Linlithgow, p. 659.
81. T.O.P. Vol. III, Linlithgow to Amery, p. 675.
82. T.O.P. Vol. III, Linlithgow to Churchill, p. 669.

83. T.O.P. Vol. III, Linlithgow to Amery, p. 681.
84. T.O.P. Vol. III, Amery to Linlithgow, p. 679.
85. Ibid.
86. See, for instance; T.O.P. Vol. III, Linlithgow to Amery, p. 668.
87. T.O.P. Vol. III, Linlithgow to Amery, p. 683.
88. Ibid.
89. *Leaders Conference: An authentic account of the Leaders Conference held at New Delhi on 19th and 20th February 1943 in respect of Mahatma Gandhi's fast.* p. 7.
90. See, for instance, T.O.P. Vol. III, Linlithgow to Amery, p. 667.
91. Ibid., p. 25.
92. Ibid., p. 10.
93. T.O.P. Vol. III, Linlithgow to Amery, p. 674.
94. Ibid., p. 46.
95. Note 1 in T.O.P. Vol. III, Linlithgow to Amery, p. 719.
96. T.O.P. Vol. III, Linlithgow to Amery, p. 719.
97. "Day by Day" in *Leaders Conference*, p. 32.
98. "Notes of a talk with Mr. Gandhi, February 23, 1943." Enclosure to # 542, T.O.P. Vol. III, p. 734.
99. T.O.P. Vol. III, Linlithgow to Amery, p. 728.
100. T.O.P. Vol. III, Churchill to Linlithgow, p. 730.
101. Ibid.
102. T.O.P. Vol. III, Linlithgow to Churchill, p. 737.
103. Ibid.
104. T.O.P. Vol. III, Churchill to Field Marshall Smuts, p. 738.
105. T.O.P. Vol. III, Churchill to Linlithgow, p. 744.
106. T.O.P. Vol. III, Linlithgow to Amery, p. 746.
107. *Leo Amery's Diaries*, p. 875.
108. Ibid.
109. *Report on Bengal*, p. 38.
110. Greenough (1982), p. 112.
111. Nanavati Papers, Testimony of N.R. Sarkar, p. 1138.
112. Ibid.
113. *Report on Bengal*, p. 39.
114. Ibid.
115. *Report on Bengal*, p. 40.
116. Greenough (1982) Table 8, p. 115. Coarse rice was selling in Calcutta at Rs. 11/4 per *maund* (82.3 pounds) on 4 January 1943 and at Rs. 22/0 per *maund* on 29 March.
117. Greenough (1982), p. 99.
118. Huq to Herbert, 9 January 1943. Reprinted in Nanavati Papers, p. 746.

119. Ibid.
120. Ibid., p. 747.
121. Ibid.
122. Ibid.
123. Ibid.
124. T.O.P. Vol. III, Linlithgow to Amery, p. 677.
125. Ibid., p. 751.
126. T.O.P. Vol. III, Amery to Linlithgow, p. 765,
127. Huq to Herbert, 26 March 1943. In Nanavati Papers, p. 750.
128. *Janayuddha*, 7 April 1943 (translation mine).
129. *Janayuddha*, 31 March 1943.
130. *Janayuddha*, 21 April 1943.
131. *The Statesman*, 23 April 1943, "River Transport".
132. *The Statesman*, 1 May 1943, "Paddy and Rice Movement".
133. Quoted in Greenough (1982), p. 115.
134. T.O.P. Vol. IV, Herbert to Linlithgow, p. 189.
135. T.O.P. Vol. III, Linlithgow to Amery, p. 862.
136. Ibid., p. 876.
137. Ibid., p. 875.
138. T.O.P. Vol. III, Linlithgow to Amery, p. 881: "I must say that the more I consider the handling of this business the more lighthearted and irresponsible it seems to me to have been. And Herbert may very well, unless he is very lucky, find himself in a position in which [Muslim League leader] Nazimuddin is unable to get a Ministry together, while Huq is in a position to claim he has a working majority behind him."
139. Ibid.
140. Out of a total of 140 members of the governing coalition, 79 were from the Muslim League, 25 from the European Group, and 20 were from the Scheduled Caste Party. The remaining 16 seats were garnered from small splinter parties who carried little weight in the Assembly. The Hindu Mahasabha, the Krishak Praja Party and Huq's Progressive Party went into the opposition, which consisted of 108 members. Shila Sen (2001), p. 173.
141. *The Statesman*, 27 April 1943, "Dr Mookerjee's Views."
142. *The Statesman*, 8 May 1943, "Warning to Hoarders".
143. Ibid.
144. T.O.P. Vol. III, Linlithgow to Amery, 3 December 1943.
145. *The Statesman*, 9 April 1943, "Bengal's Food Supply".
146. Nanavati Papers, Testimony of Major-General F.H. Skinner, p. 941.
147. See: Nanavati Papers, Testimony of Major-General F.H. Skinner, p. 939.
148. Nanavati Papers, Testimony of S.L. Hora, Director of Fisheries, Bengal, p. 984.

149. Nanavati Papers, Testimony of Representative of the Marwari Chamber of Commerce, p. 1446.

150. Ibid.

151. *The Statesman*, 14 May 1943, "Food Situation in Bengal: Government of India's Assurance".

152. Ibid.

153. *The Statesman*, 27 May 1943, "Problems of Food and Cloth Distribution".

154. *The Statesman*, 15 May 1943, "Atta to Replace Rice Rations".

155. *The Statesman*, 16 May 1943, "Howrah Meeting".

156. *Report on Bengal*, p. 50.

157. Ibid.

158. Ibid., p. 51.

159. By this time "denial" expert L. G. Pinnell had been transferred to Chittagong as Division Commissioner, and N. M. Ayyar, ICS, had been appointed Director of Civil Supplies, Bengal. Ayyar revealed that the Government of Bengal was paying Ispahani between Rupees 16 and 20 per *maund* of rice, while prices in Bihar had been considerably lower. Intensive investigation by the Famine Enquiry Commission would largely exonerate Ispahani Limited, but the rumors of embezzlement continue even to the present day.

160. *The Statesman*, 25 May 1943, "Hindu Sabha Meeting".

161. Ibid.

162. *The Statesman*, 27 May 1943, "Distribution of Rice".

163. Nanavati Papers, Testimony of Fazlul Huq, p. 744.

Chapter Four: Famine

1. *Report on Bengal*, p. 112.

2. *Biplabi*, 23 May 1943, p. 197.

3. Ibid.

4. Ibid., p. 209.

5. Ibid., p. 208.

6. Ibid.

7. An area three hundred miles northwest of Rangoon and approximately equidistant from Calcutta.

8. Stephens, p. 112.

9. The Indian National Army (I.N.A.) was an organization founded in 1942 by Mohan Singh. Its ranks were comprised of Indian soldiers who had been captured by the Japanese in Malaya and Singapore. Disillusioned with their abandonment by Britain, they organized an irregular army with the goal of invading India from the east and joining with radical national forces to over-

throw British rule in India. The I.N.A. was reorganized in early 1943 under the leadership of Subhash Chandra Bose. Its message of militant resistance to colonial rule was broadcast over "Azad Hind Radio," which reached Calcutta over the airwaves, resulting in widespread knowledge and support for the Indian National Army in Bengal. By the end of the war, it was comprised of as many as 40,000 troops.

10. Bayly and Harper, p. 274
11. Stephens, p. 115.
12. *Report on Bengal,* p. 55.
13. Ibid.
14. The use of the Home Guards, the A.R.P., and the Civic Guards in this action apparently presented no paradox to Government. That these forces, organized to deal with "enemy threat," were being used to monitor and manage the rice supply of Bengal, was in keeping with the rhetoric of "civil defence," that continued to mold all policy, and justify any means. Question about the food supply, throughout the period, were enmeshed in the rhetoric of "defence," structuring the only "code" of famine that was ever applied.
15. *Report on Bengal,* p. 56.
16. Ibid.
17. Nanavati Papers, Testimony of L. G. Pinnell, p. 547.
18. Nanavati Papers, Testimony of B. R. Sen, p. 446.
19. The evidence for this is rather anecdotal, but believable. See for instance, the testimony of the Bengal Provincial Kisan Sabha (the most extensive, non-official organization in rural Bengal during the period) in Nanavati Papers, p. 148.
20. Ibid.
21. Ibid.
22. Ibid (emphasis mine).
23. Ibid.
24. Ibid.
25. WBSA, Home Political, "Fortnightly Report for the 2nd Half of June–, 1943," file w-39/1943.
26. Ibid.
27. Ibid.
28. Ibid.
29. Ibid.
30. Ibid.
31. Ibid.
32. Ibid.
33. Ibid.
34. Ibid.

35. Ibid.

36. WBSA, Home Political, "Fortnightly Report for the 2nd Half of June–, 1943," file w-39/1943 (by "sectional famine" the magistrate is referring to a famine of considerable regional scope).

37. Hunter, p. 39.

38. *Masik Basumati*, "Khadya Samasya" Ashar, 1350 (July 1943) (translation mine).

39. T.O.P. Volume IV, Herbert to Linlithgow, p. 44.

40. Ibid.

41. Ibid.

42. Ibid., p. 45.

43. T.O.P. Volume IV, Linlithgow to Herbert, p. 41.

44. Ibid., p. 45.

45. *The Statesman*, 6 July 1943, "Bengal Assembly Meets".

46. Ibid.

47. Ibid.

48. *The Statesman*, 21 July 1943, "Mr. Huq's Criticism".

49. Ibid.

50. *Casey's Diaries*, p. 43.

51. Nanavati Papers, Memorandum of the Bosepukur Relief Committee, p. 203.

52. *Arani*, 24 Ashar, 1350 (7 July 1943).

53. Nanavati Papers, Memorandum of the Bengal Public Health Association, p. 236.

54. T.O.P. Vol. IV, Herbert to Linlithgow, 21 July 1943.

55. *The Statesman*, 31 July 1943, "Vagrancy Ordinance in Calcutta".

56. Ibid.

57. Ibid.

58. Ibid.

59. T.O.P. Vol. IV, Document # 67.

60. Ibid.

61. Ibid.

62. Ibid.

63. "de-housing" was the policy, advanced by Lindemann to bomb German cities, and particularly civilian housing complexes, not to *kill* civilians, but to leave them homeless, and thus a burden to to the Nazi state. It was a fairly cynical justification used to begin a bombing campaign against civilians in Germany.

64. *Leo Amery' Diaries*, p. 933.

65. Ibid.

66. T.O.P. Vol. IV, Linlithgow to Amery, p. 169.

67. T.O.P. Vol. IV, Linlithgow to Herbert, p. 164.

68. Ibid.
69. T.O.P. Vol. IV, Herbert to Linlithgow, p. 166.
70. Ibid.
71. Nanavati Papers, Testimony of W. H. Kirby, p. 361.
72. Ibid., p. 364.
73. *The Statesman*, 8 August 1943, "Plight of a Province".
74. Ibid.
75. Stephens, p. 180.
76. K.C. Ghosh, p. 119.
77. Stephens, p. 182.
78. Praise of *The Statesman* for publishing their photographs and "breaking" the famine, was almost universally expressed by those that I interviewed who had witnessed this period.
79. Ibid., p. 186.
80. *The Statesman*, 29 August 1943, "An All-India Disgrace".
81. Ibid.
82. T.O.P. Vol. IV, Herbert to Linlithgow, 28 August 1943.
83. Ibid.
84. T.O.P. Vol. IV, Linlithgow to Amery, p. 192.
85. Ibid., p. 195.
86. Ibid., p. 231.
87. Ibid.
88. Ibid.
89. T.O.P. Vol. IV, Auchinleck to Brooke, p. 217.
90. T.O.P. Vol. IV, War Cabinet Paper, p. 260.
91. Ibid., p. 304.
92. *Leo Amery Diaries*, p. 943 (at the same time, due to war in Greece, famine conditions were impending there).
93. T.O.P. Vol. IV, War Cabinet, W.M. (43) 131st Conclusion, Minute 1, p. 319.
94. *Medical History of the Bengal Famine*, p. 13.
95. Ibid., p. 14.
96. Ibid.
97. Ibid., p. 121.
98. Ibid., p. 48.
99. Ibid., p. 49.
100. Survey of destitutes in and around Calcutta by Department of Anthropology, Calcutta University, issued September 27, 1943. In K.C. Ghosh, pp. 83–4.
101. *Amrita Bazar Patrika*, 26 September 1943.
102. Greenough (1982), p. 121.
103. Extract from G.H.Q., India, Weekly Intelligence Report. Included in War Cabinet Paper W.P. (43) 407, reprinted in T.O.P. Vol. IV, p. 272.

104. Venkataramani, p. 30.

105. K.C. Ghosh, p. 108.

106. Ibid, p. 109.

107. Ibid, p. 90

108. Stephens, pp. 102–3.

109. *The Statesman*, 10 September 1943, "Corporation and Starvation".

110. Nanavati Papers, Testimony of D. Fraser, Inspector of Medical Services, p. 498.

111. Nanavati Papers, Memorandum of the Calcutta Relief Committee, p. 69.

112. These two organization were established before the war; the Hindu Satkar Samiti (Organization for the in 1932, and the Anjuman Mofidul Islam in 1905. They both dealt with welfare for the poor of their respective community, and both provided burial services. They became the two primary organizations for the disposal of the dead in and around Calcutta during war and famine. The Hindu Satkar Samiti doing cremations, and the Anjuman Mofidul Islam doing burials. Both organizations are still in operation today.

113. Most of the "destitutes" were, at this point, wholly or partially naked. For adult males, circumcision may have been an indicator, but for women, and small children, it is difficult to understand how distinctions were made.

114. *The Statesman*, 14 September 1943, "Lessons in Secrecy".

115. Ibid.

116. *The Statesman*, 29 September 1943, "Bengal Council Passes Vagrants Bill".

117. Ibid.

118. See T.O.P. Vol. IV, Enclosure to No. 180, p. 399.

119. K.C. Ghosh, pp. 86–7.

120. Ibid., p. 91.

121. Nanavati Papers, Testimony of F.A. Karim, p. 1375.

122. Chakrabarty, Bidyut, p. 297.

123. T.O.P. Vol. IV, Linlithgow to Amery, p. 349 (*functus officio:* finished with official duty).

124. K.C. Ghosh, p. 123.

125. It was noted in the press release that the government was also receiving "non-official aid" with the roundups, though few specifics of the organizations involved was forthcoming.

126. *The Statesman*, 1 November 1943, "Repatriating Calcutta Destitutes".

127. *The Statesman*, 6 November 1943, "Policy of Repatriation of Destitutes".

128. Nanavati Papers, Testimony of O. M. Martin, p. 529.

129. Ibid.

130. In the introduction I made reference to the works of both Sugata Bose

(1986) and Paul Greenough (1982) in relation to this wide-spread trope of passivity. In addition to being noted in much scholarship, I have heard this often repeated by the middle-class survivors of the period. It is also repeated in popular media, such as in Mrinal Sen's movie *Akaler Sadhaney*.

131. *Medical History of the Bengal Famine*, p. 16.
132. Nanavati Papers, Testimony of T. G. Davies, p. 1069.
133. Ibid.
134. Nanavati Papers, Testimony of B. K. Guha, p. 772.
135. Ibid.
136. Alan Shaw, archived in connection with the BBC oral history project "WW2 People's War." http://www.bbc.co.uk/ww2peopleswar/user/89/u894689.shtml (Last accessed May 20, 2010, 7:49 PM).
137. Nanavati Papers, Testimony of B. K. Guha, p. 772.
138. Nanavati Papers, Testimony of O. M. Martin, p. 534.
139. Nanavati Papers, Testimony of B. K. Guha, p. 772.
140. Ibid., p. 773–4.
141. Nanavati Papers, Testimony of O. M. Martin, p. 540.
142. *Report on Bengal*, p. 109.
143. The Famine Enquiry Commission's *Report on Bengal* pegged the "excess mortality" for the second half of 1943 at 1,000,000 (pp. 108–9). This estimate is the most conservative available. The University of Calcutta Anthropology Department, after extensive surveys, put the toll at 3.5 million for 1943. And exhaustive analysis of these numbers is contained in Amartya Sen's *Poverty and Famines*, "Famine Mortality: A Case Study."
144. *The Statesman*, 21 November 1943, "The Deserted Village".
145. Ibid.
146. Ibid.
147. Chittaprosad, p. 3.
148. Nikhil Sarkar, p. 5.
149. Greenough (1982), Appendix C, p. 311.
150. Ibid., p. 309.
151. Quoted in Greenough (1982), p. 182.
152. T.O.P. Vol. IV, Wavell to Amery, p. 407.
153. *The Statesman*, 27 October 1943, "Lord Wavell Sees Plight of Destitutes in Calcutta".
154. *The Statesman*, 29 October 1943, "Viceroy to Approach Army for Aid in Famine Relief".
155. T.O.P. Vol. IV, War Cabinet Paper W.P. (43) 504, p. 450.
156. *Leo Amery Diaries*, p. 950.
157. Ibid.
158. Ibid.

159. Ibid., p. 951.
160. T.O.P. Vol. IV, War Cabinet W.M. (43) 152nd Conclusion, Minute 3, p. 466.
161. *The Statesman*, 12 November 1943, "Mr. Amery on Famine Relief Work".
162. *The Statesman*, 13 November 1943, "Food Distribution in Bengal".
163. T.O.P. Vol. IV, Amery to Wavell, p. 452.
164. Ibid., p. 485
165. *The Statesman*, 5 December 1943, "Army's Help in Relief Work".

Chapter Five: Japan Attacks

1. See the introduction to Kamtekar (2002).
2. Ibid., p. 189.
3. Ibid. (Ghosh's figure is 9,965,911 tons).
4. The docks at Kidderpore and Garden Reach, together with the industrial and residential complexes that surrounded them, were referred to in Government and A.R.P. reports as "the Docklands."
5. The Essential Services [Maintenance] Ordinance of 1941 had made it a criminal offence for any worker engaged in "essential" war-related industries and enterprises from abandoning their station of employment without "reasonable excuse," under penalty of imprisonment. The rhetoric of "essential" workers, moreover, became a mantra of the colonial administration during war. See Bhattacharya, p. 41.
6. Representatives of the Bengal National Chamber of Commerce boasted at the Famine Enquiry Commission that "there was not one single case of death among industrial laborers from famine." (Nanavati Papers, p. 1089.) This presumption, I am here arguing, is highly misleading as the relative "security" of industrial laborers in Calcutta was highly contingent.
7. WBSA, Home Confidential, file W-30/43 (III).
8. Ibid.
9. *Casey's Diary*, p. 152 (emphasis mine).
10. Suranjan Das (1995), p. 62.
11. BBC oral history project "WW2 People's War." J. W. Stanworth at www.bbc.co.uk/ww2peopleswar/stories/36/a6021136.shtml (Last accessed June–, 2010, 5:25 PM).
12. Arjan de Haan, p. 159 (The figure given for factory housed workers in 1946 is 39%).
13. Ibid, pp. 158–9.
14. Kamtekar (August 2002), p. 203.
15. Mitter, p. 526.
16. Kamtekar (August 2002), p. 210.

17. Dutta and Mridula, p. 82.
18. Peter Moore, "Policing War-time Calcutta," at http://www.oldmartiniansas-sociation.co.uk/memories.html (Last accessed May 4, 2002, 1:45 PM), p. 2.
19. WBSA Home Confidential, "8th Raid," file W-30/43 (Note by Secretary of the Government of Bengal, E. W. Holland on corpse disposal.)
20. Stephens, p. 217.
21. Ibid., p. 224.
22. Ibid., p. 215.
23. Ibid., p. 216.
24. The sequence of events described below is all taken from the A.R.P. reports contained in WBSA, Home Confidential, file W-30/43, "8th Raid." A map is also included in the file, which pinpoints the locations of the bombs. A chronology of events is given in the Calcutta Fire Brigade's report in the same file. Where relevant, reference will be given to the specific documents from this file.
25. Ibid., B.N.P. Final Report.
26. Ibid., Note from B.N.R. General Manager to Government of Bengal, Home Department (emphasis mine).
27. Ibid.
28. Ibid., Port Commissioners to Bengal Secretariat.
29. Ibid.
30. Ibid., M.P.S.C.O.'s Memorandum 21/sco/80 to the Chief of the General Staff.
31. Ibid.
32. Ibid., Memo 21/SCO/80.
33. Ibid., Port A.R.P. Report.
34. Ibid., B.N.R.'s Post-Raid Report (emphasis mine).
35. Ibid., Port A.R.P. Report.
36. Ibid.
37. Ibid.
38. *The Statesman*, 6 December 1943, "Jap's First Daylight Raid on Calcutta".
39. Ibid.
40. WBSA, Home Political, file W-296/43.
41. Ibid.
42. Ibid., (emphasis mine).
43. Ibid.
44. Ibid., "Bengal Chamber of Commerce Labor Conditions".
45. Ian Stephens, in *Monsoon Morning*, remembers that clouds of smoke and ash could be seen emerging from the dock area shortly after the bombing began. Stephens was at the Statesman building, approximately two miles distant from the docks.

46. WBSA, Home Confidential, file W-30/43.

47. Ibid., B.N.R. Report.

48. *The Statesman*, 6 December 1943, "Sunday Morning".

49. WBSA, Home Confidential, file W-30/43.

50. Ibid.

51. WBSA, Home Political, file W-112/43 "Constitution of Mortuary Services under the A.R.P. Services Ordinance, 1941."

52. *Casey's Diaries*, p. 338.

53. Ibid., first reports from the Port A.R.P. and the B.N.R. A.R.P.

54. Ibid., Civil Defence Information Office, Final Report.

55. Ibid.

56. Ibid.

57. Ibid.

58. Ibid.

59. Ibid. For the assistance of sanitation workers see B.N.R. Initial Report, for losing track, see Final Report.

60. Ibid., Kitchin to Martyn.

61. Ibid.

62. Ibid., Secret Letter 56/SCO/31.

63. Ibid.

64. Ibid.

65. Bhattacharya, p. 41.

66. War Injuries Ordinance, 1941. At: http://bdlaws.gov.bd/print_sections_all.php?id=192 (Last accessed July 8, 2010; 12:32 P.M.).

67. WBSA, Home Confidential, file W-30/43, P.R.I.S. Final Report.

68. Ibid.

69. Ibid.

70. Ibid., Memo 21/SCO/80.

71. Ibid.

72. Ibid.

73. Ibid.

74. Ibid., B.N.R. A.R.P. "First Report."

75. Archived at BBC "People's War," http://www.bbc.co.uk/ww2peopleswar/stories/06/a4040506.shtml (last accessed July 8, 2010; 2:29 P.M.).

76. Ibid.

77. Ibid.

78. Bhattacharya, p. 40.

79. WBSA, Home Confidential, file W-30/43.

80. "Childhood in Calcutta," (italics mine) archived at BBC's "People's War," at: http://www.bbc.co.uk/ww2peopleswar/stories/34/a2780534.shtml (last accessed July 8, 2010; 4:50 P.M.)

Chapter Six: Second Famine

1. Narayan, p. 218.
2. Ibid., pp. 223–34.
3. *The Statesman*, 2 December 1943, "Exports of Rice and Paddy Banned".
4. *The Statesman*, 13 December 1943, "Rice Purchase By Firms".
5. *The Statesman*, 22 December 1943, "Plan for Calcutta".
6. *The Statesman*, 21 December 1943, "Lord Wavell's Assurance".
7. *The Statesman*, 18 December 1943, "Food Member Visits Dacca".
8. Ibid.
9. T.O.P. Vol. IV, Wavell to Amery, p. 646.
10. T.O.P. Vol. IV, Wavell to Amery, p. 645.
11. Ibid.
12. T.O.P. Vol. IV, Wavell to Amery, p. 645.
13. *The Statesman*, 12 January 1944.
14. Bedi, p. 22.
15. Ibid.
16. Ibid., p. 70.
17. Nanavati Papers, Testimony of K. S. Fitch, p. 680.
18. Ibid.
19. Ibid.
20. Nanavati Papers, Testimony of Major-General Wakely, p. 1023.
21. Shyama Prasad Mookerjee, for one, was using the rhetoric of an impending "second famine" freely. See, for instance, the introduction to Mookerjee's *Panchaser Manwantar*b (1350 Famine), published in January 1944.
22. Nanavati Papers, Memorandum of the Bengal Parliamentary Party, p. 18.
23. Greenough (1982), p. 190.
24. Ibid.
25. Narayan, pp. 172–3.
26. Nanavati Papers, Testimony of Tarak Nath Mukherjee, p. 910.
27. Nanavati Papers, Testimony of the Bengal Provincial Mahasabha, p. 155.
28. Ibid., p. 261.
29. Shila Sen, p. 175.
30. Nanavati Papers, Testimony of the Bengal Provincial Muslim League, p. 1373.
31. *The Statesman*, 12 December 1943, "Dar-el-Islam".
32. Ibid.
33. *The Statesman*, 28 December 1943, "Muslim League Session Concludes".
34. Basu, p. 64.
35. T.O.P. Vol. IV, Wavell to Amery, p. 808.
36. *The Statesman*, 7 January 1944, "Criticism of Food Member".

37. Ibid.
38. Ibid.
39. T.O.P. Vol. IV, Amery to Wavell, p. 609.
40. Nanavati Papers, Testimony of W.H. Kirby, p. 364.
41. T.O.P. Vol. IV, Wavell to Amery, p. 561.
42. *The Statesman*, 7 January 1944, "Criticism of Food Member".
43. Ibid.
44. Ibid.
45. *The Statesman*, 28 January 1944, "Purchase and Distribution of Foodgrains".
46. 1 *seer* = 2.057 lbs.
47. *The Statesman*, 26 January 1944, "Quota of Rice Increased".
48. Nanavati Papers, Resolution included in Testimony of Calcutta Corporation, p. 1264.
49. *The Statesman*, 26 January 1944, "Quota of Rice Increased".
50. Nanavati Papers, Testimony of the Calcutta Corporation, p. 1265.
51. Nanavati Papers, Testimony of the Official Congress Party, p. 806.
52. Nanavati Papers, Testimony of Major-General Stuart, p. 1167.
53. Nanavati Papers, Testimony of F. A. Karim, p. 1377.
54. T.O.P. Vol. IV, Wavell to Amery, p. 459.
55. Ibid., p. 616.
56. Ibid., p. 566.
57. Ibid., p. 614.
58. T.O.P. Vol. IV, Linlithgow to Amery, p. 231.
59. T.O.P. Vol. IV, Wavell to Amery, p. 434.
60. T.O.P. Vol. IV, Amery to Linlithgow, p. 191.
61. T.O.P. Vol. IV, Wavell to Amery, p. 434.
62. Ibid.
63. T.O.P. Vol. IV, Amery to Churchill, p. 488.
64. T.O.P. Vol. IV, Linlithgow to Amery, p. 296.
65. T.O.P. Vol. IV, Wavell to Amery, p. 565.
66. Ibid., p. 490.
67. Ibid., p. 434.
68. T.O.P. Vol. IV, Churchill to Casey, p. 453.
69. T.O.P. Vol. IV, Casey to Churchill, p. 454.
70. T.O.P. Vol. IV, Amery to Wavell, p. 569.
71. T.O.P. Vol. IV, War Cabinet W. M. (44) 5th Conclusion, Minute 1, p. 629.
72. Ibid.
73. T.O.P. Vol. IV, Wavell to Amery, p. 690.
74. T.O.P. Vol. IV, Amery to Wavell, p. 641.
75. Chakrabarty, Bidyut, p. 309.

76. *The Statesman*, 23 January 1944, "Casey Assumes Office as Governor of Bengal".

77. *Casey's Diary*, p. 63.

78. Amartya Sen (1981), p. 215,

79. *Report on Bengal*, p. 108 (Rates are compared to the average mortality rates for the five years prior to 1943).

80. *The Statesman*, 28 February 1944, "Sample Survey of Famine Districts".

81. Ibid.

82. Greenough (1982), p. 205.

83. T.O.P. Vol. IV, Wavell to Amery, p. 590.

84. T.O.P. Vol. IV, War Cabinet W.M. (44) 16th Conclusion, p. 701.

85. Ibid., p. 702.

86. *The Leo Amery Diaries*, p. 933.

87. T.O.P. Vol. IV, Wavell to Amery, p. 706.

88. Ibid.

89. Ibid., 707.

90. T.O.P. Vol. IV, Wavell to Amery, p. 734.

91. T.O.P. Vol. IV, Auchinleck to Chiefs of Staff, p. 737–8.

92. T.O.P. Vol. IV, War Cabinet W. M. (44) 23rd Conclusion, Minute 6, pp. 749–51.

93. T.O.P. Vol. IV, Wavell to Amery, p. 758.

94. Ibid.

95. T.O.P. Vol. IV, War Cabinet W. M. (44) 36th Conclusion, Minute 4, pp. 822–4.

96. T.O.P. Vol. IV, Wavell to Amery, p. 836.

97. Ibid., p. 900

98. T.O.P. Vol. IV, Amery to Wavell, p. 904.

99. *The Leo Amery Diaries*, p. 976.

100. Ibid., p. 979.

101. Ibid.

102. T.O.P. Vol. IV, Amery to Wavell, p. 939.

103. T.O.P. Vol. IV, Wavell to Amery, p. 941.

104. T.O.P. Vol. IV, Amery to Wavell, p. 964.

105. Ibid., p. 999.

106. T.O.P. Vol. IV, Wavell to Amery, p. 1034.

107. All information on Netai is taken from a case study included in K.S. Fitch (1947), pp. 78–9.

108. Ibid., p. 17.

109. T.O.P. Vol. IV, Amery to Wavell, p. 1175.

110. T.O.P. Vol. IV, Wavell to Amery, p. 712.

111. Ibid.

112. Nanavati Papers, testimony of Justice Braund, p. 999.
113. Nanavati Papers, Testimony of K.S. Fitch, p. 679.
114. Nanavati Papers, Memorandum of the British Indian Association, p. 224.
115. Nanavati Papers, Testimony of Representatives of the Calcutta Corporation, p. 1244.
116. Nanavati Papers, Memorandum of the Provincial Kisan Sabha, p. 167.
117. Ibid.
118. *The Statesman*, 20 April 1944, "Rise of Prices in Everyday Goods Analyzed".
119. *The Statesman*, 24 April 1944, "Paper".
120. See Greenough's interview with a village school-master, (1982) pp. 173–4
121. Nanavati Papers, Testimony of F.A. Karim, p. 1385.
122. Bose (1986), p. 199.
123. Nanavati papers, Testimony of B.R. Sen, p. 447.
124. Ibid.
125. Nanavati Papers, Memorandum of the Provincial Kisan Sabha, p. 167.
126. See Sumit Sarkar (1983), p. 409.
127. *The Statesman*, 17 November 1943, "League and Food Crisis".
128. *The Statesman*, 28 November 1943, "Dar-el-Islam".
129. T.O.P. Vol. IV, War Cabinet Paper, p. 1101.
130. T.O.P. Vol. IV, Wavell to Amery, p. 1084.
131. Rajmohan Gandhi, p. 160.
132. T.O.P. Vol. IV, Twynam to Wavell, p. 1182.
133. *Casey's Diary*, p. 346.
134. Designed to give Muslims parity with Hindus in higher education, etc.
135. *Casey's Diary*, p. 279.
136. Ibid., p. 308.
137. See: Shila Sen, p. 186.
138. Ibid., 325.
139. Ibid.
140. *Medical History of Bengal Famine*, p. 44.
141. *The Statesman*, 14 December 1943, "Cholera and Smallpox Threaten 97 Towns".
142. *Janayuddha*, 22 November 1944, "Chauler Dar".
143. *The Statesman*, 5 December 1944, "Governor Horrified by Living Conditions".
144. *The Viceroy's Journal*, p. 107.
145. T.O.P Vol. V, Casey to Wavell, p. 638.
146. Ibid.
147. Ibid.
148. Ibid., p. 641.
149. T.O.P. Vol. V, Casey to Colville, pp. 715–6.
150. T.O.P. Vol. V, Colville to Amery, p. 999.

151. *Casey's Diary*, p. 56.
152. *The Viceroy's Journal*, p. 153.
153. Ibid., p. 165.
154. T.O.P. Vol. VI, Wavell to Pethick-Lawrence, p. 295.
155. *Casey's Diary*, p. 185.
156. *Casey's Diary*, p. 148
157. *The Viceroy's Journal*, p. 143.
158. *Casey's Diary*, p. 243
159. *Casey's Diary*, p. 168
160. Ibid., p. 186
161. *Amrita Bazar Patrika*, 15 November 1945, "S.P. Mookerjee's Speech".
162. Ibid.
163. Shila Sen, p. 190.
164. *The Viceroy's Journal*, p. 141.
165. WBSA, Home Political, file W-37/45 "Confidential Report on the Political Situation in Bengal: First Half of November, 1945".
166. See publication of Calcutta Rationing Order in *Amrita Bazar Patrika*, 18 November 1945, p. 7.
167. WBSA, Home Political, file W-37/45 "Confidential Report on the Political Situation in Bengal: First Half of October, 1945".
168. WBSA, Home Political, file W-37/45 "Confidential Report on the Political Situation in Bengal: Second Half of September, 1945".
169. Ibid.
170. WBSA, Home Political, file W-37/45 "Confidential Report on the Political Situation in Bengal: First Half of November, 1945".
171. Ibid.
172. Ibid.
173. WBSA, Home Political, file W-37/45 "Confidential Report on the Political Situation in Bengal: Second Half of November, 1945".
174. *Amrita Bazar Patrika*, 22 November 1945, "Police Firing in Calcutta".
175. T.O.P. Vol. VI, Casey to Wavell, p. 725.
176. Ibid.
177. Ibid.
178. Ibid.
179. WBSA, Home Political, file W-37/45 "Confidential Report on the Political Situation in Bengal: Second Half of November, 1945".
180. *Casey's Diary*, p. 254
181. *Amrita Bazar Patrika*, 24 November 1945, "Calcutta Rationing".
182. Sumit Sarkar (1983), p. 421.
183. *Casey's Diary*, p. 254.
184. *Amrita Bazar Patrika*, 23 November 1945, "Carry Out Congress Directions".

185. T.O.P. Vol. VI Wavell to Pethwick-Lawrence, p. 602.

186. See: Sumit Sarkar (1983), p. 420.

187. T.O.P. Vol. VI, Casey to Wavell, p. 725.

188. Ibid.

189. P.K. Chatterjee, p. 163.

190. Sumit Sarkar (1983), p. 422.

191. Casey's Diary, p. 338.

192. P.K. Chatterjee, p. 167.

193. Sumit Sarkar (1983), p. 422.

194. Casey's Diary, p. 339.

195. Suranjan Das uses this term to describe the February disturbance in Das (2000).

196. T.O.P. Vol. VI, Wavell to Pethwick-Lawrence, p. 720.

197. Ibid., p. 868

198. T.O.P. Vol. VI, Pethwick-Lawrence to Wavell, p. 920.

199. Ibid.

200. T.O.P. Vol. VI, Wavell to Pethwick-Lawrence, p. 1006.

201. Ibid.

202. From the *Hindustan Times*, 3 March 1946, reprinted in T.O.P. Vol. VI, p. 1116.

203. Ibid., p. 1117.

204. Sumit Sarkar (1983), p. 423.

205. Ibid, p. 426.

206. Metcalf and Metcalf, p. 213.

207. T.O.P. Vol. VII, Wavell to Henderson, 24 April 1946.

208. T.O.P. Vol. VII, Henderson to Wavell, 4 April 1946.

209. T.O.P. Vol. VI, Wavell to King George, p. 1236.

210. Suranjan Das (1991), p. 164.

211. Bose (1986), p. 223.

212. Sumit Sarkar (1983), p. 427.

213. *Casey's Diary*, pp. 236–8.

214. T.O.P. Vol. VII, Wavell to Henderson, p. 645.

215. *The Statesman*, 1 July 1946, "Demonstration in Calcutta".

216. *The Statesman*, 1 July 1946, "Food Advisory Committee".

217. T.O.P. Vol. VIII, Wavell to Maulana Azad, 1946, p. 1114.

218. *The Statesman*, 2 July 1946, "U.S. Famine Mission Arrives in Calcutta".

219. *The Statesman*, 4 July 1946, "U.S. Food Mission Ends Bengal Tour".

220. *The Statesman*, 10 July 1946, "Rise in Calcutta Mortality".

221. *The Statesman*, 18 July 1946, "India's Food Import Needs".

222. Ibid.

223. Ibid.

224. *The Statesman*, 6 August 1946, "League Direct Action Programme Includes No-Tax Campaign".

225. Sir Arthur Waugh interviewed the Muslim League Secretary, Liaquat Ali Khan on 7 August and reported that Khan said that "shedding of British and Muslim blood would be deplorable, but that it was better than slow strangulation." (T.O.P. Vol. VII, Waugh to Abell, 7 August 1946. p. 199). That Liaquat Ali Khan foresaw possible Muslim/*British* violence is significant.

Chapter Seven: Riots

1. *The Statesman*, 7 August 1946, "Suhrawardy's Message for Direct Action Day".

2. *The Statesman*, 16 August 1946, "Discussion on Holiday".

3. *The Statesman*, 13 August 1946, "Congress Party Walk-Out".

4. *The Statesman*, 15 August 1946, "Protest Resolution Adopted".

5. *Calcutta Disturbances Commission of Enquiry* (Hereafter CDCE), Vol. V, Testimony of H.N. Sirkar, p. 58.

6. Ibid.

7. WBSA, Home Confidential, file W-351/46 (Part B 1X) "Medical Arrangements During the Civil Diturbances".

8. WBSA, Home Confidential, file W-351/46 (Part B IV) "The Work of the Fire Brigade".

9. CDCE, Vol. V, Testimony of H.N. Sirkar, p. 59.

10. CDCE Vol. II, Testimony of D.R. Hardwick, Commissioner of Police, Calcutta, p. 69.

11. Estimate of the Commissioner of Police, D.R. Hardwick in CDCE, Vol. II, p. 82.

12. T.O.P. Vol. VIII, Burrows to Wavell, p. 297.

13. Ibid.

14. Sengupta, p. 293.

15. In Suranjan Das's work (1991) he gives the "official estimate" (which I have not seen), as 4,000. In his *Struggle and Strife* (1991), P.K. Chatterjee gives the number 5,000. I do believe, from my own research, that it is likely that there were considerably more deaths. In this chapter I go into some depth as to why any accurate estimate is quite impossible given condition on the ground at the time.

16. Das (1991), p. 6.

17. Ghosh, Dutta and Ray, p. 78.

18. Ibid. (actual enumerated population in 1941: 2,070,619).

19. Exact numbers of the actual population are lacking, but according to

A.C. Hartley, Controller of Rationing, 4 million *official* residents of Calcutta were being fed by the end of 1944. Nanavati Papers, Testimony of A.C. Hartley, p. 894.

20. Ghosh, Dutta and Ray, p. 78.

21. Mintu Dutta's large family compound in south Calcutta, for one, was requisitioned in the winter of 1941. Without any prior notice, the requisitioning officers showed up at the house and told them that they had twenty-four hours to vacate the premises. The next morning, even before twenty-four hours had passed, thirty to forty military personnel arrived with mules packed down with provisions for a long stay. The family, given no other choice, hid their valuables in a cache beneath the stairwell and relocated to Dacca for the duration of the occupation of their home. When they returned in 1945, the house was a shambles, strewn with cigarette butts, empty whiskey bottles, and food wrappers. The roof was pock-marked with divots made were anti-aircraft guns had been fastened, and the garden outside had withered from a lack of care. No compensation was paid. (From an interview with Minto Dutto: 11/15/2003, Kolkata.)

22. Stephens, p. 151.

23. *The Statesman*, 1 August 1946, "Bill to Control House Rents".

24. *The Statesman*, 13 August 1946, "Congress Party Walkout".

25. Das (1991), p. 162.

26. Over the years of Calcutta's settlement, each of the many immigrant communities that had come had settled into distinct *paras* that were often, but not always, relatively homogeneous in composition. Attached to each *para* there was generally a local market, or *bazaar*, which was also recognized as a distinct commercial unit, specific to that *para*. But, because Calcutta was an almost entirely unplanned city, *paras* too were established haphazardly and without any systematic logic. A larger territorial unit, such as Beliaghata in northern Calcutta, might be comprised of a number of adjacent Hindu *paras* with a few Muslim settlements interspersed, or a single Hindu *para*, such as Ananda Pali, north of Park Circus, might exist as a "Hindu" island in the midst of surrounding Muslim *paras*. In north-central Calcutta, Hindu and Muslim *paras* were more equally scattered, sometimes bounded only by a single narrow lane. However, although they were often perceived of in communally exclusive terms, many *paras* remained only relatively homogenous. In "Hindu" *paras* in the area of Bhawanipur there would likely be some Muslim families residing, as in a "Muslim" *paras* in Mommenpur, there would be a handful of Hindu family dwellings.

27. The Maidan is a vast expanse of open fields, sometimes referred to as "the lungs of Calcutta." It was also home to Fort William, the Victoria Memorial, the Royal Calcutta Turf Club, and the Ochterlony Monument, which were

all featured prominently in imperial publications to demonstrate the grandeur of the British Raj in India. The territory of the Maidan was thus of great symbolic importance to empire. During the war, although a landing by Japanese airplanes was highly unlikely, buses were periodically parked all across the Maidan to prevent "invasion"—an exercise aimed much more at demonstrating martial control of symbolically charged territorial space than at material "defense."

28. T.O.P. Vol. VIII, Burrows to Wavell, p. 297.

29. Commissioner of Police, D.R. Hardwick in CDCE, Vol. II, p. 82/.

30. Interview with Golam Kibria (1/14/2004, Kolkata)

31. The reconstruction of events in Ananda Palit is comprised from interviews with Soumesh and Souresh Sen (11/19/2003 and 12/23/2003, Kolkata).

32. "We will fight for Pakistan!"

33. "God is great!"

34. "Bow to the Mother Goddess!"

35. Interview with Soumesh Sen

36. CDCE, Testimony of Deputy Commissioner, Calcutta Police, H.N. Sircar, Vol. V, p. 63

37. As mentioned in chapter four, it was the recurrent and plaintive moan, "Ma, phan dao" (Mother give us your rice starch) that so many Calcuttans remembered above all else.

38. Winston Churchill's friend and advisor, Lord Cherwell, pioneered the idea of "de-housing," which amounted to heavy bombing of German civilian areas in order to "de-house", and thus de-moralize the population.

39. *The Statesman* noted in an staff editorial on 20 August–, "no one will risk saying how many dwellings and business premises [were] burnt…many thousands." The lack of reliable statistics can be attributed to at least two factors; first, that there were more fires than could even be reported, or certainly fought, and second, that fire brigade workers were prevented from entering some areas by riotous mobs.

40. *The Statesman*, 20 August 1946, "The Calcutta Scene".

41. *The Statesman*, 19 August 1946, "Death Roll Now Between 2,000 and 3,000".

42. See CDCE, Testimony of H.N. Sircar, Donald Hardwick, and others.

43. WBSA, Home Confidential, file W-351/46 (Part B, VIII) "Activities of the Civil Supplies Department."

44. WBSA, Home Confidential, file W-351/46 "Report on Salvage Services." See also *The Statesman*, 19 August 1946, "Calcutta's Ordeal".

45. WBSA, Home Confidential, file W-351/46 (Part B, V), "Action Taken by the Relief Department".

46. *The Statesman*, 24 August 1946, "Troops Work in Clearing City".

47. P.K. Chatterjee, p. 170.
48. WBSA, Home Political," Fortnightly Report first half of December 1945".
49. Interview with Dolly Mukherjee. (10/30/2003, Kolkata)
50. WBSA, Home Political, "Fortnightly Report second half of December, 1945".
51. See chapter two.
52. WBSA, Home Political, "Fortnightly Report first half of December 1945".
53. CDCE, Vol. V., Testimony of H.N. Sircar, p. 83.
54. Das (1991), p. 172: "the only discriminatory element in lootings lay in Muslims exclusively pillaging Hindu shops and vice-versa."
55. ("Loot Howrah!") From WBSA, Home Confidential, file # 393/46 "Howrah and 24 Parganas, I.G.P. Report".
56. Ibid.
57. Ibid.
58. Ibid.
59. Ibid., p. 67.
60. Interview with Golam Kutubuddin (12/30/2003, Kolkata)
61. CDCE, Testimony of H.N. Sircar, Vol. V, p. 63.
62. CDCE, Testimony of Norton-Jones, Vol. IV, p. 257.
63. CDCE, Testimony of D.R. Hardwick, Vol. II, p. 94.
64. Ibid., p. 95.
65. Ibid., p. 94.
66. CDCE, Testimony of H.N. Sircar, Vol. V, p. 83.
67. Ibid.
68. Ibid., p. 60.
69. Interview with Golam Kibria (1/14/2004, Kolkata), who himself was present when the showroom was looted.
70. *The Statesman*, 18 August 1946, "Communal Riots in Calcutta".
71. Interview with Gyani Singh (11/12/2003, Kolkata), who witnessed the attack on the Grand Hotel.
72. WBSA, Home Confidential, file W-351/46 (Part B, VIII), "Activities of the Civil Supplies Department."
73. WBSA, Home Confidential, file W-351/46 (Part B, V), "Action Taken by the Relief Department."
74. WBSA, Home Confidential, file W-351/46 (Part B, VIII), "Activities of the Civil Supplies Department."
75. WBSA, Home Confidential, file W-351/46 (Part B, VIII), "Activities of the Civil Supplies Department."
76. Ibid.
77. Ibid.
78. CDCE, Testimony of H.N. Sircar, Vol. V, p. 82.

79. See the Testimonies of H.N. Sircar and P. Norton-Jones in CDCE, both recount many stories of massacres in various *bustees* throughout the city.

80. See chapter five.

81. Ibid., p. 21.

82. Ahuja, p. 16.

83. Ibid., p. 15.

84. See chapter five.

85. Entire Incident taken from WBSA, Home Confidential, file W-393/46 "I.G.P.'s Report, Howrah and 24 Parganas".

86. See Das, S. (1991), Batabyal (2005).

87. WBSA, Home Confidential, file W-398/46 "Report of the District Magistrate, Howrah".

88. See Batabyal, p. 240, note 12.

89. Das, S. (1991), p. 62.

90. Ibid.

91. Ibid., p. 61.

92. Goswami (1985), p. 244.

93. Bose (1986), p. xxx

94. Hardgrove (2002), Introduction.

95. "*Eh Marwari, khola kewari, tohre ghar mein lugga sari* (Oh Marwari, open up, there are dhotis and saris stacked in your house)" cited in, Shahid Amin, "Post-Colonial Towns Called Deoria" *Sarai Reader*, "Claiming the City," p. 50.

96. Das (1991), p. 62.

97. Ibid., (All information on this incident, unless otherwise noted is from this same file).

98. WBSA, Home Confidential, file W-392/46 "Report, Howrah and 24 Parganas."

99. The *Ananda Bazar Patrika*, for instance, ran reports that more than 600 "Hindus" had been killed.

100. WBSA, Home Confidential, file W-392/46 "Report of the District Magistrate of 24 Parganas."

101. T.O.P. Vol. VIII, Birla to Cripps, p. 278.

102. CDCE, Testimony of P. Norton-Jones, p. 300.

103. Ibid., p. 303.

104. Ibid., p. 301.

105. Ibid.

106. *Casey's Diary*, 25 November 1945. At Jallianwala Bagh, in Amritsar on 13 April 1919, Brigadier-General Reginald Dyer, had given orders to his troops to fire on demonstrators protesting against the Rowlatt Act, resulting in the massacre of 379 men, women and children, earning him the nickname "the butcher of Amritsar."

107. *Casey's Diary*, 24 November 1945.

108. See chapter six.

109. *Casey's Diary*, 4 December 1945.

110. T.O.P. Vol. VII, Burrows to Wavell, 16 August 1946, p. 240.

111. T.O.P. Vol. VIII, Burrows to Wavell, 22 August 1946, p. 302 (emphasis mine).

112. CDCE, Vol. V, Testimony of H.N. Sircar, p. 58.

113. CDCE, Vol. V, Testimony of S.N. Mukherji, p. 167.

114. Ibid., p. 126.

115. Ibid.

116. CDCE, Vol. II, Testimony of D.R. Hardwick, p. 83.

117. CDCE, Vol. IV, Testimony of E.K.G. Sixsmith, p. 155.

118. See: Sumit Sarkar (1983), p. 432.

119. T.O.P. Vol. VIII, Burrows to Wavell, 22 August 1946, p. 296.

120. CDCE, Vol. IV, Testimony of P. Norton-Jones, p 242.

121. Ibid.

122. *Casey's Diary*, 6 May 1944.

123. CDCE, Vol. V, Testimony of H.N. Sircar, p. 62.

124. CDCE, Vol. II, Testimony of D.R. Hardwick, p. 64.

125. CDCE, Vol. IV, Testimony of P. Norton-Jones, p 265.

126. *The Statesman*, 18 August 1946, "Communal Riots in Calcutta".

127. WBSA, Home Confidential, file W-351/46 (Part B, IX), "Activities of the Public Health Directorate."

128. WBSA, Home Confidential, file W-352/46 (Part B, V), "Action take by the Relief Department."

129. *The Statesman*, 23 August 1946, "War Was Never Like This".

130. WBSA, Home Confidential, file W-351/46 (Part B, IX), "Activities of the Public Health Directorate."

131. WBSA, Home Confidential, file W-352/46 (Part B, V), "Action take by the Relief Department."

132. WBSA, Home Confidential, file W-351/46 (Part B, VIII), "Activities of the Civil Supplies Department."

133. Ibid.

134. Ibid.

135. WBSA, Home Confidential, file W-351/46 (Part B, X) "Action Taken by the Publicity Department."

136. Ibid.

137. Ibid.

138. *The Statesman*, 21 August 1946, "Only Stray Cases of Assault".

139. See CDCE, Vol. V, Testimony of S.N. Mukherji, p. 152.

140. *The Statesman*, 21 August 1946, "Only Stray Cases of Assault".

141. Ibid.
142. WBSA, Home Confidential, file W-393/46 "Howrah and 24 Parganas, I.G.P. Report."
143. Ibid.
144. WBSA, Home Confidential, file W-351/46 (Part B, IX) "Action Taken by the Department of Health and Labor." (all information and quotes on burial are taken from this file unless otherwise noted.)
145. Interview with Mintu Dutto (11/15/2003, Kolkata)
146. WBSA, Home Confidential, file W-351/46 (Part B, IX) "Action Taken by the Department of Health and Labor."
147. *The Statesman*, 26 August 1946, "Ghastly Experience of August 16th Victim".
148. Interview with N.K. Mukherjee (Kolkata)
149. *The Statesman*, 21 August 1946, "Only Stray Cases of Assault".
150. WBSA, Home Confidential, file W-351/46 (Part B, IX) "Action Taken by the Department of Health and Labor."
151. CDCE, Vol. V, Testimony of S.N. Mukherji, p. 152.
152. Interview with Soumesh Sen (11/19/2003, Kolkata)
153. Interview with Ashoke Mukherjee (11/21/2003, Kolkata)
154. Interview with Gopal Banerjee (11/10/2003, Kolkata)
155. CDCE, Vol. XI, S. A. Masud, p. 244.

Chapter Seven: Riots

1. See p. 57.

BIBLIOGRAPHY

Archival Primary Sources

Center for Studies in Social Sciences (Calcutta)

Jadanath Sarkar (1870–1958) Collection of Personal Papers.
Photographs by Ahmed Ali.

West Bengal State Archives (WBSA)

Home Confidential Files.
Home Political Files.
Intelligence Branch Files.

National Archives of India (New Delhi)

Nanavati Papers.

British Library, India Office Records (London)

Bengal Secretariat Files (R/3/2).
Economic and Overseas Department Files (L/E/8).
Financial Department Collections (L/F/7).
Indian Police Collection (Mss. Eur F161).
Information Department Collections (L/I/1).
Governor's Reports (L/P&J/5).
Personal Diary of Richard Casey (Photo Eur 48).
Political Department Files (L/P&J/7).
Political Department Collections (L/P&J/8).
Political 'Internal' Department Collections (L/P&S/13).
Private Office Papers (L/PO).
Service and General Department Files (L/S&G/7).
War Staff Files (L/WS/I).

Bibliography

Interviews (Calcutta)

Dolly Mukherjee, 29 & 30 Oct., 3, 6 & 11 Nov. 2003.
Gopal Banerjee, 10 & 14 Nov. 2003.
Konika Das, 8 Nov. 2003.
Somnath Mukherjee, 9 Nov. 2003.
Gyani Guraban Singh, 12 Nov. 2003.
Sipra Chowdhury, 13 Nov. 2003.
Mintu Dutta, 15 Nov. 2003.
Kali Saha, 15 Nov. 2003.
Ashoke Mukherjee, 17 & 21 Nov. 2003.
Soumesh, 19 Nov. 2003.
Abdul Sattar Khan, 23 Nov. 2003.
Khagendranath Brahma, 13 Dec. 2003.
Manab Dutta, 13 Dec. 2003.
Souresh Sen, 23 Dec. 2003.
Golam Kutubuddin, 30 Dec. 2003.
Aurobindo Ghosh, 31 Dec. 2003.
Mazhar Beg, 1 Jan. 2004.
Tarun Mitra, 3 Jan. 2004.
Basanta Kar, 3 Jan. 2004.
Sabita and A.K. Chatterjee, 10 Jan. 2004.
Golam Kibria. 14 Jan. 2004.
Amalendu Dey, 16 Jan. 2004.
Purnima Dutta, 17 Jan. 2004.
Dr. Devi Banerjee and Dr. Sunil Ranjan Banerjee, 20 Jan. 2004.
Komal Kumar Chatterjee, 23 Feb. 2004.
Narendra Krishna Mukherjee 14 July 1999–1 Oct. 2001.

Newspapers and Periodicals

English:
Amrita Bazar Patrika (Calcutta).
Dawn (Calcutta).
Harijan (Bombay).
The Statesman (Calcutta).
The Star of India (Calcutta).

Bengali:
Ananda Bazar Patrika (Calcutta).
Bangashri (Calcutta).
Biplabi (Calcutta).
Dipali (Calcutta).

Bibliography

Dainik Basumati (Calcutta).
Janayuddha (Calcutta).
Mouchak (Calcutta).
Masik Basumati (Calcutta).
Prabasi (Calcutta).
Rangmashal (Calcutta).

Published Primary Source Materials

Agar, William. "Food or Freedom: The Vital Blockade," in pamphlet series *America In a World At War* (New York: Farrar & Rinehart, inc, 1941).

Amery, L. S, and John Barnes. *The Leo Amery Diaries.* (London: Hutchinson, 1980).

Anand, Mulk Raj. *Letters On India.* (London: G. Routledge & sons, ltd., 1942).

Anonymous. *India Ravaged [Being an Account of Atrocities Committed under the British Aegis, Over the Whole Sub-Continent of India in the Latter Part of 1942]* (Place and Publisher Unknown, January 1943).

Banerjee, Taransankar. *Pancham Gram (Five Villages.)* (Delhi: Manohar Books Services, 1973 [1943]).

Beard, Richard, and Reva Beard. *From Calcutta With Love: the World War II Letters of Richard and Reva Beard.* (Lubbock: Texas Tech University Press, 2002).

Bedi, Freda. *Bengal Lamenting* (Lion Press: Lahore, 1944).

Bengal Famine Code (Revised Edition of 1913.) (Calcutta: The Bengal Secretariat Book Depot, 1913).

Bhattacharya, S. "World War II and the Consumption Patterns of the Calcutta Middleclass." *Sankhya: The Indian Journal of Statistics*, Vol. 8, No. 2 (Mar., 1947) pp.197–200.

Calcutta Disturbances Commission of Enquiry. (Calcutta: Government of West Bengal, 1947) 11 Volumes.

Chakrabarty, Bidyut editor and translator. *Biplabi: A Journal of the 1942 Open Rebellion* (Kolkata: K.P. Bagchi & Company, 2002).

Chattopadhyay, Kashinath, editor. *Uposhi Bangla: Samayikpatre Panchasher Manwantar.* (Calcutta: Sariban, 2007).

Chittaprosad. *Hungry Bengal: A Tour Through Midnapur District, by Chittaprosad, in November, 1943.* (Bombay: New Age, 1943).

Churchill, Winston, and Robert Rhodes James. *Winston S. Churchill: His Complete Speeches, 1897–1963.* (New York,: Chelsea House Publishers, 1974).

Das, Tarashankar. *Bengal Famine (1943) as Revealed in a Survey of the Destitutes in Calcutta.* (Calcutta: University of Calcutta, 1949).

Dutt, T.K. *Hungry Bengal.* (Lahore: India Printing Works, 1944).

Bibliography

Famine Inquiry Commission of India, *Report on Bengal* (New Delhi: Government of India, 1945).

Fitch, Lieutenant-Colonel K.S. *A Medical History of the Bengal Famine, 1943–44.* (Calcutta: Government of India Press, 1947).

Gandhi, Mahatma. *Quit India.* (Bombay: Padma Publication Ltd., 1942).

Gandhi, Mahatma and Anand T Hingorani. *My Appeal to the British.* (New York: The John Day Company, 1942).

Geddes, Arthur. "The Population of Bengal, Its Distribution and Changes: A Contribution to Geographical Method." *The Geographical Journal,* Vol. 89, No. 4 (Apr., 1937), pp. 344–61.

Ghosh, Kali Charan. *Famines In Bengal, 1770–1943.* (Calcutta: Indian Associated Publishing Co, 1944).

Hodson, Henry Vincent. *Autobiography.* (Athelstane E-Texts, http://www.athelstane.co.uk/hvhodson/hvhbiogr/index.htm, last retrieved 19 Apr. 2011, copyright 2003).

International Conciliation: Documents for the Year 1945. (New York: Carnegie Endowment for International Peace, 1946).

Jinnah, Mahomed Ali, and Mirza Abol Hassan Ispahani. *M. A. Jinnah—Ispahani Correspondence, 1936–1948.* (Karachi: Forward Publications Trust, 1976).

Leaders Conference: an Authentic Account of the Leaders Conference Held At New Delhi On 19th And 20th February 1943 In Respect of Mahatma Gandhi's Fast. (New Delhi: Convenors of the Conference, 1943).

Mahalanobis, P.C., Ramkrishna Mukherjea, and Ambika Ghosh. "A Sample Survey of After-Effects of the Bengal Famine of 1943." *Sankhyā: The Indian Journal of Statistics,* Vol. 7, No. 4 (Jul., 1946), pp. 337–400.

Majumdar, D.N., C. Radhakrishna Rao, and P. C. Mahalanobis. "Bengal Anthropometric Survey, 1945: A Statistical Study." *Sankhyā: The Indian Journal of Statistics,* Vol. 19, No. 3/4, (Jun., 1958), pp. 201–408.

Mansergh, Nicholas, and Esmond Walter Rawson Lumby. *Constitutional Relations Between Britain And India; the Transfer of Power, 1942–7.* (London: His Majesty's Stationery Office, 1970–80).

Mukherjae, Ramkrishna. "Note on Concentration of Agricultural Wealth in Bengal." *Sankhyā: The Indian Journal of Statistics,* Vol. 7, No. 4 (Jul., 1946), pp. 442–4.

Mukherjee, Ramakrishna. "Economic Structure of Rural Bengal: A Survey of Six Villages." *American Sociological Review,* Vol. 13, No. 6 (Dec., 1948), pp. 660–72.

Mukhopadhyay, Syamaprasad. *Panchaser Manwantar* ("The Famine of 1350.") (Calcutta: Bengal Publishers, 1350 B.S.).

Narayan, T.G. *Famine Over Bengal.* (The Book Company: Calcutta, 1944).

Bibliography

The Imperial Gazetteer of India, 1907–1909 (Clarendon Press: Oxford, 1909).

Thompson, Edward John. *Enlist India for Freedom!* (London: V. Gollancz, ltd., 1940).

Wavell, Archibald Percival Wavell, and Penderel Moon. *Wavell: the Viceroy's Journal.* (London: Oxford University Press, 1973).

WWII People's War: An Archive of World War II Memories—Written by the public, gathered by the BBC. (at: http://www.bbc.co.uk/ww2peopleswar/ last accessed 19 Apr. 2011).

Other Sources

Action Against Hunger, ed. *The Geopolitics of Hunger, 2000–2001: Hunger And Power.* (Boulder: L. Rienner, 2001).

Agamben, Giorgio. *Homo Sacer: Sovereign Power and Bare Life.* (Stanford: Stanford University Press, 1995).

———. *State of Exception.* (Chicago: University of Chicago Press, 2005).

Ahmed, Rafiuddin. *The Bengal Muslims: 1871–1906: A Quest for Identity.* (Delhi: Oxford University Press, 1981).

Ahmed, Rafiuddin, ed. *Understanding the Bengal Muslims: Interpretive Essays.* (New Delhi: Oxford University Press, 2001).

Ahuja, Ravi. "Networks of Subordination—Networks of the Subordinated," in Harald Fischer Tine ed., *The Limits of British Colonial Control in South Asia: Spaces of Disorder in the Indian Ocean Region* (New York: Routledge, 2008).

Amin, Shahid. *Event, Metaphor, Memory: Chauri Chaura, 1922–1992.* (Berkeley: University of California, 1995).

Arnold, David. "Industrial Violence in Colonial India." *Comparative Studies in Society and History* Vol. 22, No 2 (Apr., 1980), pp. 234–55.

Asad, Talal. "On Torture, or Cruel, Inhuman and Degrading and Inhuman Treatment." *Social Research* Vol. 63, No. 4 (1996), pp. 1081–109.

Azad, Maulana Abul Kalam. *India Wins Freedom.* (New Delhi: Orient Longman, 2004).

Bailey, Sydney D. "Administration in Bengal: The Rowlands Report." *Far Eastern Survey*, Vol. 15, No. 6 (Mar. 27, 1946), pp. 90–2.

Baker, Nicholson. *Human Smoke: The Beginnings of World War II, the End of Civilization.* (New York: Simon & Schuster, 2008).

Bandyopadhyay, Samik. trans. *In Search of Famine, a film by Mrinal Sen.* (Calcutta: Seagull Books, 1985).

Bandyopadhyay, Sandip. *Itihaser Dike Phire, Chechallisher Danga* ("Looking Back at History: The Riot of 1946"). (Calcutta: Utsa Manus, 1992).

Bandyopadhyay, Sekhar. *Caste, Politics and the Raj: Bengal 1812–1937.* (Calcutta: K.P. Bagchi, 1990).

Bandyopadhyay, Tarashankar. *Manwantar* ("Famine"). (Calcutta: Sahityo Prakash, 1990).

Bibliography

Barton, William. *India's Fateful Hour*. (London: J. Murray, 1942).

Basu, Rita. *Dr. Shyama Prasad Mookherjee and an Alternative Politics in Bengal.* (Kolkata: Progressive Publishers, 2002).

Batabyal, Rakesh. *Communalism in Bengal: From Famine to Noakhali, 1943–47.* (New Delhi: Sage Publications, 2005).

Bayly, C. A. "The Pre-History of 'Communalism'? Religious Conflict in India 1700–1860." *Modern Asian Studies* Vol. 19, No. 2 (1985), pp. 177–203.

Bayly, C. A, and T. N Harper. *Forgotten Armies: the Fall of British Asia, 1941–1945.* (Cambridge: Harvard University Press, 2005).

Benjamin, Walter. "Critique of Violence." In *Reflections*. (New York: Schocken, 1986), pp. 277–300.

Bhadra, Gautam. "Four Rebels of 1857," in Ranajit Guha, ed. *Subaltern Studies IV: Writings on South Asian History and Society* (Delhi: Oxford University Press, 1985), pp. 229–75.

Bhattacharya, Sanjoy. *Propaganda And Information In Eastern India, 1939–45: a Necessary Weapon of War.* (Richmond: Curzon, 2000).

Birkenhead, Frederick Winston Furneaux Smith. *The Prof In Two Worlds: the Official Life of Professor F. A. Lindemann, Viscount Cherwell.* (London: Collins, 1961).

———. *The Professor And the Prime Minister: the Official Life of Professor F. A. Lindemann, Viscount Cherwell.* (Boston: Houghton Mifflin, 1962).

Biswamoy Pati, ed. *Turbulent Times, India, 1940–44.* (Mumbai: Popular Prakashan, 1998).

Biswas, Oneil. *Calcutta and Calcuttans.* (Calcutta: Firma KLM Private Ltd., 1992).

Blechynden, Kathleen. *Calcutta Past and Present.* (Thacker, Spink and Co.: Calcutta, 1905).

Bose, Sugata. "The Roots of 'Communal' Violence in Rural Bengal. A Study of the Kishoreganj Riots, 1930." *Modern Asian Studies*, Vol. 16, No. 3 (1982), pp. 463–91.

———. *Agrarian Bengal: Economy, Social Structure, and Politics, 1919–1947.* (Cambridge: Cambridge University Press, 1986).

———. "Starvation amidst Plenty: The Making of Famine in Bengal, Honan and Tonkin, 1942–45." *Modern Asian Studies*, Vol. 24, No. 4 (1990), pp. 699–727.

———. *Peasant Labour and Colonial Capital : Rural Bengal Since 1770.* (Cambridge: Cambridge University Press, 1993).

Bose, Sugata and Ayesha Jalal. *Modern South Asia: history, culture, political economy.* (New York: Routledge, 1998).

Brewis, Georgina. "'Fill Full the Mouth of Famine': Voluntary Action in Famine Relief in India 1896–1901." *Modern Asian Studies*, Vol.44, No.4 (2010), pp.887–918.

Bibliography

Cannon, Walter B. *Bodily Changes In Pain, Hunger, Fear And Rage: an Account of Recent Researches Into the Function of Emotional Excitement.* (College Park, Md.: McGrath Pub. Co., 1970).

Castro, Josué de. *The Geography of Hunger.* (Boston: Little, Brown, 1952).

———. *The Black Book of Hunger.* (New York: Funk & Wagnalls, 1968).

Césaire, Aimé. *Discourse On Colonialism.* (New York: Monthly Review Press, 1972).

Chakrabarty, Dipesh. "On Deifying and Defying Authority: Managers and Workers in the Jute Mills of Bengal circa 1890–1940." *Past & Present*, Vol. 100, no. 1 (Aug., 1983), pp. 124–46.

———. *Rethinking Working Class History: Bengal, 1890–1940.* (Princeton: Princeton University Press, 1989).

Chandrasekhar, S. "Population Pressure in India." *Pacific Affairs*, Vol. 16, No. 2 (Jun., 1943), pp. 166–84.

Chatterjee, Partha. *Bengal 1920–1947: The Land Question.* (Calcutta: K.P. Bagchi and Company, 1984).

Chatterjee, Partha. *The Present History of West Bengal: Essays in Political Criticism.* (Delhi: Oxford University Press, 1998).

Chatterjee, Pranab Kumar. *Struggle and Strife in Urban Bengal 1937–1947.* (Kolkata: Das Gupta & Co., 1991).

Chatterjee, S.P. *Bengal in Maps.* (Kolkata: National Atlas and Thematic Mapping Organisation, 2003).

Chatterji, Bankim Chandra. *Anandamath.* Basanta Koomar Roy, trans. (New Delhi: Vision Books [1881] 1992).

Chatterji, Joya. *Bengal Divided: Hindi Communalism and Partition 1932–1947.* (New Delhi: Cambridge University Press, 1995).

Chattopadhyaya, Haraprasad. *Internal Migration in India: A Case Study of Bengal.* (Calcutta: K.P. Bagchi, 1987).

Chattopadhyay, Suchetana. "War, Migration and Alienation in Colonial Calcutta: the Remaking of Muzaffar Ahmad," *History Workshop Journal*, Issue 64, No. 1 (2007) p. 212–39.

Chattopadhyaya, Tapan. *The Story of Lalbazar: Its Origin and Growth.* (Calcutta: Firma KLM Private Ltd., 1982).

Clune, Frank. *Song of India.* (Sydney: Invincible Press, 1947).

Cohen, David William and E.S. Atieno Odhiambo. *The Risks of Knowledge.* (Athens: Ohio University Press, 2004).

Crapanzano, Vincent. "Hermes' Dilemma: the Masking of Subversion in Ethnographic Description." In *Writing Culture: the Poetics and Politics of Ethnography*, James Clifford & George E Marcus eds. (Berkeley: University of California Press, 1986), pp. 51–76.

Das, Nilanjana. *Of Dust And Distress.* (Delhi: Indian Publishers' Distributors, 2004).

Bibliography

Das, Suranjan. *Communal Riots in Bengal: 1905–1947*. (Delhi: Oxford UP, 1991).

———. "Nationalism and Popular Consciousness: Bengal 1942." *Social Scientist*, Vol. 23, No. 4/6 (Apr.–Jun., 1995), pp. 58–68.

———. "The 1992 Calcutta Riot in Historical Continuum: A Relapse into 'Communal Fury'?" *Modern Asian Studies*, Vol. 34, No. 2 (2000), p. 281–306.

Das, Tarakchandra. *Bengal Famine (1943): As Revealed in a Survey of Destitutes in Calcutta*. (Calcutta: University of Calcutta, 1949).

Datta, Pradip Kumar. *Carving Blocs: Communal Ideology in Early Twentieth-century*. (New Delhi: Oxford University Press, 1999).

Davis, Mike. *Late Colonial Holocausts: El Nino Famines and the Making of the Third World*. (London and New York: Verso, 2002).

De, Amalendu. *Pakistan Prostab O Fazlul Huq* ("The Pakistan Call and Fazlul Huq"). (Calcutta: Ratna Prakashan, 1972).

De, Bikramjit. "Imperial Governance and the Challenges of War: Management of Food Supplies in Bengal, 1943–44." *Studies in History*, Vol. 22 (2006), pp. 1–43.

Dutta, Partha. *Urbanization, Local Politics, and Labour Protest: a Case Study of Jute Mills Area of 24-Parganas (North), 1900–1959*. (Malda: Dipali Publishers, 2008).

Datta, Syamaprasad and Mridula. *Interaction, Confrontation, Resolution: The Economic Issues in Bengal Legislature (1921–51)*. (Calcutta: Bibasha, 1998).

Dewey, C.J. "The Education of a Ruling Caste: The Indian Civil Service in the Era of Competitive Examination." *The English Historical Review*, Vol. 88, No. 347 (Apr., 1973), pp. 262–85.

Drèz, Jean, Amartya Sen and Athar Hussain. *The Political Economy of Hunger: Selected Essays*. (Oxford: Clarendon Press, 1997).

Ewing, Ann. "The Indian Civil Service 1919–1924: Service Discontent and the Response in London and in Delhi." *Modern Asian Studies*, Vol. 18, No. 1 (1984), pp. 33–53.

Fanon, Frantz. *Black Skin, White Masks*. (New York: Grove Press, 1967).

———. *The Wretched of the Earth*. (New York: Grove Press, 1965).

Farmer, Paul. *Pathologies of Power: Health, Human Rights, and the New War on the Poor*. (Berkeley: University of California, 2003).

Feldman, Allen. *Formations of Violence: The Narrative of the Body and Political Terror in Northern Ireland*. (Chicago: University of Chicago, 1991).

Fort, Adrian. *Prof: the Life of Frederick Lindemann*. (London: Jonathan Cape, 2003).

Gandhi, M.K. *Hind Swaraj and Other Writings*. Anthony J. Parel, ed. (Cambridge: Cambridge University Press, 1997).

————. *An Autobiography: The Story of My Experiments with Truth*. Mahadev Desai, trans. (Boston: Beacon Press, 1993).

Gandhi, Rajmohan. *Eight lives: a Study of the Hindu-Muslim Encounter*. (Albany: State University of New York Press, 1986).

Ghosh, Kali Charan. *Famines in Bengal, 1770–1943*. (Calcutta: National Council of Education, 1987).

Ghosh, Murari, Alok Dutta and Biswanath Ray. *Calcutta: A Study in Urban Growth Dynamics*. (Calcutta: Firma KLM Private Limited, 1972).

Glendevon, John Hope. *The Viceroy At Bay: Lord Linlithgow In India, 1936–1943*. (London: Collins, 1971).

Gondhalekar, Nandini and Sanjoy Bhattacharya. "The All India Hindu Mahasabha and the End of British Rule in India, 1939–1947." *Social Scientist*, Vol. 27, No. 7/8 (Jul.–Aug., 1999), pp. 48–74.

Goswami, Omkar. "Collaboration and Conflict: European and Indian Capitalists and the Jute Economy of Bengal, 1919–39." *Indian Economic Social History Review*, Vol. 19 (1982), pp. 141–79.

————. "Then Came the Marwaris: Some Aspects of the Change in the Pattern of Industrial Control in Eastern India." *Indian Economic Social History Review*, Vol. 22 (1985), pp. 225–49.

————. "*Sahibs, Babus* and *Banias:* Changes in Industrial Control in Eastern India, 1918–50." *Journal of Asian Studies*, Vol. 48, No. 2 (May 1989) p.289–309.

Greenough, Paul R. "Indian Famines and Peasant Victims: the Case of Bengal in 1943–44." *Modern Asian Studies*, Vol. 14, No. 2 (1980), pp. 205–35.

————. *Prosperity And Misery In Modern Bengal: the Bengal Famine of 1943–44*. (Oxford: Oxford University Press, 1982).

Guha, Ranajit. *A Rule of Property for Bengal: an Essay On the Idea of Permanent Settlement*. (Paris: Mouton, 1963).

————. *Elementary Aspects of Peasant Insurgency in Colonial India*. (Delhi: Oxford University Press, 1983).

————. "Discipline and Mobilize", in Partha Chatterjee and Gyanendra Pandey, eds. *Subaltern Studies VII* (Delhi: Oxford University Press, 1992), pp. 69–120.

————. *Dominance Without Hegemony: History and Power in Colonial India* (Cambridge: Harvard University Press, 1997).

Gupta, Partha Sarathi. *Radio and the Raj, 1921–1947*. (Calcutta: K.P. Bagchi, 1995).

Grant, Kevin. "The Transcolonial World of Hunger Strikes and Political Fasts, c. 1909–1935", in Durba Ghosh and Dane Kennedy (eds), *Decentering Empire: Britain, India, and the Transcolonial World*. (New Delhi, Orient Longman, 2006), pp. 243–69.

Bibliography

Haan, Arjan de. *Unsettled Settlers: Migrant Workers And Industrial Capitalism In Calcutta.* (Hilversum: Verloren, 1994).

———. *A Case for Labour History: the Jute Industry In Eastern India.* (Calcutta: K.P. Bagchi & Co., 1999).

Hardgrove, Ann. *Community and Public Culture: The Marwaris in Calcutta 1897–1997.* (www.gutenberg-e.org: Columbia University Press, 2002).

Harriss-White, Barbara. *Rural Commercial Capital: Agricultural Markets in West Bengal.* (New Delhi: Oxford, 2008).

Hore, Somnath. *Visions: Paintings And Sculptures by Somnath Hore, Ganesh Pyne, Bikash Bhattacharjee, And Jogen Chowdhury.* (Calcutta: Ladies Study Group, 1986).

———. *Somnath Hore.* (New Delhi: Lalit Kala Akademi, 1988).

———. *Bronzes.* (Kolkata: Centre for International Modern Art (*CIMA*) Gallery, 1992).

Hunter, W.W. *The Annals of Rural Bengal.* (London: Smith, Elder and Company: 1883).

Islam, M. Mufakharul. *Bengal Agriculture, 1920–1946: a Quantitative Study.* (Cambridge: Cambridge University Press, 1978).

Jalal, Ayesha. *The Sole Spokesman: Jinnah, the Muslim League and the Demand for Pakistan.* (New York: Cambridge University Press, 1985).

Kabir, Hamayun. *War Against the People: A Sharp Analysis of the Causes of Famine in Bengal.* (Calcutta: Peoples' Book Club, 1944).

Kafka, Franz. *The Penal Colony.* (New York: Schocken, 1961).

Kamtekar, Indivar. "A Different War Dance: State and Class in India, 1939–1945." *Past and Present,* No. 176 (August 2002) pp. 187–221.

Kamtekar, Indivar. "The Shiver of 1942." *Studies in History* Vol. 18 (2002), pp. 81–102.

Kar, Bimal. *Dewal* ("The Wall"). (Calcutta: Ananda Publishers, 2003).

Kirsch, Stuart. *Reverse Anthropology: Indigenous Analysis of Social and Environmental Relations in New Guinea.* (Stanford: Stanford University Press, 2006).

Knight, Henry. *Food Administration In India, 1939–47.* (Stanford: Stanford University Press, 1954).

Kosuge, Nobuko. *Japan And Britain At War And Peace.* (London: Routledge, 2009).

Majumdar, R.C. *History of Modern Bengal.* (Calcutta: G. Bharadwaj & Co., 1981).

Malkki, Lisa. *Purity and Exile: Violence, Memory, and National Cosmology Among Hutu Refugees in Tanzania.* (Chicago: University of Chicago, 1995).

Metcalf, Barbara. *Islamic Revival in British India: Deoband, 1860–1900* (Princeton: Princeton University Press, 1982).

Bibliography

Metcalf, Thomas. *Ideologies of the Raj*. (Cambridge: Cambridge University Press, 1996).

Metcalf, Barbara D. and Thomas R. *A Concise History of India*. (New York: Cambridge University Press, 2002).

Misra, A.M. "'Business Culture' and Entrepreneurship in British India, 1860–1950." *Modern South Asian Studies*, Vol. 34, No. 2 (May 2000), pp. 333–48.

Mitter, S.C. *A Recovery Plan for Bengal*. (Calcutta: The Book Company, 1934).

Mueggler, Erik. *The Age of Wild Ghosts: Memory, Violence, and Place in Southwest China*. (Berkeley: University of California Press, 2001).

Mukerjee, Madhusree. *Churchill's Secret War: The British Empire and the Ravaging of India During World War II*. (New York: Basic Books, 2010).

Nand, Brahma. *Famines in Colonial India: Some Unofficial Historical Narratives*. (New Delhi: Kanishka Publishers, 2007).

Pandey, Gyanendra. *The Construction of Communalism in Colonial North India*. (New Delhi: Oxford University Press, 1990).

———. "In Defense of the Fragment: Writing about Hindu-Muslim Riots in India Today", in Ranjit Guha ed. *A Subaltern Studies Reader: 1986–1995*. (New Delhi: Oxford UP, 1997), pp. 1–33.

Roll of Ipsden, Eric Roll. *The Combined Food Board: a Study In Wartime International Planning*. (Stanford: Stanford University Press, 1956).

Ray, Anandashankar, ed. *Chorha Samagra* ("The Ocean of Rhymes"). (Calcutta: Mudrakar, 2003).

Roy, M. N. *Poverty Or Plenty?* (Calcutta: Renaissance publishers, 1944).

Samaddar, Sivaprasad. *Calcutta In Other Tongues*. (Calcutta: Sahitya Samsad, 1995).

Sarkar, Nikhil. *A Matter of Conscience: Artists Bear Witness to the Great Bengal Famine of 1943*. (Calcutta: Punascha, 1998).

Sarkar, Sumit. *The Swadeshi Movement In Bengal, 1903–1908*. (New Delhi: People's Pub. House, 1973).

———. *Modern India, 1885–1947*. (New Delhi: McMillan, 1983).

Scarry, Elaine. *The Body in Pain: The Making and Unmaking of the World*. (New York: Oxford University Press, 1985).

Scott, James. *Weapons of the Weak: everyday forms of peasant resistance*. (New Haven: Yale University Press, 1985).

Sen, Amartya. *Poverty And Famines: an Essay On Entitlement And Deprivation*. (Oxford: Clarendon Press, 1981).

———. *Development as Freedom*. (New York: Anchor Books, 1999).

Sen, Arun and Anukul Chandra Moitra. *Police Officers: Being the Law Relating to Police Officers with Reference to their Powers and Duties*. (Calcutta: Eastern Law House, 1938).

Bibliography

Sen, P.K. *Six Years of Howrah A.R.P.* (Calcutta, 1945).

Sen, Shila. *Muslim Politics in Bengal, 1937–1947.* (Kolkata: Viswakos Parisad, 2001).

Sengupta, Debjani. "A City Feeding on Itself: Testimonies and Histories of 'Direct Action' Day." *Sarai Reader*, 2006. Retrieved, April 18, 2011.

Seth, Hira Lal. *"Quit India" Re-examined.* (Lahore: Indian printing works, 1943).

Sinha, Narendra Krishna. *The Economic History of Bengal.* (Calcutta: Firma KLM Private Limited, 1985).

Sinha, Pradip. *Calcutta in Urban History.* (Calcutta: Firma KLM Private Limited, 1978).

Smith, Colin. *Singapore Burning: Heroism And Surrender in World War II.* (London: Viking, 2005).

Snow, C. P. *Science And Government.* (Cambridge: Harvard University Press, 1961).

Stephens, Ian Melville. *Monsoon Morning.* (London: Ernest Benn, 1966).

Tagore, Rabindranath. *The Visva-bharati Quarterly.* (Calcutta, The Visva-bharati quarterly, 1943).

Tagore, Saumyendranath. *Resurgence of Tribal Savagery in Calcutta.* (Calcutta: Ganabani Publishing House, 1946).

Thorne, Christopher G. *Allies of a Kind: the United States, Britain, And the War Against Japan, 1941–1945.* (New York: Oxford University Press, 1978).

Tinker, Hugh. "A Forgotten Long March: The Indian Exodus from Burma, 1942" *Journal of Southeast Asian Studies*, Vol. 6, No. 1 (Mar., 1975), pp. 1–15.

Tuker, Sir Francis. *While Memory Serves.* (London: Cassell, 1950).

Venkataramani, M.S. *Bengal Famine of 1943: The American Response.* (Delhi: Vikas Publishing House, 1972).

Vernon, James. *Hunger: A Modern History.* (Cambridge: Harvard University Press, 2007).

Winick, Myron. *Hunger Disease: Studies by the Jewish Physicians in the Warsaw Ghetto.* (New York: John Wiley & Sons, 1979).

Zweiniger-Bargielowska, Ina. *Austerity In Britain: Rationing, Controls, And Consumption, 1939–1955.* (Oxford: Oxford University Press, 2000).

Films

Akaler Sadhaney ("In Search of Famine"). Dir. Mrinal Sen. Perf. Smita Patil, Radhamohan Bhattacharya. Gita Sen, and Dhritiman Chatterjee. D.K. Films, 1980.

Ashani Sanket ("Distant Thunder"). Dir. Satyajit Ray. Perf. Soumitra Chatterjee, Babita, Ramesh Mukherjee, and Chitra Banerjee. Balaka Movies, 1973.

INDEX